THE CONSTITUTION AS SOCIAL DESIGN

GRETCHEN RITTER

The Constitution as Social Design

Gender and Civic Membership in the American Constitutional Order

STANFORD UNIVERSITY PRESS

STANFORD, CALIFORNIA 2006

Stanford University Press
Stanford, California

Printed in the United States of America on acid-free,
archival-quality paper

Library of Congress Cataloging-in-Publication Data

Ritter, Gretchen.
    p.   cm.
    Includes bibliographical references and index.
    ISBN-13: 978-0-8047-5378-4 (cloth : alk. paper)
    ISBN-10: 0-8047-5378-4 (cloth : alk paper)
    ISBN-13: 978-0-8047-5438-5 (pbk : alk. paper)
    ISBN-10: 0-8047-5438-1 (pbk. : alk.paper)
    1. Women's rights — United States — History.
2. Women — Legal status, laws, etc. — United
States — History. 3. Political rights — United
States — History. 4. Feminism — United States —
History. 5. Constitutional history — United States.
I. Title.

HQ1236.5.U6R57   2006
342.7308'78 — dc22   2006005156

Typeset by BookMatters in 10/14 Janson

In **memory** *for*
    Lora Romero (1960–1997)
    and
    Karl Holfelder Ritter (1957–1997)

and in **hope** *for*
    Rose and Lukas

Contents

Acknowledgments

I have accumulated many debts, both personal and intellectual, in the time taken to write this book. My thanks to Sandy Levinson, Ruth O'Brien, Martha Fineman, Reva Siegel, Jordan Steiker, Vicki Schultz, Martha Minow, Kim Scheppele, Gerald Torres, and Zipporah Wiseman for teaching me about law. One of the works that first inspired me to think about constitutional law as a system for ordering social relations was Karen Orren's brilliant book *Belated Feudalism*, which remains, in my view, one of the greatest works in American politics published in the past twenty years.

Others have given me thoughtful input on the project as it has progressed. Among my colleagues at the University of Texas at Austin, I wish to thank Kamran Ali, Kit Belgum, Cathy Boone, David Braybrooke, Evan Carton, Michael Churgin, Jane Cohen, Ann Cvetkovich, Willy Forbath, Sue Heinzelman, John Higley, Juliet Hooker, Gary Jacobsohn, Allison Martens, Lisa Moore, Allison Perlman, H. W. Perry, Sharmila Rudruppa, Larry Sager, Sean Theriault, Gerald Torres, Jeff Tulis, Debra Umberson, Sarah Weddington, Kurt Weyland, and Jacqui Woolley, as well as Deans Bill Powers and Richard Lariviere. Beyond my home university, I would like to thank Eileen Boris, Michael Brown, John Coleman, Nancy Cott, Mary Dudziak, Martha Fineman, Michael Hanchard, Hendrick Hartog, Nancy Hirschmann, Mary Katzenstein, Ira Katznelson, Linda Kerber, Alice Kessler-Harris, Desmond King, Dan Kryder, Rob Lieberman, Eileen McDonagh, Uday Mehta, Suzanne Mettler, Carol Nackenoff, Anne Norton, Julie Novkov, Ruth O'Brien, Karen Orren, Ann Orloff, Carole Pateman, Virginia Sapiro, Clare Sheridan, Theda Skocpol, Reva Siegel, Rogers Smith, and Kathleen Sullivan.

Parts of this book have been presented as lectures at different universities.

The feedback I have gotten from those public presentations has done a great deal to sharpen my arguments. My thanks to the organizers and audiences members at the American Political Development Colloquium at the University of Wisconsin; the American Politics Workshop at Harvard University; the Center for History, Society, and Culture at the University of California, Davis; the Department of Political Science at UCLA; the Feminist Legal Theory Workshop at Cornell Law School and at Emory's Law School; the Fulbright Colloquium at the CUNY Graduate Center; the Government Department at Cornell University; the Human Rights Colloquium at the University of Texas Law School; the Institute for Women and Gender Studies at Columbia University; the Law and Public Affairs Program at Princeton University; the Miller Center at the University of Virginia; and the Twentieth Century American Politics and Society Workshop at Columbia University. I would also like to acknowledge the assistance I received from the National Endowment for the Humanities, which provided me with fellowship support in 2001. My thanks as well to the Public Policy Clinic at UT Austin and its former director, Dr. Gary Freeman, for support of this project.

I am blessed to have many smart and generous friends, who have put up with my musings and meanderings for a long time. A few deserve special mention. Among them are Christine Williams, a wonderful reader and committed feminist, who inspires me by her ability to live her politics. Katie Stewart has read many drafts and listened to many of my half-baked ideas. She always pulls out the best in what I am doing and encourages me to build upon it. Ruth O'Brien has given me the benefit of her formidable knowledge of law and theory, and has always encouraged me to reach for the prize. Debra Umberson has shown me that it is possible to be both a productive scholar and an effective administrator while still being there for your kids. Kit Belgum has reminded me of the joys of research and writing. Ann Cvetkovich has offered many thoughtful comments on my work, and the inspiration of someone who is willing to follow her muse. These wonderful friends have guided me through the journey of creating this book.

My family has provided inspiration, distraction, and support for this book. Sean Keel spent many hours entertaining our kids while I went into to my office to look over yet another set of court cases. As I traveled further into the realm of law, I came closer to the world of my father, David S. Ritter, who is a judge in New York State. My father has taught me many valuable lessons, including the importance of having work that you love. I would also like to thank my mother and her husband, Sandy and Warren DuBois, for their support and encouragement. My brothers and their families — Andy Ritter and Karen Ritter, Matt Ritter, and Alex and Tyler Ritter — offered me their love and good humor throughout. My friends and family members have sustained me with their kindness and patience. This book is dedicated to the memories of two people I have lost — my brother Karl Ritter, and my friend Lora Romero. Both were bright lights, and the world is a bit dimmer without them. The book is also dedicated to my children, Rose and Lukas, who animate my hopes for democracy, and who teach me every day that, as one radical feminist wrote, "love, justice, and equality are the solution."

THE CONSTITUTION AS SOCIAL DESIGN

ONE

The Constitution as Social Design

A constitution not only constitutes a structure of power and authority, it
constitutes a people in a certain way. It proposes a distinctive identity and
envisions a form of politicalness for individuals in their new collective capacity.

— SHELDON S. WOLIN, *The Presence of the Past*

Harriet Stanton Blatch was committed to woman suffrage. When her
mother, Elizabeth Cady Stanton, passed away in 1902, Harriet returned
from England to carry on her mother's work. Winning the vote became
Harriet's full-time mission until the Nineteenth Amendment was adopted in
1920. The amendment was a personal as well as a political victory. It represented the fulfillment of a long-held family dream that American women
would become full and equal citizens. Yet for Harriet, like her mother
before her, the vote was merely a starting point in the campaign for true
democracy. Reflecting on the seventy-fifth anniversary of the 1848 Woman's
Rights Convention at Seneca Falls, Blatch confided, "My mother could not
conceive of suffrage as standing by itself, as an issue unrelated to other issues.
For her it was inseparable from the antislavery agitation, from women's
demand for entry into the field of labor, into the universities and profes-
sions" (DuBois, 1997, 226). Blatch was well aware that women's fight for
equality did not end with the vote. Women's inclusion in the electorate did
little to change their status of economic dependency. As wives, mothers, and

1

workers, American women remained economically subordinate, and the political system was ill equipped to address the problems of industrial exploitation and legal discrimination that made them so.

By her eightieth birthday, in 1936, Blatch was still looking to the future: "The failures of a decade cannot shake my faith in democracy and liberty," she declared to the friends and family who had gathered in New York to celebrate with her. "I am here to represent the feminist side in this discussion of the future of democracy," she said (DuBois, 1997, 5). Blatch must have known when she passed away in 1940 that much remained to be done. Women still suffered legal discrimination. Even with the gains made during the New Deal, American social provisioning paled in comparison to the social policy regimes emerging in Western Europe. Under the leadership of Franklin Delano Roosevelt, American democracy was more vibrant than it had been when women first won the vote in 1920. Yet it seemed that there were limits on how much American democracy could expand. Both Elizabeth Cady Stanton and Harriet Stanton Blatch had operated within a constitutional order which made the achievement of a more expansive, enriched democracy difficult.

This book is about the contribution that generations of feminists made to the promise of American democracy. It is also about the constitutional order that both constrained and inspired their democratic ambitions.

When did women achieve full civic membership in the Unites States? Was it in 1789, when the Constitution was adopted? Or was it in 1868, when the Fourteenth Amendment defined national citizenship for the first time? Was it in 1920, when women finally received the right to vote? Or in the 1960s and 1970s, when women were granted new rights in employment and education? Or, perhaps, did the failure to adopt the Equal Rights Amendment in the early 1980s illustrate that women are still not recognized as full and equal members of the polity? The absence of a clear answer to this question is indicative of women's ambiguous place in the American civic order.

For much of the nation's history, women's presence in the community of "the People" was assumed but not specified. Before the twentieth century, women's place in the American political community was conceived of relationally. As wives, daughters, servants, and slaves, women were represented in public affairs through their husbands, fathers, and masters. They had no

independent civic status. Then, in the late nineteenth century and throughout the twentieth century, women gradually came to be seen as individuals.
Individualism seems essential for civic recognition in America, a nation
whose public philosophy is premised on liberalism and natural rights.[1]
American women's claim to an autonomous legal and political status has
been hard-fought; in many ways they are still not fully recognized in those
terms. Yet autonomy is not an unambiguously positive status for women. It
remains uncertain what it would take for women to secure a civic membership that provides them with equal rights and status, and that is more fully
expressive of their social identities, experiences, and concerns.

This book is about gender and civic membership in American constitutional politics, from the adoption of the Nineteenth Amendment through
second wave feminism. There are two central concerns that motivate this
work. First, it examines how American civic membership is gendered, and
how the terms of civic membership available to men and women shape their
political identities, aspirations, and behavior. Second, this book explores the
dynamics of American constitutional development through a focus on civic
membership, which is understood here as a legal and political construct at
the heart of the constitutional order. In other words, this is a book about
gender politics and constitutional development, and about what each of
these can tell us about the other.

Within the American constitutional order women have undergone a shift
from a civic status based upon marriage, family relations, and economic
dependency to one based upon the principles of liberal individualism and
legal personhood. Yet the attainment of a liberal civic status remains partial;
in the struggle to achieve standing as public-realm individuals, women still
face resistance to the idea that their sex does not matter to their civic membership. The federal government and many in the broader society will go
only so far in granting women constitutional equality. Many prefer to think
that it is appropriate for women to be recognized as relational beings, tied to
their children and spouses, who are situated and shaped by their lives in the
domestic realm.

The shift from a citizenship based on domesticity and dependency to one
that is imperfectly based on liberal individualism and legal personhood cor-
responds to the nation's emergence as a modern liberal constitutional order.[2]
By considering the constitutional transition from a common law system of
social governance to a modern liberal system of social governance, we can

better understand how our modern institutions sometimes alleviate social hierarchies and sometimes reformulate them. Many of these hierarchies contain changing conceptions of the household and the place of its members in politics. I contend that the modern liberal order that took hold in the United States in the twentieth century retained imprints from the earlier common law system of governance, meaning that status hierarchies connected to marriage, labor, and race were modernized under such rubrics as privacy, autonomy, and federalism. Put positively, despite the problematic way in which it is conceived, individualism (a status that for women is premised on their separation from domestic relations) affords some members of previously subordinated groups new opportunities for political efficacy and social mobility.

Approaching constitutional development through debates over civic membership allows for new insights into one of the central paradoxes of American history — namely, how it is that a nation founded on universalist principles of equality is so marked by a history of hierarchy, subordination, and exclusion. How can Thomas Jefferson be both the author of the Declaration of Independence and the master (and father) of slaves? How can the legacies of slavery, coverture, immigrant exclusion, Indian extermination, and relocation camps be reconciled with a history that includes the Declaration, the Bill of the Rights, the Emancipation Proclamation, the Four Freedoms, and the "I have a dream" speech? Many resolve this contradiction by imagining that liberal individualism and equality constitute the core truth about America, while practices of subordination do not represent the nation's spirit or destiny and are better understood as historical remnants that eventually were swept away by the power of American political ideals. Such a portrait is seductive, not least for the subordinated groups who invoke it to advance claims of inclusion.[3] Yet it is also a troublesome misrepresentation for a nation that often proves willing not only to retain and reformulate certain forms of social hierarchy, but to generate new institutions and practices of political and social exclusion. It makes more sense, then, to begin with the premise that both hierarchy and equality have been central to the principles and practices of the American constitutional order.

We can begin to make sense of the duality of the American political experience by looking comprehensively at the constitutional order as a social design that expresses and manages, through the terms of civic membership, the competing principles of individual rights and concerns with social order. The polity is shaped by a civic order that affords different terms of rights and recognition and that demands different duties from various groups within the nation. Variations in the terms of civic membership accord with the civic standing and social place of particular social groups. The focus of the book's analysis is debates on gender and civic membership. For, as both a central and long-subordinated group in American politics, women's civic membership reveals the boundaries and nature of the constitution order. The first part of the book considers the impact of the Nineteenth Amendment and finds that, while suffrage provided women with a claim to an identity as engaged citizens and legal persons, marriage remained a defining element in the civic status of women and men. Part II focuses on the 1940s, and finds that the new validations of labor status and military status worked to elevate the civic position of American men over women. Part III examines the impact of second wave feminism on civic membership. Inspired by the civil rights revolution, the 1960s and 1970s were decades when women's citizenship expanded under the rubric of equality. Yet, since many Americans remained convinced that sex differences run more than skin deep, and that women's social roles should involve more than their individual ambitions, there was a limit to how far equality pursuits could go. In areas like contraception and abortion, privacy became an alternative principle for expanding the rights of women. What emerges from this analysis is the long, uneven, and still unfinished process of claiming the status of full legal personhood for women. The conclusion of this book offers an alternative vision of civic presence for women based on an embodied, public form of civic membership.

Theoretical Framework

A vast comparative literature on citizenship and civic membership has emerged in recent years. This literature arose in response to large-scale historical events in the late twentieth century, such as the birth of new nations following the collapse of the Soviet Union; the rise of globalization and attendant changes in political and economic relations; the growth in political formations and claims based on race, gender, ethnicity, and religion; and an increase in claims of civic dualism associated with new patterns of migration and the expansion of transnational governing institutions. These events have changed and complicated the terms of civic membership away from the stable patterns established after World War II in the industrial West.

Understanding this shift away from industrialism, nationalism, and legal individualism as foundations for civic membership has led many scholars to consider the role that institutions play in organizing political identities and the relationship between the populous and the state. Some of this work, including this book, takes the form of historical inquiry into where we have been in order to clarify our view of where we are going.

This study of U.S. civic membership and gender politics is situated within the framework of constitutional politics. *Civic membership* refers to the legal and political status of all persons under U.S. political authority. In addition to citizens, this category would include slaves, wards (e.g., Native Americans), permanent residents, immigrants in the process of naturalizing, colonized subjects (e.g., the populations of the Philippines and Puerto Rico following the Spanish American War), and women who lost their U.S. citizenship through marriage to foreign nationals. In contrast, *citizenship* is conceived of here in the formal sense, as a legal status. One either is or is not a citizen of a nation. Since the adoption of the Fourteenth Amendment in 1868, all persons born in the United States, or naturalized by the federal government, are considered American citizens. Specific legal rights typically attach to citizenship, such as the right to vote or to serve on a jury. Certain duties are expected of citizens, including the duty to defend the nation in times of war. Governments typically provide certain social benefits to their citizens as well, often in recognition of their civic service — such as social security, veterans' benefits, and Medicare. Though not all citizens have these rights, benefits, and duties, citizenship is typically used as a legal marker for their assignment. Throughout this book, references to citizenship are narrowly specified in terms of formal legal status.

Civic membership also refers to the broader political, legal, and social meanings that attach to one's place within the polity. It is conceived of dynamically and historically, as involving everyday political practices and processes in which the state and its members both enact and contest members' rights, duties, and civic statuses within different institutional and discursive settings. Civic membership is located in all of the places where the state and the populous intersect: in the legal realm, the regulatory and policy realms, and the realm of political representation and popular culture. Within the nation the experience of civic membership varies, both according to the institutional or ideological site where interaction occurs (in a voting booth, before a court of law, on a welfare line, or in a classroom where stu-

dents pledge allegiance to the flag), and according to the social group represented in that experience. The positions of various social groups come
together in a larger civic order, where the civic standing of each is defined
relative to the rest.

The *constitutional order* of the United States refers to the role of the
Constitution, constitutional discourse, and constitutional law in structuring
the polity institutionally and socially.[4] Appeals to constitutional laws and
norms represent appeals to foundational law and to fundamental political
commitments that bind us across generations. The community invoked and
created in the phrase "We, the People," stands at the center of the institutional framework and political community that the Constitution defines. On
the one hand, the Constitution outlines the power and offices of the national
government. On the other hand, the Constitution suggests a civic order in
which the government and "the People" have a set of rights and duties
toward one another. Civic membership, to the extent that it speaks to the
reciprocal relationship between the people and the government, is at the
heart of the constitutional order. Usually in American politics, the overall
terms of civic membership are assumed, but occasionally they are deeply
challenged, either internally (by social movements and political realign-
ments) or externally (by wars or economic depressions), in ways that affect
the structure of the larger constitutional order and the relationship of various social groups to one another within constitutional politics.

Some scholars suggest that it is useful to see the Constitution as contain-
ing both social and structural elements. The structural elements (e.g.,
Articles 1–3) provide an institutional design for the federal government, des-
ignating the division of labor between the branches, the organization and
operation of different offices, the areas of governing authority, and the relationship with the states. The social elements of the Constitution reflect the
normative commitments contained in the document (e.g., the Preamble; the
Guaranty Clause), address issues of political membership (e.g., Article 4,
Section 2; Amendments XIII–XV, XIX, XXIV, and XXVI), and provide for
individual rights and popular sovereignty (e.g., the Bill of Rights). I contend
that this division between the structural and social elements of the Constitution relies upon a false dichotomy.

Even in its structural elements, the Constitution provides a social design,
both when it creates a body politic and when it provides the means for its
social recognition and regulation.[5] Aspects of this social design include: the

purpose of government is to serve the people; the power of government derives from the consent of the governed; different forms of democratic representation provide for the expression of different social interests in government; federalism allows for and endorses the social-ordering authority of states; and the guaranteeing of certain rights expressed in various amendments suggests support for certain social roles, forms of social organization, and types of political engagement. Further, both the Bill of Rights and the checks-and-balances mechanisms of the Constitution express an eighteenth-century concern with limiting the authority of the government over *the people*. This social-design perspective may be applied to understanding constitutional development in the debates over civic membership.

The constitutional order creates legal persons and a political community; it orders relations among the members of that community; and it provides a purpose or mission for that community.[6] In this regard, the constitutional order invokes and creates a body politic that is both bounded and internally ordered. At the interface between the polity and society, by recognizing and rewarding certain social roles and relationships, the constitutional order helps to constitute society itself. Of course, not all aspects of our social roles and relations are generated by our civic membership. But to a greater extent than is typically recognized, who we are, what we do, and who we are attached to are contingent upon our constitutionally inscribed place in the polity.[7]

Constitutions do not just call upon social identities; they help to create and regulate a *social order*. All communities are structured around different social roles — those of husbands and wives, parents and children, masters and servants, teachers and pupils, and so on. These roles find expression in politics through the government's recognition and regulation of these social relationships in legal codes dealing with marriage, morality, family relations, racial segregation, and labor relations. In American politics, social-order concerns typically are treated as matters of state law when they are regulated under the authority of a state's police power.[8] But at various times in our national politics, social roles prove pertinent to civic membership, sometimes explicitly and sometimes implicitly. Community and social regulatory concerns governed under the police power are often in tension with constitutional guarantees of individual liberty. Thus social-order interests may oppose liberty interests, an opposition made particularly visible in cases considering the civic status of subordinate groups like women and African

Americans. These groups' contributions to social ordering sometimes outweigh claims to liberty and individual rights, a tendency that leaves governing authorities with the task of finding the constitutional means to justify this preference for order over liberty. *The constitutional order acts as an instrument of social design when social roles are made pertinent to civic membership, and when the terms of civic membership are used to regulate social relations.*

This function is not just a matter of federal judges ceding authority to the states. More important are instances when constitutional actors uphold social arrangements for substantive reasons. When Congress and the courts express a preference for certain forms of marriage — monogamous, intraracial, or heterosexual — they connect this preference to the health and character of the body politic. Sometimes governing authorities do not just recognize certain social roles; they also reward particular roles — like the roles of head of household, husband, or worker — with political privileges or social benefits. The terms of civic membership are attached to these social identities and functions. Finally, the courts may give constitutional validation and purpose to laws that regulate social relations in the interest of upholding a certain kind of social order, for instance when they affirm antimiscegenation laws.

Some constitutional orders make their social-order commitments clear and unambiguous features of their constitutional texts.[9] That is not the case with the U.S. constitutional order. The text of the U.S. Constitution sets out general social-ordering principles (popular sovereignty, principles of personal liberty, etc.) and only occasionally provides explicit terms for the Constitution as social design — in the Three-Fifths Clause, the Voting Amendments, and the Prohibition Amendment, for instance. The elaboration of the constitutional order as social design happens mostly elsewhere: in court rulings, congressional debates, presidential declarations, and social-movement pronouncements on the meaning of the Constitution. Sometimes these elaborations become authoritative and are institutionalized — meaning they shape the terms of civic membership for the broader community — and sometimes they do not.

The process of elaboration has changed over time. During the first hundred-plus years of constitutional experience, preference for particular social arrangements was clearly stated by constitutional actors; in time, in the course of the twentieth century, the terms of articulation became more remote. Looking across American constitutional history, one can see a shift from the articulation of express social-ordering concerns to a more neutral, liberal language that stresses individualism, achievement, and choice. Once governing authorities spoke in terms of women's perpetual dependence (*Muller v. Oregon*, 208 U.S. 412 [1908], 421); "the degraded condition of" an "unhappy race" (*Dred Scott v. Sandford*, 60 U.S. 393 [1857], 409); women's natural entitlement to "special considerations" (*Breedlove v. Suttles*, 302 U.S. 277 [1937], 282); or of "a race so different" it was excluded from citizenship (*Plessy v. Ferguson*, 163 U.S. 537 [1896], 561). Later, their language evolved to include references to a group's failure to assimilate (*Hirabayashi v. U.S.*, 320 U.S. 81 [1943], 96); the "usages, customs and traditions" that justified segregation (*Plessy v. Ferguson*, 550); privacy as the value that protected domestic life (*Griswold v. Connecticut*, 381 U.S. 479 [1965]); and the "attitudes, interests and beliefs" which prevented women's economic advancement (*EEOC v. Sears, Roebuck and Co.*, 839 F.2d 302 7th Cir. [1988], 321). Sometimes the shift to a language of liberalism was accompanied by an expansion in rights and political power for subordinate groups; sometimes it represented a recoded justification for social hierarchy. This book traces the changes in the way that social-ordering concerns have been constitutionally articulated over time and considers how these changes have affected the terms of civic membership.

Many of the struggles over civic membership have revolved around the tension between social-order concerns and individual liberty. The two main founding documents of the American constitutional order — the U.S. Constitution and the Declaration of Independence — tend to be read as emphasizing different political values and interests.[10] From a social-design perspective, the Declaration speaks to the rights of the individual, while the Constitution begins with an invocation of community. Both documents begin with "We."[11] But in the Declaration the weight of the main text, and the presumption that provides legitimation for self-governance, lies in the "truth" that "all men are created equal." That is the part of the Declaration that has historically sparked the political aspirations of different groups. In contrast, the Preamble of the Constitution focuses on the political interests of the community for whom a government is created that will "promote the general welfare." Political elites and governing authorities have relied on the Preamble in their efforts to identify the boundaries of the American political community. This distinction in emphasis is captured by the shorthand phrases we commonly use to invoke these documents. That phrase for the

Constitution is "We, the People," while for the Declaration it is "all men are created equal." Throughout American history, these two central texts have been given meaning by the political actors who have laid claim to them, articulating their "constitutional aspirations" (Hartog, 1987) with reference to them.

Much of the writing about the role of liberalism in American political development considers whether the political recognition of social arrangements is at odds with the individualist, autarkic presumptions of liberalism. Some contend that concerns about social order appear as a remnant from an earlier stage in political development, as represented, for instance, in the ongoing vitality of the common law tradition of domestic relations in American politics (Orren, 1991; Tomlins, 1995; Zeigler, 1996a and 1996b). For others, liberal theory, with its presumption of possessive individualism, offers an insufficient account of how society should be organized, leaving itself open to illiberal programs for ordering society (Tocqueville, 1945; R. M. Smith, 1997; Hartz, 1955). Finally, there are those who think that liberal philosophy has an implicit sociology connected to it, in which groups are organized hierarchically between rational, public individuals, and the irrational, dependent others who are under the public and private authority of autonomous individuals (Mehta, 1999). Within feminist theory, many scholars seek to uncover and analyze the ways that liberal politics and institutions fail to promote gender equity or are premised on the social and political disempowerment of women (W. Brown, 1995; Pateman, 1988).

The duality of American experience — the struggle between social order and individual rights — is often expressed in debates over civic membership. A couple of examples will illustrate this point. Prior to the Civil War, Abraham Lincoln thought that slavery was wrong and corrupting, and believed that African Americans were human beings entitled to the recognition and protection of the Declaration of Independence. Yet the prospect of civic or social equality for African Americans was also unimaginable for him. As William Cain writes, "Lincoln insisted that while blacks were covered by the terms of the Declaration of Independence, they could not permanently dwell in the nation. . . . Given his doubts about blacks ever becoming full-fledged U.S. citizens, it appears that Lincoln was 'a pessimist on the subject of the possibility of an interracial, egalitarian society' " (Cain, 1996, 57–58). So while African Americans deserved recognition as human beings under the terms of the Declaration, they would not make good members of the political community invoked by the Constitution. Lincoln favored recolonizing former slaves in Africa.

Women offered a more difficult problem for managing the tension between individualism and social order. They were necessarily a part of the political community, since it was a living, expanding community in which women bore and raised the next generation of citizens. But women were members of that community indirectly, as attachments to men. In this sense, they fell under the terms of the Preamble to the Constitution from the beginning, but their inclusion in the Declaration took generations. What these debates also suggest is the double meaning that inheres in the phrase "We, the People." "The People" may be seen as a community of equals, who are also the rights-bearing individuals of the Declaration. Because of the pre-sumption of meaningful equality, Lincoln was unable to imagine African Americans as members of the constitutional community of "the People." Or, "the People" includes the unequal dependents of rights-bearing individuals, who together constitute the nation as a social body. So one could be a mem-ber of the community invoked by the Constitution without falling under the terms of the Declaration.

Likewise, civic membership had a double meaning: in nineteenth-century America, it meant either all those recognized as members of the national community (anyone entitled to an American passport), or only the rights-bearing individuals entitled to full civic status and political participation (those who could vote, hold office, etc.). Women, if they were native-born and white, were always civic members in the first sense, yet they campaigned for decades to become civic members in the second sense as well, a campaign that lasted far longer for nonwhite women.[12] Subordinated political groups typically have sought to change the terms of their civic membership and claim inclusion by invoking the Declaration of Independence.[13] This claim to personhood and equality also implies a reconceptualization of "the People" in whose name the polity operates. Who is a part of "the People," and on what terms, has been a central question in the overall meaning and purpose of the constitutional order.

This approach to thinking of the Constitution as social design contrasts with several others that appear in the literature. Often scholars of American political development focus on the workings of state institutions while giv-ing less attention to points of intersection between state institutions and public action. Such studies might approach civic membership in terms of immigration policy (King, 2000), or the extension of political rights to new groups (Orren, 1991; Kryder, 2000), or the development of social provisioning bureaucracies (Skocpol, 1992; Lieberman, 1998). The theoretical literature on gender and civic membership (Yuval-Davis, 1997; Burgett, 1998; Lister, 1997), or race and civic membership (Yu, 2001; Gilroy, 1993; Lipsitz, 1998), frequently is framed in terms of the construction of political identity or a broadly conceived notion of the public sphere. Such literature pays relatively little attention to places where civic members interact with state institutions, or to the ways in which their political identities and actions are formed by those institutions. Some studies, however, are at the intersection of political science, historical sociology, and legal history, and examine in detail how state institutions form civic membership and how civic membership is enacted or contested by various social groups (Mettler, 1998; McDonagh, forthcoming; Novkov, 2001). This book is clearly indebted to this scholarship, which tends, nonetheless, to be more specific regarding the groups, institutions, or periods on which they focus. The present study endeavors to create a more historically and theoretically comprehensive account of the role of governing institutions in shaping the terms of civic membership for men and women in the United States.

In analyzing constitutional development through debates over civic membership, this book considers how the changing terms of civic membership shift the polity *institutionally* as well socially. Such institutional changes may involve new mandates for government action in support of newly recognized rights; shifts in the balance of authority between levels of government or branches of government; or restrictions on the actions of government as interferences with the rights of citizens. In its focus on debates over civic membership, this book outlines several instances where developments in the institutional and social aspects of the constitutional order reflect one another, such as the shift that occurred in the 1930s and 1940s when the Supreme Court found that the recognition of civic difference between men and women was constitutionally acceptable as part of the shift from a negative-rights to a positive-rights regime in labor law.[14] The acceptance of civic difference had broad implications for the organization of the social insurance programs developed in support of social citizenship under the New Deal. This example, and others, are elaborated in an analysis that views the Constitution as an instrument of social design in order to highlight both the shifting institutional commitments of government and the changing terms of membership in the community of "We, the People."

The next section analyzes a constitutional movement that occurred at the end of the Civil War along with two significant Supreme Court cases from that period, considered here for two reasons. First, it is essential to understand the nature of the constitutional order that emerged from Reconstruction, since that order provides the framework for the constitutional struggles over civic membership in the twentieth century. A great deal of excellent scholarship already exists on this period in American constitutional development. The particular focus of this inquiry is on the role that the Woman Rights movement played in shaping the interpretation of the Reconstruction Amendments. Second, this analysis is meant to be exemplary, demonstrating what it means to think about constitutional development and struggles over civic membership as reflective of one another.

The Civil War Legacy

The American constitutional order was remade in the aftermath of the Civil War. Three constitutional amendments — which abolished slavery, defined national citizenship, and protected the right to vote against racial discrimination — grounded this new constitutional order. Relative to the states, the authority of the federal government had been greatly expanded in the wake of secession. The new constitutional order that emerged from Reconstruction provided the framework for subsequent conflicts over the terms of civic membership for various social groups. With the incorporation of the freedmen into the citizenry, the composition of "We, the People" was forever changed, although their place within the polity remained a subject of much conflict and debate. Women, too, sought to change their place within the political community of the nation, and demanded recognition as full, rights-bearing civic members under the terms of the Reconstruction amendments. Those demands were rejected: women's political exclusion lasted until the adoption of a new constitutional amendment in 1920. Yet even today the three amendments adopted between 1865 and 1870 supply much of the framework for civic membership.

With the end of the Civil War and the adoption of the Reconstruction

Amendments, national citizenship was defined and specified by the Constitution for the first time. As the terms of the new constitutional regime were elaborated in Congress and the courts, one question with which these governing institutions grappled was what the new civic order meant for women. Previously, women were presumed to lack independent civic standing; they were represented in the public realm by their fathers, husbands, and masters. Were women to be included under the new terms of civic membership, as national citizens with the same rights and privileges as others? If so, what impact would this have on the terms of social ordering? Just as this issue emerged, the suffrage movement moved forward with a campaign to claim for women all the rights and privileges of national citizenship under the Fourteenth Amendment.

Within the postbellum constitutional context, the status of African American women was often obscured in constitutional and political discussions. African American women participated in the suffrage movement and civil rights movements of the nineteenth and early twentieth centuries. Yet their participation was frequently neglected, derided, or obscured by leaders of the civil rights movement and the mainstream suffrage movement (Terborg-Penn, 1998). The exclusionary character of these movements was also reflected in the federal courts and Congress, where the discussions typically referred to *men* for African Americans and *whites* for women. This book seeks to specify which groups are being discussed in these legal and political texts and highlights places where concerns about race intersected with concerns about gender status.

The Thirteenth Amendment was adopted just as the Civil War ended in 1865, abolishing slavery and involuntary servitude throughout the United States and empowering Congress to enforce the amendment's provisions. After the adoption of the Thirteenth Amendment, questions remained about the status of the freedmen. There was growing concern about the mistreatment of African Americans in the South, where there was considerable resistance to the idea of civic equality across the races. Seeking to secure the civic status of former slaves, Congress passed the Fourteenth Amendment, which was adopted in 1868 and declared that all "persons born or naturalized in the United States, and subject to the jurisdiction thereof, are citizens of the United States and of the State wherein they reside." This sentence that opens the amendment makes all those born in the United States, regardless of race or gender, citizens of both the nation and of their state.

The Fourteenth Amendment also sought to protect these newly made citizens from hostile or discriminatory action by the states. The second sentence of Section 1 includes three key clauses. The first clause forbids the individual states from "abridg[ing] the *privileges and immunities* of *citizens* of the United States." The Privileges and Immunities Clause is the only one of the three that specifically addresses the rights of *citizens*, yet this clause was narrowly interpreted, so it proved less relevant to the efforts of rights advocates to expand civic membership. Echoing the Fifth Amendment, the second clause prevents states from depriving "any *person* of life, liberty or property without *due process* of law." Due process jurisprudence became a significant and controversial source of rights development both early on and later in the twentieth century. Finally, the third clause commands the states not to "deny to any person within its jurisdiction the *equal protection* of the laws." This last clause proved vital to the expansion of civil rights in the twentieth century.

The terms of the Fourteenth Amendment are both general and specific. Generally, the amendment establishes national and state citizenship for all persons born in the United States. More specifically, the Fourteenth Amendment provides protection to all persons from hostile or discriminatory state action — particularly relevant for the newly freed slaves, whose civil rights the amendment was meant to secure. The second section, which addresses the issue of political rights, calls for a reduction in national political representation for states that deny voting rights to any males over the age of twenty-one. This addition of the word *male* to the Constitution was derided by women's rights advocates, who demanded equal treatment for all civic members, regardless of race or sex. Eventually, this amendment became the foundation for a civic membership based on equality and individual rights.

The last Reconstruction Amendment, the Fifteenth Amendment, provides that the right to vote may not be abridged on account of race or previous condition of servitude. While this amendment does not provide a positive right or a direct grant of suffrage, it does protect that right (which emanates from the states) from discrimination wherever it exists. The reference to subordinate status also links the Fifteenth Amendment to the Thirteenth Amendment. Prior to the adoption of the Fifteenth Amendment in 1870, there was uncertainty over whether the Fourteenth Amendment provided for the right to vote. Most believed that the amendment secures civil rights but not political rights, though some thought that political rights are necessarily implied by the amendment. The passage of the Fifteenth Amendment was read as evidence that the Fourteenth Amendment did not include the right to vote. Yet some link between suffrage and the Fourteenth Amendment was retained with the addition of the Fifteenth Amendment. To many, the vote implied full civic status. Suffrage also was viewed as an instrument of political self-defense for the other rights and interests of citizenship. Although many leading suffragists worked with the abolition movement prior to the war, some opposed the Fourteenth and Fifteenth Amendments since they were viewed as impediments to women's rights. Eventually, the language of the Nineteenth Amendment was patterned on the language of the Fifteenth Amendment. Nonetheless, the courts found that the Nineteenth Amendment had less impact on the civic status of women than the Fourteenth and Fifteenth Amendments had on the civic status of African American men (Ritter, 2000a and 2002).

THE NEW DEPARTURE

Early women's rights activists, such as Lucretia Mott, Susan B. Anthony, Paulina Wright Davis, and the Grimke sisters, began their activist careers in the antislavery cause in the early 1840s. The natural rights and religious humanist philosophy of the movement (as well as the discriminatory attitudes of many male leaders) inspired these activists to call for the recognition of women's rights and humanity. The woman destined to become the intellectual giant of the movement, Elizabeth Cady Stanton (then a young mother of several small children, not yet including Harriet), called a convention in the small Upstate New York town of Seneca Falls in 1848, thus launching the Woman Rights movement. The gathered assembly of men and women issued a declaration (paraphrasing the Declaration of Independence) demanding different rights and protections for women, including suffrage. After a flurry of activity in the 1850s, the work of the movement was put on hold for several years while attention was devoted to the Civil War and abolition. As the war ended, many former allies were divided over whether to pursue universal rights for all Americans or to focus first on the position of the freedmen in the South. After the Thirteenth and Fourteenth Amendments had been adopted, two large women's rights organizations were formed to promote the cause of suffrage for women. The more radical group was the National Woman Suffrage Association (NWSA), headed by Stanton and Anthony. The more reformist organization was the American Woman Suffrage Association (AWSA), headed by Lucy Stone and Harry Blackwell.

Despite opposition by the radicals, the Fourteenth Amendment was adopted. So at the 1869 NWSA annual convention Virginia Minor unveiled a new strategy for securing the vote:

> I believe that the Constitution of the United States gives me every right and privilege to which every other citizen of the United States is entitled. . . . [A]ll rights and privileges depend merely on the acknowledgment of our right as citizens, and wherever this question has arisen the Government has universally conceded we are citizens; and as such, I claim that if we are entitled to two or three privileges, we are entitled to all. (Stanton, Anthony, and Gage, 1969, 409–10)

Minor's speech and accompanying resolutions marked a radical departure for the woman suffrage movement. These suffragists now asserted that as citizens (under the Fourteenth Amendment) women were already entitled to vote. This change in strategy was heralded as the "New Departure" (DuBois, 1987 and 1995; Winkler, 2001).

The New Departure sought to demonstrate that under the Reconstruction Amendments, women were national citizens with all of the rights and privileges of other national citizens, including the right to vote. The effort failed, but an analysis of the campaign reveals how the new American constitutional order tolerated distinctions between groups of citizens. The distinction between state and national citizenship was used to recognize equality in national citizenship, while differences in rights and duties were retained among the ranks of state citizens. Since the New Departure took place just as the federal courts began interpreting the Reconstruction Amendments, I suggest that the campaign promoted a more restrictive interpretation of the Fourteenth Amendment that weakened the link between voting and civic membership, delayed the adoption of woman suffrage, and limited the impact of the Nineteenth Amendment once it was secured.

The New Departure campaign lasted from 1869–75, ending with a firm rejection of its key argument by the Supreme Court in *Minor v. Happersett*,

88 U.S. 162 (1874). Prior to this ruling, the advocates of the New Departure employed four tactics in their campaign to secure the vote: the first was *publicity*, in the form of speeches, pamphlets, and newspaper articles, circulated in hope of creating a public dialogue about the cause of women's suffrage and the rights of women as citizens; the second was *legislative*, aimed particularly at Congress in the form of memorials and testimony calling for resolutions to recognize women's inherent right to vote or laws to punish states that discriminated against women in the right to vote; the third was *direct action*, as women around the country attempted to register and vote, sometimes successfully; and the fourth was *judicial*, because as a result of women's efforts to vote, cases came before the state and federal courts on the question of whether women possessed the right of suffrage as an aspect of citizenship (Stanton, Anthony, and Gage, 1969, chaps. 23–25).

The most insightful and innovative advocates of the New Departure (such as Anthony and Stanton) interpreted the Fourteenth Amendment as a mandate for civic inclusion and rights. First, they claimed that since women were born in the United States and were persons, they were citizens of the national government. Second, as citizens, women were entitled to all of the rights and privileges of citizenship. Next came their key and most controversial claim — that under the Privileges and Immunities Clause of the Fourteenth Amendment, all citizens were entitled to vote. This claim rested on three assumptions: first, that national citizenship was superior to state citizenship; second, that voting was a privilege of citizenship; and third, that the voting privilege was protected under national citizenship.

In testimony before Congress, Stanton rejected the view that states could infringe on the rights of national citizens: "While the Constitution of the United States leaves qualifications of electors to the several states, it nowhere gives them the right to deprive any citizen of the elective franchise . . . hence those provisions of the state constitutions that exclude women from the franchise are in direct violation of the Federal Government" (Stanton, Anthony, and Gage, 1969, 411–12). Stanton contended that control of the franchise was a matter that concerned both the state and the federal governments, yet the federal government reigned supreme here. States could regulate qualifications for the franchise but they could not arbitrarily disenfranchise large groups of people.

How is voting a privilege of citizenship? Here Stanton looked beyond the Fourteenth Amendment to the principles expressed in the Preamble. "Even the preamble recognizes, in the phrase 'We, the people,' the true origin of all just government" (Stanton, Anthony, and Gage, 1969, 412). Women were members of the political community whose consent legitimated the government. The New Departure advocates linked their expansive, inclusive view of "the People" with the guaranty of a republican government (assumed to imply a representative government) contained in Article 4. Finally, the suffragists read the Constitution through the Declaration of Independence. As Anthony said prior to her trial for voting in the 1872 presidential election, "The Declaration of Independence, the National and State Constitutions, . . . all alike propose to protect the people in the exercise of their God-given rights. . . . [H]ere, in this very first paragraph of the Declaration, is the assertion of the natural right of all to the ballot; for, how can 'the consent of the governed' be given, if the right to vote be denied?" (Stanton, Anthony, and Gage, 1969, 631). Women were a part of the political community recognized by the Declaration and the Constitution. They had *always* had the right to vote, even if earlier generations of men failed to recognize that right. The constitutional order that Stanton and Anthony envisioned went beyond the intentions of the founders or even the words of the constitutional text. It was an order founded in the *principles* expressed in both the Constitution and the Declaration — an order in which all of the people had certain natural and inalienable rights, including the right of suffrage.

RESPONSE TO THE NEW DEPARTURE

The response to the New Departure by Congress and the courts was to insure that the new terms of civic membership did not disturb gender roles within the social order. The understanding of the right of suffrage that existed prior to the Civil War was more classically republican or corporatist than liberal in nature, as spelled out in the various state constitutions and laws.[15] Electors were typically defined as male inhabitants, freeholders, taxpayers, freemen, and (especially in the South) white. Property qualifications for voting were gradually removed during the antebellum era, but the requirement that a voter be a taxpayer or a householder was often retained. These freeholders or householders may not have owned medieval estates, but they did represent all members of their household in the public realm. Under the common law of domestic relations, the master of a household held authority over his wife, children, wards, servants, and slaves, and it was in the interest of all of these people that he spoke in the public realm. In nineteenth-century America, when free white men entered the public realm, they met there as members of the social compact and as liberal individuals enjoying equal rights. But in their households, they were republican masters.

Women, then, held a border status. The civic identities of women in the nineteenth century were governed primarily under coverture (explicitly for wives and implicitly for single women who were treated as would-be wives), which left many antebellum state judges to struggle with the question of whether women were citizens (Kettner, 1978). After the Fourteenth Amendment, it was clear that women were citizens. What remained unclear was their relationship to the state: Was it mediated or was it direct? Were they individuals and legal persons, or were they dependents of their fathers and husbands? What position did they hold, exactly, in the community of "We, the People"? With the end of the Civil War and the adoption of the Reconstruction Amendments, the racial order of the United States was remade (though the extent of that remaking was sharply debated). Yet Congress and the judiciary moved to limit the degree to which this new political structure disturbed the remainder of the social order (Stanley, 1988). That desire to limit the amendments' impact on the broader social order was expressed most strongly in connection to gender. Government authorities clearly asserted that the Reconstruction Amendments were not intended to and did not change the political status of women. How did the courts and Congress manage to preserve gender hierarchy within the old social and political order while still acknowledging the changes wrought by the war and Reconstruction in race relations?[16] The key to that puzzle lays in their interpretation of the Privileges and Immunities Clause of the Fourteenth Amendment.

On the same day in the early 1870s, the Supreme Court handed down two cases that provided the first major interpretations of the Fourteenth Amendment. The Court's ruling in the *Slaughter-House Cases*, 83 U.S. 36 (1872), sharply limited the scope of the Privileges and Immunities Clause of the Fourteenth Amendment. The second case was *Bradwell v. Illinois*, 83 U.S. 130 (1872), where the Court upheld Myra Bradwell's exclusion from the Illinois bar. This case is remembered especially for the notorious concurrent opinion of Justice Joseph P. Bradley. It is illuminating to read these two cases together, for not only did *Slaughter-House* provide the means by which the gender order was left undisturbed by the Fourteenth Amendment in

Bradwell, but *Bradwell* may provide part of the explanation for the motivation behind the Court's ruling in *Slaughter-House*.

The complaint in *Slaughter-House* was brought by a group of Louisiana butchers to protest the state government's establishment of a monopoly on facilities for animal slaughtering in New Orleans. The butchers contended that the new slaughtering facilities violated their rights as citizens to pursue a calling or livelihood. The key questions in the case concerned the relationship between state and federal citizenship, and what constituted a privilege or immunity of citizenship. The majority opinion is prefaced by a summary of the plaintiff's argument before the Court, which states: "The purpose [of the Fourteenth Amendment] is manifest, to establish through the whole jurisdiction of the United States ONE PEOPLE, and that every member of the empire shall understand and appreciate the fact that his privileges and immunities cannot be abridged by State authority" (83 U.S. 53). Writing for the majority, Justice Samuel F. Miller rejected this interpretation because he saw a different purpose in these amendments, emphasizing "the one pervading purpose found in them all, . . . we mean the freedom of the slave race, the security and firm establishment of that freedom, and the protection of the newly-made freeman and citizen from the oppressions of those who had formerly exercised unlimited dominion over him" (83 U.S. 71). While the Fourteenth Amendment defined national citizenship and protected the privileges that attached to it, it did not disturb the terms of state citizenship. "It is quite clear, then, that there is a citizenship of the United States, and a citizenship of a State, which are distinct from each other, and which depend upon different characteristics or circumstances in the individual" (83 U.S. 74). It was through federalism, then, that the "different characteristics or circumstances in the individual" were expressed in relation to civic membership. Federalism allowed the Court to preserve a differentiated social order while proclaiming an egalitarian national citizenship designed to protect the freedmen. The privileges of national citizenship, at least for white butchers, did not include professional or employment rights.

In his dissent, Justice Stephen J. Field took a different view of the relationship between national and state citizenship: "A citizen of a State is now only a citizen of the United States residing in that State" (83 U.S. 95). By implication, civic rights resided in national citizenship: "The fundamental rights, privileges, and immunities which belong to him *as a free man* and a free citizen, now belong to him as a citizen of the United States, and are not dependent upon his citizenship of any State" (83 U.S. 95, emphasis mine). For Field (who went on to quote from the Declaration), as for Anthony and Stanton, the rights of citizens did not derive from the Constitution. Rights were merely expressed in the Constitution and protected by it. Yet for Field, these rights were still gendered — they were the rights of a "free man."

In the Supreme Court journal, the conclusion of *Slaughter-House* is followed on the next page by the start of the Court's opinion in *Bradwell*, which considered whether women have the right to practice law. Although Myra Bradwell was an esteemed member of the Chicago legal community and the editor of Chicago's daily legal journal, she had been denied admission to the Illinois bar. Arguing the case before the Supreme Court, Senator Matthew Hale Carpenter opened by saying, "The question does not involve the right of a female to vote" (83 U.S. 133). This statement was a clear attempt by Carpenter to distance himself from the advocates of the New Departure. Yet Carpenter's disavowal of the New Departure position did not protect him from the Court's narrow construction of national citizenship. Writing again for the majority, Justice Miller rejected Carpenter's claim that professional licensing was a privilege of citizenship protected under the Fourteenth Amendment, noting that the "opinion just delivered in the *Slaughter-House Cases* renders elaborate argument in the present case unnecessary" (139). Rather, as the logic of the prior case suggested, "the right to control" professional licensing was "not transferred for its protection to the Federal government, and its exercise is in no manner governed or controlled by citizenship of the United States in the party seeking such license" (139). Once again, federalism allowed for differentiated terms of civic membership.

That explains the *how*, but still leaves open the question of *why*. Why did the federal courts tolerate such differences in civic membership? Justice Bradley's infamous concurrence gives us the answer to this question. At issue, wrote Bradley, was the claim that "under the fourteenth amendment" it is "one of the *privileges and immunities of women as citizens* to engage in any and every profession, occupation, or employment in civil life" (140; emphasis mine). Bradley made a subtle shift in his opinion from referring to "citizens of the United States" to discussing the rights of "women as citizens." Women citizens were a distinct category, with their own privileges and immunities, which conformed to the common law (that is, coverture), the civil law, and "nature itself." The opinion continues, "On the contrary, the civil law, as well as nature herself, has always recognized a wide difference in the respective spheres and destinies of man and woman. Man is, or should be, woman's protector and defender. The natural and proper timidity and delicacy which belongs to the female sex evidently unfits it for many of the occupations of civil life" (141). Women were unfit for the activities of the civil, or public, sphere. There was a "harmony" of "interest" within the family, represented as its own governing unit, separate from the civil sphere. Yet if women were citizens, and were barred from the civil sphere, how were their interests and concerns to be represented there? They were represented by their husbands, since under common law "a woman had no legal existence separate from her husband, who was regarded as her head and representative in the social state" (141). Though citizens, women were not legal persons. They were members of the community recognized by the Constitution but not, yet, persons recognized by the Declaration. They had no legal existence apart from their husbands, who represented them in the "social state." The Fourteenth Amendment did not displace coverture as the source of women's civic status. What of unmarried women? The norm of coverture covered them as well, since "the paramount destiny and mission of woman are to fulfill the noble and benign offices of wife and mother" (141). Unmarried women were seen as exceptional and abnormal, and their lack of representation in the public sphere was deemed of little concern.

Bradley's opinion is all the more striking when read alongside his dissenting opinion in *Slaughter-House*. There, he wrote that the Fourteenth Amendment affirmed "that citizenship of the United States is the primary citizenship in this country," while state citizenship was "secondary and derivative" (83 U.S. 112). Further, this newly strengthened national citizenship brought with it many "*traditionary* rights and privileges" that "the government, whether restricted by express or implied limitations, cannot take away or impair" (114). Among the rights that made citizenship meaningful, according to Bradley, was the "right to choose one's calling" (116). When writing generally about national citizenship, Bradley quoted the Declaration and wrote in universalistic terms about fundamental rights. When he imagined white bakers and the new freedmen, Bradley saw national citizenship as a status that held a broad range of privileges and immunities, such as the right to pursue a calling. But when he envisioned women's civic membership, this universalism and individualism faded. Women were particular kinds of citizens, who were not individuals or legal persons, but people whose special calling placed them in the domestic realm.

After *Slaughter-House* and *Bradwell* national citizenship was narrowly construed to include a few civil rights, such as the right to travel. My contention here is *not* that the Court's response in these cases was entirely motivated by their abhorrence of the New Departure. Nor do I argue that the New Departure's vision of the Constitution was likely to become authoritative in the late nineteenth century. Rather, my modest claim here is that the movement influenced the *severity* of the Court's reaction and contributed to a particularly narrow interpretation of the Privileges and Immunities Clause. This movement had an impact on constitutional development, therefore, but the impact was negative; it inspired a more restrictive understanding of civic membership within the new constitutional order.[17]

Despite these developments, suffrage advocates pushed forward the claim that voting was necessary to protect citizens in the exercise of all of their civic rights. If voting was implied by the Fourteenth Amendment (something left in doubt by the new Fifteenth Amendment), then this right was likely to be found in the Privileges and Immunities Clause. Once that clause was narrowly interpreted by Justice Miller, it was easy for the lower state and federal courts to dismiss the claims of the New Departure movement — something they did on a regular basis in the early 1870s. Anthony hoped to have her name on the case that went before the Supreme Court on the question of woman suffrage (as mentioned above, she was arrested and tried for voting in the presidential election of 1872), but a federal judge in New York ended her dream by dismissing her claim to a right to vote under the Fourteenth Amendment.

The case that settled the suffrage question was brought by Virginia Minor. Francis Minor (Virginia's husband) argued the plaintiff's position before the Court in *Minor v. Happersett*, 88 U.S. 162 (1874). In his brief before the Court, Francis Minor contended that the franchise was a necessary privilege of national citizenship, since it was "preservative of all rights and privileges; and especially of the right of the citizen to participate in his or her government" (164). The majority was not persuaded. As part of the people who formed the United States, the Court found, women had always been citizens, though before the war they were never explicitly acknowledged as such. Going further, the Court proclaimed that "*sex has never been made one of the elements of citizenship* in the United States. In this respect men have never had an advantage over women. The same laws precisely apply to both" (170; emphasis mine). Within the realm of national citizenship the

Court denied that there was, or had ever been, a civic hierarchy based on sex. That denial was used to dismiss the relevance of the Fourteenth Amendment as a basis for defending women's citizenship or defining her privileges and immunities.

Suffrage was a state matter. According to state law, suffrage rights were open to differences between the sexes. The Reconstruction Amendments neither created nor added to the rights of national citizens; they only protected rights that were already present. "The amendment did not add to the privileges and immunities of a citizen. It simply furnished an additional guaranty for the protection of such as he already had. No new voters were necessarily made by it" (171). For suffrage to be a necessary part of national citizenship, the Court reasoned, it must have been an absolute right of citizenship in all the states at the time of the founding. The style of argument here is similar to the reasoning used in the majority opinion in *Dred Scott v. Sandford*, 60 U.S. 393 (1856).[18] Like Justice Roger B. Taney before him, Justice Miller reasoned inductively to uncover the balance between social-order concerns and individual rights within the constitutional order. The evidence from which both judges drew to determine the terms of civic membership were prior laws and practices governing subordinate social groups. Since women were citizens but not voters in virtually all the states since the founding, then suffrage could not be a necessary right of citizenship.

The Court also intuited the nature of American civic membership from the second section of the Fourteenth Amendment: "if suffrage was necessarily one of the absolute rights of citizenship, why confine the operation of the limitation to male inhabitants?" (174). This question was central, and clearly expressed the tension between liberty and social order. On the one hand, Section 2 protected liberty and individual rights by punishing states that infringed on the right to vote. On the other hand, Section 2 implicitly recognized the relevance of gender to civic membership by denying protection to women as would-be voters. Even worse, for the advocates of woman suffrage, was the Fifteenth Amendment. "If suffrage was one of these privileges or immunities [under the Fourteenth Amendment], why amend the Constitution [with the Fifteenth Amendment] to prevent its being denied on account of race, &c.?" (175). This view was taken in contrast to the arguments made in *Slaughter-House*, where each new Reconstruction Amendment confirmed and enforced the rights expressed in the previous amendment. In *Slaughter-House* voting was a right that protected all other civic rights. But in *Bradwell* voting was something different — it was separate from the civil rights of citizenship, and it was a grant from the states to those citizens who contributed to the public good. Voting was no longer viewed as coextensive with democratic citizenship. As a result of these cases, the meaning of national citizenship was narrowed as political rights were separated from and made secondary to civil rights.

THE LONG-TERM IMPACT OF THE NEW DEPARTURE

The irony of this story, then, is this: partly in response to the New Departure, the courts established a constitutional framework in which suffrage did not define civic status more broadly. This demarcation occurred at a time when, popularly, voting *was* regarded as the central right of citizenship and as the crucial marker of civic status within the ranks of citizens (Baker, 1984; Burnham, 1974; McGerr, 1986). The inclination of the courts during Reconstruction was to substantiate the importance of suffrage as an aspect of national citizenship for the freedmen. To make this argument, the courts relied heavily on the Fifteenth Amendment, stressing its connection to the Fourteenth Amendment. But, having downplayed the significance of the participatory rights of citizens (through their interpretation of the Privileges and Immunities Clause) in the Fourteenth Amendment, and having separated the civil and political rights of citizens in response to the claims of the suffragists, the courts created a framework in which it was easy to limit political rights.

In the two decades around the turn of the century, many states passed new constitutional provisions restricting the right to vote through such mechanisms as the poll tax and the literacy test (Keyssar, 2000; Kousser, 1999). By the time *Giles v. Harris*, 189 U.S. 475 (1903), was handed down, suffrage was a virtually unenforceable right in the South. As Richard Pildes writes, "notwithstanding the Fourteenth and Fifteenth Amendments, *Giles* carves out from them the category of 'political rights' and holds such rights unenforceable" (Pildes, 2000, 298). After the Nineteenth Amendment, the right of suffrage for women was not deemed unenforceable, but the significance of this right was greatly reduced by a constitutional structure that made voting an insignificant aspect of citizenship and democracy. Again from Pildes: "*Giles* reflected and shaped a constitutional culture in which the large issues of democratic governance and institutional structure were, like unknown territories on a medieval map, cast as threatening monsters and placed outside the known domains of constitutional law" (318). All American citizens lost something when participatory rights were displaced from the constitutional core of civic membership. When the women's rights movement was revitalized in the 1960s and 1970s, it focused less on political rights like voting and more on civil rights like equal treatment before the courts. This focus made for a less deliberative and more elite-driven democracy than we might otherwise have had.

Conclusion

Generations of American women — Elizabeth Cady Stanton, Harriet Stanton Blatch, and Nora Blatch among them — fought to expand the constitutional order and make it more democratic. Their efforts propelled constitutional development in the United States. The chapters that follow trace American constitutional development over much of the twentieth century. Starting with the right to vote and advancing through privacy and the protection of reproductive rights, the account that follows outlines a gradual shift from a constitutional order in which women's civic membership was based on domesticity and dependency to one in which they are mostly seen as autonomous, rights-bearing members of the polity. The emergence of this new civic status for women was marked by the institutional arrangements and norms of the prior constitutional order. Despite the advantages available to many women under these new terms of civic membership, there is growing evidence of the discrepancies and disadvantages that derive from individualism and equality as they are cast in this modern, liberal constitutional order.

The discussion undertaken in the previous section illustrates how this approach to the Constitution as social design illuminates the process of constitutional development in the decades after the Civil War. Debates over the citizenship of African Americans and women prompted the Supreme Court to assert that the Reconstruction Amendments were meant primarily to assist the freedmen, and to take a conservative view of the general framework of citizenship established by the amendments. Institutionally, this stance led the Court to rely heavily on the structure of federalism in order to differentiate the rights of male and female citizens. The general content of national citizenship was made virtually null in *Slaughter-House*, as the Privileges and Immunities Clause was found to be of little value to those claiming that their rights as citizens had been violated. Civic membership remained primarily rooted within the states. Socially, the Court validated a structure of civic membership in which the rights and position of African American men were protected, while women, both black and white, remained under the cloak of coverture in domestic harmony with their husbands. Yet this bifurcated structure provided weak protection for African American men, since political rights had only limited significance in the structure of national citizenship, and since state governments retained their authority to differentiate among ranks of citizens, albeit not directly along the color line.[19] Not surprisingly, a constitutional structure that made social ordering by sex allowable was used to assert and protect social differences along the lines of race as well.

The failure of the New Departure movement provides important background for the analysis undertaken in Part I on the impact of the Nineteenth Amendment. Scholars are often puzzled by the apparent failure of the Nineteenth Amendment either to provide women with equal citizenship or, more broadly, to remake the American constitutional order (Shklar, 1991). The contention here is that the impact of the Nineteenth Amendment was limited by the constitutional framework created during Reconstruction. In their early rulings on the meaning of the Reconstruction Amendments, the Court parsed political and civil rights in the overall structure of citizenship. At the time that rights advocates first called for women to be granted the right to vote, it was the central right of citizenship, both politically and legally (e.g., see the main opinion in *Dred Scott*). But by the time the Nineteenth Amendment was finally adopted, the significance of suffrage had declined, to be gradually replaced by other institutional links between the citizens and the government (Ritter, 2002). Consequently, the norms of coverture — which gave women a dependent and indirect position within the civic community of "We, the People" — were only partially displaced by the Nineteenth Amendment.

PART I

The Impact of the Nineteenth Amendment

Voting

After a seventy-two-year campaign, in 1920 the Nineteenth Amendment to the Constitution granted American women the right to vote. One scholar calls the campaign for the franchise "the greatest independent political movement of modern times" (Susan Kinsley Kent, quoted in Pateman, 1994, 331). The suffrage movement was broadly based and it provoked rich public debate. When the amendment passed, women were perhaps the most organized and effective political force in American society. Yet this tremendous change in the body politic left surprisingly little imprint on American politics. The absorption of this new block of voters scarcely altered the organization of electoral or party politics. Nor did the amendment change the way that the Constitution was understood or interpreted. Some would say the Nineteenth Amendment was one of the great nonevents in American political history (Shklar, 1991). The chapters in Part I of this book explore the limited impact of the Nineteenth Amendment, and analyze the changes in women's civic membership following their incorporation as voters. This chapter's focus is the relationship between voting and civic membership.

Most recent scholarship on the Nineteenth Amendment does not address its limited impact on women's civic membership or the general constitutional order. Several studies in political science deal with the effect of the Nineteenth Amendment on American electoral politics (Andersen, 1996; Burnham, 1974; Graham, 1996; Harvey, 1998; Shklar, 1991). They find that it took decades for women to be fully incorporated into the electoral system, and that women did not exhibit an independent voice in electoral politics until quite recently. Historians examining the effect of the Nineteenth Amendment on the Woman Rights movement conclude that the success of the suffrage campaign resulted in division and disorganization among women's rights activists (Chafe, 1972; Lemons, 1973; O'Neill, 1971). Yet others from both history and political science seek to demonstrate that the long campaign for the vote *did* result in substantial gains for the advocates of women's rights (Andersen, 1996; Cott, 1987 and 1998; Wheeler, 1995).

For democratic theorists, the inclusion of such a large group into a system of democratic representation is taken as a major advance in democratic governance (Nussbaum, 1999). Some scholars of American political development also regard the Nineteenth Amendment as a moment in the progression of American liberal politics toward a more egalitarian and universalist political system (R. M. Smith, 1997). Until recently, however, few scholars of constitutional development have considered the Nineteenth Amendment (but see Siegel, 2002). Most theories of constitutional development, whether they theorize development through the lens of constitutional moments (Ackerman, 1998), debate the impact of social movements and political contexts on the Constitution (Strauss, 2001; Forbath, 1999), or discuss the emergence of new constitutional orders (Tushnet, 2004), would be at pains to explain the limited impact of the Nineteenth Amendment. As Richard Pildes writes, "In the conventional constitutional canon, democracy is nearly absent as a systematic focus of study in its own right" (Pildes, 2000, 295). So while there is some disagreement about the nature of the suffrage victory in political terms, there is little clear focus on what this amendment meant in terms of constitutional development and women's civic membership.

We begin with the vote. What is the relationship between voting and civic membership? This question may be approached philosophically, constitutionally, or politically, and I will consider all three perspectives. Philosophically, some view voting as a guarantee of democratic accountability and an expression of the capacity for self-governance. Others regard voting as a form of social solidarity and an expression of civic virtue. Constitutionally, voting is protected against discrimination in several amendments (the Fifteenth, Nineteenth, Twentieth, and Twenty-fourth). It is also associated with the guaranty of the republican form of government in Article 4, and with the Due Process and Equal Protection Clauses of the Fourteenth Amendment. Nowhere in the Constitution is suffrage named as a specific right of citizenship. Finally, from a political perspective, many view voting in instrumental terms as a means of expressing political preferences and providing protection from abuses of governmental authority. For the women's rights advocates, the vote was understood in both instrumental and solidaristic terms. It provided a claim to full civic status and allowed women's political interests to be heard. But for both cultural and constitutional reasons, the vote did little to elevate women's civic standing.

Political Theories of Voting

THE SUFFRAGIST DISCOURSE ON VOTING AND CIVIC MEMBERSHIP

How was the relationship between voting, democracy, and civic membership imagined and practiced in the United States? Many political visions were mobilized behind the cause of suffrage in the seven decades that it took to secure women's right to vote. Within the movement, over time, there was an array of views about the meaning of the vote and its relationship to civic membership (Kraditor, 1981). There were, however, two strong themes that emerged repeatedly in discussions of the vote: the instrumental value of the vote, and the role of the vote in conferring civic status. In relation to this first theme, many suffrage leaders expressed what may be characterized as liberal or natural rights views regarding voting and civic membership.

Liberal political philosophy is premised on the view that humans are naturally equal and equipped with reason, therefore capable of self-governance (Locke, 1980). Robert Dahl writes, regarding the relationship between voting and democracy, that "voting equality at the decisive stage is necessary in order to provide adequate protection for the intrinsic equality of citizens" (Dahl, 1989, 109). A further presumption for liberals is that individuals are aware of their own interests and seek to act on those interests. John Stuart Mill wrote that "each is the only safe guardian of his own rights and interests — is one of those elementary maxims of prudence, which every person, capable of conducting his own affairs, implicitly acts upon, wherever he himself is interested" (Mill, 1991, 245). Voting brings these two presumptions together in the context of representative democracy by affording an equal vote to every citizen, and by seeing the vote as an expression of self-interest that protects citizens from domination by other citizens or the state. This is why no one can be excluded: "Men, as well as women, do not need political rights in order that they may govern, but in order that they may not be misgoverned" (Mill, 1991, 329). Government is created to secure the rights of citizens. The people serve as the source of government's legitimate authority (Declaration of Independence). Finally, many liberals believe that the vote not only conveys policy preferences or political interests, but it also protects the exercise of basic civil rights. As Frederick Douglass said in defense of the Fifteenth Amendment, "The negro needs suffrage to protect his life and property, and to ensure him respect and education" (Stanton, Anthony, and Gage, 1969, 311). For Douglass, it was precisely because the position of African Americans as citizens was so precarious that they needed suffrage to secure their civic status.

The Declaration of Sentiments, adopted by the Woman's Rights Convention at Seneca Falls in 1848, was the Woman Rights movement's founding document. The document opens with a paraphrase of the Declaration of Independence. "We hold these truths self-evident: that all men and women are created equal" (Stanton, Anthony, and Gage, 1881, 70). Further on in the text is a reference to women's exclusion from governance: "Now, in view of this entire disenfranchisement of one-half of the people . . . we insist that they have immediate admission to all the rights and privileges which belong to them as citizens of the United States" (Stanton, Anthony, and Gage, 1881, 71). Among the resolutions adopted at Seneca Falls was one that called for women "to secure to themselves their sacred right to the elective franchise" (Stanton, Anthony, and Gage, 1881, 72). These were rights that belonged to women as *citizens* and as *human beings* in a democracy — as equal individuals. There was also a clear instrumental element to their protestations contained in the Declaration, since these women felt themselves "aggrieved" and "oppressed" by the "unjust laws" that were imposed on them without their consent or participation.

Other elements of the suffragist discourse on voting were compatible with the republican vision of voting and civic membership. Within republicanism, the relationship between voting and civic membership is solidaristic; as Aristotle put it, "Man is by nature a political animal" (Aristotle, 1943, 54). In association with other men, in the pursuit and administration of justice, men express their highest virtues — and citizenship is defined by participation in politics: "He who has the power to take part in the deliberation of judicial administration of any state is said by us to be a citizen of that state" (Aristotle, 1943, 127). This expectation of participation has led many to contend that in a republic, citizens are necessarily voters. Historically, republicans also have tended to define the community of citizens narrowly, by dividing the population governed by the state between citizens (who participate in politics) and subjects (who are governed by their masters and by the state). The subjects include slaves, wives, children, and servants. Citizenship requires virtue, which is cultivated through education and engagement within the political community, to insure that political participation is motivated by the pursuit of the general good (Rousseau, 1972). Montesquieu (whose work was often cited by the founders — see, for instance, *The Federalist Papers*) modifies republicanism's demanding view of citizenship by including a concept of representative government that was the basis for the model developed in England after their Civil War (Montesquieu, 1949; Dahl, 1989; Riesenberg, 1992). This modification makes republicanism more adaptable to large societies, and increases the significance of voting as the central act of political participation. Today, the communitarians stress the participatory aspects of civic membership and view the right of suffrage as a marker of civic status (or its absence as a marker of civic exclusion) (Sandel, 1982; Katz, 2000).

The suffragists believed that political participation was developmental. As one speaker said at the 1916 convention of the National American Woman Suffrage Association (NAWSA), "If I were asked to give one reason above all others for advocating the enfranchisement of women I should unhesitatingly reply, 'The necessity for the complete development of woman as a prerequisite for the highest development of the race' " (Harper, 1922, 492). The suffragists also connected voting to civic status. Voting was so central to civic membership for the suffragists that it was definitional. Explaining why working women supported suffrage, Elizabeth Schauss said at the 1910 convention of the NAWSA, "Although she gives the same quality and the same amount of work yet she cannot command the same wage, and why? Simply because she is not a recognized citizen by virtue of the ballot" (Harper, 1922, 301–2).

Women could not act as citizens or be recognized as full civic members until they became voters. The reason that the Woman Rights movement focused on the franchise, then, was not just instrumental, it was also normative. Women wanted the vote not just because of how they might use it, but because with it they would be civic members in the full sense of the term.

Not all suffragists were broadly democratic. Like classical republicans, many suffragists believed that there were segments of the population that were not qualified for political participation. This view was particularly resonant in the late nineteenth and early twentieth centuries, as the discourse of scientific racism became prevalent in popular culture. Some white suffragists resented that their class (the class of educated white women) was excluded from the franchise, when others, including immigrants and African American men, were given the franchise.[1] Such members of the suffrage movement typically favored literacy qualifications for voting. Mrs. Desha Breckinridge spoke on this subject at the 1911 NAWSA convention in Louisville, Kentucky. "If the literate women of the South were enfranchised it would insure an immense preponderance of the Anglo-Saxon over the African, of the literate over the illiterate, and would make legitimate limitation of the male suffrage to the literate easily possible" (Harper, 1922, 330). White suffragists did not object to a stratified political order in the determination of civic rights. Rather, many simply felt that women's natural place in that order (with white women historically ahead of nonwhite men) had not been properly recognized or rewarded.

What this cursory review of the suffragist discourse illustrates is both a preoccupation with the instrumental value of the vote to provide self-protection for a previously subordinated group, and a view of the franchise as a marker of civic membership. Sketching the suffragists' seemingly contradictory views about voting brings us closer to understanding why the Nineteenth Amendment had so little impact, for it helps to make sense of the peculiar relationship between voting, civic membership, and the constitutional order of the early twentieth century. To a large extent, the suffragists wanted the vote for status reasons — because they believed that with the vote they would be regarded as first-class citizens. Further, they gave little concrete thought as to how they would use the vote once they had it. To the extent that the suffragists did regard the vote instrumentally, the political identity they attached to instrumental voting (that of liberal individualism) was contrary to the political identity that activist women had developed, prior to suffrage, as public-minded, group-oriented citizens, and as women. Their views about voting and nonpartisanship left women's rights activists poorly positioned to act effectively within the electoral arena. Finally, the mixture of republican and liberal thinking about voting meant that throughout the history of the suffrage campaign movement leaders voiced *both* the language of universalism and the language of political order, or exclusion. That mixture was present as well in juridical expressions regarding the relationship of voting to citizenship, where the apparent contradiction between equal, universal citizenship and government recognition for hierarchical social relations was contained under the rubric of federalism.

VIEWS ON VOTING AND THE CIVIC STATUS OF WOMEN IN THE 1920S

Women are trying to vote as citizens rather than as women.

— GRACE ABBOTT (1925)

What effect did suffrage have on women's place in the American political order? In her lectures on American citizenship, Judith Shklar notes that women finally going to the polls turned out to be the biggest nonevent in our electoral history: "Women wanted their standing as citizens, but they were neither an ascriptive social group nor a distinct political class. They were just like the men in their class — good enough citizens, no more and no less" (Shklar, 1991, 60–61). Shklar argues that women sought the right to vote because it implied a change in their political standing. Without suffrage women had had no civic personalities. In the nineteenth century, the vote helped to define the civic identities of white men partly because black men and all women were excluded from voting. So while the achievement of suffrage for women implied a change in their political standing and recognition in the public realm, it did not necessarily foster political participation. Indeed, the terms of incorporation may have deprived women of the ascriptive identity they needed to act as a "distinct political class."

The issue for women, then, was not so much that suffrage made them voters, but that having the vote made them full citizens. It is not entirely surprising that there was some confusion over the use of the vote after the passage of the Nineteenth Amendment and, more generally, the change in women's civic membership. Women's prior attitudes toward electoral politics, the weakened state of the party system, the terms on which the regular parties accepted women voters, broader social expectations about the nature and behavior of women voters, and confusion within women's political organizations over how to utilize the vote — all of this contributed to the difficult transition women faced in becoming voters. The remainder of this section considers how both the public and women political leaders understood the relationship between the vote and women's civic standing in the years after the enactment of the Nineteenth Amendment.

Once they were granted suffrage, women's rights activists had to articulate a position for themselves within the political arena. In her effort to outline the role of women as voting citizens, former suffrage leader Carrie Chapman Catt recommended changing the culture of voting by altering the location of voting polls from masculine to feminine settings. "Wherever there is a school-house in a precinct or election district it ought to be a polling place, and where there is a church parlor . . . you should stand for having the polling place there." The setting would change the meaning of voting: "For the cleaner, the more airy, the pleasanter the place in which the election is held, the more of a patriotic function it will become, and that is what voting ought to mean to every man and every woman" (Catt, 1920, 580). This image of the pure, patriotic voting was contrasted with the traditional voting environment, where the voter "comes into a place with the air thick with tobacco smoke and with every window and door closed tight" (Catt, 1920, 581). In these smoky back rooms, self-interested machine voting thrived, while in clean, feminine electoral settings, the higher call of the national good was heard (see also Savage, 1924). By changing the voting context as well as the social identity of the electorate, Catt believed that the normative meaning of the vote could also be changed.

Like Catt, the public also believed that women brought a new gendered sensibility to political life. Women voters were viewed as less partisan and self-interested in their outlooks than male voters. As Corra Harris wrote, "Do not for a moment imagine that men conferred citizenship upon you from an awakened sense of justice. . . . They need you, a newer, cleaner element, in political life" (Harris, 1921, 16). Harris's comment is typical, both in its equation of suffrage with citizenship and in its assumption that women have distinctive political sensibilities. More specifically, women were assumed to support social welfare measures such as child labor legislation, temperance, education, and maternity and infant health care provision

("Women Voters," 1922). Some observers also suggested that women's political outlooks were local, since they were animated by women's practical experience ("Education for Citizenship," 1921). Yet mostly, women's distinctive political interest was presented as almost natural, rather than programmatic or organizationally based. Gendered identity did not translate readily into an organized political identity for women in the electorate.

A woman's domestic role not only informed her politics, according to some social commentators, but it also took priority over politics. As the *Ladies Home Journal* editorialized just after the adoption of the Nineteenth Amendment,

> Influence the world over is more potent than authority, and if women surrender the advantage they possess in the family relation for what they can gain in imitation of men or in competition with men, then they will gamble away their great opportunity . . . women's distinctive public as well as private service, whether rendered through the ballot or otherwise, will be rendered not man fashion but rather in ways that are distinctive to women. ("Wives, Husbands," 1920, 1)

As voters, women would remain distinctly gendered, since gender identity trumped the power of political influences on women. Their contributions to politics would be gendered just as their family roles were. Women's contribution to the public realm should remain subordinate to their private obligations. The editors further assumed that the possibility of party activism and office holding should be put aside by women until their children reached adulthood.

Though gendered in their public sensibilities, women were warned against forming a distinctive political block. Even if gender difference was unavoidable, it should not be emphasized or highlighted within the American liberal political system. Civic equality after suffrage required that women reject the prospect of being "a class apart." The message was that the moment that gender became a divisive political identity, it ceased to operate in the public interest. Many of these warnings were directed against the National Women's Party (NWP) and the League of Women Voters (LWV) (Jordan, 1920). The largest women's political organization of the 1920s, the LWV was created from the National American Woman Suffrage Association. The NWP was the radical rump group (formerly the Congressional

Union) that promoted sex solidarity in voting and campaigned for an Equal Rights Amendment to the Constitution to complete the promise of equality that remained unfulfilled after the Nineteenth Amendment. Members of the LWV were no fans of the NWP, particularly because of its efforts to promote sex solidarity in voting and pass "blanket" equality legislation (Becker, 1987). Most politically active women in the 1920s believed that they were now obligated to act as nonpartisans within the electoral realm. For many, that meant avoiding association with a women's political party.

Despite these contradictory messages about partisanship and political identity, activist women remained committed to the view that the value of the vote lay in its effect on women's political status and self-esteem. Quite frequently, both men and women equated women's obtaining the vote with their becoming citizens, a new civic status that separated women from other, less desirable social classes. Asking whether women were disappointed with politics in 1923, Catt wrote, "I have heard of no woman who is disappointed enough to want to go back with the paupers, insane and criminals who compose the disenfranchised classes" (Catt, 1923, 14). In a series of interviews in *The Woman Citizen* in 1924, women activists evaluated the meaning of suffrage for women and for the nation. In one, Winifred Lenihan suggested that suffrage indicated changes that had already taken place. "Woman's suffrage is not a cause of anything. . . . It is an effect, the outcome of a great change in women's status that has altered her attitude toward men, toward work, toward life. It is evidence of how far womankind has progressed" ("Is Woman Suffrage Failing?" April 5, 1924, 9). Several interviews praised the educational effect of women's suffrage. Others spoke of suffrage in terms of recognition and justice. Molly Lifshitz stated, "*Of course*, it makes a difference to women to have the vote. It is a mark of recognition. But it is only right and fair that they should have it. I don't think they should be expected to accomplish any particular thing with it" ("Is Woman Suffrage Failing?" March 22, 1924, 8). Among the more critical comments were those made by working-class women leaders (e.g., Rose Schneiderman and Mary Scully), who pointed out the failure of women's organizations to reach out to women like them ("Is Woman Suffrage Failing?" March 22, 1924, 9, and April 19, 1924, 15). Some of those interviewed also noted the loss of momentum and the lack of independent women's leadership in the postsuffrage era.[2] Yet overall these women made clear that regardless of how it was used, or whether it was used, the vote changed their civic standing.[3]

At the end of the decade, women political leaders offered a more meas-ured view of the effects of suffrage on their civic status. For the tenth anniversary of the Nineteenth Amendment, Judge Florence Allen wrote,

> Whether or not the ballot is exercised at all, whether it is exercised foolishly, there is a potential power in the franchise which makes its holder more influential than the one who does not have the vote. . . . [U]nder our system, prior to ten years ago, one half of the adult population possessed the potential power of the ballot, and one half of the adult population did not possess that power; in other words, American born women were as aliens within their own country. (F. E. Allen, 1930, 5)

Allen's comments suggest that there was no specific political program that women brought into politics, but that suffrage allowed women to defend their interests and to obtain civic recognition. That last view was echoed by Mabel Vernon of the NWP, who wrote that the vote "has certainly made a big dent in the traditional idea that women are to be set apart as a class, — that there are certain selected activities in which they cannot properly take part — and had helped to open the way for women in any line of endeavor they choose to enter" (Vernon, 1930, 227). As a privileged right that belonged to first-class citizens, suffrage helped to make women into public persons.

Before the passage of the Nineteenth Amendment, women sought the vote for both instrumental and normative reasons — to defend their politi-cal interests and to elevate their civic standing. Both of these changes, they imagined, would provide them with a stronger and more egalitarian civic membership. By the time that suffrage was adopted, greater emphasis was placed on voting's effect on women's civic status than on its instrumental value. During the decade following the adoption of the franchise, women were presumed to be distinct in their political outlooks and interests. However, they were discouraged from expressing those differences in an organized and programmatic way, since that would be contrary to the pub-lic's expectations of the appropriate role for liberal individual citizens in the electoral realm. Unfortunately for women political leaders, voting's effect on women's civic standing was also limited by the view of the federal courts regarding the constitutional relationship between voting and civic membership.

Judicial Interpretation of the Nineteenth Amendment

The first chapter set out the constitutional understanding of the relationship between voting and civic membership that emerged from Reconstruction. This chapter examines the effect that the Nineteenth Amendment had on the terms of civic membership within the American constitutional order of the early twentieth century. At first it appears that the Nineteenth Amendment left no trace within constitutional law. Only three Supreme Court cases from the early 1920s commented on the amendment. Two of these cases dealt with the amendment's legality. The third case, *Adkins v. Children's Hospital* (1923), addressed the amendment in passing, as it dealt mainly with the exercise of state authority under the police power and the right-of-freedom of contract under the Fifth Amendment. Nevertheless, this third case is the most pertinent for understanding the impact of the Nineteenth Amendment on women's civic membership. Beyond the federal courts, state cases also looked at whether the Nineteenth Amendment made women eligible for jury service and public office. Other cases, concerning the rights of married women, addressed the normative influence of the Nineteenth Amendment on women's civic membership within the states. While the next two chapters examine married women's rights and women's eligibility for jury service, this chapter considers the impact of the Nineteenth Amendment on women's constitutional status, particularly in the areas of voting rights and eligibility for public office, and closes with an analysis of a 1930s voting rights case. The Supreme Court's ruling in *Breedlove v. Suttles* (1937) demonstrates the ongoing relevance of social-ordering concerns in determining the political rights of both men and women.

The Supreme Court ruled on the legality of the Nineteenth Amendment in *Leser v. Garnett*, 258 U.S. 130 (1922). The same day the Court handed down *Leser*, it denied another challenge to the amendment in *Fairchild v. Hughes*, 258 U.S. 126 (1922), finding that the plaintiff lacked standing. The argument of the plaintiffs in *Leser* was that the Nineteenth Amendment was an illegal amendment for several reasons, two of which the Court addressed. First, the plaintiffs claimed "that so great an addition to the electorate, if made without the state's consent, destroys its autonomy as a political body" (136). The Court responded by noting, "This amendment is in character and phraseology precisely similar to the Fifteenth" (136). Since the Fifteenth

Amendment was valid, so was the Nineteenth. The plaintiff's second argument was that the amendment was improperly ratified by several states, especially Tennessee and West Virginia. The Court answered this claim by pointing out that other states had since ratified the amendment, so that even without Tennessee and West Virginia it was still valid (37).

Two aspects of the Court's response to the first argument are significant. First, the Court recognized the parallel between the Nineteenth and Fifteenth Amendments. This recognition raises questions about the constitutional effect of the two amendments. Did each amendment provide for political rights in the same way? Did the Nineteenth Amendment recognize women's position as a historically subject group in the same way that the Fifteenth Amendment did for African Americans? Finally, is there an implied relationship between the Nineteenth and Fourteenth Amendments for women, as there is between the Fourteenth and Fifteenth Amendments for African Americans? Second, the Court never substantively responded to the state sovereignty argument made by the plaintiffs. The state that brought this case was Maryland, which, along with several other southern states, rejected the woman suffrage amendment. In the South, state sovereignty was the terminology used to defend racial segregation from federal intervention. Many southern states feared that the Nineteenth Amendment would enable African American women to vote (O'Neal, 1920). Implicit in this concern was a specific conception of "the People" who constituted the body politic invoked by the Constitution. The Court neither denied nor affirmed this vision; it merely addressed the legitimacy of the procedures by which the body politic might be reordered. Both the Fifteenth Amendment parallel and the state sovereignty argument point to the role that race and other social-ordering concerns played in constitutional considerations of women's suffrage.

In an article on the constitutional history of jury service, Vikram Amar (1995) argues that the constitutional amendments that protect the right to vote (the Fifteenth, Nineteenth, Twenty-fourth, and Twenty-sixth) should be seen as protecting the broader political rights of citizens. Amar's arguments help to sharpen our consideration of the parallels between the Nineteenth and Fifteenth Amendments. He contends that the authors of the Fifteenth Amendment understood the distinction between civil, political, and social rights, and subsumed other political rights — such as the right to serve on a jury or hold elective office — under voting. Amar also shows that the suffragists associated the right to vote with the right to serve on juries. Yet, as Chapter 4 demonstrates, the federal courts failed to connect voting to jury service for women in the way that they connected these two rights for African Americans in *Neal v. Delaware*, 103 U.S. 370 (1881). Further, the state courts were mixed on the question of whether the Nineteenth Amendment implied a right to hold elective office. Overall, it appears that the Fifteenth Amendment had been given more constitutional weight with regard to the broader political rights than the Nineteenth Amendment. Yet neither amendment had been recognized as providing equal political status for African Americans or women.

Nor were women and African Americans recognized as subject groups in the same way. Coverture was not considered comparable to slavery, and while the distinctions between the sexes and races were still juridically understood as "natural," the social subordination of women took a different form than the social subordination of African Americans (Siegel, 1997). Until the 1970s, women were not covered by the Equal Protection Clause of the Fourteenth Amendment in the same way that African Americans were.[4] Only recently have sex classifications in state or federal law come to be seen as constitutionally suspect.[5] Although the Fifteenth Amendment failed to build fully on the Fourteenth Amendment to create equal rights for African Americans, this failure is even more apparent in the connections made between the Fourteenth and Nineteenth Amendments for women's rights. As Justice Ruth Bader Ginsburg comments:

> There was always a view that once the Nineteenth Amendment was passed and it made women full citizens, that was in effect an Equal Rights Amendment. Women were always citizens. They were always people within the meaning of the Equal Protection Clause and always citizens but they didn't have the most basic right of citizenship, the right to vote, until 1920. Many people thought that you could put the Fourteenth Amendment together with the Nineteenth Amendment and that was essentially the Equal Rights Amendment. But it didn't happen. (R. B. Ginsburg, 1994, 45)

Rather than interpreting the Nineteenth Amendment as having completed women's civic membership — as building political rights on top of the civil rights recognized in the Fourteenth Amendment — the Supreme Court retained a parsed and narrow view of women's civic standing.

It might have been otherwise, as suggested by the Court's ruling in
Adkins. At issue in this case was the constitutionality of the District of
Columbia's minimum wage law for women. In overturning the law, the
Supreme Court partially reversed a series of cases that upheld protective
labor legislation for women. These prior cases (particularly *Muller v. Oregon*;
see Chapter 5) relied upon multiple theories of gender difference in justifying the distinctive legal treatment of working women. One theory was that
women were naturally or biologically weaker than men. Another view
emphasized women's structural inequality; since women were legally and
economically discriminated against, it made it harder for them to compete in
the marketplace. The third theory of gender difference focused on women's
maternal role, and the burdens — both physical and social — which weighed
on working mothers.

The Court in *Adkins* chose to consider only one of these theories of gender difference in explaining their rejection of a minimum wage law that
applied only to women workers. Noting the changes in women's political and
legal status, the majority wrote: "In view of the great — not to say revolutionary — changes which have taken place . . . in the contractual, political,
and civil status of women, culminating in the Nineteenth Amendment . . .
we cannot accept the doctrine that women of mature age, *sui juris*, require or
may be subjected to restrictions upon their liberty of contract which could
not lawfully be imposed in the case of men under similar circumstances"
(553). Here the Court viewed the Nineteenth Amendment as the culmination of changes in the "contractual, political, and civil status of women." This
standpoint was precisely what the suffragists had hoped to achieve with the
Nineteenth Amendment — a signal change in women's civic membership status that completed the gradual changes made over previous decades. But this
view turned out to be more ideal than real. The broader constitutional effect
of the Nineteenth Amendment at the federal level was limited to this case, a
case in which women were found entitled to the same negative freedom of
contract rights as men (Gillman, 1993). Even in contemporary commentaries on the case, there were numerous suggestions about what the Supreme
Court missed in this decision.

Most of the critical commentaries, like Justice Holmes's dissenting opinion in *Adkins*, accused the majority of ignoring the physical differences
between the sexes. Because of these differences, disparate legal treatment was
constitutionally justified.[6] Beyond these exclamations of women's physical

weakness, a few law review notes offered a more nuanced view of what was wrong with the majority opinion. One writer in the *California Law Review* suggested that the justices had overlooked women's economic inequality.

> Will the learned justices of the majority be pardoned for overlooking the cardinal fact that minimum wage legislation is not and never was predicated upon the political, contractual or civil inequalities of women? It is predicated rather upon the evils to society, resulting from the exploitation of women in industry, who *as a class labor under a tremendous economic handicap.* The problem is one of economic fact, not of political, contractual or civil status. ("Constitutional Law," 1923, 353)

The changes in women's civil and political status had not remedied their economic subordination. Similarly, a comment in the *Columbia Law Review* suggested, "Finally, the court's contention that the modern movement for the civil emancipation of women, culminating in the Nineteenth Amendment, has so fortified her contractual capacity as to render gratuitous any legislation of this type, can only be regarded as the sheerest judicial persiflage" ("Constitutionality of Minimum Wage," 1923, 565). While this comment may be read in various ways, one possible reading focuses on concerns over the contractual rights of women after the Nineteenth Amendment. That is, this note might be arguing that women still lacked the status of a *sui juris* — that they were not yet autonomous legal persons. Certainly married women did not have the same civil rights and capacities as men. Under such circumstances, as critics of the Equal Rights Amendment would argue, to impose a procedural standard of equality on women might actually increase substantive inequality between men and women.

State cases that addressed the impact of the Nineteenth Amendment on office holding reveal a range of views about the amendment's effect on women's civic membership. Some courts denied any link between suffrage and office holding, citing the continuing relevance of common law constructions of women's civil and political disabilities, and contending that historical precedent went against the claims of rights advocates. Other courts confirmed the link between office holding and suffrage, revealing the normative influence of the Nineteenth Amendment on judicial reasoning about women's place. In a few instances, state courts cited the parallels between the Nineteenth and Fifteenth Amendments. The broadest construction credited the Nineteenth Amendment with creating a new political status for women. Although women were generally found eligible for office holding, once the appropriate statutes were passed, most state and federal courts retained a narrow view of the effect of the Nineteenth Amendment on women's civic membership.

Many high courts issued advisory opinions on women's eligibility for office holding either to the governor or the state legislature. In *Opinion of the Justices*, 113 A. 614 (1921), the court advised the Maine governor that he could now appoint women as justices of the peace. The justices' reasoning was threefold. First, they noted the parallel between the Fifteenth and Nineteenth Amendments: "The privileges conferred upon women by the Nineteenth Amendment are precisely the same as those conferred on the colored race by the Fifteenth" (615–16). Noting that in *Neal*, and *Ex parte Yarbrough*, 110 U.S. 651 (1884), the Supreme Court found that the Fifteenth Amendment conferred broader political rights (in those cases, the right of jury service) on African Americans, the Maine court reasoned that the same should be true for the Nineteenth Amendment's effect on women. Second, the court saw a direct link between voting and office holding. "The continuation of those [public] offices should at all times be placed in the hands and administration of those who might be duly intrusted in after days with their 'continued existence and preservation' " (616). In other words, those responsible for maintaining public offices through their votes were best qualified to serve in those offices. Finally, there was the direct effect of the Nineteenth Amendment on the state constitutions. "Every political distinction based upon the consideration of sex was eliminated from the Constitution by the ratification of the amendment. Males and females were thenceforth, when citizens of the United States, privileged to take equal hand in the conduct of government" (617). Following the Nineteenth Amendment, it was no longer possible to distinguish the political rights, or civic membership, of men and women.

The Maine high court came closest to viewing the Nineteenth Amendment as completing women's civic membership. The opinion of the Massachusetts Supreme Judicial Court in 1922 was narrower. In the case *In re Opinion of the Justices*, 135 N.E. 173, that court denied the link between suffrage and office holding: "The right to hold office is not necessarily coextensive with the right to vote" (174). Noting that it was up to the states to determine qualifications for office holders, and that other qualifications besides being an elector were imposed on state offices, the court implied that the state could provide a qualification based on sex if it chose to do so. Yet there were no sex-based qualifications in the statutes. Instead, "When the fundamental law is silent as to the qualifications for office, it commonly is understood that electors and electors alone are eligible" (176). Thus, when the Nineteenth Amendment eliminated the sex restriction on voting, it had made women electors, and as such they became eligible for office once the legislature passed an enabling law. The court concluded, "The constitutional situation has become so changed by the supervention of the Nineteenth Amendment" that the court's old ruling which barred women from public office was no longer in force (176). It was not by its breadth that the Nineteenth Amendment made women eligible for public office in Massachusetts, but only by its direct effect on the state constitutional qualifications for office.

The third state court opinion on women's eligibility for office holding came from Texas. In 1924, Miriam "Ma" Ferguson was elected governor of Texas. During the campaign, her candidacy was challenged in *Dickson v. Strickland*, 265 S.W. 1012. The case was brought by Charles Dickson, who sued state election officials, claiming that Miriam Ferguson was ineligible for office and should be stricken from the ballot. According to Dickson, Ferguson was a figurehead candidate, standing in for her husband and campaign manager, James "Pa" Ferguson. James Ferguson was impeached while serving as governor of Texas a few years earlier, so he was no longer eligible for that office. Dickson also claimed that Miriam Ferguson was ineligible both as a woman and a wife to hold public office. The state supreme court denied these claims, and a few days later Miriam Ferguson was elected governor.

With regard to sex, the court ruled that women were (and perhaps had always been) eligible for public office in Texas. "A careful analysis of the . . . Constitution . . . makes it entirely clear that the electors of this state have left themselves free to choose a Governor without regard to the sex or coverture of the person of their choice" (1020). The justices denied the specific relevance of the suffrage amendments. Indeed, they implied that a constitutional restriction of office holders to electors would have barred women from eligibility since women were not electors when the constitution was adopted. Further, the court denied that the common law rules of coverture were in force in Texas. The state had *not* adopted the common law principle of marital unity which would "deprive a married woman of her separate identity, her discretion, and her will, and subject her to her husband's dominion, so as to disqualify her from holding public office" (1022). Finally, the court acknowledged the normative influence of the Nineteenth Amendment.

> In fact, it is to blind one's eyes to the truths of current history not to recognize that the last vestige of reason to sustain a rule excluding women from office was removed when she was clothed with equal authority with men, in the government of the state and nation, through the ballot. When the reason for the rule of exclusion has failed, the rule should no longer be applied. (1023)

The reasoning given here is the opposite of the view expressed by the Massachusetts court two years earlier. While denying the direct effect of the Nineteenth Amendment on the state's rules regarding eligibility of office holding, the Texas court gave credit to the normative influence of the amendment on judicial thinking about women's rights.

The last office-holding opinion was issued by the high court of New Hampshire. According to the justices in the case *In re Opinion Justices*, 139 A. 180 (1927), the state constitution was built upon the common law. Therefore, the "framers of the Constitution understood that office holding was limited to men by that document, although no mention of the subject was made therein" (182). At the same time, the court agreed that there was a connection between suffrage and office holding. "The fundamental idea was and is that the rights of electing and being elected are equal, save for the specific constitutional limitations as to certain offices" (182). Consequently, suffrage made women eligible for elective office. That connection pertained only to elective office, however, and in the case of appointive office, the common law restriction against women (who were said to lack discretion) applied. Yet since the Constitution was silent on the matter, legislation could be enacted "to remove the common-law disability" on women's eligibility for appointive office (184).

Several things are apparent from these cases. First, the courts proclaim the continued relevance of the common law except in instances where it is specifically superseded by statutory law.[7] Second, the courts engage in interesting interpretive dances in relation to the state constitutions. Little is said in these constitutions about sex qualifications, and much is necessarily made by the state courts of the little that is said. Further, there is the striking ability of different state courts to reach opposite conclusions from similar provisions in their constitutions.[8] Third, the particular meaning of the Nineteenth Amendment is interpreted in at least three different ways: specifically, by the language of the amendment and its direct effect on the state constitution; normatively, by the overall effect that the amendment had on judicial reasoning; and historically, by analogy to the Fifteenth Amendment. It is in the last sense that the court comes closest to reading the amendment as implying a broader set of political rights that would elevate women's civic membership. Finally, it should be noted, that while none of the courts fully credits the Nineteenth Amendment with the creation of equal civic membership, all of them rule that the amendment had made women eligible for public office to a greater or lesser degree.

Seventeen years after the adoption of the Nineteenth Amendment, the Supreme Court handed down its ruling in *Breedlove*, which upheld Georgia's poll tax law that exempted women from paying back taxes. The plaintiff, a white man, argued that the law was "repugnant to the equal protection clause and the privileges and immunities clause of the Fourteenth Amendment and to the Nineteenth Amendment" (280). The Court disagreed. The Fourteenth Amendment "does not require absolute equality" (281), wrote the Court, and the Nineteenth Amendment had nothing to do with a state's right to tax its citizens. Nor was voting protected under the Privileges and Immunities Clause of the Fourteenth Amendment. Instead, the Court offered this endorsement of the Georgia law:

> The tax being upon persons, women may be exempted on the basis of special considerations to which they are naturally entitled. In view of burdens necessarily borne by them for the preservation of the race, the state reasonably may exempt them from poll taxes. The laws of Georgia declare the husband to be the head of the family and the wife to be subject to him. To subject her to the levy would be to add to his burden. (282)

Evidently, little had changed in the sixty years since Justice Bradley issued his concurrent opinion in *Bradwell v. Illinois* (1872). Neither the Fourteenth nor the Nineteenth Amendments (or the two together) were sufficient to make women into full legal persons. Because of their "natural" differences, and their positions as wives and mothers, women were entitled to special consideration. Their civic membership was still based in gender difference. In support of this position, the Court cited *Muller v. Oregon*, 208 U.S. 412, the 1908 case that originally exempted women from the freedom-of-contract regime, making it possible for them to be protected by labor laws. Social roles and relations, then, continued to define civic membership. The Nineteenth Amendment did not displace a constitutional order in which the privileges and immunities of national citizenship were limited, political rights were secondary to civil rights, and women's domestic roles shaped the terms of their civic membership.

What *Breedlove* also illustrates is that the link between voting and civic membership in the American constitutional order was severely attenuated by the rise of Jim Crow, and the Court's acquiescence to the rise of racial segregation in the South (Klarman, 2004; Pildes, 2000). The severance of voting from other constitutional rights (originally performed in the distinction between the Fourteenth and Fifteenth Amendments) allowed for a narrow reading of the rights afforded under the Fourteenth Amendment and of the affiliation between voting and civic membership. When the political climate was more favorable and the Court was more assertive in the aftermath of the Civil War, then a more connected vision of constitutional rights across the Reconstruction Amendments seemed possible, at least for African Americans (e.g., in *Strauder v. West Virginia*). But the Court also demonstrated an early willingness to view these rights in a more parsed fashion when it came to women (e.g., in *Bradwell* and in *Minor v. Happersett*). By the early twentieth century, neither the political climate nor the courts favored a robust, connective view of the relationship among constitutional rights or of the importance of voting in the overall structure of citizenship. And both women and African Americans were the losers for it.

The Changing Electoral Context

While the constitutional order in which the Nineteenth Amendment took effect was grounded in Reconstruction, the political regime in which women became citizens was rooted in the electoral realignment of 1896 (Burnham, 1974; Ritter, 1997a). The defeat of Populist and Democratic candidate William Jennings Bryan by Republican stalwart William McKinley in 1896 signaled the end of a political era characterized by deep partisan attachments, competitive state and national elections, and high levels of voter participation (Kleppner, 1987; McGerr, 1986). Contrary to the view of the federal courts, voting was popularly seen as the premier right of citizenship in the late nineteenth century, which explains why women's rights advocates were intent on winning the vote for women. Not only did the vote organize the body politic in the late nineteenth century — it also organized the state in an era when the federal government was run as a distributive patronage system (Skowronek, 1982).

Prior to the Nineteenth Amendment the activities of men largely defined politics, even though women were energetically engaged in lobbying campaigns for distinct social policies (Skocpol, 1992). Politics, in the nineteenth century, meant parties and elections. The political realm changed in the early twentieth century, making it more accessible to women and their political styles. When women finally entered the electoral realm they were determined to do so in a new way — they sought to remake that realm in the interest of good government through educational campaigns and a more enlightened, critical partisanship. As Kristi Andersen writes, "both men and women believed women to have distinct political preferences" (Andersen, 1996, 218). However, women failed to form a cohesive political block. The terms on which women's political preferences would be expressed, and what this meant for their political identities, were open to question (Andersen, 1996; McGerr, 1990; Clemens, 1993).

Women were not entirely divorced from electoral politics and partisanship in the late nineteenth century. In general, the Republicans were friendlier to the cause of women's rights than were the Democrats. Several smaller reform parties, including the Populists and Prohibitionists, also advocated for woman suffrage, which is one reason why suffrage first took hold in the West, where the reform parties were most competitive (McConnaughy, 2004). Part of the division between the NWSA (led by Susan B. Anthony and Elizabeth Cady Stanton) and the AWSA (led by Lucy Stone and Henry Blackwell) was over the question of partisan alignment: the AWSA favored the Republican party while the NWSA did not. Rebecca Edwards (1997) argues that the major parties in the postbellum era offered distinctive visions regarding the proper organization of the family and the relationship between male and female citizens and the state. Particularly with regard to how to govern the territories (where the shield of federalism was not available), the national parties were explicit in their views about what constituted a proper social order — as evidenced in the Republican campaign against polygamy (S. B. Gordon, 2002) and the Democratic campaign against miscegenation (Novkov, 2002). To the extent that they were allowed a public voice in these matters, activist women often aligned themselves with these distinctive partisan visions of social order, and in the context of movements like the Women's Christian Temperance Union, offered their own views about the way that gender relations should be governed in society (Gilmore, 1996).

Yet suffragist women constituted their claim for the right to vote against male traditions of partisanship. As historians Paula Baker (1984) and Michael McGerr (1986) show, in the nineteenth century partisanship was regarded as an expression of masculinity. The high point for political participation in the United States was the period after the Civil War, when partisan identity was organized according to war allegiances; veterans' groups such as the Grand Army of the Republic were virtual adjuncts to the parties. Baker contends, "Men granted women the vote when the importance of the male culture of politics and the meaning of the vote changed. Electoral politics was no longer a male right or a ritual that dealt with questions only men understood" (81). Not only the right to vote, but partisanship — the exercise of the vote — was gendered in the nineteenth century.

After Bryan's defeat, the national electoral system was characterized by low voter turnout, noncompetitive elections, one-party rule, declining levels of partisanship, the rise of interest group politics, and the emergence of a federal bureaucratic government. The decline in turnout was due to both changes in the party system and heavy legal restrictions on voting (Burnham, 1974; Kousser, 1974 and 1999; Piven and Cloward, 1980). The loss in electoral competitiveness and the emergence of one-party rule in different areas of the country, particularly the South (Kleppner, 1987; Key, 1949), was associated with the exclusion of large groups of voters from participation. The decline in voting and partisanship created a political space for the gradual rise of interest group politics and a bureaucratic regulatory state (McCormick, 1986; Clemens, 1993). This shift in the governance structure was accompanied by a shift from voters and parties to interest groups and lobbyists. It was at the pinnacle point of many of these changes that women were granted suffrage. During the 1920s, the value of the vote (gauged by participation, partisanship, and both electoral and, more broadly, political effect) was at perhaps its lowest point in the twentieth century. Consequently, the practical gain for women was limited, and in some respects even negative, since the move to electoral politics contributed to the disaggregation of women's activism in the nonelectoral realm (for a contrasting view, see Cott, 1995a). Women activists went from being a highly effective, gender-identified political force in the realm of nonpartisan, interest group politics, to being individual liberal voters within the ranks of the regular parties.

WOMEN AND PARTISANSHIP AFTER THE VOTE

Once they had the franchise, women had to create new political identities for themselves as voting citizens. The nature of these new identities was the subject of a great deal of debate and dialogue among both activists and observers. How would these millions of newly enfranchised voters organize and identify themselves within the electoral arena? How would women relate to the major political parties? How would women's identities as citizens or as gendered citizens be brought to bear on questions of partisanship and participation?

Early scholarship on women's post–Nineteenth Amendment behavior presented women's suffrage as a failure. The first evaluations from the 1920s and subsequent scholarly analyses in the 1970s criticized women voters in the postsuffrage era for their lower levels of political participation and lack of an independent vote. Political scientist Charles Edward Russell concluded in his 1924 article "Is Woman Suffrage a Failure?" that, with suffrage, "the number of docile ballot-droppers has approximately been doubled" (Russell, 1924, 35). Half a century later, Stanley Lemons (1973) echoed this view when he wrote that during the suffrage campaign "more had been promised ... than could be delivered" (112). William Chafe (1972) concurred with this assessment, suggesting that when women voted, they voted by their class and by the wishes of the men around them.

More recently, political scientists and political historians have offered a more optimistic assessment of the impact of women's suffrage on the American electoral system in the 1920s. Looking at data from Illinois, Walter Dean Burnham (1974) downplayed the significance of women's suffrage for the decline in voting that occurred in the 1920s. Similarly, Paul Kleppner (1982) found that women were less integrated than men into the electoral system, partially as a result of political conditions at the time, which depressed men's rates of participation as well. The electoral system of the early twentieth century lacked the vitality of the highly competitive and participatory system of the late nineteenth century. Sara Alpern and Dale Baum (1985), in their examination of women's participation in the 1920 presidential election, show that women's voting behavior was somewhat distinct from men's (in one region they favored Harding, in another they favored Cox). Yet the distinctions were not consistent and there was no women's voting bloc. Finally, they suggest that contemporary commentaries on the "failure" of women's suffrage, while often inaccurate, nonetheless contributed to a public view of women as less vigorous in their performance of civic duties.

Addressing this earlier scholarship, both Anna Harvey (1998) and Kristi Andersen (1996) have contributed to our understanding of women's electoral participation after the Nineteenth Amendment. Harvey focuses on the institutional and organizational constraints women activists faced in dealing with the regular parties. Her work shows that women activists entered into an already structured arena of electoral competition that rendered difficult their own early efforts to achieve political effectiveness there. Harvey's book, however, fails to consider the noninstrumental value of suffrage that motivated many rights activists to seek the vote. Some women wanted the vote to have a voice in policy matters. Others wanted the vote because of its expected effect on women's political standing. During the nineteenth and early twentieth centuries, women wanted the vote because they believed it would make them full citizens, both legally and culturally.

Andersen's excellent book *After Suffrage* evaluates women's electoral participation and political standing after the Nineteenth Amendment. Yet she does not consider the impact of the Nineteenth Amendment in other domains of women's civic membership. Since women's rights advocates sought the right to vote because of its anticipated impact on women's civic standing more generally, much can be learned from an analysis of the amendment's impact on other civil and political rights, such as married women's rights and the right to serve on juries (see Chapters 3 and 4). This broader view makes for a richer and more pessimistic analysis of the impact of suffrage on women's civic membership. The vote did not substantially alter women's position in the constitutional order. Even Andersen's excellent analysis of women's behavior in the electoral realm leaves unresolved the puzzle of why the Nineteenth Amendment had such a limited impact on women's civic membership.

Before the passage of the Nineteenth Amendment, women political activists debated what electoral standing would mean for women. What they agreed on was what they did not want it to mean — traditional male partisan politics. After years of criticizing the regular parties, writers in *The Woman Citizen* (the journal of the League of Women Voters) were hard put to explain why women should join the regular parties now that they were voters. The early, habituated response of the journal was expressed in a front-page editorial that appeared on October 23, 1920 — just two months after the Nineteenth Amendment was adopted. Under the heading "Blessed Are the Bolters," the editors wrote:

> It is no wonder that some millions of citizens decide to escape the task of finding an intellectual trail through the bewildering fog of conflicting views and complacently join a party and take the views its leaders give forth as unimpregnable wisdom and truth, to swear for or to die for. It is the easiest way. Yet it is the bolters who have made history, led the world's progress, made new epochs, compelled evolution. Women suffragists were bolters, and they bolted to gain an end and gained it. . . . Blessed are the bolters, for in them lies the promise of a new and better order. ("Blessed," 1920, 565)[9]

To these editors, good civic membership required breaking the bonds of party loyalty. Only through political independence was real progress was to be made.

Under fire from the political establishment for their antipartisan stance, women's rights activists began to promote enlightened partisanship instead. Explained LWV chairperson Maud Wood Park,

> We feel that it is a mistake to have a separate women's party and from the time of our organization last February, we have urged our members to enroll in the party of their choice. The League is the common meeting ground for women of all parties, where they may gain information and education conducive to the intelligent use of the ballot, and where they may plan together how they shall work for what women want. (Parks, 1920, 152)

Members of the League included prominent partisan activists like Harriet Taylor Upton (Republican) and Emily Newell Blair (Democrat), who tried their best to pursue feminist agendas through partisan channels. Initially it seemed that the parties would accommodate women with committee appointments and so forth. But by the latter part of the decade, many party activists were disillusioned. The difficulty of maintaining a nonpartisan partisanship became quite evident to activist women.

In a series of essays on citizenship for *The Woman Citizen*, Carrie Chapman Catt considered the question of partisanship. Catt began by articulating a conditional defense of partisan activity for women. "Now we are urging you, and you are going to urge other women to take up politics as a patriotic duty, and consequently do you realize that we must make quite respectable the 'lady politician'? We cannot afford to have that old view of the man politician continue; for we cannot afford to have it directed towards the women who go in politics" (Catt, 1920, 582). For women to find their place in the electoral realm the public view of partisanship had to be regendered. Women had to support other women as they brought a different voice to political competition. How would this change occur? Catt had an idea:

> You will get those men who are in charge of political committees (once you have proven to them that this is a nonpartisan school, that you are not going to give a lift to one party over the other) to send their own party workers to the school, which is the most important result you could possibly anticipate, for political workers are often badly trained and most pitiably misinformed. (Catt, 1920, 582)

This suggestion was astonishing from the woman considered the brilliant tactician of the suffrage movement. After years of fighting for the vote, Catt imagined that local women would bring party workers into their schools to be educated on the political process. This hard-nosed feminist exhibited a seemingly naive faith in the ability of education to produce enlightenment, and thereby right past wrongs. One can only imagine how amused party bosses were with Catt's suggestions.

Ironically, the call for nonpartisanship was used to attack and regulate women political activists. The ability of activist women to engage the parties on substantive terms was constrained by partisans who brandished the stick of nonpartisanship alongside the club of partisan loyalty. Controversy erupted in 1921 when New York's Governor Miller denounced the LWV. "There is no proper place for a league of women voters, precisely as I should say that there was no proper place for a league of men voters. I have a very firm conviction that any organization which seeks to exert political power is a menace to our institutions, unless it is organized as a political party" ("A Teapot," 1921, 949). In calling for nonpartisan partisanship, Miller put organizations like the LWV in a difficult position. Miller attacked the apparent partisanship of a *women's* league. There should be no distinctive groups in politics — just loyal citizens pursuing the national good through the party system. Further, the party system had room only for obedient followers and not for fickle independents. Parties were necessary for political accountability — outside the parties were only unaccountable political organizations that were a "menace to our institutions" ("A Teapot," 1921, 949). Nonpartisan principles were used to secure a compliant partisanship. Apparently many of the well-trained citizens in the LWV agreed with Governor Miller and quit the organization. The failure of activist women to articulate a notion of a programmatic women's partisanship in the 1920s made them vulnerable to such attacks ("A Teapot," 1921; Lemons, 1973).

To be sure, the League of Women Voters and its leaders were entirely naive about the regular parties. Like many progressive reformers, these former suffragists were critics of partisanship. They advocated a shift to a new style of politics, based on education and independent political action. Over time, such a shift occurred, so that the partisan world of the twentieth century was a pale replica of the partisan world of the late nineteenth century. But in advocating for a politics of nonpartisanship at a time when partisan structures still played a large role in organizing politics, the women's movement lost much of its previous political effectiveness.

By the end of the decade many women were acting from within the circle of partisanship, yet there remained a great deal of ambiguity about the role and identity of women as partisan voters. An interesting exchange between Sarah Schuyler Butler and Emily Newell Blair was published in 1931. Both had risen to high offices within the regular parties. For seven years in the 1920s, Blair was vice chairman of the Democratic National Committee. Discouraged by her experience, she wrote, "I am disappointed with what politics has done for women. . . . Now at the end of ten years of suffrage I find politics still a male monopoly" (Blair, 1931, 20). Most of the women promoted to leadership positions in the parties, Blair charged, were not independent-minded and had little or no gender consciousness. These women "participate in politics by ignoring other women. . . . Such women never bother with so-called women's measures or movements. They have no use for feminism" (21). Much of the difficulty, Blair admitted, lay in the inability of women leaders to mobilize women voters *as women*. Just as "Men could run as men, and do," women must learn to run as, and vote for, women. Further, they should be urged "to vote for the feminist, that is the woman who wants to widen the opportunities for women, instead of for the tool of some man" (22). This call for a gender-conscious electoral politics did not present women as essentially feminine or maternal, but it did suggest that women live in a gender-differentiated world where they have reason to claim political power for themselves.

A rather different view came from Butler, the young vice chairman of the New York State Republican Committee. Butler expressed no disappointment when she announced that "there is no such thing as a 'woman vote' " (Butler, 1931, 14). She argued that "American women are no less individualist than American men. They have gone about their political affairs as individuals, not as a group" (14). So the test of women's success should be individual as well. As women became more experienced, they would be more fully included: "The fact remains that women are little by little finding their way into the party councils and into public office" (39). No mention was made by Butler of feminism or women's issues. Nor was there any suggestion that women candidates should make political claims on the basis of their gender. Instead, Butler admonished, "as citizens we should be just as concerned with the representatives of the opposite sex as with those of our own" (40). Unlike Blair, Butler called for women to shed their gender identities as they entered the party councils.

Perhaps it was disappointment with the failure of women to mobilize and use the vote instrumentally that led former suffragists to emphasize the normative value of the vote. *Equal Rights*, the journal of the NWP, published a series of essays in 1930 reflecting on the tenth anniversary of the Nineteenth Amendment. To the question "What have women accomplished with the vote during these ten years?" Mabel Vernon responded, "The answer to this question undoubtedly disappoints those who expected women to reform politics" (Vernon, 1930, 227). Yet she reminded readers that "many suffragists who worked hardest for the vote never claimed that great changes would be made and reforms effected by the vote in the hands of women." Instead, she concluded, these "women based their appeal on the justice of their cause" (Vernon, 1930, 227). Suffragists believed the vote would make them first-class citizens and effective political participants. After 1920, some were discouraged at the low voter turnout and the failure to mobilize women voters into an effective electoral force (Andersen, 1996). But many remained comforted by women's new civic standing.

Women's relation to partisanship remained unsettled a decade after they won the franchise. Prior to the adoption of the Nineteenth Amendment, women's civic membership was clearly gendered. After the vote was granted, women's political standing changed and a measure of political equality was gained. Before the Nineteenth Amendment, suffrage campaigners derided the traditional partisanship that was associated with male politics. Yet they failed to clearly delineate whether or how women might retain a gendered identity as voting citizens. Nor was it in the interest of the major parties to assist them in that effort. Women were absorbed instead as ungendered, less experienced, and less motivated individual voters.

In *After Suffrage*, Andersen discusses women's political position before the New Deal and attempts to unravel the puzzle of why suffrage appeared to have so little impact on American politics. She writes, "At the same time it is clear that the boundary which had been drawn to exclude women from electoral politics was not erased but was renegotiated, so that women, for the most part, had a special and relatively powerless place in American party and electoral politics by the end of the 1920s" (Andersen, 1996, 142–43). The weak terms of women's inclusion were shaped by many things, including: the efforts of the regular party organizations to absorb the new voters as ungendered party loyalists (as Harvey, 1996, shows); longer-term changes in the nature of electoral politics and the role of the state that diminished the importance of partisanship to political identity; and women's prior understandings about partisanship and their subsequent confusion about their own proper relationship to the parties. The years after the Nineteenth Amendment *did* witness a change in the culture of voting (from casting ballots at saloons to voting at schools, and from "campaigns of mobilization" to "campaigns of education and advertising") and a decline in the gendered distinctiveness of men and women's civic membership. Outside the electoral realm, in what Robyn Muncy (1991) terms the "female dominion" of women's bureaus and organizations, where women retained more gender distinction, they were more politically effective. Ironically, then, women's civic membership may have been redefined by the vote at the cost of their political identities as women.

Conclusion

This chapter has addressed the ways in which women's civic membership was reconceived after the passage of the Nineteenth Amendment. The focus here has been on what suffrage meant for women's political standing and place within the American constitutional order. In the nineteenth century, women were regarded as politically distinct from men, and the main marker of that difference was the absence of the vote. The vote symbolized public autonomy for women. Prior to the Nineteenth Amendment, women's civic membership was conceived of in relational terms and they were represented in the public realm by male family members. Once women won the right to vote, the distinction between men's and women's civic membership diminished, and women moved toward inclusion as liberal individual citizens. Yet this change was partial and uneven, as expressed in both the juridical and political understandings of women's civic membership after suffrage.

Why did the Nineteenth Amendment have such a limited impact on women's civic membership and the broader constitutional order? This chapter has highlighted four reasons. First, suffrage took effect in a constitutional context where political rights were divided from civil rights, and voting was not regarded as a defining aspect of one's civic status. Ironically, this constitutional context formed partly in response to an earlier effort by the suffrage movement to claim voting as a right of citizenship under the Fourteenth Amendment. Second, within the political context of the early twentieth century, the instrumental value of the vote declined as the nation shifted to a party system with low voter turnout, noncompetitive elections, and lessened partisan allegiances. Third, the suffragists were not well suited to function in this electoral environment, since the women's movement promoted nonpartisan, interest group politics as an alternative to traditional partisanship. They adapted poorly to their new roles as liberal, individual voters. Fourth, and finally, even within this constitutional and political context, the normative impact of suffrage could have reshaped the civic standing of women, as suggested by the *Adkins* decision. But instead, women's civic identities remained invested with the normative values of coverture, as illustrated by the Court's opinion in *Breedlove*. The next chapter examines the ongoing impact of coverture on women's civic membership in the early twentieth century.

Beyond the impact of the Nineteenth Amendment, this examination of the relationship between suffrage and women's civic membership illuminates many key lessons. The first concerns the relationship between voting and civic membership in representative democracies. The analysis in this chapter suggests that this relationship depends on the specific political and constitutional context of a particular nation. In the United States, the relationship between suffrage and civic membership was configured differently in different historical epochs and for different groups. During the nineteenth century, the vote was a crucial boundary marker within the ranks of citizens, between those regarded as first-class citizens and those who were seen as more remote and politically dependent. By the time that women were granted the right to vote, the relationship between voting and civic membership had been reconfigured both constitutionally and politically, so that it was no longer such a determinate signifier of overall civic status. Along with this change went shifts in the instrumental value of the vote — which narrowed the electoral choices available to many voters and insulated the emerging regulatory bureaucracy from direct electoral pressures. This change left citizens with less ability to express their policy and political preferences through the electoral process. Consideration of rights and of belonging both matter to our understanding the relationship between voting and civic standing.

The other lesson that emerges here concerns the process of constitutional development. In her wonderful and comprehensive essay "She, the People" (2002), Reva Siegel examines the puzzle of why the Nineteenth Amendment had so little impact on the constitutional status of women. Siegel contends that the Nineteenth Amendment should be read synthetically with the Fourteenth Amendment, in order to foster a view of civic equality that allows for government intervention into the private realm, as she believes suffragists intended. Yet, was this indeed what the suffragists intended? My own reading suggests that suffrage activists were more interested in making women public persons than in altering their status as private wives. Perhaps more significantly, the analysis here provides a less optimistic reading of the potential of the Nineteenth Amendment as an instrument for a broader civic equality. The reasons for this relative pessimism are twofold. First, I contend that the search for equality within liberal political structures will always lead to problematic and limited outcomes for women (see Chapter 9 and W. Brown, 1995). Second, from an institutional and developmental perspective, this analysis gives greater weight to the constraints within the postbellum constitutional order — limits that could not readily be overcome with a new interpretation of the Nineteenth Amendment. The key problem is not with the narrow construction of the Nineteenth Amendment, but with the construction of the Fourteenth Amendment. Since the 1870s, the Privileges and Immunities Clause of the Fourteenth Amendment has been rendered virtually meaningless as an instrument for expanding civic membership. Unless the terms of civic membership are substantively reimagined on new constitutional terms — a reimagination that must be rooted in broader political changes in American society — then there is little likelihood that "equal" citizenship within the current constitutional order will provide women with a satisfactory civic membership.

THREE

Marriage

In the nineteenth century, marriage defined one's role in the social order and, through this, one's rights and responsibilities in the polity. The notion that marriage was a private matter, beyond the reach of government recognition and regulation, was not evident in the rulings of the federal or state courts. Rather, marriage was viewed as being important to the state. It provided social stability. It held men economically responsible for the well-being of women and children. The exercise of that responsibility was taken as evidence of a man's civic capacities — it qualified him for the exercise of the rights and duties of citizenship. Within marriage, women provided not only care and comfort, they also inculcated civility and civic virtue in their husbands and sons. Wives' dependency made them legal nonentities under the rules of coverture, giving them little claim to direct representation in democratic politics. Rather, husbands represented their wives within the public sphere. For women, marriage both dictated their contribution to the polity and provided them with indirect representation there.

What effect did the Nineteenth Amendment have on the link between marriage and civic membership? The Nineteenth Amendment recognized women as political participants and legal persons. As voters, women were seen as separate, autonomous, and public. Yet marriage remained a defining element of the civic membership of women and men in the decade after the suffrage amendment was adopted. This was true not only despite women's transition to the status of voting citizens, but despite the influx of women into the paid labor market. Even the development of social provisioning and the emergence of a modern bureaucratic state failed to sever fully the link between marriage and civic membership; rather, their relationship was transformed and reconfigured within American constitutional politics in the twentieth century. By the mid-1940s, marriage had become, if anything, *more* central in defining the rights and responsibilities of American civic members, though in new ways and places than before.

Why did marriage retain a vital role in shaping civic identity? One factor was the challenge of social diversity within the body politic. Debates over how to manage and regulate social diversity were prevalent in the Progressive Era. The influx of immigrants, the start of the great migration of African Americans into the urban North, and new proposals for the civic incorporation of Native Americans all provoked broader discussions, sometimes in constitutional terms, about civic membership and social order in the United States. Further, although women gained political rights in this period, voting had a limited impact on their civic standing in the polity (see Chapter 2). Finally, in the area of labor law, the Supreme Court applied the doctrine of substantive due process to questions of civic liberty, and found that most efforts to regulate working conditions were unconstitutional violations of the principle of freedom of contract. Under the *Lochner* regime (as this jurisprudential tradition was called), the relationship between labor status and civic identity was configured differently for men than for women. Women workers were considered as a special case, more deserving of state protection, and this differentiated status was consistent with regarding marriage as definitive of women's civic membership. Thus, the jurisprudence of rights in this period was understood in gendered terms.

Coverture

By marriage, the husband and wife are one person in law: that is, the very being or legal existence of the woman is suspended during the marriage, or at least is incorporated and consolidated into that of the husband: under whose wing, protection and *cover*, she performs everything. . . . Upon this principle, of the union of person in husband and wife, depend almost all the legal rights, duties, and disabilities that either of them acquire by the marriage.

— SIR WILLIAM BLACKSTONE, *Commentaries on the Laws of England*

When the United States was founded, the law governing citizens in their daily activities drew upon English common law. The common law tradition that governed marriage in most states created a different set of civil rights for married women than for men or single women. The civil disabilities of married women under the common law slowly were lifted over the course of the nineteenth century as wives gained property rights and the right to retain their own earnings. These changes owed much to the efforts of the Woman Rights movement. Although constitutional law designated the terms of civic membership, common law principles continued to shape married women's civic membership well into the twentieth century. After the passage of the Nineteenth Amendment, women political activists sought to complete the project of civic equality by eliminating the common law rules governing married women.

The standard work on the common law used by American jurists was Sir William Blackstone's *Commentaries on the Laws of England*, quoted above, which synthesized the common law tradition in four volumes. This work was first published in the 1700s and gained a wide following in the American colonies (Basch, 1982, chap. 2). In the first volume, Blackstone addresses the rights of persons and details the mutual obligations inherent in four relations, namely: master and servant, husband and wife, parent and child, and guardian and ward. The relationship between husband and wife was founded, according to Blackstone, in nature. The moral content of that relationship was governed by the church. Yet the rights and duties of marriage were governed under common law as a civil contract. The guiding principle for the rights and duties of husbands and wives was the principle of marital unity.

Under the common law, women ceased to legally exist upon marriage. Their identities were absorbed into, or covered by, their husbands. As Blackstone wrote, "her condition during her marriage is called her *coverture*" (1978, 1:442). Without recognition as legal persons, wives suffered a series of civil disabilities: they could not own property, they could not make out wills (for they had no will), they could not enter into legal contracts (except for necessities). They could not sue in their own names, and wives also lacked authority over their children. Women regained their civic existence when they were widowed or, the legal equivalent, "where the husband has abjured the realm, or is banished: for then he is dead in law" (443). After the death of a husband, women reverted from being *feme coverts* to *feme soles*. Widows were also entitled to the *dower*, a one-third interest in their husband's estate from the time of his death until their own death or remarriage.

Having absorbed the civic existence of his wife, the husband took responsibility for his wife's possessions and actions. He gained title to her property and he was accountable for her debts. Her public actions were presumed to represent him — he was held responsible for them. Wrongs done to a wife were an affront to her husband, and it was his right to sue the transgressor. The children she bore were under his legal authority. A widower was entitled to *curtesy*, which gave him full interest in his wife's estate from her death until his own.

Civically, married women were nonexistent. Domestically, husbands and wives had duties toward each other, and the wife was under the authority of her husband. A wife owed her husband domestic service, sexual access, affection, companionship, and care for him and their children. A husband owed his wife support and protection. Husbands had the right to chastise moderately (physically punish) their wives for misbehavior. She was obliged to follow him in his choice of a domicile, or legal residence.

Finally, the marital relation was based on a notion of mutuality. Husbands and wives could not contract with one another, not only because wives lacked a civic presence, but also because it was thought to interfere with their domestic bonds. Marital law reforms of the late nineteenth and early twentieth centuries gave wives the right to contract with their husbands, but not over things within the domestic realm, such as housework (Siegel, 1994b). Nor could husbands and wives testify for or against each other in court, "partly because it is impossible their testimony should be indifferent; but principally because of the union of person" (Blackstone, 1978, 1:443). When legal reforms allowed for spousal testimony, the area of marital communication — confidential conversation between husbands and wives — remained protected (*Funk v. United States*, 290 U.S. 371 [1933]). The domicile presumption also spoke to this notion of marital union: the domicile is the place where the home is made.

Three aspects of the common law rules on marriage are worth highlighting. The first concerns the issue of civic existence. In the American system, where political rights are built upon civil rights, it followed that wives, lacking an independent civic identity, also lacked political presence (Siegel, 1994b). The antisuffragists claimed that husbands represented their wives within the political realm, so wives needed no separate vote (Kraditor, 1981). Second, within the domestic realm, husbands had authority over their wives. Although within the civic realm wives lacked status as legal persons, within the domestic realm their status was clear and distinct: they were subordinate to their husbands. Prior to the twentieth century, this element of the patriarchal domestic order was constitutive of the broader social order (Cott, 2001; Kann, 1991; Kerber, 1998). Inevitably, then, as the relationship between civic membership, social relations, and the constitutional order was restructured, so too the status of wives was affected in the domestic sphere. Third, law played an understood role in preserving the sanctity of the marital union. As Jürgen Habermas points out in *The Structural Transformation of the Public Sphere* (1989), there is tension over the role of the family in bourgeois democracies as both the site of patriarchal authority and as the place of affective human relations that stands apart from the state and the marketplace. Just as the public realm was remade, partly through the admittance of women into the electoral realm, changes in the domestic realm were also underway as the balance between affective intimacy, domestic hierarchy, and social order was renegotiated.

Marriage in the American Constitutional Order

Some might argue that marriage has no bearing on constitutional politics. After all, marriage traditionally is regarded as a matter of state statutory law and common law. Yet the governance of marriage is central to the establishment and maintenance of social order. The presence of social-order concerns in constitutional politics was quite evident in the nineteenth century, as the nation confronted the issue of slavery, engaged in westward expansion into new territories, and addressed the civic status of various religious and racial minorities that were incorporated through territorial expansion. Later, as the United States entered the world stage and Americans traveled and intermarried with foreign nationals, the government addressed the connection between political and personal allegiance. In various Supreme Court cases from the late nineteenth and early twentieth centuries, the link of marital status to civic membership and the constitutional order became apparent.

Two themes are evident in the constitutional cases dealing with marriage. The first expresses the centrality of marriage to civic status and the importance of marriage as a social-ordering tool in a democracy. The second reveals a concern over federalism, as the Court endeavored to specify the proper role of both the state and national governments in regulating marriage. Sometimes the federal government made evident its authority to regulate marriage, and stated clearly that marital status was central to civic membership. This position emerges in cases from the territories or in immigration cases. But in other instances the federal courts deferred to the states in regulating marriage. After the passage of the Nineteenth Amendment, the courts again took up marriage in defense of the rights of individuals against state intrusion. Yet, implicit within this defense of liberty were clear presumptions of proper social ordering that the courts made manifest.

Dred Scott v. Sandford, 60 U.S. 393 (1857), is the leading antebellum case on citizenship. At issue in the case was a claim to freedom by Dred and Harriett Scott, a slave couple held by the Sandford family of Missouri. In their pleas before the Court, the Scotts asserted that their earlier residence in a free territory had ended their enslavement. The Court used the case to consider the relationship between race and citizenship. Writing for the majority, Chief Justice Roger Taney asked, "Can a negro, whose ancestors were imported into this country, and sold as slaves, become a member of the political community formed and brought into existence by the Constitution of the United States, and as such become entitled to all the rights, and privileges, and immunities, guarantied by that instrument to the citizen?" (404). Citizenship was equated with political membership in the community of "We, the People." Such membership was bounded and exclusionary, and implied full rights and recognition for those who held this status. Given this vision of citizenship, it is no surprise that the majority concluded (on the eve of the Civil War) that African Americans could not be citizens.

Since citizenship was not defined in the Constitution prior to the Fourteenth Amendment, Taney examined other indicators of political membership and civic status. One of the indicators that he focused on was marriage. After reviewing the antimiscegenation laws that existed in the colonies at the time of the Revolution, Taney observed that these laws "show that a perpetual and impassable barrier was intended to be erected between the white race and the one which they had reduced to slavery, and governed as subjects with absolute and despotic power" (409).[1] For Taney, then, the bar against marriage was also a bar against political membership for the "degraded" race — those of African descent.

This controversial case produced several concurring and dissenting opinions. In his dissent, Justice Benjamin Curtis also treated marriage as a marker of civic status, but this time it was taken as an indicator of the civic capacity (and therefore civic membership) of Dred Scott. Curtis noted that Dred Scott had married Harriett Robinson with the consent of his master, Dr. Emerson, while they resided in the free territory of Wisconsin. "In that Territory they were absolutely free persons, having full capacity to enter into the civil contract of marriage" (599). Scott's capacity for consent was indicative of his ability to act as a legal person. Nor was this an ordinary contract.

> What, then, shall we say of the consent of the master, that the slave may contract a lawful marriage, attended with all the civil rights and duties which belong to that relation; that he may enter into a relation which none but a free man can assume — a relation which involves not only the rights and duties of the slave, but those of the other party to the contract, and of their descendants to the remotest generation? (599)

Scott was acting not just as a free legal person, but as a *free man* who assumed the rights and duties that are afforded to a person of that status. Scott's status as a husband demonstrated his civic capacity not only because he exercised rights as an individual, but also because he exercised rights for his wife and children ("a relation which involves not only the rights and duties of the slave, but those of the other party to the contract, and of their descendants"). The dependency of his wife and children on him demonstrated Scott's capacity for freedom and civic membership.

Yet even as a free man, Scott was still marked by race. As Curtis wrote, "In my judgment, there can be no more effectual abandonment of the legal rights of a master over his slave, than by the consent of the master that the slave should enter into a contract of marriage, in a free State, attended by all the civil rights and obligations which belong to that condition" (599–600). In a final twist on the relationship between social order and civic member-ship, Justice Curtis stressed "the consent of the master" in making Scott a free man. Even within the ranks of citizens, race and social authority still shaped one's civic place.

While the relationship between race and civic membership was remade by the Reconstruction Amendments, the relationship between gender and civic membership remained disputed. Had the Fourteenth Amendment recon-figured the political status of women? Previously, women were seen as hav-ing a mediated relationship to the state; the civic dependency of married women was made explicit by the rules of coverture. Once the Fourteenth Amendment was passed, with its promise of privileges and immunities for all citizens, did coverture recede as the normative foundation for women's civic membership? As Justice Bradley made clear in his concurrence in *Bradwell v. Illinois*, 83 U.S. 130 (1872), the answer to this question was no. In that case, Bradley recalled that it was "a maxim of that system of jurisprudence [the common law] that a woman had no legal existence separate from her hus-band, who was regarded as her head and representative in the social state" (141). That rule was not changed by the new amendments — "this cardinal principle still exists in full force in most States" (141). The Fourteenth Amendment had not displaced coverture, which still provided the "cardinal principle" that women were not legal persons and had no place in the "social state," or public sphere.

In *Dred Scott*, Taney cited the laws of marriage to conclude that only those with full civic status were recognized as citizens, or as members of "We, the People." For Curtis, on the other hand, the community of "We, the People" was more expansive and included gradations of civic status. Supposedly, the Reconstruction Amendments stood for the principle that there was *only one political grade*, and that all national citizens had the same rights and privileges. As the discussion in Chapter 1 indicates, Bradley's opinion in *Bradwell* sug-gests the way that the views of Taney and Curtis were combined in the post-bellum period to allow for both visions of "We, the People" (the equal and exclusive vision versus the graded and inclusive vision) to exist simultane-ously in the American political order, through the use of federalism as con-stitutive of civic difference among the ranks of civic members. But an appeal to federalism was unavailable when the issue of civic status arose in the territories, which were under federal authority. Discussions of marriage and civic status in the territories made clear the national government's investment in creating and maintaining certain social arrangements.

Congress passed several laws in the late nineteenth century punishing the practice of polygamy.[2] At that time there were large Mormon settlements (the Mormons were the main target of the antipolygamy laws) in the Utah territory, and Utah's application for statehood was resisted by the federal government because of concerns over polygamy. Utah resident John Reynolds appealed to the Supreme Court, after his trial and conviction for bigamy, charging that the law under which he was convicted (the Poland Act of 1874) was an unconstitutional interference with his freedom of religion. In *Reynolds v. United States*, 98 U.S. 145 (1878), the Court rejected the plaintiff's argument by drawing a distinction between religious beliefs, which were protected, and religious practices, which were not. The Court majority also affirmed the significance of marriage for social ordering. "Marriage, while from its very nature a sacred obligation, is nevertheless, in most civilized nations, a civil contract, and usually regulated by law. Upon it society may be said to be built, and out of its fruits spring social relations and social obligations and duties, with which government is necessarily required to deal" (165). Marriage was a contract, but a special and particular kind of contract, in that it provided the foundation for other "social relations and social obligations and duties" — in other words, it made people into responsible members of the broader community. This formative aspect of marriage was what made it so important to government and what linked it to the structure of the polity more generally. As the Court continued in *Reynolds*, "In fact, according as monogamous or polygamous marriages are allowed, do we find the principles on which the government of the people, to a greater or less extent, rests" (165–66). The social practices that shaped "the People" also shaped the government.

Congress also perceived this connection between marriage and civic order, and in its efforts to stamp out polygamy, it legislated that polygamists should be denied the right of suffrage. After several men and women filed suit against the registrar for refusing to place their names on the voter rolls, the Court found in *Murphy v. Ramsey*, 114 U.S. 15 (1885), that marital status was an allowable qualification for suffrage.[3] "It would be quite competent for the sovereign power to declare that no one but a married person shall be entitled to vote" (43). Further, the Court went on to draw a distinction between the rights that belonged to all persons as citizens, and political privileges, which were discretionary and under the authority of the state or federal legislatures. "The personal and civil rights of the inhabitants of the territories are secured to them, as to other citizens, by the principles of constitutional liberty, which restrain all the agencies of government, state and national; their political rights are franchises which they hold as privileges in the legislative discretion of the congress of the United States" (44–45). In support of this distinction and the discretionary nature of political rights, the Court cited the *Dred Scott* decision (45). Clearly, the Reconstruction Amendments had not abrogated the link between marriage and civic membership.

Once westward expansion was complete and the continental territories were all converted into states, issues of civic membership revolved around immigration questions. The large influx of immigrants in this period brought with it a growing number of marriages between American nationals and foreign nationals, raising questions of citizenship, which Congress addressed first by granting automatic citizenship to foreign women who married American men (in 1855), and later (in 1907) by depriving American women of their U.S. citizenship when they married a foreign national. Such was the case of Ethel Mackenzie.

Ethel Mackenzie was born and raised in the United States. In 1909 she married Gordon Mackenzie, a British national, after which she and her new husband continued to live in California, where she always had resided. When California granted women the right of suffrage in 1913, Ethel Mackenzie, who had been an active suffragist, attempted to register as a voter but was denied registration because she was not deemed to be a U.S. citizen. Mackenzie filed suit and the case went to the Supreme Court as *Mackenzie v. Hare*, 239 U.S. 299 (1915). In her complaint, Mackenzie argued that Congress had violated the Fourteenth Amendment when it stripped her of her citizenship without her consent. The Court disagreed. In a passage reminiscent of Bradley's concurrence in *Bradwell*, the Court cited the continued importance of coverture ("the identity of husband and wife") in determining a woman's civic membership.

> The identity of husband and wife is an ancient principle of our jurisprudence. It was neither accidental nor arbitrary, and worked in many

instances for her protection. There has been, it is true, much relaxation of it, but in its retention as in its origin it is determined by their intimate relation and unity of interests, and this relation and unity may make it of public concern in many instances to merge their identity, and give dominance to the husband. (311)

By birth, heritage, residence, and professed allegiance, Ethel Mackenzie was an American citizen. As such, she had laid claim to the status of voter — to be recognized as a public, autonomous person with individual political interests. But Congress and the Supreme Court rejected that claim and deemed her instead to be a dependent appendage of her husband. In one of the first tests of the significance of suffrage versus coverture in determining a woman's political status, coverture took precedence. The political identities of women in the early twentieth century continued to be formed by their personal identities.

Reforming Marriage

Many former suffrage advocates were disappointed with the limited impact of the Nineteenth Amendment on women's civic status. Beyond the vote, the suffrage amendment did little to alter the rights or recognition afforded to women by the courts or legislatures. This adherence to the status quo was particularly the case for married women, who still operated under a variety of legal disabilities connected to coverture. Consequently, the National Women's Party (NWP) determined to pursue full legal equality for women so that they would be treated as autonomous rights-bearing individuals. The means they settled on to achieve this goal was an Equal Rights Amendment to the Constitution. At the NWP's 1921 reorganization conference, the party committed itself to removing "all the remaining forms of subjection of women" (quoted in Becker, 1981, 18). The women from the League of Women Voters (LWV) and various social-feminist and feminist labor organizations determined instead to pursue a piecemeal approach of removing the legal disabilities of married women while preserving laws that were beneficial to women in labor regulation and other areas.

The debate over the ERA was a defining issue for the women's rights movement from the 1920s to the 1960s. Equality proponents sought to abolish all legal classifications based upon sex and to have women treated as individual, autonomous citizens with the same rights and duties as men. They focused on two barriers to equality as central and as justifying the pursuit of an amendment to the federal constitution. One was the legacy of coverture, which continued to define women's civic status in the early twentieth century, and the other was federalism, which made the pursuit of legal equality enormously difficult. Social feminists opposed the ERA for fear that it would abolish protective legislation. These activists had spent decades developing special labor and social welfare legislation that applied solely to women and was premised on the presumption of women's physical weakness and social dependency. Whereas working men had unions and could better defend their own interests without the assistance of the government, working women were far more vulnerable to employer exploitation. Given the community's interest in preserving the health and well-being of the nation's mothers (and future mothers), the government was called upon to regulate women's working conditions.[4]

In 1920, Alice Paul, the founder and leading figure of the National Women's Party, first contemplated seeking some form of blanket legislation to remove all of the legal disabilities on married women. Over the next three years, Paul and her allies in the NWP moved from a proposal for blanket equality legislation with an exemption to preserve industrial legislation for women, to advocating a constitutional amendment that might have negated protective labor legislation. In contrast, Florence Kelley (the secretary of the National Consumers League) and other leading social feminists went from a shared interest in equality legislation to firm opposition to the ERA (Zimmerman, 1991).[5] As time passed, the division between feminists on the issue of constitutional equality only deepened. Because of a constitutional structure that cast rights in negative terms (this period was the *Lochner* era of "freedom of contract") and imagined equality as sameness in terms of a male standard, there were no easy answers to the question of how to advance the political interests and civic standing of women.

The motivation behind the ERA was to rid the nation of the legal disabilities that remained attached to the status of being a wife. Both the League of Women Voters and the National Women's Party were involved in state-by-state campaigns to eliminate legal discriminations against married women, since the most obvious and most numerous sex-based legal classifications were rooted in marriage law (League of Women Voters, 1924 and 1930). As one commentator said in reference to the normative effects of common law discriminations: "The old medieval laws have a deadly effect on the minds of our people . . ." (U.S. Senate, 1929, 22). In reviewing the achievements of activist women in the decade after suffrage, an NWP attorney observed, "The attention of women is strongly concentrated on the marital relation, and it is not surprising that the greatest effort of women has been toward putting marriage on a partnership level. . . . Despite the steady advance to free women from the shackles of the common law, the statutes and decisions of the United States reflect the inferior position of women" (Matthews, 1930b, 53). The campaigns to abolish discrimination against married women proved difficult and time consuming, so the National Women's Party began to consider a more permanent, encompassing, and effective solution to the problem of legal discrimination. Several of the early drafts of the ERA included specific reference to marriage. The first section of the proposed amendment read, "No political, civil or legal disabilities or inequalities on account of sex, or on account of marriage unless applying alike to both sexes, shall exist within the United States or any place subject to their jurisdiction" (Kelley, 1922, 14). Although the reference to marriage was eventually dropped from the amendment, the proponents of the ERA remained committed to overcoming an understanding of women's civic status as relational and dependent — an understanding which was rooted in the coverture tradition.

The proponents of the ERA had a liberal, aspirational vision of the role of law. They believed that by establishing sex equality as a foundational principle in the nation's "supreme law" they would be advancing expectations and opportunities for women. They compared their campaign to the effort of the abolitionists to secure the Fourteenth Amendment. Further, they contended that their vision of women's rights was inspired by the original proponents of rights for women — by the signers of the Declaration of Sentiments, which was written by Elizabeth Cady Stanton and adopted at the Seneca Falls convention in 1848. In a paraphrase of the Declaration of Independence, the Declaration of Sentiments listed, among the "injuries and usurpations" committed by mankind against womankind, a reference to marriage. "He has made her, if married, in the eye of the law, civilly dead" ("Declaration of Sentiments," n.d.). Like their nineteenth-century foremothers, the equality advocates of the 1920s advocated a philosophy of natural and individual rights in which sex difference was irrelevant to one's civic and social status.

In contrast to this philosophy of rights, according to the equality proponents, protective legislation was premised on a diminished understanding of women and their social capacities. As Burnita Shelton Matthews wrote in a 1926 essay, restrictive labor legislation "fortifies the harmful assumption that to labor for pay is a prerogative of the male, and that women are a class apart who are only allowed to engage in paid work at special hours, under special supervision, and subject to special government regulation" (Matthews, 1926, 125). What was problematic about protective legislation, and what led the NWP to call for its abolition, was that by positing the view that women were socially and biologically distinct, these laws justified treating them as civically distinct as well. Whereas in the nineteenth century presumptions about women's dependent and relational natures were expressed in marital law, in the twentieth century these same presumptions were being shifted onto labor and social welfare laws. Further, in the twentieth century, women's civic difference was attached not only to their role as wives, but increasingly to their role as mothers as well. In both centuries, legal presumptions of gender difference had a broad impact on the civic identities that underlay women's civic membership.

Social feminists believed that proponents of the ERA were privileging "theoretical" equality over the real concerns and experiences of working women. As the head of the Women's Bureau, Mary Anderson, said, "rights must be interpreted for women workers as something concrete, and we must start from the world where it is today" (quoted in Kessler-Harris, 1982, 210). Although many of the advocates of protective legislation initially favored laws that would apply to both working men and working women, they found that the federal courts rejected labor regulations that applied to male workers. Such laws were typically found to violate the freedom-of-contract right of male citizens — a right that the courts attributed to the liberty component of the Due Process Clauses of the Fifth and Fourteenth Amendments. However, as the social feminists and their allies discovered in *Muller v. Oregon*, 208 U.S. 412 (1908), the courts were willing to tolerate laws that regulated the working conditions of women only, since women were seen as physically weaker and socially less able to defend themselves in bargaining relations with their employers. Having found a way to secure labor benefits for women, social feminists were willing to accept the characterization of women as "so constituted that she will rest upon and look to him [men] for protection" (422), even when they had the same contractual rights as men. Because of a woman's "physical structure" and her "performance of maternal functions," the Court determined in *Muller* that "she is properly placed in a class by herself" and could be treated as constitutionally different from men (421). To the social feminists, civic difference (or inequality) was an acceptable price to pay for economic protection. Few feminists were willing to tolerate a notion of gender difference that was attached to marital status, but a more "natural" conception of gender difference — signaled by women's capacity to mother — was acceptable to the social feminists.

The first four decades of the twentieth century witnessed a major change in the way that gender difference was legally conceptualized and related to civic membership. Central to this shift was the emergence of new understandings about how marriage, labor status, and motherhood affected what the state owed its citizens, and what citizens owed the state. In *Muller*, early versions of those new understandings are visible. The Court in *Muller* still portrays women as dependent upon the men in their lives, but men are evidently not as reliable a source of protection and support as they once were, so now the state may act to defend and protect women workers from abusive bosses. Why should the state do this? Not only because working women are more vulnerable than their labor brethren, but also because they are the "mothers of the race." In the early twentieth century, then, maternalism joined with marital status in grounding women's civic difference. Further, although gender difference continued to ground civic difference for women, it now became a source of civic inclusion and rights rather than a means of civic exclusion, as it was under the terms of coverture. Because of gender difference, women without able-bodied husbands were entitled to state protection. Further, because of gender difference, women with and without husbands would be entitled to state provision.[6] For men, marital status continued to serve as a positive foundation for civic status, but more in the realm of social provision and positive rights than in terms of political rights and constitutional liberty.

Muller both reflected the sense that men's and women's civic membership were different, and gave further depth to those differences by clearly placing women outside of the regime of freedom of contract. Yet these differences might have diminished if, as the social feminists had hoped, the *Muller* decision represented merely the first assault on the freedom of contract doctrine. There was reason to be hopeful about this possibility when the Court handed down *Bunting v. Oregon*, 243 U.S. 426 (1917), on the eve of the passage of the Nineteenth Amendment. *Bunting* appeared to apply the logic of

Muller to men, as the Court upheld a law regulating the labor conditions of men. Yet the reasoning in *Bunting* was quite different. As Judith Baer summarizes the National Consumers League's brief in *Bunting*, "The brief quotes economists, social reformers and other authorities who argue that short hours are beneficial to individuals and society because workers can then educate themselves by going to libraries, night schools, university extension courses, and public lectures. It is also argued that such education is necessary for good citizenship and the intelligent use of the vote" (Baer, 1978, 90). While *Muller* upheld protective labor legislation for women because they were not full citizens, *Bunting* upheld labor legislation for men precisely because they were full citizens. The distinction between men's and women's civic membership in relation to their labor status continued. The freedom-of-contract doctrine had been narrowed, not overturned, when the Nineteenth Amendment was passed in 1920.

The *Bunting* opinion suggested a constitutional path for transcending the difficult choice between equality with negative rights or civic difference with positive rights. What is hinted at in *Bunting* is the prospect of civic equality and positive rights for both men and women. That vision might have been realized had the Courts and Congress viewed woman suffrage as a change not only to women's political rights, but also to the terms of civic membership in the broader constitutional order. Yet in the one case where the Supreme Court offered a broader reading of the impact of the Nineteenth Amendment, *Adkins v. Children's Hospital*, 261 U.S. 525 (1923), it managed to further entrench the division between civic equality and positive rights. The *Adkins* case recalls a legal tradition that cited women's dependence on men and their role as mothers to justify protecting them as workers. Further, *Adkins* was central to the debate between equality feminists and social feminists, who pursued different approaches to remedying the civil disabilities that attached to women's marital status.

At issue in *Adkins* was a federal law that established a board which set minimum wages for women workers in the District of Columbia. The Supreme Court found the law unconstitutional. With the advent of the Nineteenth Amendment, women's civic status changed, as did the ability of the government to regulate women's working conditions. The last chapter considered the impact of the *Adkins* case from the perspective of the impact of the suffrage amendment. The focus of this chapter is on marriage and other social roles that cast women as dependent and civically disabled.

Coming just three years after women were granted the right to vote, the *Adkins* decision threatened to end the exception for women under the *Lochner* freedom-of-contract regime, at least in the case of minimum wage laws. Discussing the earlier ruling that had created this exemption, the Court wrote of *Muller*:

> The decision proceeded upon the theory that the difference between the sexes may justify a different rule respecting hours of labor in the case of women than in the case of men. It is pointed out that these consist in differences of physical structure, especially in respect of the maternal functions, and also in the fact that historically woman has always been dependent upon man, who has established his control by superior physical strength. (552–53)

Nature and law made women weak and dependent upon men. But law, at least, was subject to change. Legal changes "in the contractual, political, and civil status of women" (553) had taken place. Women were now men's equals in civic status, so they were no longer entitled to state protection of their working conditions. The broader change wrought by the Nineteenth Amendment affected women's civic membership, but not the larger constitutional order. It was a transformation that brought women partially into the negative-rights regime already occupied by men.[7]

Adkins signaled a further erosion of the common law regime that governed women's civic standing in the nineteenth century (Cott, 2001). Yet, whether the rules of domestic relations were truly vanquished or merely refashioned under privacy rights is open to question (Siegel, 1994a). At the very least, *Adkins* contributes to the complex picture that appears regarding women's civic membership in the 1920s. Women were being recognized as public-realm beings with civic standing, but the costs of this recognition were quite apparent to social feminists, who fought to retain protective legislation and therefore fought against the ERA. Ambivalence about equality, especially with regard to civil rights and civic duties that impinged upon domestic duties, grew in response to *Adkins*. Presumptions about women's civic identity that were related to women's domestic roles continued to inform their civic status after suffrage, but often in new forms and places within the law.

Finally, in an interesting response to the ERA proposal, the social feminists offered another alternative amendment in the 1920s. In addition to fighting against state laws that legally discriminated against married women, they sought to change the way in which marriage was constitutionally governed, advancing an amendment to enable Congress to regulate marriage nationally. In her endorsement of Senator W. L. Jones's resolution calling for a marriage amendment, Grace Raymond Hebard asked, "We naturalize our citizens through our Federal Courts; why not marry and divorce by the same judicial procedure?" (Hebard, 1913, 1310). Recognizing the ongoing connection between marriage and civic status, social feminists hoped to put marital status issues in the same legal and judicial realm as suffrage, so that they might better control the influence of marriage on civic status more generally.[8]

The Cable Act

Until the twentieth century, the nationality of American women did not depend on their marital status. Then, in 1907, Congress passed a law that deprived American women of their national citizenship upon marriage to a foreigner. The law was passed in the interest of conforming to international standards that favored family unity in nationality and achieved such unity by making a wife's nationality derivative of her husband's. The law was also aimed at making American policy consistent, since the United States since 1855 had granted the foreign wives of American men automatic U.S. citizenship upon their marriage. When objections were raised to the 1907 law, speakers in Congress expressed their disdain for women who would choose a non-American husband, thereby betraying their political allegiance to their birth country. No such concern was expressed when American men married foreign women—since it was assumed that the husbands would succeed in Americanizing their brides (Bredbrenner, 1998).

Yet the passage of the Nineteenth Amendment challenged the theory of family unity that lay behind these laws when it cast women as autonomous political actors. In their campaign for the vote, suffragists had called for an educated, nonpartisan citizenry, and had played to concerns over the "uneducated" political participation of immigrants. Women's rights activists contended that this ignorant, immigrant vote would be offset when the suffrage amendment added native-born, middle-class women to the electorate. The extension of the vote to women in 1920 was part of a larger process, in which the boundaries of inclusion and exclusion were redrawn in the United States following the First World War. Other elements of this reordering of civic membership included the passage of the Quota Act of 1921, the Married Women's Act (or Cable Act) of 1922, the Indian Citizenship Act in 1924, and the National Origins Act (or Johnson-Reed Act) of 1924. Further, many states in the 1920s passed laws removing the right to vote from legal residents who were not yet citizens.[9] The common theme behind these laws was the move toward a clearer separation between citizens and noncitizens, and the granting of full rights to those who were considered citizens.[10] In this reordering, the demands of political membership were made more rigorous; for women, Native Americans, and immigrants, the movement toward rights and political participation was accompanied by civic education and Americanization campaigns. Meanwhile, in the area of immigration, race was becoming a more significant barrier to inclusion.

The Cable Act expressed this mix of concerns over civic membership. When the National American Woman Suffrage Association reorganized as the League of Women Voters in 1920, reforming the 1907 law was one of the main items on their agenda. Many women remained incensed by the Supreme Court's 1915 ruling in *Mackenzie* that stated that marriage to a foreigner amounted to consent to expatriation for American women.[11] Among the six planks that the LWV agreed to at its inaugural convention was one concerning the citizenship of married women: "Believing . . . that alien women should not acquire citizenship by marriage with Americans, but rather by meeting the same requirements as those posed for the naturalization of American men" ("First Woman's Platform," 1920). The plank went on to ask for independent status for women's citizenship. Many women activists of the 1920s connected the advancement of women's rights to the unique character of American women's civic membership, which they characterized as intelligent, considered, and ever conscious of the national good. They argued that the long, hard suffrage campaign set native-born women apart from immigrant women. Before such women were awarded the high privileges of citizenship and voting, the suffragists argued, they too should be expected to undergo a process of education and enlightenment that would allow them to make good use of their votes. As activist American women sought to develop a new civic identity, they retained their vision of the exclusive character of women's politics. As the constitutional order was remapped in the aftermath of the Nineteenth Amendment, not only were the terms of women's civic membership resituated, but the place of native-born white women was repositioned relative to that of other groups in the civic order.

After two years of intensive lobbying by leading women's organizations (orchestrated by the Women's Joint Congressional Committee) the Cable Act was passed and signed into law in 1922. The central purpose of the law was to revert to independent citizenship for women, so that native-born women would retain their American citizenship after wedding foreigners and so that foreign women no longer would automatically be granted U.S. citizenship upon marriage to American men. Yet the details of the law added many qualifications and exemptions to these provisions, which reflected an ongoing concern with family unity and the continued belief that husbands and a family's place of residence deeply influenced the political loyalties of wives.

Contrary to the view that the Cable Act was but one more step toward the inclusion of women as liberal individuals, the law contained racial exceptions to its recognition of women's autonomous political standing. Any woman who married an alien ineligible for American citizenship (e.g., Chinese) lost her American citizenship as long as she remained married. When an American woman of Chinese descent married a Chinese nationalist man, she lost her citizenship permanently. Indeed, racial restrictions on immigration and citizenship were becoming more elaborate, as represented in the Quota Act of 1921 and the National Origins Act of 1924. Even among women who retained their American citizenship after marriage to a foreigner who was eligible for U.S. citizenship, their civic status changed: they ceased to be "natural" citizens and became "naturalized" citizens instead. Practically, this distinction meant that when an American woman married to a foreign man resided abroad for two years, she forfeited her American citizenship. This provision was significant symbolically as well, for it suggested that while birth established a permanent national identity for American men, the political identity of American women was mutable by marriage. As the debates about the Cable Act made clear, any American woman who would marry a foreign man (the criticism was particularly directed at elite American women who married into the European nobility) was herself regarded as unnatural and suspect (Sapiro, 1984; R. M. Smith, 1989).

The earlier history of married women's citizenship further illuminates the connection between marital status and civic membership. As Virginia Sapiro (1984) observes, the restrictions on married women's citizenship rights were expanded in the late nineteenth century. Prior to 1855, and following the common law tradition of birth allegiance, a woman's civic membership was constituted by birth rather than marriage. In was in the midst of a period of intense nativism, in 1855, that Congress made the alien brides of American men automatically eligible for citizenship. The new law was justified as an expression of concern for the children of American men residing abroad. By extending citizenship to the wives of these men, U.S. authorities thought they would encourage these women to aid their husbands "in instilling the proper principles in his children." Through this extension of citizenship a wife, it was thought, "at once conform[ed] to the political character of her husband" (Sapiro, 1984, 10). Then, in 1907, during another upswing in nativism, Congress extended the same principle to American women who married alien men. As the Supreme Court confirmed in *Mackenzie*, matrimony was a contract in which women voluntarily "merge[d] their identity" with their husbands, not merely socially or civilly, but also politically (Sapiro, 1984, 10–11). Thus, liberal principles of contract and voluntarism were used to deny the separate identity of married women, and to confer upon them a restrictive status through which they could be denied citizenship.

Clearly, women's rights leaders saw the Cable Act as a further extension of the equality principle embodied in the Nineteenth Amendment. They argued that the Nineteenth Amendment changed the political standing of American women more broadly. After the passage of the suffrage amendment, women's organizations had made independent citizenship a top priority, since they believed, as Maud Wood Park said, that "a woman is as much an individual as a man is, and her citizenship should be no more gained or lost by marriage than should a man's" (quoted in Cott, 1987, 99). Such views (along with concern over the status of immigrant women) were crucial to the law's passage. As one congressman reported, "there was no particular force in the demand for this bill until the Nineteenth Amendment became part of the organic law of the land. . . . At that moment the doctrine of dependent or derived citizenship became as archaic as the ordeal of trial by fire" (Sapiro, 1984, 12). To a greater extent than before, the Nineteenth Amendment made women "independent individuals" in the civic realm. As they ceased to be subjects to the state, the political relevance of their subjection to their husbands was also in question. Yet this change did not lessen the desire to use marriage as a means of providing social order in other realms.

The Cable Act is significant for our discussion of gender and civic membership in the 1920s in several respects. First, it illustrates dual aspects of civic membership. Civic membership under the liberal political system of the 1920s was concerned with the rights and responsibilities of independent individuals, including married women. Yet the debates about civic membership also reflected the continued relevance of social order, both in the concerns about the political composition of the nation and in the persistence of marital status as a condition that marked civic membership. Second, the Cable Act demonstrates that women's incorporation into the voting citizenry should not be understood simply as an expansion of liberal principles of inclusion. Rather, in simultaneously denying rights to immigrant women and to women who married "ineligible aliens," the Cable Act offset its inclusions with political exclusions. Third, analysis of the Cable Act affects our understanding of American political development in this period. Some scholars have characterized the decade after World War I as an era of contractive conservatism, while others see it as a time of continued (though slowed) democratic progressivism. These two images might be brought together by characterizing the 1920s as a period of political reordering, in which the terms of civic membership were being reconceived for all Americans. Finally, the story of the Cable Act reinforces Carole Pateman's arguments regarding women under the social contract. Both status and contract helped to define married women's unique political position in American civil society. By consenting to marry, women agreed to their place in civil society, yet the position or status they agreed to denied them equal standing with men (Pateman, 1988).

Adjudicating Marriage and Civic Status
After the Nineteenth Amendment

STATE CASES

In his 1935 casebook on husband and wife law, Chester Vernier asked, "have married women won their struggle for equality?" and answered that "they have succeeded very substantially but not completely" (4). The author noted that while there were then equal rights statutes in twelve states, "nine states still declare that the husband is 'the head of the family' " (4). Further, as the scholars who have studied coverture reform in the nineteenth century have shown, legislative enactments and judicial enforcements are two different matters. Only through a detailed examination of state cases can we determine the status of the marital unity principle a decade or so after suffrage. This section proceeds with a consideration of cases that address married women's rights at the general level, and more specifically in the area of domicile.

To indicate the range of responses by the state courts to the new equality laws, I will discuss four cases briefly. Responding to that state's Married Woman's Act, the Minnesota court addressed the question of whether a wife could be prosecuted for stealing from her husband. In *State v. Arnold*, 235 N.W. 373 (1931), the court stated, "In our opinion the status of marriage has not been modified by the Married Woman's Act, and only property rights and contracts are affected thereby" (374). While some of the features of coverture may have changed, a woman's status as a wife remained the same. The high court of Mississippi had offered a similar view when they wrote in *Austin v. Austin*, 100 S. 591 (1924), "It was not the purpose of the makers of our Constitution nor of the Legislature to entirely destroy the unity of man and wife with all the incidents flowing therefrom" (592). Marital unity was still a guiding legal principle. Contrast these views with the one expressed by the state court in Wisconsin, in *First Wisconsin National Bank v. Jahn*, 190 N.W. 822 (1922). Regarding the state's new equal rights law, the court found,

> The purpose of these statutes in general was to remove the limitations imposed by the common law upon married women, and at the same time leave them with such protection as it afforded. . . . By recent legislation in this country, the sexes have been brought to an absolute equality of right and privilege before the law, but that does not and should not strike down sex as the basis of classification in the enactment of laws relating to the health, morals, and general well-being of our people. (824–25)

The Nineteenth Amendment and laws like it had created an equal political and civil status for women that changed the status of wives within marriage. These laws did not, however, eliminate sex classification in law.

The response of the Wisconsin court in *First National Bank* represents the progressive end of the range of responses taken by the state courts regarding the Nineteenth Amendment's effect on married women's rights. As the discussion of the debate on women's eligibility for jury service suggests (see Chapter 4), most state courts did not construe the Nineteenth Amendment as having created a political status for women that made them equal to men.

Yet it can be argued that the Nineteenth Amendment had a normative influence that created an environment in which statutory change was more likely. What still has to be determined is the overall effect of these statutory changes on women's civic membership.

In Georgia, the husband was deemed the head of the household. Yet even in this deep South state, the climate of equality was influential. In *Curtis v. Ashworth*, 142 S.E. 111 (1928), the state supreme court held that husbands were no longer responsible for torts committed by their wives, since recent legal changes had "greatly modified the principle that the civil existence of the wife is merged in that of the husband. It robbed the principle of much of its effect. It has resulted in the destruction of the subjection of the wife to the husband" (113). While the law did not explicitly address the issue that the court was considering, the justices felt justified in this broad construction partly because of recent laws granting women the right to vote and to hold office. Consequently the court found, "The wife is now made, in all important affairs of life, the equal of the husband. While the husband is still declared by state to be the head of the family he, like the King of England, is largely a figurehead" (113).

Comparing *Curtis* to *Arnold* allows for a couple of observations. First, such a comparison reinforces the significance of judicial construction. Though the Minnesota legislature committed the state to equal rights for married women and the Georgia legislature continued to uphold the principle of a husband's authority, in effect, thanks to the courts, the law was more progressive in Georgia than it was in Minnesota. Second, in neither state was there real equality for married women. No state was willing to abrogate fully the principle of marital unity or coverture, even though both courts and legislatures asserted women's civil equality. Formally, the rules of coverture were changing, but informally the principles behind coverture often remained in place, and marital status continued to have political significance.

DOMICILE

Consideration of the changes in the common law rule concerning domicile demonstrates the complexity of this issue. According to Albert Leavitt, a leading legal scholar on the subject in the 1920s, "The domicil is the legal home. It is the place where the law can act upon the status of the individual no matter where the person may be *in corpore*" (quoted in Breckinridge, 1931, 7).

Persons' legal existence, their civic being, was located in their domicile. Taxation, political representation, and their legal estate all were attached to the person's domicile. Under the common law, a married woman's domicile was her husband's, regardless of where she actually lived. As women gained an independent civic presence with the Nineteenth Amendment, it seemed reasonable to expect that they would be recognized as having an autonomous domicile when they lived apart from their husbands. To some extent, they were granted this right in the years after suffrage. But the common law principles covering a married woman's domicile continued to have influence, suggesting once again the law's effort to preserve women's domestic status while recognizing their rights in the political realm.

Even when married women were clearly winning rights in other areas, the decade after suffrage saw little progress in the area of domicile. Sophonisba Breckinridge was a feminist activist and social scientist at the University of Chicago who had done a great deal of work surveying the legal status of women (married and single) in the years after suffrage. In her monograph published in 1931, *Marriage and the Civic Rights of Women: Separate Domicil and Independent Citizenship*, she concluded, "What has not been recognized is her right to establish separate domicil for other purposes [besides divorce or marital difficulty], for any purpose that seems reasonable and suitable to her and her husband, when there is no question of discord, but when for various reasons it may seem well for the two to live for considerable periods of time in different localities" (5). Just as Breckinridge wrote these lines, two court cases did precisely what she called for: they allowed women to establish separate domiciles even when there was no marital discord. These cases reveal a great deal about the nature of women's civic membership in the years after the Nineteenth Amendment.

The first case, *McCormick v. United States*, 57 Treas. Dec. 117 (1930), concerning a French woman married to an American man, came from the United States Customs Court, Third Division. The woman was charged a customs fee upon entering the United States on the presumption that she was legally a U.S. resident since her domicile was her husband's, who lived in Chicago. However, she was then, and had always been, a resident of Paris. In ruling in favor of the woman, the court wrote,

> During the past couple of generations or so the legal status of a married woman has gradually and definitively changed. The common law theory of

marriage has largely ceased to obtain. The wife is now a distinct legal entity. She now stands in most, if not all, of the States on terms of equality with her husband in respect to property, torts, contracts, and civil rights. This has been accomplished by statute and by decisions of the courts. (118)

A woman's legal identity was no longer subsumed under that of her husband. She was now a "distinct legal entity" with equal rights in many areas. The court came close to concluding that the common law theory of marital unity was now dead.

As a result, the court was ready to recognize a woman's right to a separate domicile even when there was no marital discord. Reviewing other court rulings in which a married woman's right to contract with her husband was recognized, the court said, "Since she has the right to make a contract with her husband, she may contract with him upon the subject of domicile. The husband may consent to a change of domicile for the wife and such consent may be express or implied" (120). Wives could acquire separate domiciles provided their husbands consented to it. Thus, women were civic entities and as such could make contracts — even contracts with their husbands over aspects of the marital relationship. Yet the areas in which such contracts could be made and the terms that guided them were still beholden to the rules of marital status. Not all areas of the marital relationship were open to contract. Even when they were open, often the husband was presumed to retain authority over his wife. Indeed, in the area of domicile, the court made it clear that, "Though modified, the rule that a husband's domicile is the domicile of the wife still obtains" (119).

A very different view was offered in the concurrence to this opinion, where Justice Cline argued for equal civic membership regardless of sex. "A denial of the right of any free person of either sex who is of mature age, *sui juris*, to choose for all purposes his or her domicile or legal residence, is repugnant to the fundamental principles of the Constitution of the United States" (125), he began. Cline tied the amendment directly to a woman's right to establish her own domicile. "I believe it covers the right of woman to select and establish a residence wherever she chooses to vote" (125). (Indeed, by 1929 eight states had reached a similar verdict — a point that will be returned to below.) Further, Cline made clear his broad interpretation of the Nineteenth Amendment by citing the decision in *Adkins v. Children's Hospital*. In light of the Nineteenth Amendment, the *Adkins* court had ruled against special labor legislation for women, saying "woman is accorded emancipation from the old doctrine that she must be given special protection or subjected to special restraint in her contractual and civil relationships" (125). Though the Nineteenth Amendment figured prominently in Cline's interpretation, he did not rely solely on this amendment in arguing for constitutional equality. Rather, he suggested that the Nineteenth Amendment merely provided recognition for rights that women already held as citizens. "It is significant that the nineteenth amendment vests no new right in women, but gives written recognition to an existing right, and prohibits the State or Federal sovereign from denying or abridging that right" (126). This view of the Nineteenth Amendment echoed that of the early suffragists who argued that women already had all the rights of citizenship, including the right to vote and the right to serve on juries, under the Fourteenth Amendment. Yet despite *Adkins*, this view was not widely shared by the American judiciary.

More common than Cline's dissent was the opinion of the majority in *McCormick* or of the majority opinion in *Commonwealth v. Rutherford*, 169 S.E. 909 (1933). Handed down by the Supreme Court of Appeals of Virginia, *Rutherford* concerned Helen Rutherford, resident of New York, and her husband, John Rutherford, resident of Virginia. The state of Virginia had assessed income taxes against Helen Rutherford, claiming that her domicile was the same as her husband's, which made her a resident of Virginia. Since the time of her marriage to John Rutherford in 1927, Helen Rutherford had lived, voted, and paid taxes in New Rochelle, New York. Mrs. Rutherford was a financially independent woman who maintained her separate residence with her husband's consent, and their marriage was amicable.

In ruling in favor of Helen Rutherford's claim that she was a legal resident of New York, the court concurred with the argument that to do otherwise "would deprive her of her property in derogation of the Fourteenth and Nineteenth Amendments of the Constitution of the United States" (909). The court reviewed the history of the common law's rule regarding a wife's domicile and considered the erosion of the theory of marital unity in Virginia. Except for "the right of curtesy" and a husband's "marital rights," the justices found that in Virginia the court had already "wiped aside every vestige of control the husband ever had under the common law" (912). Thus, the Court in the *Rutherford* case appeared to be building on firm precedent when it rejected the "obsolete and vanishing common-law fiction" of marital unity (913). Yet the Court did not desire that this fiction should vanish completely. "The authorities are not uniform, they are diverse; but we think that the statutory invasion of the fiction, certainly in this state, has broken it down as far as the political, civil and property rights of the wife are involved; but as to purely domestic relations it is, at least in part, preserved and it ought so to be" (913). Thus, the Court presented a complex picture of women's civic membership a decade after suffrage. Women's civic rights under the Fourteenth and Nineteenth Amendments were broad. With their new civic standing, even women's status within marriage was affected. The most progressive courts were ready to declare the death of coverture and of the theory of marital unity. Yet these same courts provided an escape clause from the new promise of equal civic membership. In the arena of "purely domestic relations," the old rules of marital unity and of a husband's marital rights were "preserved," as "it ought so to be." The reasons for this rule were vague. Where once there was hierarchy and an explicit recognition of male authority, now there was privacy and marital harmony.[12]

Several law journals commented on the *Rutherford* case. Most concluded, as the *Harvard Law Review* said, that "the case constitutes a foreseeable culmination of the liberalism of many American courts in modifying the strict common-law rule preventing the acquisition of an independent domicile by a married woman" ("Conflict of Laws," 1934, 348–49). The political status of women had changed, and along with it so had their rights within marriage. But just as women's rights advocates prepared to celebrate this further modification of the rules of coverture, the *Minnesota Law Review* provided a note of caution.

> However, the instant decision is a logical result of the modern tendency to place the wife on an equality with her husband. But the court deciding the principal case seems to have assumed that the only theory underlying the rule that a married woman's domicile follows that of her husband is the common law fiction of identity. The other theory upon which the principle partially is based is the policy of the law of preserving the unity of the home. ("Recent Cases," 1933, 477)

The "unity of the home" had come to replace the rule of the husband as the justification for women's subordinate domestic role (Siegel, 1996).[13]

In the years after suffrage, judicial decisions on married women's rights

indicated that a woman's position in civil society was governed by both status and contract. As the Louisiana Supreme Court stated in *Moulin v.
Monteleone*, 115 S. 447 (1927), "It is true that marriage is something more
than an ordinary contract in which the parties alone are concerned, for it is
a status, in which society itself is concerned. . . . In Louisiana, the wife, by
virtue of several recent emancipation laws, has practically every prerogative
that the husband has" (450). The political emancipation of women had
affected the status of wives, giving them (almost) as many prerogatives as
their husbands had. But the statuses of husband and of wife continued to
exist and be governed by broader social interests — interests that continued
to dictate women's responsibility to the domestic sphere.

As this brief sample of court cases on married women's rights suggests, the
Nineteenth Amendment had a significant but complex impact on women's
civic membership. The principle of coverture was being eroded. Yet a married woman's status as a wife continued to influence her public standing. This
change is captured by the laws passed in several states in the 1920s that
allowed married women to establish a separate domicile for the purpose of
voting (League of Women Voters, 1930). Such laws were regarded as a mere
modification to the common law principle that a wife's domicile follows her
husband's. It was as if the courts were offering women two different civic
memberships, one for the public realm and one for the private realm. As a
public-realm citizen, a woman was an independent person with the right to
vote and to establish her own domicile, but within the domestic sphere, she
remained a wife beholden to her husband.

SUBSTANTIVE DUE PROCESS

Two important developments occurred in the area of substantive due process
jurisprudence in the 1920s that reflected larger changes in the constitutional
order of citizenship. One involved the incorporation of women under the
freedom-of-contract doctrine in the *Adkins* case, discussed above. The other
was the extension of substantive due process reasoning in the direction of
privacy (see also Fineman, 1999; Woodhouse, 1992). This later doctrinal
development is evident in the majority opinions in *Meyer v. Nebraska*, 262
U.S. 390 (1923), and in *Pierce v. Society of Sisters*, 268 U.S. 510 (1925), both
of which were written by Justice James C. McReynolds. In each case, the
Court ruled that constitutional protections of liberty invalidated particular

state laws regulating education. More specifically, the Court was protecting the right of parents to secure a fitting education for their children. These cases would appear, then, to continue the line of reasoning expressed in *Adkins*, in which the authority of the government to regulate the social order was challenged by the proponents of individual interests. Yet on closer examination, the outcomes in *Meyer* and *Pierce* are quite distinct from the end result in *Adkins*. Whereas *Adkins* did advance an understanding of women as public, capable individuals, the Court's rulings in *Meyer* and *Pierce* ultimately succeeded in doing the opposite — they opened a new domain for the articulation of social-order concerns within constitutional politics. Among the social-design elements expressed by the development of this doctrine was an affirmation of the institution of marriage.

At issue in *Meyer* was a state law that barred instruction in foreign languages prior to the eighth grade. The plaintiff was a parochial schoolteacher convicted of teaching German to his young students. The statute under which Meyer was convicted was challenged as an unreasonable infringement of his liberty as protected under the Due Process Clause of the Fourteenth Amendment. In considering the issue, the Court noted that there was no exact definition of liberty, but ventured to suggest some of the things connoted by the term.

> Without doubt, it denotes not merely freedom from bodily restraint but also the right of the individual to contract, to engage in any of the common occupations of life, to acquire useful knowledge, to marry, establish a home and bring up children, to worship God according to the dictates of his own conscience, and generally to enjoy those privileges long recognized at common law as essential to the orderly pursuit of happiness by free men. (399)

Under the first two aspects of liberty detailed here — freedom of contract and freedom of employment — this case was connected to other freedom-of-contract cases, like *Adkins*. In that context, the right claimed was given the legitimacy of well-developed doctrine. But after that, the list turned toward personal, private matters like childrearing and marriage, which were represented as markers of individualism and as the rights of a free man. Indeed, even the presentation of religion was characterized as a matter of personal conscience. Nonetheless, what is portrayed here as individualism and liberty had its roots in organized forms of social regulation. Religion, education, marriage, parenting — all involve social institutions that order the community through a series of authority relations, such as pastor and congregant, teacher and student, husband and wife, and parent and child. The Court recognized this aspect of the liberty rights being protected when it cited "those privileges long recognized at common law as essential to the orderly pursuit of happiness." What initially appeared as a contest between liberty and order, then, was actually an affirmation of social ordering framed as concern for individual liberty.

A similar coupling of liberty and order is expressed in *Pierce*. In that case, a private religious school challenged an Oregon law that commanded parents and guardians to send their children to public schools. The Supreme Court ruled that under the precedent set in *Meyer*, the law was an unconstitutional infringement on "the liberty of parents and guardians to direct the upbringing and education of children" (534). Further detailing the rights and duties of parents to educate their children, the Court continued,

> The fundamental theory of liberty upon which all governments in this
> Union repose excludes any general power of the state to standardize its
> children by forcing them to accept instruction from public teachers only.
> The child is not the mere creature of the state; those who nurture him and
> direct his destiny have the right, coupled with the high duty, to recognize
> and prepare him for additional obligations. (535)

Implied here is the right of the state to regulate the education of children — though that right is limited to the extent that the government cannot "standardize *its* children." Further, the recognition of a parental right to direct their child's education was immediately reframed as a "high duty" — one that would lead a parent to prepare their child for "additional obligations." Just what sort of obligations might these be? The Court did not say, but it seems reasonable to suppose that they are social obligations (such as work, civic involvement, religious participation, as well as marriage and parenting) that concern a child's place in the larger community *he* is destined to join as an adult.

If this analysis is correct, then it raises an obvious question: why should the Court use the liberty component of the due process doctrine to affirm social ordering? While this issue is discussed more fully in Chapter 8, for present purposes a brief outline of this early shift in the Constitution as a social design will suffice. There were three reasons for the reliance on substantive due process liberty. First, the advent of the Nineteenth Amendment may be read as part of a larger process in which constitutional governance shifted from a more corporatist form (that is, the Curtis view of "We, the People," in which there are a variety of political grades included in the polity that have relational standing toward each other), to a more modern, liberal form.[14] As a liberal system of governance, the constitutional order was clearly concerned with the rights of individuals. Such a system placed increased emphasis on the idea of individual liberty. Second, what was left behind in this transition was a prior system of social governance encoded in the common law of domestic relations. Time and again in the state cases, judges wrote about the erosion of coverture. Elsewhere, the authority of masters over their servants was being eroded in labor law (Orren, 1991), and the status of other dependent people, formerly understood as wards, also was being recast in the direction of voluntarism and autonomy.[15] As Henry Maine suggested in a different context, the legal recognition of status relationships appeared to be on the wane, while contract was on the rise (Maine, 1972; Dolgin, 2002). As a means of ordering society, common law status relations were no longer readily available to the courts, so other alternatives needed to be found. Third, and finally, it made sense for the Court to invoke liberty, because liberty as privacy marked the domestic space in which these common law status relations previously resided. The household that had previously contained a master who governed over his wife, children, servants, and wards according to legal prescription, was now a home in which this free man apparently was left to re-create those private authority relations without government intrusion. To the extent that such relations were re-created to the satisfaction of the community (through marriage and parenting, and with the aid of the schools and churches), individuals were at liberty to do so with less direct government intrusion.

Conclusion

When women's rights activists gathered at Seneca Falls in 1848, they called upon the public to recognize women as individuals with natural rights, entitled to equality and political representation. At the time, the main impediments to this goal were the law and norms attached to coverture, which positioned women as relational and dependent. Many of the indictments contained in the Declaration of Sentiments were aimed at the oppressive aspects of marriage and its effect on women's civic membership. To remedy this situation, the signatories of the Declaration called for educational access, marital reform, and legal rights. The one plank that stirred great controversy among the assembled delegates was the call for woman suffrage. What made the call for suffrage so radical was its implied rejection of a social and political universe built around the principles found in the common law of domestic relations. Instead of social hierarchy between men and women, there would be equality. Instead of the containment of women in the domestic sphere of home and family, they would be present in the public sphere of politics and commerce. Instead of regarding women as relational beings attached to husbands and children, they would be seen as autonomous individuals with separate political interests. What was radical about the vote was that it threatened to change women from wives into persons.

But did it? When suffrage was finally adopted seventy-two years after Seneca Falls, were women no longer seen — in civic terms — as wives? The answer is neither a clear "yes" nor a clear "no." After the adoption of the Nineteenth Amendment, marriage played a less significant role in defining women's civic membership, but it remained part of the substratum of their civic rights, duties, and identities. Marital status continued to impact directly women's civil rights in many states, and it affected indirectly the expectations and treatment that government officials accorded to women. In the realm of labor laws and nationality, many government officials still exhibited the belief that women depended on men, and that personal relations were likely to affect a woman's political allegiances. In some areas, women came to be seen and acknowledged as public, independent individuals. In other areas, they continued to be understood as relational and dependent upon the men around them.

Nor was this tension merely a matter of remnants that had yet to be cleared away in the aftermath of the suffrage amendment. Marital status did not shape women's civic membership only in relation to the old rules of coverture — most of which were slowly but surely being swept away by the courts and the legislatures. Marital status was coming to affect new legal formations in constitutional law and in statutory law. This shift occurred because the constitutional order in the United States continued to shape the social order — the Constitution continued to operate as social design, albeit on new terms. Marriage emerged as an important feature of social provisioning legislation, where the calculation of who deserved government assistance and on what terms was often made with reference to marital status. Constitutionally, space was being made for the recognition of individual rights among the previously subordinated and for the affirmation of acceptable social-ordering institutions, including marriage. This shift occurred in the domain of substantive due process jurisprudence. Particularly important to the project of harmonizing social relations within a modern liberal governance structure were contracts with implied social statuses connected to them, such as the marital contract and the employment contract. Gender — in relation to social-ordering institutions like marriage — continued to imply civic difference after the Nineteenth Amendment.

FOUR

Jury Service

After women gained the right to vote they expected to be treated as first-class citizens, with all the rights and duties of full civic membership. Yet instead of this, women confronted continued resistance to their participation in civic obligations such as jury service. State after state, from 1910 through the 1920s, considered the impact that suffrage had had on women's eligibility for jury service. When the question arose regarding the relationship between the statuses of elector and juror, most courts and legislatures conceived the question narrowly, as a matter to be settled by statute. Some acknowledged that suffrage signaled a normative recognition of women as public persons. Yet many suggested that outside of the realm of suffrage, common law principles still determined women's civic identities and made them legally ineligible for jury service. Only a few courts addressed the question in constitutional terms by examining the relationship between specific rights and women's broader civic status.

The last two chapters have brought us closer to understanding the limited impact of the Nineteenth Amendment on women's constitutional standing.

This chapter continues this inquiry by examining the nineteenth-century and early-twentieth-century campaigns for women's jury service. After suffrage was granted, women's rights activists claimed that their new position as voters entitled them to other rights, such as the right to serve on juries. Their arguments paralleled the arguments of an earlier generation of suffragists, who claimed in the 1870s that the Reconstruction Amendments to the Constitution entitled women to all of the rights and privileges of citizenship, including jury service and voting. In both of these campaigns, rights advocates articulated their understanding of the relationship between voting and jury service within the broader context of civic membership. Thus, tracing the campaign for jury service in connection to the campaign for suffrage reveals a great deal about the changing structure of women's civic membership.

Constitutionally and historically, jury service raised broader questions about the structure of American civic membership. In the United States, jury service historically has been tied to voting. In most states, a common prerequisite for undertaking jury service was having the status of elector, that is, being a citizen with the right to vote — a criterion that also fit with the nineteenth-century Woman Rights movement's conception of civic membership. As voters, women would obtain all of the rights and privileges of other first-class civic members. Among those rights was the right to serve on a jury, the most significant right or duty, after voting, that citizens commonly filled. Jury service was democracy in action — it was direct governance by the citizens. Women's exclusion from this role suggested that even with the vote, they had yet to obtain the status of civic equality. In the nineteenth century, women's rights activists hoped to build on Supreme Court rulings regarding jury service and civic status for African American men in light of the Fourteenth and Fifteenth Amendments. After the Nineteenth Amendment passed, many former suffragists argued that women were automatically eligible to serve on juries. Yet the state courts typically disagreed.

This chapter considers the relationship between jury service and women's civic membership before and after the Nineteenth Amendment. What the debate over women's jury service reveals is that the Nineteenth Amendment did little to displace the constitutional structure of civic membership founded upon the Reconstruction Amendments. That structure separated political from civil rights, gave narrow influence to political rights status, and failed to include women under the equal protection provision. So while the

Nineteenth Amendment did help to lessen the distinctiveness of men's and women's civic membership, and gave women some recognition as public persons, it did not create civic equality for men and women. In a series of cases about women's jury eligibility after suffrage, numerous state courts ruled that the Nineteenth Amendment applied only to voting. The Nineteenth Amendment did have some normative influence on lawmakers and other government officials who were inclined to grant women new civil and political rights in light of their new status as voters. But even here, the influence was greater in the years leading up to the adoption of the national amendment than in the decade following the amendment's passage. This debate over women's jury service gives more texture to the portrait that appeared over the last two chapters regarding the incomplete, incoherent character of women's civic membership after the Nineteenth Amendment.[1]

The Nineteenth Amendment might have transformed women's civic standing in two ways, the first more doctrinal, the second more political. Doctrinally, the courts might have found that within the larger structure of the Constitution, the Nineteenth Amendment had a broad impact that went beyond the question of the vote. For the most part, that interpretation did not materialize.[2] Politically, the adoption of the Nineteenth Amendment might have signaled a broader public commitment to gender equality in law and politics. Certainly some of the normative impact of the Nineteenth Amendment translated into related legal and institutional reforms, but here, too, the effect was fairly limited. Neither through the courts nor through popular political channels were women's rights activists able to secure full civic standing with the Nineteenth Amendment. What the jury service campaign makes more apparent is that the judicial failure of suffrage to provide civic equality was due to the existence of a constitutional structure that devalued political rights like voting. That structure was developed partly in reaction to the efforts of earlier rights advocates to claim full civic membership (including voting and jury service) under the Reconstruction Amendments.

Another objective of this chapter is to consider the relationship between jury service and women's civic membership more generally. The debates over jury service illuminate the connections between the civil and political rights of citizenship. Jury service may be regarded as either a political right, that is, as a form of democratic participation in the exercise of law and justice, or as a civil right — a matter of individual protection against state authority. Women's rights activists of the nineteenth century understood this dual character of jury service and thought of political and civil rights as intimately connected, political rights providing a mandate for the broader claims of civil rights. But by the early twentieth century, rights activists began to conceive of civil and political rights more discretely, and the character of jury service began to be cast more narrowly as a civil right. This shift occurred partly in response to the narrow and discrete casting of civic rights (including jury service) by the Supreme Court in the late nineteenth century.

Further, I contend that the concept of jurors as peers suggests very different ways of thinking about what women bring to the exercise of their civic duties. For women, jury service raises the issue of what it means to be a peer (as in, "a jury of one's peers") — whether in a formal legal sense, or as something deeper and more substantive, which speaks to the ways that women bring their lived experiences to the exercise of their civic duties. Further, jury service is a more substantial commitment, in terms of time and effort, to civic participation — a commitment that brings people more fully into the workings of the state and more intimately into contact with other citizens. As such, it raises questions about whether women's public duties affected their ability to meet their private obligations in the domestic realm. In contrast to men, women in the nineteenth and early twentieth centuries were never seen as fully public beings, and public-realm activities such as jury service were sometimes thought to impinge negatively on their private identities and activities as women (W. Brown, 1995). Civic membership, in connection to the performance of substantial civic duties such as jury service, was regarded as a public identity. Gender intersects with civic identity differently for women than it does for men.

Jury Service and Civic Status: The Nineteenth-Century Debate

With the exception of voting, for most citizens the honor and privilege of jury
duty is their most significant opportunity to participate in the democratic process.

— *Powers v. Ohio* (1991)

What is the relationship between jury service and civic membership? The common law tradition of trial by jury is meant to serve as a guarantee of liberty against abusive exercises of governmental authority. Yet, not only do juries help to protect individual liberty, they also serve as an institution of self-government in which civic members apply the law to members of the community. As part of the Bill of Rights, under the Sixth Amendment, the Constitution guarantees all criminal defendants a right to trial by an impartial jury. The right to serve on juries has been considered most prominently under the Fourteenth Amendment's Equal Protection Clause. In addition to concern about the rights of defendants and the rights of potential jurors, the concept of a "jury of one's peers" connects jurors to defendants around the issue of civic status. What determines who a defendant's peers are? Must they have the same civic status and political rights? Should they belong to the same community as the defendant and have a shared sense of justice? Should race or gender matter in determining one's peers? In all these respects — regarding the rights of defendants, the rights of potential jurors, and the concept of jurors as peers — jury service is connected to civic membership.

In the nineteenth century, the connection between jury service and civic membership was explored most prominently with regard to the Reconstruction Amendments. After these amendments were passed, there were competing views regarding their scope and meaning, about which it was left to the Supreme Court to make a judicial determination. What was the scope of national citizenship and to whom did it apply? How did a history of subjugation or civic exclusion affect the rights granted to different groups within the polity? As the Court sought to answer these questions they dealt, among other matters, with jury service and voting, and their relationship to civic membership.

This was the constitutional context that the Woman Rights movement faced as it made claims for women's right to vote and to serve on juries. According to the state and federal courts, women were ineligible to serve on juries for at least four reasons. The most direct constraint was the common law tradition that made women ineligible for jury service. In Blackstone's *Commentaries*, a jury is defined as consisting of "twelve free and lawful men, *liberos et legales hominess*" (Blackstone, 1978, 3:352). The text goes on to state, "Under the word *homo* also, though a name common to both sexes, the female is however excluded, *propter defectum sexus*" (Blackstone, 1978, 3:362). In other words, the sex of women constituted a defect that barred them from jury service. Second, setting aside this direct prohibition, most women were not regarded as persons before the law under the rules of coverture. A third, more narrow and more readily overcome constraint concerned women's electoral status. Most states defined the pool of eligible jurors as electors. Thus, until women could vote, they could not serve on juries. Finally, some states had specific statutory or constitutional provisions that explicitly limited the class of eligible jurors to men.

Yet the Woman Rights movement offered its own interpretation of the Reconstruction Amendments and jury service as they related to women's civic membership. First, on the basis of the Fourteenth Amendment, rights advocates argued that citizenship entitled women to vote and serve on juries. Second, activist women of this period built their arguments about the Fourteenth Amendment upon the foundation of an earlier argument they had developed about the role of jurors as peers, contending that women defendants were entitled to have women jurors as their peers. Finally, as the suffrage movement met with some success in the late nineteenth century, suffragists stressed the connection between electoral status and jury service. This dialogue about jury service and civic membership within the Supreme Court and the Woman Rights movement reveals sharply contrasting visions of national civic membership, its privileges and immunities, and the role of political rights in civic life.

In contrast to the more limited view of political rights and the privileges of citizenship that the Supreme Court offered in the *Slaughter-House Cases*, 83 U.S. 36 (1872); *Bradwell v. Illinois*, 83 U.S. 130 (1872); and *Minor v. Happersett*, 88 U.S. 162 (1874) (see Chapter 1), the Court took a more expansive and synthetic approach in *Strauder v. West Virginia*, 100 U.S. 303 (1879). The *Strauder* case was important for its recognition of the right to serve on juries under the Fourteenth Amendment. In *Strauder*, the Supreme Court found a West Virginia statute barring African Americans from jury service to be unconstitutional: "The very idea of a jury is a body of men composed of peers or equals of the person whose rights it is summoned to determine; that is, of his neighbors, fellows, associates, persons having the same legal status in society as that which he holds" (308). Denying African Americans the right to sit on juries would serve to place "practically a brand upon them, affixed by law, an assertion of their inferiority" (308), which would result in unequal civic status. Jury service was treated as a civil right — the Court stated that the purpose of the Fourteenth Amendment was to grant the freedmen "all the civil rights that the superior race enjoy" (306).[3] Jury service was also considered a right that reflected a broader civic status. The Court wrote that the Fourteenth Amendment created a right to "exemption from legal discriminations, implying inferiority in civil society" (308). Although the opinion was framed doctrinally as an equal protection matter, the Court referred repeatedly to jury service as a right or an immunity, and stressed its interest in protecting the citizenship status of the freedmen. Yet the opinion went on to assert that other characteristics — like age and *sex* — were acceptable criteria for jury qualification. According to the Court, the Fourteenth Amendment was intended to protect the citizenship of African Americans, and to prevent racial discrimination, not gender discrimination.

From these 1870s cases emerged the beginnings of a national framework for civic membership, a framework that stressed the distinction between civil and political rights and made political rights secondary. Further, in its rulings in *Slaughter-House* and *Bradwell*, the Court narrowed the meaning of the Privileges and Immunities Clause (the clause that speaks most directly and generally to the rights of citizens), and asserted that the progressive power of the Equal Protection Clause applied only to African Americans. On what were these interpretations based? The Court used history (that is, the intentions of Congress in passing the amendments) and doctrine (prior Court cases that discussed the Privileges and Immunities Clause present in Article 4 of the Constitution) to justify its findings. But it is clear from the dissenting opinions in these and related cases, as well as in congressional reports on the amendments, that other interpretations were possible, if less likely.[4] Further, the opinion in *Strauder* makes plain that the narrow reading of civic membership offered here was partly provoked by the judiciary to ensure that these amendments were not used to reorder social relations (particularly gender relations) more broadly. In a few more years, the Court would retreat from its commitment to use these amendments even to reorder race relations (Brandwein, 1999).

The emerging framework for national citizenship articulated by the Supreme Court also influenced the state and territorial courts in their treatment of women's claims that voting and jury service are rights of citizenship. In an early pair of cases from the 1880s, the territorial government of Washington considered the consequences of women's suffrage for the right to serve on juries. After suffrage was established for women in Washington, in *Rosencrantz v. Territory*, 5 P. 305 (1884), the Supreme Court of Washington Territory upheld women's right to sit on juries. Just three years later (after a change in personnel), however, the same court reversed this decision in

Harland v. Territory, 13 P. 453 (1887). The latter opinion is interesting for several reasons, the most relevant for the present study being its treatment of women's civic membership rights under the Fourteenth Amendment. The court opinion approvingly cited Justice Bradley's concurrence in *Bradwell*, a case in which women were found to be citizens and entitled to the rights thereof, but it was decided that professional licensing (Myra Bradwell had applied for admission to the bar in Illinois) was not a privilege or immunity of citizenship. As discussed in Chapter 1, Justice Bradley wrote of the restrictions on women's citizenship: "So firmly fixed was this idea [of women's dependence] in the common law that it became a maxim of that system of jurisprudence that a woman had no legal existence separate from her husband" (141).

In its comment on this case, the Washington court in *Harland* concluded, "Thus we see that the Fourteenth Amendment, which certainly spreads its protecting shield over females, because females are citizens, is yet not strong enough to overcome the implied limitations of prior law and custom with which it was brought into association when it was adopted" (456). According to this court, it seemed that for women to obtain all available rights and duties of citizenship and to gain standing as civic persons, more than the Fourteenth Amendment or a grant of suffrage by the territory was required. Rather, women would continue to be governed by "prior law and custom," particularly the common law tradition which granted women "no legal existence separate from her husband." Thus, the court found, women could be excluded from jury service.

The state courts also addressed the question of whether the privileges and immunities of citizenship included jury service. There were three ways of understanding jury service in relation to citizenship: as a right (or privilege), as a grant, or as a duty. The New Departure view was that jury service was a right of citizenship. The second view was that jury service was a grant to some citizens and not a natural right inherent in citizenship. The Court applied this view to both suffrage and (to a lesser extent) jury service in the late nineteenth century. The third view saw jury service as a duty of citizens — like paying taxes or serving in the military — rather than as a legal right citizens might seek to employ or protect. Some state courts acknowledged the ambiguous status of jury service by calling it a "privilege or duty," while others sought to deny jury service to women by terming it a duty and not a privilege of citizenship. However it was conceived, eligibility for jury service was a significant marker of political standing.[5]

To the extent that the Supreme Court had in mind women's claims to the rights of citizenship when it narrowly interpreted the Privileges and Immunities Clause of the Fourteenth Amendment in the 1870s, the rights movement helped to shape the post–Civil War constitutional order, albeit in a conservative and narrowing direction (Hoff, 1991; Stanley, 1988; Stanton, Anthony, and Gage, 1969; DuBois, 1987; Kerber, 1995; Holland, 2001). Out of the Reconstruction Amendments to the Constitution came a framework for national civic membership within which the debate over women's rights and jury service took place. One effect of that framework was to make political rights secondary in the constitutional order of civic membership (V. D. Amar, 1995). Further, the framework that grew out of the Reconstruction Amendments allowed for a hierarchy of political standing in which women were not granted the same civil or political rights (including jury rights) as other citizens. This denial was partially done through the Court's refusal to apply the Equal Protection Clause to women. Finally, this framework incorporated an older conception of women's civic membership, grounded in coverture, in which women had no presence within the public realm. This framework made necessary the campaign for a suffrage amendment, and ultimately helped to limit the impact of the Nineteenth Amendment on women's civic membership.

JURORS AS PEERS

The *Strauder* opinion connected jury service to civic membership through the concept of a peer. To explicate this concept more, it is useful to consider Marianne Constable's (1994) analysis of the mixed jury. In premodern England, a mixed jury was invoked in cases when two different communities, and two different senses of justice, were at issue. Its history is used by Constable to reveal a different way of thinking about law and justice. According to Constable, the mixed jury embodied "a principle of personal law" (2), in which persons were judged according to the standards of their communities. Since the members of different communities understood the customs and principles of justice within their communities, community standards were brought to bear through jury selection. In cases involving a native and either an alien or a member of another group with its own customs and beliefs (such as Jews or merchants), juries were selected with equal representation from both communities.

Constable contrasts this system with modern-day ideals about juries. In modern practice, a "jury of one's peers" consists of six or twelve individuals with the same formal legal status as oneself. Under modern legal doctrine, concerns about jury service are concerns about exclusion rather than inclusion. Thus, our understanding of juries as an aspect of civic membership has been reduced, as has our sense of community and how communities participate in justice. The "other" that we are concerned with today is a racialized or gendered other, since racial and gender differences speak to differences in interests (rather than differences among communities and their sense of justice) in the American political order.

This reduced "otherness" in contemporary legal doctrine points out an interesting conundrum for the lawyers and judges seeking to apply the Fourteenth Amendment's Equal Protection Clause. Constable (1994) frames the issue this way: "How is one to identify parts of the population without differentiating between what are formally recognized only as equals?" (41). Thus, our justice system faces a Foucaultian (1990) problematic of producing the identity of difference it then seeks to regulate. Difference becomes a check-off box on application forms, or a category on one's birth certificate or driver's license. It's an officially ascribed factor of an individual's identity. Presumably such an identity stands for more — stands for lived experience and community membership — but in the administration of justice such links become tenuous and the categories take on their own meanings.

Thus, Constable contrasts two notions of justice represented in different ideals about juries. Under the system of the mixed jury, the defendant's peers were members of his or her community whose practical understanding of justice and everyday experiences were similar to that of the defendant. In contrast, the modern notion of jurors as peers is that of persons who share the same formal political status as the defendant. For U.S. citizens, this means a jury composed of other citizens. In the first view, social difference provides positively to a jury's substantive understandings of justice. In the second view, social difference is problematic and can contribute to bias in the practice of law. Thus, even an all-white, all-male jury is treated in terms of difference — to the extent that it differs from an ideal jury that represents the racial and gender composition of society. The perfect modern jury is a jury that is socially neutral with no substantive preconceptions that might interfere with its determination of the facts.

The more substantive notion of jurors as peers represented in the mixed jury recalls another (now defunct) English common law institution — the matrons' jury. Although women were generally barred from jury service, in some special instances their participation was not just allowed but demanded, in which case a matrons' jury was formed. If a woman convicted of a crime and sentenced to capital punishment claimed she was pregnant, then a jury of twelve matrons was called to determine whether in fact she was. If the woman was found to be pregnant, the death sentence was delayed until after the child was born. Matrons' juries represented a transition from the personal law concept associated with the mixed jury and the positive law philosophy of the modern jury (Blackstone, 1978, 3:394–95).

Women were called upon to serve on a matrons' jury because of their knowledge as women. Even more specifically, these were juries of matrons rather than maids, since married women and mothers presumably would recognize from their own experiences the physiognomy of pregnancy. Since the matrons' jury called for the positive inclusion of women for their shared practical knowledge, it resembled the mixed jury. Yet there were differences as well. Matrons were not called upon to offer justice, but to establish the facts. Even in this role, the women jurors were supervised by an equal number of male jurors who were present during the physical examination of the convicted. (This practice suggested, perhaps, some doubt about how women might perform this role and what conclusions they would offer without the supervision of men.) The role of matrons' juries was quite limited, in that it did not allow for women's knowledge of other women to extend to judgment of the crime. Before the common law, English juries offered verdicts that "spoke the truth" (ver-dict, from the Latin, "speaks the truth") to determine not only the facts, but more broadly what was just (Constable, 1994, 2). Modern juries are charged merely with establishing the facts of a case. It is left to the courts to apply the law.

Despite the limitations of the matrons' jury, its history is suggestive. Some records exist of the use of matrons' juries in the American colonies (Taylor, 1959, 225). Indeed, there may have been instances on either side of the Atlantic when a women's jury was called upon to do more than establish pregnancy. In the late 1600s, a women's jury was impaneled in Virginia to hear "a case involving the morals of a young woman" (Taylor, 1959, 225). Four hundred years later, an English court called a women's jury together "for a case involving manslaughter of a baby" (Weisbrod, 1986, 60). As these examples illustrate, women's substantive knowledge was called upon to consider crimes against women or specific crimes such as infanticide. This practice suggests a notion of peers as something more than those with the same formal legal standing, but also as those sharing common experiences and insights into social conditions. These commonalties might provide the basis for shared political interests and a shared sense of justice.

The Woman Rights movement in the middle and latter parts of the nineteenth century stressed that American women were denied the right to a trial by a jury of their peers. Even the demand for the vote had to do with being made the political peers of men. At the 1854 Woman Rights Convention in Albany, New York, it was resolved "that women are human beings whose rights correspond with their duties; . . . and that men who deny women to be their peers, and who shut them out from exercising a fairshare [*sic*] of power in the body politics, are arrogant usurpers" (Stanton, Anthony, and Gage, 1881, 594). Women's natural rights as human beings entitled them to a political status as men's peers. Two years earlier, at the Syracuse National Woman Rights Convention, Rev. Antoinette L. Brown had addressed the issue of peerage specifically in relation to the law: "The law is wholly masculine; it is created and executed by man. . . . The law then could give us no representation as woman, and therefore no impartial justice even if the present lawmakers were honestly intent upon this; for we can be represented only by our peers. . . . Common justice demands that a part of the law-makers and law executors should be of her own sex" (Stanton, Anthony, and Gage, 1881, 594–95). As the legal subjects of men, women had no representation within the civic realm. For there to be justice, women should be represented at bar, bench, and jury box by their legal equals — other women. When the territorial government of Wyoming gave women the right to vote and made them eligible for jury service in 1869, the *New Orleans Times* commented that women "cannot sit as the peers of men without setting at defiance all the laws of delicacy and propriety" (Stanton, Anthony, and Gage, 1887, 735; Rodriguez, 1999). This southern newspaper was concerned that a change in women's political status, making them men's peers, would result in a change in their "feminine nature." While for many women activists in the 1850s, the demand for women jurors was a demand for justice by their peers (a group that did not then include men), others recognized that in making women jurors their status changed to make them the peers of men.

Two different conceptions of women as peers animated the debate over women's rights and jury service in the nineteenth century. The first, represented in the preceding discussion, was concerned with peerage as a legal status. Antoinette Brown and Susan B. Anthony each denied that women were able to receive justice, since they were not the peers, but the legal inferiors, of the men who populated the courtroom. One remedy was to recognize this difference in status and provide women with a jury of their legal peers. As Elizabeth Cady Stanton said in a plea to the New York State legislature in the 1850s, "The noble cannot make laws for the peasant; the slaveholder for the slave; neither can man make and execute just laws for woman, because in each case, the one in power fails to apply the immutable principles of right to any grade but his own" (Stanton, Anthony, and Gage, 1881, 597). If women ranked lower than men, then they deserved their own justice. Likewise, if women *were* men's equals, then they could not be excluded from the jury stand. In either case — whether women formed a separate grade requiring the inclusion of women on juries, or an equal grade that did not permit their exclusion from juries — peerage was regarded in the first instance as a formal legal status.

The second concept of women as peers referred not to their legal status but to their social knowledge. Again, from Stanton's testimonial to the New York State legislature:

> Shall the frenzied mother, who, to save herself and her child from exposure and disgrace, ended the life that had just begun, be dragged before such a tribunal [a judge and jury of men] to answer for her crime? How can he judge of the agonies of soul that impelled her to such an outrage of maternal instincts? . . . Shall laws which come from the logical brain of man take cognizance of violence done to the moral and affectional nature which predominates, as is said, in woman?" (597–98)

In this passage, Stanton suggested that the experience of women makes them better prepared to understand the nature of certain crimes, such as infanticide. Further, she contended that women jurors are more likely to appreciate the prior implicit crime against the accused woman, and to hold to account the man who left her pregnant and without aid. Stanton also gestured (ironically, perhaps, with the words "as is said") to essential gender differences that make a woman better equipped to understand another woman. Whether due to commonalities in experience or in nature, women were needed on juries to determine the crimes of other women and the injuries done to women.

Not only does their knowledge make women better positioned to determine the facts in crimes that involve other women, it also renders them better able to apply justice. In its comment on women's jury service in Wyoming in 1870, the *Cincinnati Gazette* wrote, "How can men justly judge a woman? They cannot have the knowledge . . . requisite to the judgment of motives and temptations. . . . Furthermore, many of the crimes of men are against women. How can men appreciate their injury? . . . How can justice be expected from those who instinctively combine to preserve their privilege to abuse women?" (Stanton, Anthony, and Gage, 1887, 738). Understanding the circumstances under which women were likely to commit crimes or the damage done when men committed crimes against women, women were better positioned to offer justice in their determinations of guilt and influence on sentencing.

The Woman Rights movement of the nineteenth century sought to defend the right of women civic members to a jury of their peers. For these women activists, the term "peer" reflected both their concern with women's legal and political status and their desire to have the benefit of other women's experiences and social outlooks in the courtroom. In both these respects, we see a fuller sense of civic membership being developed and offered in the early fight to make women eligible for jury service. Implicit in the conception of peerage as a legal status is a critique of American civic membership as an institution tolerant of social inequalities. An institution that allowed women to be excluded from the rights and privileges that men held in civil society was one tolerant of hierarchy in the political order. Further, while women demanded equal status with men, they expected to bring to the performance of their citizenship the benefits of women's particular social experience and knowledge. For this reason, women ought to be included positively in the community of "the People."

VOTING, CIVIC MEMBERSHIP, AND JURY SERVICE

Is jury service, like voting, one of the political rights of citizenship? Women's rights advocates were not successful in claiming the right to vote and serve on juries under the Fourteenth Amendment. They had more success in claiming that electoral status entitled them to the other rights and privileges of civic membership. Some states and territories that granted women suffrage in the late nineteenth century also allowed them to serve on juries (Rodriguez, 1999). The basis for this link was both general and narrow. At the general level, jury service could be regarded as a political right like voting and office holding. As Vikram David Amar (1995) argues, such a view was developed in connection with the Fifteenth Amendment, which guaranteed African Americans equal voting rights. Some of the authors and interpreters of the Fifteenth Amendment argued that the possession of the vote necessarily implied the possession of these other political rights. Or, in a creative interpretation, some women claimed that marriage was like slavery, so the Fifteenth Amendment ("The right of citizens . . . to vote shall not be denied . . . on account of . . . previous condition of servitude") also applied to women, at least if they were or had been married. The more narrow view was that voting status was an explicit qualification for jury service in many states, so that the extension of the suffrage to a new group made them eligible for jury service. In any case, the treatment of African American men under the Fifteenth Amendment in the late nineteenth century set important precedents for how courts decades later would interpret the Nineteenth Amendment.

The Founders regarded juries to be both a necessary protection against governmental encroachments upon liberty and a form of republican self-government. As Alexander Hamilton wrote in Federalist Paper 83, "The friends and adversaries of the convention, if they agree in nothing else, concur at least in the value they set upon the trial by jury: or if there is any difference between them, it consists in this; the former regard it as a valuable safeguard to liberty, the latter represent it as the very palladium of free government" (Hamilton, Madison, and Jay, 1961, 424). The view that jury service was a form of political participation that educated citizens for other forms of political participation, such as voting, was articulated by Tocqueville: the jury "should be regarded as a free school which is always open and in which each juror learns his rights, . . . and is given practical lessons in the law. . . . I think that the main reason for the . . . political good sense of the Americans is their long experience with juries in civil cases" (V. D. Amar, 1995, 221). The jury box was a place where Americans learned the virtues of self-governance.

Amar regards jury service as part of a plenary political right that includes the right to vote and to hold office. He contends that this plenary right is grounded constitutionally in the four voting amendments to the Constitution (the Fifteenth, Nineteenth, Twenty-fourth, and Twenty-sixth). "Jury service," writes Amar, "like voting and office holding, was conceived of as a political right, as distinguished from a civil right, and political rights were excluded from the coverage of the Fourteenth Amendment. Instead the Constitution speaks to the exclusion of groups from jury service most directly through the voting amendments" (V. D. Amar, 1995, 204). Why is jury service a political right like voting? Jurors vote on whether to convict; they apply the law, thereby governing the society. In the process, they often go beyond a finding of fact to offer their own sense of what is just. Therefore, they make normative choices as a community of citizens. In this regard, the role of a juror is the role of a citizen (and not merely a person) who actively participates in the governing process.

For women's rights advocates, jury service and suffrage were not just civic activities but also markers of civic status. The role of voter and juror served not only to distinguish between citizens and noncitizens, but also between those citizens who had political rights and those who did not. Further, in contrast to T. H. Marshall, who saw civil rights as the foundation of citizenship, women's rights advocates saw voting as the preeminent right of citizenship, from which other rights followed (Marshall, 1950). If women were secured the right to vote, they would be more likely to be recognized as first-class citizens and accorded other political and civil rights, including the right to serve on juries. If their elevation to the status of elector did not enable women to hold office and to serve on juries, then it appeared to many that they still were being denied first-class citizenship.

Prior to the Nineteenth Amendment, some courts found the link between electoral status and voting status persuasive as narrowly construed, particularly with regard to African American men. The key case for this position was *Neal v. Delaware*, 103 U.S. 370 (1881), in which the Court found that African Americans were now entitled to vote by the Fifteenth Amendment: "Therefore, a statute confining the selection of jurors to persons possessing the qualifications of electors is enlarged in its operation so as to embrace all those who . . . are entitled to vote" (387). Once the Fifteenth Amendment made African Americans qualified electors, they became eligible to serve on juries. Yet while the Fifteenth Amendment provided the constitutional basis for this decision, it was the Fourteenth Amendment which gave the Court's opinion its normative thrust. The Court wrote, "The question thus presented is of the highest moment to that race, the security of whose rights of life, liberty, and property, and to the equal protection of the laws, was the primary object of the recent amendments to the national Constitution" (389). The extension of citizenship to African Americans after the Civil War secured for them a claim for equal civil rights. Despite its immediate effect of allowing jury service on the basis of electoral eligibility, the ruling in *Neal* (contrary to Amar and the Woman Rights movement) is indicative of the remote and disunited nature of political rights in relation to civic membership.

The debate over whether electoral status qualified citizens for jury service raises several issues about the political and civil rights of citizenship. First, it raises the question as to whether jury service is a political or civil right. It is both, but despite the efforts of the Woman Rights movement to cast it as a political right, the Supreme Court saw it primarily as a civil right that only narrowly was related to voting. Second, it raises the issue of what the relationship is between civil and political rights. Do civil rights or political rights provide the foundation on which other rights follow? Here again, both possibilities historically were present, but the claim for a plenary political right failed to win a judicial mandate in the late nineteenth century. Finally, this matter raises the issue of whether particular rights have a larger normative effect on one's civic status. Does voting create a status of civic equality that entitles one to broader recognition by the courts and legislatures? As we will see in the next section, the answer to this question depends on the movements making such claims and the political context in which they are made, as well as on the doctrinal understandings of the role of particular rights within the larger structure of citizenship. The courts in the late nineteenth century seemed willing to grant only a narrowly construed relationship between the right to vote and the right to serve on juries that neither recognized the existence of a plenary political right of the sort Amar imagines, nor allowed for voting as a determinative right from which other rights followed. But earlier and later, the courts saw jury service and its relationship to suffrage differently.

This section has discussed the nineteenth-century debate over jury service for women as it relates to women's civic membership. In concluding, it may be useful to reflect on what the struggle for jury service tells us about women's civic membership before the Nineteenth Amendment, and whether jury service should be conceived of as a political right. The struggle for jury service illuminates the significance of the framework for civic membership set by the Reconstruction Amendments to the Constitution, a framework that made the struggle for political rights more difficult and allowed a hierarchy of civic standing to remain in place. Further, the discussion of jurors as peers illuminates how the struggle for rights was also a struggle for civic status, and suggests ways in which the movement imagined that women would substantively contribute to the body politic. Finally, the effort to make women eligible for jury service was influenced deeply by the effort to obtain suffrage for women both conceptually and politically.

Is jury service a political right of citizenship? Yes, but the realization of that right depends on the political and historical context. It may be, for instance, that in the early national period jury service was conceived of, politically enacted, and judicially defined as a political right. Yet within the context of the late nineteenth century, the political conception of jury service had faded a great deal. While jury service continued to be seen as a valuable safeguard of liberty and as a marker of civic status (as in *Strauder*), it was no longer readily regarded as a form of democratic participation like voting. This shift says as much about the constitutional framework of civic membership at that time as it does about juries and jury service per se. When the terms of civic membership changed yet again in the early twentieth century, as women received the right to vote, the question of whether jury service was a political right, and voting's overall relationship to civic membership, was raised once again. That is the subject of the next section.

From the nineteenth-century debate over jury service, we learn not only about women's civic membership but also about the civic order more generally. The drawing of many parallels between the situation of women and that of African Americans was at times beneficial to women in their arguments for civic equality, and at times it was limiting. Both the Fourteenth Amendment and *Strauder* demonstrate this ambiguity. The occasion for establishing the constitutional definition of national citizenship and the protection of the privileges and immunities guaranteed within it was one of the racial politics at the settlement of the Civil War. Consequently, American citizenship is forever imprinted with matters of race (Holland, 2001). A broad interpretation of the Fourteenth Amendment, such as the one claimed by the advocates of the New Departure, might have anchored women's claims to full civic status on similar moorings. But that was not to be, given the Supreme Court's narrow interpretations of what national citizenship meant (privileges and immunities), and who had it (that the Equal Protection Clause did not apply to women). Similarly, in *Strauder* we see the Supreme Court articulating a broadened ideal of democratic civic status and clearly linking this ideal to the social standing of an oppressed group. Yet the *Strauder* Court refused the opportunity to extend this view to women, thereby preserving the tiered gender hierarchy of social standing within American national citizenship. It seems unsurprising, then, that from the end of the Civil War until the passage of the Nineteenth Amendment and beyond, white activist women and black activist men found themselves articulating race- and gender-exclusive notions of civic membership (DuBois, 1987). By doing so, they were simply repeating the language that the Supreme Court had already spoken to them.

Jury Eligibility and the Nineteenth Amendment

We're voters all, we would be free
Maryland, my Maryland;
To fullest meed of liberty,
Maryland, my Maryland;
We seek the right denied for years
To sit as jurors and as peers,
Forget your Mid-Victorian fears,
Maryland, my Maryland.

— FLORENCE E. KENNARD,
"MARYLAND WOMEN DEMAND JURY SERVICE"

Examining the debate over jury eligibility for women clarifies the consequences of the Nineteenth Amendment for women's civic membership in ways that an examination of women's electoral politics does not. In particular, it shows that the narrow and compartmentalized understanding of citizenship that was elaborated by the courts in the late nineteenth century continued to inform public and judicial understandings of women's political status after 1920. Court rulings from the 1870s and 1880s articulated a view of women's civic membership under the Fourteenth Amendment as providing only limited rights. Further, the common law understanding of women (particularly married women) as lacking civic personalities was incorporated partially under the Fourteenth Amendment. The jury eligibility debates of the 1920s reveal that the Nineteenth Amendment only partially altered this conception of women's civic status.

Jennifer Brown (1993) also has written about the jury eligibility cases of the period from 1910 through the 1920s as a reflection on women's political status after suffrage. She argues that the state courts vacillated between an "incremental" and "emancipatory" view of the Nineteenth Amendment, in which the amendment solely addressed women's right to vote or more broadly concerned their civic status. Brown's essay offers useful insights into the 1920s movement for jury service. However, this argument differs from Brown's in two respects. First, rather than regard women's civic membership in holistic terms as equal or as different from men's civic membership (or as progressing from difference toward equality), the argument here conceives of women's civic membership as partialized and historically contingent. Women were regarded as "equal" in some areas and not others. Further, the trend toward rights was not always progressive — there were historical examples of reversals. In this regard, Brown's dichotomy between an incremental and emancipatory approach belies the more complex nature of women's civic membership in this period. Second, Brown writes on the effort to let "women into the Constitution," as if they were not there before the Nineteenth Amendment (J. K. Brown, 1993, 2204). This contention implies a belief in the liberal, egalitarian soul of the Constitution that I do not fully share. In contrast, the argument here shares the view of Rogers Smith (1997), Catherine Holland (2001), and others (Kerber, 1998; Hoff, 1991; Siegel, 1994b), that the Constitution has been historically tolerant and inclusive of unequal, ascriptive statuses — such as the status of slaves until the Thirteenth Amendment, or the status of women until (and after) the Nineteenth Amendment. Thus, my differences concern Brown's assumptions about the overall nature of women's civic membership and the American political order.

THE CAMPAIGN FOR WOMEN'S JURY SERVICE

Although the women's movement of the 1920s fractured in the aftermath of the Nineteenth Amendment, all the rights activists supported the jury service campaign. As jury service activist Burnita Shelton Matthews commented, "If there is one subject which all the woman's organizations are agreed upon, it is, probably, jury service for women" (Matthews, 1929). Around the time that the Nineteenth Amendment was passed, fourteen states granted women the right to serve on juries. In half of these cases, women were found to be automatically eligible for jury service once they became electors. In the other seven cases, new laws were passed which made women eligible to serve on juries. Yet despite vigorous campaigns by the League of Women Voters, the National Women's Party, and many other groups, only one new state and the District of Columbia were added to the list of jurisdictions where women served on juries during the rest of the decade. By the middle of the 1920s it was increasingly evident that the courts and legislatures were resistant to further extensions of women's rights in this area (L. M. Young, 1989).

Part of this resistance may have reflected the movement's growing ambivalence over how to pursue civic equality in the wake of the Court's decision in *Adkins v. Children's Hospital* (1923). This was the case in which the Court found that women's civic status changed with the advent of the Nineteenth Amendment, and so did the ability of the government to regulate the conditions under which they labored. What were *Adkins*'s implications for the jury service debate? *Adkins* may be read as signaling a further erosion of the common law regime that governed women's civic standing in the nineteenth century (Cott, 2001). Yet whether the rules of domestic relations were being truly vanquished or merely refashioned on new terms (as suggested in Chapter 2) was still open to question (Siegel, 1994a). Ambivalence about equality, especially with regard to civil rights and civic duties that impinged upon domestic duties, grew in response to *Adkins*. The opponents of women's jury service were quick to argue that it was a civic duty that drew women away from their domestic obligations.

The arguments for jury service echoed those made by nineteenth-century women's rights proponents. In particular, advocates emphasized the role of women jurors as the legal and social peers of women defendants, and highlighted the role of juries as a bulwark of liberty. But there was also a new stress on the political circumstances of recently enfranchised women. The 1920s campaigners continued to express an aspiration for full civic membership in light of their suffrage status. They were also sometimes despairing about the limited impact of the Nineteenth Amendment on their civic standing. Further, they asserted that jury service was a civic duty they were obligated to perform — a duty that better equipped them for the performance of their other civic duties. Finally, since jury service was a more substantial and intimate form of civic participation, it provoked discussions of whether sex differences mattered to the performance of civic status.

Like the earlier generation of rights activists, the new cohort of jury service proponents stressed the importance of juries in a democratic system and the need for women jurors as peers. Within the structure of civic membership, jury service was regarded as a fundamental civil right, necessary for the protection of other rights; "the right of trial by a jury of one's peers is more important than any other guaranty of liberty" (McCulloch, 1920, 488). Further, women were entitled to a jury of their peers — a jury that included other women. As Catherine Waugh McCulloch (1920) explained, "In cases where women are interested parties, women would have greater protection if they were wronged if there were other women on the jury" (488). As citizens and as women who were citizens, women were entitled to service on juries and to have a jury of their peers.

In their reflections on women's civic standing after the Nineteenth Amendment, women's rights activists were alternately aspiring and despairing. The National Woman Party's "Declaration of Principles" stated, "Women shall no longer be deprived of their right of trial by a jury of their peers, but jury service shall be open to women as to men" (Pell, 1931, 326). Given their position as electors, women were entitled to be and act in the public realm — just as they did in business and politics. As Rabbi Edward L. Israel, testifying in favor of a women's jury service bill in Maryland stated, "We have to face the fact that women are a part of our life as never before, they are in our business life, our political life, our professional life" (Kennard, 1931). Yet after a decade of suffrage, the exclusion of women from the jury box was seen as a sign of their continued civic inequality. As one activist wrote in 1930, "The legal status of women is still not equal to that of men, however, it has been said that 'women are now the peers of men politically' " (Matthews, 1930a, 124).

Women's rights activists of the 1920s were concerned, after the Nineteenth Amendment, with women's civic performance. Some argued that women must not just enjoy civic privileges, but should also share in civic duties. Helen Sherry of the State Federation of Republican Women testified before the state legislature in Maryland — "now that women have the vote, [they] are ready to assume the burdens as well as the benefits of citizenship" (Kennard, 1931). Jury service was seen as contributing to women's civic education. Judge Robert Marx of Cincinnati commented in 1925, "Since women vote their service upon the jury is a broadening experience to them and increases their capacity for civic usefulness. While this is not immediately a contribution to the improvement of the jury system, it is an advantage to the body politic" (Sheridan, 1925, 795). The hope and expectation was that the right to vote had made women first-class civic members, but for this to be the case, they had to be allowed to serve on juries. "Since the adoption of woman suffrage, women have arrived, so to speak, and are demanding the why and wherefore of their exclusion from jury service" (Matthews, 1929). Armed with new rights and ready to perform their civic duties, women wondered why they were still denied full civic membership.

Unlike their predecessors, the last generation of suffragists had moved away from natural rights arguments to stress women's inherent differences from men and to use this as an argument for suffrage. A similar position was taken with regard to juries. Women's service was needed on juries to ensure that justice would be served, especially in cases involving women or children as defendants or plaintiffs. Judge John Walsh wrote of women jurors, "I have found them less inclined to give way to impulses or emotions, if you prefer to call it such, than many of our male jurors, and this condition stands out most prominently in the criminal cases which involve the morals or chastity of a woman child under the age of consent in our State, whereas in such cases I have found men to be moved by sentiment and resentment rather than the facts and the law in the case" (Walsh, 1927, 411). It was the differences between men and women civic members that warranted the participation of women in jury service.

THE COURTS AND LEGISLATURES RESPOND

Evident in the discussion above is the aching sense among the postsuffrage rights activists that the goal of obtaining civic equality for women had yet to be achieved, despite the Nineteenth Amendment. Rather, it seemed, while the courts and legislatures conceived of the Nineteenth Amendment as having established a public-realm presence for women, they only were granted a limited perch there. Doctrinally, this view expressed itself in terms of the narrow impact accorded to the Nineteenth Amendment with regard to other civic rights for women. Further, there was still a conception of women's civic standing (fostered by some in the women's movement itself) as remaining partly rooted in women's private-realm obligations. As a result, the majority of states that made women eligible for jury service provided them with exemptions for childcare. Finally, the jury service debate brings out the complexity of the argument within the women's movement and among the public at large over what equality really is and whether women should have it.

Were women public persons and first-class citizens after the adoption of the Nineteenth Amendment? Burnita Shelton Matthews, who wrote a series of articles on women's jury service in *Equal Rights* in 1929 and 1930, believed the courts were historically ambivalent about whether women were persons. In the first article, Matthews reviewed the *Strauder* case. There, according to Matthews, the Court ruled that barring African American men from jury service "would brand them as an inferior class of citizens" (26). This doctrine should also apply to women, since "the Constitution guarantees that protection to persons and not merely to negroes" (26). Yet the doctrine was not applied, because of "the curious ability which judges of the male persuasion have manifested to regard women as persons at one time and not as persons at another" (Matthews, 1929, 26).

That ambivalence, it seemed, persisted a decade after the Nineteenth Amendment was adopted. In considering the influence of the Nineteenth Amendment on women's jury service, the Massachusetts Supreme Court was faced with a statute that listed all qualified voters as eligible jurors (*Commonwealth v. Welosky*, 177 N.E. 656 [1931]). But in finding that this law did not include women, the court wrote, "The Nineteenth Amendment to the Federal Constitution conferred the suffrage on an entirely new class of human beings. . . . It added to qualified voters those who did not fall within the meaning of the word 'person' in the jury statutes" (670). With the Nineteenth Amendment, women became persons before the law in a way they had not been before. Yet the legacy of their legal nonpersonhood remained. As the Massachusetts judges summarized, "The change in the legal status of women wrought by the Nineteenth Amendment was radical, drastic and unprecedented. While it is to be given full effect in its field, it is not to be extended by implication" (670). In other words, women were now legal persons — beings within the public realm. But the extent of their public presence was assumed to be limited to the area of suffrage.

Around the country, state courts were asked to interpret the impact of suffrage on women's other citizenship rights and duties. Their rulings varied. Considering the cases in which the state courts took up this issue, three different views were offered regarding the effect of suffrage on women's eligibility for jury service. The first, and most common, was the view that the Nineteenth Amendment had no effect on women's jury eligibility. Some courts reasoned that the common law restriction on women's jury service still held. Typical was the ruling of the New Jersey Court of Appeals (*State v. James*, 114 A. 553 [1921]), which stated, "This constitutional guaranty as to the right to jury trial has been held to be trial by jury at common law. A common-law jury consisted of 'twelve free and lawful men'" (555). Thus, suffrage did not make women eligible for jury service. Reasoning from a different perspective, a New York court reiterated the traditional conservative view of the citizenship rights found in the Fourteenth Amendment. The New York court denied that women's new suffrage status made a difference, since "jury service was not a matter of right, either civil or political, but a matter of duty," and concluded that "women were not entitled as citizens to act as jurors" (*In re Grilli*, 179 N.Y.S. 795 Kings Co. S. Ct. [1920], 797; see also *Harper v. State*, 234 S.W. 909 [1921]). In any event, several state courts agreed that while the Nineteenth Amendment made women eligible to vote, it did not overcome prior legal limitations on their jury service (*In re Opinion of the Justices*, 130 N.E. 685 [1921]).

Second, some courts acknowledged women's status as electors under the Nineteenth Amendment, but suggested that this did not make them automatically eligible to serve on juries. Several state courts considered whether the laws on jury eligibility described eligible voters in terms that implied just one sex. That was the approach taken in Idaho (*State v. Kelley*, 229 P. 659 [1924]), Illinois (*People ex rel. Fyfe v. Barnett*, 150 N.E. 290 [1925]), and Massachusetts (*In re Opinion of the Justices*). More sympathetic courts found that women's new status as electors was permissive, making them eligible for legislative entitlement to serve on juries. The Massachusetts high court virtually called upon the state's general court to pass a law making women eligible for jury service (*In re Opinion of the Justices*, 685).

Finally, under the third view, women automatically became eligible for jury service when they became electors. This last view gave the greatest weight to elector as a civic status that commanded other privileges and duties. Several courts linked voting status to jury service by way of *Neal*. Since *Neal* made African Americans eligible for jury service in their status as electors under the Fifteenth Amendment, it would seem that the Nineteenth Amendment would do precisely the same for women. That, indeed, was the conclusion that the courts came to in four of the five cases where *Neal* was considered. Only the Massachusetts court found differently. Beginning with Nevada, and going through Michigan, Iowa, and Indiana, the other four courts concluded that *Neal v. Delaware* had recognized suffrage as a political status to which privileges and duties might be attached (*Parus v. District Court*, 174 P. 706 [1918], *People v. Barltz*, 180 N.W. 423 [1920], *State v. Walker*, 185 N.W. 619 [1921], and *Palmer v. State*, 150 N.E. 917 [1926]). This interpretation was stated most clearly in *Barltz*:

> What was the purpose and object of the people in adopting the constitutional amendment, striking out the word "male" from the Constitution? . . . We think there can be but one answer to this question, and that is that the purpose was to put women on the same footing as men with reference to the elective franchise. . . . The moment a woman became an elector under the constitutional amendment she was entitled to perform jury duty, if she was possessed the same qualifications that men possessed for that duty. In other words, she was placed in that class of citizens and electors, from which class jurors were, under the statute, to be selected. (425)

The Nineteenth Amendment, like the Fifteenth before it, placed women in a new citizenship class — the class of citizen electors. It was from this class that jurors in most states were drawn. In this narrow and direct way, states were willing to grant the Nineteenth Amendment impact, though they did not go as far as did the Supreme Court in *Neal* and use the suffrage amendment to bring women more firmly within the ambit of the Fourteenth Amendment.

Yet a stronger version of this view appears in the *Parus* case. Here, jury service is presented as a political right of citizenship, like voting or holding office.

> Can we reasonably say that although woman, on whom has been conferred the right of electorship, the right to enjoy public office, the right to own and control property, and on whom has been imposed the burden of taxation in a common equality with men, is nevertheless deprived of the privilege of sitting as a member of an inquisitorial body, the power, scope of inquiry, and significance of which affects every department of life in which she, as a citizen and elector, is interested and of which she is a component part? (708)

Not only does jury service appear here as a political right, it is also part of a recognition of women's newly won status as public-realm beings, as active citizens and property owners. But the language of the *Parus* ruling is quite unusual. More typical were court rulings that denied a wider impact to the Nineteenth Amendment or that asserted the continuing significance of maternalist conceptions of women's place (Sheridan, 1925).

In many of the states that granted women's eligibility for jury service, women were provided with automatic exemptions, so that a woman had to affirmatively register her willingness to serve on a jury before she was added to the list of prospective jurors. Needless to say, in such states, the proportion of women jurors was very low. Other states provided that any woman who requested an exemption be excused, while still others allowed women who had young children or other dependent family members to be excused. Such policies reflected not only a reluctance to allow women to serve on juries (generally, it was the opponents of women's jury service who insisted on exemptions), but also the continued presumption that women's identities were more firmly rooted in the private than in the public realm. Either the obligations of motherhood were thought greater than the obligations of citizenship, or the duties of motherhood were taken to be women's contribution as citizens. One popular ditty that expressed the public's discomfort with women's jury service in this period went, "Baby, baby, don't get in a fury, Mama gone to serve on the jury" ("First Jurywomen," 1930, 27). Although there was some debate regarding how extensive the exemptions for women jurors should be, in the decades after the Nineteenth Amendment there was general agreement on the superior virtues of the motherhood role.

Since the women's rights advocates of the early twentieth century had themselves often invoked maternalist arguments in their discussions of women's potential contribution to the public realm, it seems no surprise that the courts concurred with them. While the early Woman Rights movement relied more heavily on individual natural rights arguments, by the turn of the century activist women were more inclined to resort to the ideology of domesticity. According to the latter view, women were indeed different, and in many ways better (more virtuous, moral, and cooperative) than men. Further, women's identities were rooted firmly in the private realm of home and family. Their virtues as citizens, then, were the virtues of good mothers. The public behavior of female citizens was expected to be an extension of their private identities. The antisuffragists, and later opponents of women's jury service, argued against conferring upon women any citizen duties seen as an impediment to the fulfillment of their private obligations (Skocpol, 1992; Muncy, 1991; Mink, 1995).

The debate over equality after the Nineteenth Amendment was illuminated by the division, among jury service proponents, over whether women jurors differed in any predictable way from men. Most believed women did differ, and feminists often used this argument to claim that women jurors would provide a different sense of justice that would be particularly beneficial to women and children. The popular and political journals of the 1920s contain many discussions of the differences between male and female jurors, with several concluding that a mixed jury offered the greatest assurance of justice. Indeed, the state legislature of Oregon passed a law in 1921 instituting a mixed jury by mandating that in criminal cases involving a minor, half of the jury must be women (Chapter 273, Oregon Laws of 1921). This law faced practical difficulties that prevented its effective enactment, particularly because Oregon also provided for broad exemptions of women from jury service that created a shortage of women in the venire. Both the law and the exemption policy reflect particular conceptions of women as citizens.

When this law was challenged, the state supreme court upheld it (*State v. Chase*, 211 P. 920 [1922]). The court explained why, in its opinion, this policy was justified: "Any one who has occupied the Circuit bench and seen a poor frightened girl, a stranger to the court room, forced to detail the facts in regard to her injury or shame to a jury composed of strange men, has felt that the presence of a few mothers of children in the jury box would be more in accordance with humanity and justice" (922). The reasoning here sounds much like the reasoning in Stanton's plea to the New York State Legislature in cases of infanticide. It is a woman's understanding — of children, and of the sexual wrongs done to innocent women or girls by men — that justifies a positive demand for women's inclusion on juries. Despite the high court's approval, this experiment with mixed juries was abandoned in 1923 because the state's exemption policy made it too difficult to secure enough women jurors. The stress on difference highlighted women's distinctive civic contributions, but it also tended to excuse them from public participation.

This section has examined the postsuffrage campaign to obtain jury service for women in order to understand the impact of the Nineteenth Amendment on women's citizenship. Analysis of the campaign shows that the Nineteenth Amendment failed to create equal citizenship for women at either the level of civic status or the rights and duties of citizenship. The national citizenship framework created in the late nineteenth century limited the impact of suffrage on citizenship. The court decisions regarding jury service reveal how reluctant state courts were to grant the Nineteenth Amendment much influence over women's rights and duties in other areas. This reluctance was consistent with a structure of citizenship in which political rights were considered secondary to civil rights, and in which women's status as persons before the law remained ambivalent. The impact of the amendment was more normative (and short-term) and less constitutional. The Nineteenth Amendment did make women into civic beings, but their presence within the public realm was seen as limited and often as secondary to their obligations in the private realm. It was clear by the end of the 1920s that the feminist movement's dream of making women men's peers as first-class citizens was still far from being realized.

Women's Citizenship: The Nineteenth Amendment and Beyond

The struggle to secure equal jury service for women went on through the 1970s. As late as 1961, the Supreme Court upheld Florida's practice of automatically exempting women from jury service (*Hoyt v. Florida*, 368 U.S. 57). Shortly after the *Hoyt* ruling, the women's liberation movement emerged. This movement had two different wings: the liberal feminists, associated particularly with the National Organization for Women, and the radical feminists, associated with the style and organizations of the New Left. The liberal feminists took up the project of more fully articulating an ideal of equal public-realm citizenship for women, which they sought to enshrine in the Constitution with the Equal Rights Amendment — an effort that failed in the early 1980s. The radicals rejected the ideal of liberal citizenship for women and even argued that women ought to give back the vote as a reflection on the good it had brought them. Whether they sought to complete or reject the citizenship they received from their foremothers, neither group of feminists in the 1960s and 1970s were satisfied with what they had been given (Echols, 1989).

As amended by the Nineteenth Amendment, women's citizenship was at best an imperfect vehicle for their political articulation and mobilization. It did little to restructure the citizenship created after the Civil War. In the nineteenth century, the vote was regarded by many as the central right of citizenship. But despite the rhetoric of the Declaration of Independence, not all Americans were regarded as equal. Instead, the community of the nation was ordered by race and by gender. That order was reflected in the distinctive terms of citizenship found among these various groups. Even as an inclusive liberal polity in the twentieth century, the terms of citizenship as defined under the Fourteenth, Fifteenth, and Nineteenth Amendments continued to speak to the differential political standing of whites and blacks, and of men and women.

Viewed through the lens of electoral politics, the historical failure of women to lay claim to the rights of citizenship after the Nineteenth Amendment remains somewhat mysterious. The continued particularities of women's citizenship are made clearer in the struggle for jury eligibility, which reveals that the narrow, parsed structure of national citizenship as established under the Fourteenth Amendment remained intact. It is part of my argument here that the effort of the Woman Rights movement in the post–Civil War period to construct a progressive vision of the Reconstruction Amendments helped inspire the Supreme Court to do just the opposite. To insure that these amendments would never be used to upend sex discrimination, the courts diminished the scope of national citizenship, downplayed the power of political rights within citizenship, and addressed the progressive power of the Equal Protection Clause primarily to African Americans. This was the legacy left to the suffragists in the early twentieth century. The creative constitutionalism of their foremothers had begotten a framework of national citizenship that greatly diminished the likelihood that suffrage would ever transform women's citizenship more broadly. The rights advocates of the 1920s quickly recognized the inadequacies of what they had won, and were drawn into other campaigns, including the campaign for jury service. Once women had the vote, they were supposed to be full citizens. Yet this did not occur.

The citizenship established for women under the Nineteenth Amendment carried with it all the limitations found in the judicial interpretations of the Fourteenth Amendment. It was a citizenship of limited rights, limited expectations, and broad space for state regulation of its specifics — one that left women little room for the elaboration of a public, distinctly feminist politics. The alternative (and never realized) vision articulated by rights advocates was of a citizenship grounded in political rights, like voting and jury service. Instead they got a citizenship in which, at the barest level, women were men's equals and could not be excluded from voting, or eventually, from serving on juries. But the failure to exclude did not constitute an argument for inclusion. Indeed, the political identity that women held as nonvoters prior to the Nineteenth Amendment may have provided them with a better basis for a public women's politics. Not until the 1960s would women forcefully address the terms of their citizenship again and seek to move beyond the Nineteenth Amendment.

Striking parallels surfaced in the terms of citizenship deemed available to white women and black men (black women were most often left out of consideration by the courts, civil rights groups, and women's rights groups), but important differences as well. African American men were recognized as having broader claims for the protection of their citizenship rights, and their status as electors was recognized as a political status that implied other rights, including the right to serve on juries. For women, both suffrage and jury service were deemed grants rather than rights of citizenship. Further, when women's jury eligibility was established, it was done in terms that neither recognized women as political peers in the fuller, more substantive way that many nineteenth-century activists had imagined, nor allowed for their consideration as a previously excluded political class, as had been suggested for African Americans in the *Strauder* case. Instead, women's formal standing in the public realm was regarded as secondary to their more essential private-realm activities. When women were no longer formally or informally excluded, it was because of a defendant's right under the Sixth Amendment to a jury that reflected a fair cross section of the community. It was not, in other words, a matter of a woman's political rights — either to a jury of her peers, or to participate in political governance through her jury service.

Indeed, suggested in the nineteenth-century debates over women jurors as peers is another implicit model of citizenship. In contemporary feminist-theory literature, there is a debate over whether women's citizenship should be premised on equality or on difference. Often, the advocates of the difference position ground their claims in the maternalist attributes women are purported to share. The advocates of equality are often concerned with the ways that formal equality can be made meaningful through government social programs or adjustments in the private division of labor between men and women. On each side of this debate, the positions tend to reify around competing principles of justice (Bock and James, 1992; Butler and Scott,

1992; Fraser and Bartsky, 1992; L. F. Goldstein, 1992; Gunew and Yeatman, 1993; Hirschmann and Di Stefano, 1996; Jones, 1993; Phillips, 1993 and 1995; Shanley and Pateman, 1991; Weisbarg, 1993).

In contrast, the nineteenth-century discussion of jurors as peers suggests the positive good that would result if women brought their substantive, lived experiences with them to the exercise of their public citizenship. In this model, women's maternalism and their sexuality are contextualized and problematized (e.g., in discussions of infanticide or rape), rather than elevated and celebrated. And while the expectation is that women's specific experiences will inform women's outlook, these roles are not designated as legitimating women's political role, nor are they used to exclude women from certain political functions.

In contrast to women's citizenship based on equality or on difference, there is a move to get beyond the one-or-two-sizes-fits-all models of citizenship. This alternative demands neither sameness nor difference, but expects substantive experience to provide the basis for community justice on whatever terms that will occur. This ideal of citizenship is closer to the one elaborated by Constable in her discussion of the mixed jury and personal law (Constable, 1994; Ritter, 1997b). It is an ideal of citizenship that views difference as socially made, rather than demographically assigned, and that expects community norms and practices — on juries and elsewhere — to provide the basis for politics and justice in society. The danger of this approach is that community norms could be used to impose conservative or conformist values on individuals. The promise of this approach lies in the ability of women to bring their lived experiences to their civic lives, thereby bridging the private/public distinction in the direction of public activism. This is the legacy of the long struggle for women's right to serve on juries — it clarifies the nature of women's citizenship after the Nineteenth Amendment, and provides the basis today for reimagining the relationship between citizenship and democracy.

PART II

War and Civic Membership in the 1940s

FIVE

Labor

In the United States, work is central to civic status. The independent yeomen and farmers of the early American republic found their virtue in their distinctiveness from European aristocrats and African American slaves. Their economic autonomy made them striving democrats, with no material obligations to their betters or their lessers. Economic freedom and opportunity — what Lincoln's generation called "free labor" (Foner, 1995) — defined the American spirit of entrepreneurship and political self-governing. According to Judith Shklar (1991), Americans retained a "vision of economic independence, of self-directed 'earning,' as the ethical basis of democratic citizenship. . . . We are citizens only if we 'earn' " (67). Yet, as Alice Kessler-Harris (2001) reminds us, work status did not pertain to women's civic standing in the same way as it did to men's. In the nineteenth century, women's civic identities were rooted in the domestic realm. This left women, and especially wives, in the category of dependent members of the polity. Like slaves, they were outside the realm of civil society. Over the course of the twentieth century, as more and more women entered gainful employment, the nation was forced to contend with the reality of working women. Women were treated differently from working men, as less capable and more vulnerable, less deserving of a decent wage or union membership, and more deserving of legal protection. So long as work defined men's civic membership, as earning and producing formed the foundations for civic standing, then women were cast apart. But the Great Depression called the relationship between work and civic membership into question for both men and women.

The 1930s witnessed profound changes in the labor rights of American citizens. With the passage of the National Labor Relations Act of 1935 (commonly referred to as the Wagner Act), workers were guaranteed the right to organize and bargain collectively. Within the realm of social provisioning, the Social Security Act of 1935 provided for Old Age Insurance (OAI) as a reward for a lifelong record of full-time employment. Civic members who contributed their labor to society were to be recognized with a guarantee of protection against poverty in old age. Labor standards, which set minimum wages and maximum hours for many hourly workers, were established by the federal government under the Fair Labor Standards Act (FLSA) of 1938. These three major acts of legislation were premised on a profound constitutional reconceptualization of the relationship between work and civic membership. No longer were workers' rights understood in purely individualistic terms. Workers were seen instead as members of broader social communities that were vulnerable to economic forces beyond their individual control, and that collectively contributed to the general welfare of the larger society. Further, workers were recognized as having positive rights, protected and supported through government action, rather than simply negative rights, such as the right to "freedom of contract" that was shielded by the courts from the threat of legislative intrusion. In short, the concept of liberty and its relationship to labor and civic status was rethought to mean protection against economic insecurity, the right to act collectively, and a positive vision of the federal government as empowered by democratic representation to act in the interest of the larger public.

Some scholars (e.g., Novkov, 2001) have suggested that the constitutional construction of American civic membership was "feminized" during the late New Deal because women went from being the exception to the rule of "freedom of contract" from 1908 through the 1920s, to being the standard for a new rule in the 1930s and 1940s.[1] The new rule (or judicial doctrine) allowed for government regulation of the working conditions of American women *and men* — something that had previously been rejected as an infringement on the autonomy of men's civic membership. Yet this "feminization" of American civic membership did not lead to a dismantling of gendered hierarchy in civic membership. Rather, that hierarchy was reformulated, along with the larger civic order. Whereas, in the nineteenth century, civic membership was primarily defined by political rights, in the twentieth century it became more defined by social rights. With the decline in voting and of the partisan distributive state in the early twentieth century, and with the establishment, under the New Deal, of old-age insurance, unemployment insurance, veteran's benefits, agricultural adjustments, and aid to dependent families, the relationship between the people and the national government became thickest in the area of social provisioning. Just as the organization of civic membership shifted from the political to the social realm, so too did the gendering of civic membership shift from political and civil rights to the area of social rights. Labor status was central to the reorganization and regendering of civic membership in the late 1930s and 1940s.

The use of substantive due process reasoning to prohibit labor regulations (under the doctrine of freedom of contract) ended with the case of *West Coast Hotel Co. v. Parrish*, 300 U.S. 379, in 1937. The Court became more deferential to the legislatures, now theorizing that the federal government could act under the Commerce Clause to regulate labor conditions and to recognize the rights of workers to organize and bargain collectively. Indeed, by the 1940s, these positive labor rights were being hailed by the Court as central to the meaning of modern civic membership. Having lost the old means for men to express masculine autonomy as workers and civic participants under the logic of freedom of contract, union leaders and government officials searched for new ways to articulate a positive relationship between labor status, civic membership, and masculinity. What came to replace the "freedom of contract" doctrine was recognition and reward for the role of men (as workers and soldiers) as family providers. Being a family provider became a civic virtue that was used as a premise for the organization of Social Security benefits and veterans' benefits.[2] Women, under the logic of the family-provider philosophy, were seen *not* as workers or military personnel (though many served in these roles in the 1940s), but as men's dependents.

Meanwhile, there was another stream of substantive due process reasoning that survived the constitutional shift to the New Deal. The Due Process Clause of the Fifth and Fourteenth Amendments may be read either procedurally or substantively. Under a substantive reading, emphasis is put on the fundamental rights that are protected from government action, as follows — "nor shall any State deprive any person of *life, liberty, or property*, without due process of law" (U.S. Constitution, Fourteenth Amendment). In the shift to a new constitutional understanding in the 1930s, the economic version of substantive due process — that is, the freedom-of-contract doctrine — was rejected. But the more social stream of the doctrine remained, and would eventually grow into the constitutional doctrine of privacy.

Starting in the 1920s (*Meyer v. Nebraska*, 262 U.S. 390 [1923], *Pierce v. Society of Sisters*, 268 U.S. 510 [1925]), and continuing in the 1940s (*Prince v. Massachusetts*, 321 U.S. 158 [1944]), this social stream of substantive due process cases emerged in response to the liberal modernization of the national constitutional order. Social-ordering principles could no longer be easily expressed through the distribution of civil rights in relation to the status hierarchies contained within the common law of domestic relations. Now, as traditional status hierarchies were being modernized (Siegel, 1994b), social-ordering principles were expressed and located differently in the constitutional order. With the growing belief in civic equality, it was no longer readily acceptable to suggest that women as wives had no legal personality or civil rights. Instead, social-ordering concerns now were expressed through doctrines like privacy and family provisioning, and were located beyond the reach of national citizenship through federalism, or within the social rights of citizenship, through policies like Social Security. Finally, social differences that could be naturalized, made voluntary or traditional, and treated positively through incorporation, provided other means for the expression of social-ordering concerns, even under the rubric of equal protection.

The "Feminization" of Civic Membership

During Roosevelt's first term in office, the Supreme Court strongly resisted the administration's effort to move to a new constitutional understanding that would allow the federal government to act aggressively in addressing the economic depression. Several major pieces of New Deal legislation were overturned in the mid-1930s. But the Depression persisted and FDR was reelected by a landslide in 1936. In his campaign for a second term, the president made a point of criticizing the Court for its recalcitrance. Finally, in 1937, the Court appeared ready to allow the federal government more freedom of action in addressing the nation's economic woes. Central to the shift away from the *Lochner* era of jurisprudence was the establishment of a new conception of the relationship between labor and civic membership. In moving to a new vision of this relationship, the Court looked to the situation of women workers to offer an exit from the freedom-of-contract regime. Since women had been only loosely incorporated into the freedom-of-contract regime since *Adkins v. Children's Hospital*, 261 U.S. 525 (1923), they provided the easiest point from which to break from that regime and move toward a new conceptualization of due process liberty, under which state regulation of labor conditions did not necessarily violate the civic autonomy of workers.

During the *Lochner* era, the Supreme Court held that under the Due Process Clauses of the Fifth and Fourteenth Amendments, citizens were entitled to make free contracts without government intrusion. As a result, most government efforts to regulate the terms of work (e.g., wages, hours, and working conditions) were found to be unconstitutional. Yet, for many years in the early twentieth century (beginning with the ruling in *Muller v. Oregon*, 208 U.S. 412 [1908]), women were thought to be an exception to this freedom-of-contract rule, not only because they were physically weaker than men (and, as the mothers of the race, deserved special protection), but because they did not possess as many rights and could not bargain for good labor contracts as effectively. As a result, protective labor legislation that applied only to women typically was upheld by the courts. During the early twentieth century, one of the main distinctions between men's and women's civic membership was premised on this differential constitutional treatment of their labor status. After the Nineteenth Amendment was adopted in 1920, this gender exception was lifted partially with the *Adkins* decision of 1923. There, the Court found that women's new political rights equipped them to bargain more effectively, so that the states could no longer afford them paternalistic assistance in the form of minimum wage laws. Women were now men's equals, but the equality they received was a negative one, in which they too were denied government protection against abusive labor conditions.

Adkins may be read as signaling a further erosion of the common law regime that governed women's civic standing in the nineteenth century (Cott, 2001). *Adkins* signaled that women were increasingly seen by the courts as public-realm beings, both politically and economically. But it was not yet clear whether the norms of coverture truly were being vanquished, or merely refashioned as issues of privacy and family provisioning (Siegel, 1994b). This is where things stood at the start of FDR's second term, when the *West Coast Hotel* case was heard (Baer, 1978; Lipschultz, 1996). Like *Adkins* fourteen years before it, the controversial *West Coast Hotel* case, which highlighted the dispute over women's civic equality, concerned the constitutionality of a minimum wage law for women, this time in the state of Washington. Women's organizations filed *amicus* briefs for both the plaintiffs and the defendants. The Supreme Court made very clear at the beginning of its ruling what was at stake. "We are of the opinion that this ruling of the state court demands on our part a re-examination of the *Adkins* Case" (389–90). The Court was prepared to reconsider the *Lochner* regime in the area where the freedom-of-contract regime seemed weakest — with regard to protective labor legislation for women.

The Court began its assault on the *Lochner* regime by questioning the concept of freedom of contract: "The Constitution does not speak of freedom of contract. It speaks of liberty. . . . But the liberty safeguarded is liberty in a social organization which requires the protection of law against the evils which menace the health, safety, morals, and welfare of the people" (391). The Court had come to view rights as historically situated and dependent upon public understandings. Within the context of the Great Depression, liberty of contract — to the extent that such a right even existed — was to be applied with an eye toward the public welfare. As for due process considerations, the Court stated that "regulation which is reasonable in relation to its subject and is adopted in the interests of the community is due process" (391). Having redefined liberty and recognized the right of the legislature to regulate contracts, the Court went on to find that the parties to employment contracts were not equal, and cited *Holden v. Hardy*, 169 U.S. 366 (1898), in support of its argument: "And we added that the fact 'that both parties are of full age, and competent to contract, does not necessarily deprive the state of the power to interfere, where the parties do not stand upon an equality, or where the public health demands that one party to the contract shall be protected against himself'" (394). Inequality or public health demands could justify state regulation of labor contracts.

Nowhere did such concerns apply more fully than in the situation of women, who were physically weaker than men and also, since they were less unionized, economically more vulnerable: "It is manifest that this established principle is peculiarly applicable in relation to the employment of women in whose protection the state has a special interest" (394). *Muller* had been resurrected. The Court did not care to uphold a "fictitious equality" in the case of women workers. Further, regulations that were applied to women workers were meant not simply for their benefit, but for the benefit of the whole community. Yet the Court did not set women as an exception to a general rule — regarding public welfare and conditions of inequality — that could be applied to male workers as well. The rule was merely applied more readily to women. So while *Muller* had been resurrected and women could once again be "properly placed in a class by herself," this class was no longer so distant from the class of men. It would be a short step from protecting women to protecting workers as a class when the differences between men and women were just a matter of degree. "The argument that the legislation in question constitutes an arbitrary discrimination, because it does not extend to men, is unavailing. . . . The Legislature 'is free to recognize degrees of harm and it may confine its restrictions to those classes of cases where the need is deemed to be clearest' " (400). In the process of considering the relationship between labor status and gender status in *West Coast Hotel*, the Court began remaking the civic order by bringing the *Lochner* era to an end. At this crucial turning point in American political development, gender played a key role.

The *West Coast Hotel* case overturned *Adkins* and began the New Deal constitutional revolution. In its ruling, the Court upheld a law establishing a minimum wage for working women, and criticized the principle of freedom of contract more generally. Four years later, the logic of this opinion was extended when the FLSA was upheld in *United States v. Darby*, 312 U.S. 100 (1941). In this case the Court stated simply its finding from the earlier one, "Since our decision in *West Coast Hotel Co. v. Parrish* it is no longer open to question that the fixing of a minimum wage is within the legislative power and that the bare fact of its exercise is not a denial of due process under the Fifth more than under the Fourteenth Amendment" (125). Then they offered this extension: "the statute is not objectionable because applied alike to both men and women" (125). Men's civic membership was "feminized" when the logic of labor autonomy was abolished. In terms of labor, gender, and civic membership, the implications of these cases were twofold. On the one hand, the Court made claims for equality for women more attractive when equality no longer meant access to negative freedoms, such as the freedom of contract, but the Court made claims for treating women as different than men more constitutionally acceptable as well. Differential standards of civic rights for men and women had returned. In the decade following this ruling, both tendencies would be visible, though ultimately a more gender-distinctive order of civic membership in the area of labor rights would emerge.

Social Provisioning and the Citizen Worker Ideal

The differential treatment of men and women workers was apparent in the area of social policy as well as in judicial rulings. As previous scholarship has established, women workers were much less likely to receive benefits under the terms of the Old Age Insurance Program (which was established under the Social Security Act of 1935), both because the program excluded many job categories in which women were the majority (such as domestic workers and nonprofit workers) and because part-time workers or workers with irregular work histories did not qualify for benefits. The statute had a strong (though implicit) racial component to its benefits awards as well. The program was designed with full-time (typically white and unionized) male workers in mind, rather than women or minority workers. Likewise, under the FLSA, most women workers were excluded, even though they were the ones who were most likely to benefit from the modest minimum wage standards initially set (Mettler, 1998). The model of the *citizen worker* that took form in government social policy in the late 1930s was applied to women as workers at best only to a limited extent. Rather, according to this model, men were cast as family providers and women were recognized and rewarded as the dependent wives and widows of working men. Beginning with the 1939 amendments to the Social Security Act, wives and widows were entitled to spousal benefits under the updated Old Age and Survivors Insurance Program.

When the Social Security Act was passed in 1935 it was intended to provide a foundation for a comprehensive system of social provisioning. The initial act had ten titles. Of these, the first, second, fourth, and ninth titles were the most significant. The first title provided for Old Age Assistance (OAA), a public welfare program administered by the states and jointly funded by the state and federal governments. The second title set up the contributory pension system, Old Age and Survivors Insurance (OASI after 1939), which was administered by the federal government and financed with a payroll tax. Title IV expanded on the state-based system of mother's pensions created during the Progressive Era to create Aid to Dependent Children (later Aid to Families with Dependent Children, or AFDC), another public assistance program administered by the states but jointly financed by the federal government. Finally, Title IX created a joint federal-state unemployment insurance system that was financed by a payroll tax paid by employers. When this system was created, it was believed that the two insurance measures (Titles II and IX) would predominate over the assistance categories in political legitimacy and public funding. In the short term, at least, that was not the case. The Roosevelt administration also hoped to add medical insurance to the social security system at a later date.

The division between assistance and insurance was essential to the way that social provisioning under Social Security was conceived. While FDR favored an extensive system of social policies to provide Americans with economic security from "the cradle to the grave" (Perkins, 1946, 283), he was conservative in his views about public assistance. Yet while the president may have been clear about the important philosophical differences between relief and insurance, the public, at first, was not. During the 1930s several social movements promoted pensions for the elderly. Pensions were more attractive to many citizens than an uncertain insurance program. In terms of the number of recipients and expected levels of funding (initially it was expected that the first OAI pensions would be paid in 1942, after the trust fund had accumulated contributions for several years), OAA benefits far exceeded anticipated OAI benefits in the first few years of the Social Security Program (Berkowitz, 1980, 56). Further, the political popularity of OAA threatened to undermine support for OAI.

The Roosevelt administration responded to this problem by calling for a commission that would reform the social security system. The proposals of the Federal Advisory Commission (established in 1937) provided the basis for the 1939 amendments to the Social Security Act, which were designed to strengthen OAI and curtail OAA. By adding coverage for the widows, wives, and orphaned children of contributors, OAI was transformed into OASI.

Further, the starting date for OASI pensions was moved up to 1940, so that contributors could begin to benefit from the program sooner. Finally, eligibility and funding restrictions were placed on OAA (Altmeyer, 1966, chap. 4).

Why was the recipient base for the insurance program expanded through the addition of women as dependents? Other alternatives were considered. One was to add new categories of workers (which would include many women workers) to the rolls. Another was to add women not as men's dependents, but as separately entitled recipients who received benefits on the basis of their private (or household) labor contributions. The first alternative was rejected by Congress primarily because of the desire of southern legislators to maintain labor discipline among African Americans.[3] Further, there was resistance to providing social benefits to women workers (particularly married women) during the Depression because their place in the labor market was thought to disadvantage men seeking employment. The second alternative, advocated by the women members of the Federal Advisory Commission that developed the proposal for the amendments, was rejected because there was not strong support in the commission or in Congress for seeing household labor as creating an independent civic entitlement (Kessler-Harris, 1995).[4]

Rather, the commission articulated the distinction between civic independence and civic dependence in a particular way. Men's roles as providers for dependent women and children, it seemed, helped to secure their stature as independent civic members — in other words, employment and family were related to male civic membership. As the head of the Federal Advisory Commission, Paul Douglas, said in introducing the proposals before Congress in 1939, "At the base of American civilization is the concept of the family and the perpetuation of that concept is highly important" (quoted in Kessler-Harris, 1995, 105). The inclusion of the families of male workers was acceptable in 1939, more so than the extension of benefits to women on their own terms for their public or private labor. But it should be emphasized as well that the survivors' benefits concept emerged out of the need to strengthen OAI by broadening its base, and was not motivated originally by a desire to create family-oriented social policies.[5]

By strengthening OAI in this conservative way, the 1939 amendments also worked to preserve the dual nature of social provisioning in the United States. OASI was a national insurance program. Following the model of mothers' pensions, Aid to Dependent Children (ADC) was a state-based assistance program. OAA was also a state-administered assistance program, though vastly more popular and well funded than ADC. Despite the desire by many New Deal policymakers to provide more support for ADC, the efforts to curtail assistance and valorize insurance affected not only OAA but ADC as well. The changes to OASI moved better-off widows and orphans out of ADC. As Suzanne Mettler (1998) writes, "In effect the amendments rescued mostly white, middle-class women and their children from the miserly benefits and intensive scrutiny of ADC and granted them coverage in a program with national, uniform standards, and rights-based benefits" (167). Dependent women and children, recognized through their connection to male citizen workers, were deemed worthy, while single mothers and the children of unemployed and minority parents were left behind. What this policy also indicates is not only that previously developed policies (such as mothers' pensions) affect the development of subsequent policies, but that the development of conjoining policies may have a great, and perhaps unintended, impact on existing policies. Women remained primarily defined by their status as wives and mothers, rather than by their increasing presence in the workforce.

The Equal Rights Amendment

During the Great Depression, public support for equal rights for women was at a nadir and activists had to battle efforts to remove married women from the labor force. All of that changed when women's contributions to the war effort, both in uniform and on the production lines, revitalized the argument for equality. At the end of the 1930s, women constituted 25 percent of the labor force; by 1945, women's proportion of the civilian labor force had risen to 36 percent (Hartmann, 1982, 18, 21). Women's wartime employment challenged several presumptions about their social roles. First, it challenged ideas about what constituted women's work. As the manpower demands for war production grew, industries that had previously been all male domains, such as shipbuilding, began to admit substantial numbers of women workers. Second, women's war work brought into doubt protective legislation laws. Many of the laws designed to protect women workers were suspended or relaxed during the war, with little ill effect. Third, the need for workers helped to lower barriers against the employment of married women or women with young children. To aid working mothers, the federal government and private employers subsidized or created day care centers at many work sites. Fourth, the war substantially broadened women's participation in the labor movement. Heavy-industry jobs were more likely to be unionized, so as women moved into this field they came into contact with the unions. Finally, assumptions about women's pay were challenged by the movement to grant equal pay for equal work (Hartmann, 1982, chaps. 4 and 5).

All of these consequences of women's wartime employment increased support for finally obtaining civic equality for women. Citing women's wartime contributions, allies of the National Women's Party introduced the ERA into Congress once again. This time, the initiative was received much more positively. The American Association of University Women and the General Federation of Women's Clubs both came out in support of the proposal. At their 1944 conventions, the Republican and Democratic parties also went on record in support of constitutional equality for women. Many governors and President Harry Truman endorsed the measure. Further, the connection between gender and protective legislation appeared to have been judicially neutralized by *United States v. Darby*, 312 U.S. 100 (1941), which upheld the minimum wage law for both men and women. The ERA was passed in committee and reached the House and Senate floors. Finally, in 1946, the Senate voted thirty-eight to thirty-five in favor of the ERA. This vote was short of the two-thirds majority needed, but it was better than the amendment had ever done before. The Equal Rights Amendment came closer to adoption in the mid-1940s than it would again until the 1970s.

In the debate over the Equal Rights Amendment in the mid-1940s, the conflicting trends in women's labor status and civic membership are apparent. The opponents of the ERA included supporters of traditional family roles, social feminists, some labor progressives, as well as labor activists interested in protecting male prerogatives in the paid work realm. Supporters of the ERA included liberal feminist organizations, professional women's groups, feminist legal scholars, as well as their allies in both the Democratic and Republican parties. Some of the supporters were internationalists committed to advancing the cause of human rights and international cooperation. This issue divided many traditional allies — including the women's movement, supporters of the New Deal, and political progressives more generally. The details of the debate offer a revealing take on the civic position of women at the end of the Second World War.

Much of the congressional opposition to the ERA was articulated in terms of protecting the family and the role of women as mothers and wives. Thus opponents of the amendment introduced a statement by Silas Strawn (former president of the American Bar Association) contending that "the amendment would inevitably invalidate many of the State laws protecting the American home" (*Congressional Record*, July 17, 1946, S9223). Similarly, Senator Overton of Louisiana offered the following criticism of the ERA (posed, in accordance with debate rules, as a question): "in view of the fact that women are not as physically able to take care of world affairs . . . can it be said that the State laws could continue to keep the husband as the head and master of the community?" (*Congressional Record*, July 18, 1946, S9311). In Overton's view, it was right that state governments should take a benevolent and paternalistic attitude toward women, and that women ought to reside primarily in the domestic realm, away from the worries of public life.

That was not what concerned Senator Robert Wagner of New York and his progressive labor allies. Both Wagner and Frances Perkins (Roosevelt's secretary of labor and a longtime ally of the social feminists) went on record in opposition to the ERA. For these labor progressives, the danger of passing the ERA was that it would make unconstitutional many of the protective labor laws and social provisioning laws that assisted women. In his floor comments, Wagner stated that (unlike some of his southern colleagues) he would "sympathize, of course, with the effort to do away with State laws which give married women rights inferior to those enjoyed by their husbands" (*Congressional Record*, July 18, 1946, S9293). Yet Wagner felt that women were already protected by the Equal Protection Clause of the Fourteenth Amendment, and that in its application of that provision in *Muller v. Oregon*, the Court had properly "recognized that 'woman's physical structure and the performance of maternal functions place her at a disadvantage in the struggle for subsistence' " (*Congressional Record*, July 18, 1946, S9293). Preserving this view on the part of the Court was "especially important," not just in order to preserve protective labor legislation, but also to continue the administration's work in "develop[ing] our social-insurance program in the field of maternal care, widows', old-age, and survivors' insurance" (*Congressional Record*, July 18, 1946, S9294). Wagner's comments indicate that even though constitutional understandings were changing regarding the relationship between labor status and citizenship (labor regulatory laws were now held to be constitutional when applied to men as well as women), the notion of gender difference still permeated the federal government's understanding of the link between work and citizenship. Now, ideas of gender differences were used to justify and defend a set of social policies that rewarded working men and (at a reduced level) their dependent wives and widows under a model of family provisioning.

The advocates of the ERA cited several reasons for their support of the amendment. The legitimacy of their cause was presented as principled: equality was an American value that ought to apply fully to all citizens. ERA advocates wanted to have gender equality clearly inscribed into the Constitution, as the repository of our political norms. Along these same lines, they stressed the likely effect the amendment would have on women's civic status, and hoped that the ERA would finally elevate women to the rank of first-class citizens. There was also a practical concern behind the amendment. For many years, women had fought state by state to overturn discriminatory laws and to enact laws that would make women more equal. These efforts were slow and often frustrated by resistant local judges or legislators. An amendment to the Constitution would correct a broad pattern of legal discrimination in one sweeping gesture. On the issue of protective labor laws and social insurance programs, some defenders of the ERA argued that the Constitution would continue to tolerate gender distinctions in these areas, while others contended that such provisions and protections ought to be extended equally to men and women. Finally, women's rights advocates and their congressional supporters also stressed the role of international norms and opinions in their advocacy of the ERA (see also Chapter 6).

It was certainly the case, as the critics charged, that the majority of women who supported the ERA were professional women, rather than hourly workers or union members. Yet it is also true that the General Federation of Women's Clubs (GFWC) threw its support behind the amendment, suggesting that many nonworking advocates of women's rights were also supportive. The organization that led the effort to ratify the ERA was, as it had been since the 1920s when the amendment was first introduced, the National Women's Party. For this group, as for the GFWC, the ERA represented an effort to complete the campaign for civic equality that had been an aspiration since the suffrage movement a generation earlier.

As Emma Guffey Miller of the NWP stated in one of the hearings, "We women want to be persons now because we are still not persons in the Constitution of the United States" (U.S. Senate 1945a, 4). Miller's reference to "persons" simultaneously invoked the protection of the equal rights of persons within the Fourteenth Amendment and women's loss of legal status as persons under coverture.[6] These points were explained further in a pamphlet prepared by the NWP and issued as a Senate document in 1946, entitled *Questions and Answers on the Equal Rights Amendment.* To the question of whether women already had equal rights after the passage of the Nineteenth Amendment, the pamphlet's authors answered, "Supreme Court decisions have established the fact that the only right women won under the suffrage amendment was the right to vote. . . . Without the amendment, the attainment of this equality of citizenship is only a theoretical possibility" (U.S. Senate, 1946, 18–19).

Constitutional equality would affect not only women's legal position, but also their psychological self-awareness and political participation. In the pamphlet it was asked, "What would be the psychological effect of the amendment?" The answer was, "To raise the status of all women" (U.S. Senate, 1946, 11). Later in the same pamphlet, it was suggested that the amendment would result in greater political participation and a greater presence of women in the public realm. "With wider participation of women in our political, civil, and economic life, and more power in the hands of women, greater aid would undoubtedly be given to mothers" (U.S. Senate, 1946, 14). In this vision, politics would be feminized by the ERA (in a way that was quite different than that described above), as women's concerns would find significant voice in the public realm. Further, this new civic and political status was something women deserved in light of their war service.

Women's rights advocates favored an ERA not just for reasons of status or principle, but also because of the practical insecurity and strategic difficulty involved in undertaking dozens of state-level campaigns to achieve legal equality. As Jane Norman Smith of the NWP testified, "I know that it would be an endless task to secure an equal status for women in the laws of this entire country, one by one, State by State, as some opponents of the equal rights amendment have recommended" (U.S. House, 1945a, 16). Women must be secured not just in their political rights, as they were under the Nineteenth Amendment, but also in their civil rights. They must be brought under the protective wing of the Fourteenth Amendment. To be effective, equality must be written into the nation's fundamental law, and made a foundational right not subject to women's changing political fortunes. This goal could only be achieved, the advocates argued, with a constitutional amendment.

Both sides in this debate focused on the Fair Labor Standards Act (FLSA) and the Social Security Act (SSA) in discussing the merits and demerits of an equality standard. New Deal supporters and labor progressives such as Secretary Perkins and Senator Wagner saw in the FLSA the development of a labor rights regime that recognized and rewarded differing gender roles through direct national programs, or through the distinctions between state and federal labor regulations. As discussed earlier, the FLSA established a national system of wage and hour regulations for wage workers. In the process, the act "feminized" civic membership by abolishing the notion that civic independence required a total absence of government regulation or support in the work realm. Yet, while both men and women workers were now under the protection of national regulation, a dual system of labor standards remained that operated through the mechanism of federalism.

The dualism in labor standards preserved under federalism was justified by labor progressives who cited the physical differences between men and women, their different social roles, and their differences as workers. According to Frances Perkins, these laws were developed in recognition of the distinctive experiences of working women.

> It is well established that, as a class, women workers are more susceptible to exploitation by unscrupulous employers than are men. This is because, typically, they are not the primary family breadwinners and, in order to supplement the family income, will work for a lower wage than men; because they are frequently casual workers, and as such are not as well organized in unions as men; and because of blind and unreasonable prejudice against women workers. (U.S. House, 1945a, 88)

For Perkins, the situation of women workers should be recognized and addressed in ways that met their immediate needs and protected them from employer discrimination. Yet the labor progressives failed to see the ways in which gender-based labor laws *promoted* many of the differences in labor conditions that Perkins cited as justifications for these laws.

On the issue of the differences between state and national labor standards, Perkins suggested there was also a difference in interstate versus intrastate working conditions that was occluded by the war. The FLSA applied only to interstate industries. "When the war emergency is at an end millions of these women now working under the wage protection of the Fair Labor Standards Act in interstate industries will return to intrastate service industries and other occupations where the wage rates have historically been low and working conditions deplorable" (U.S. House, 1945a, 89). According to this logic, the limited coverage of the FLSA became an argument not for broadening the standards of labor regulation for all — rather, it favored retaining gendered labor standards in the harsher working environment of intrastate industries. Attorney Marvin Harrison went further in explicitly opposing common protective labor standards for men and women. In the context of many of the differences between men and women workers cited by Perkins, Harrison argued, "it will be extremely difficult — if not indeed impossible — to draw a minimum wage law fair and adequate to the one and not wholly useless as to the other" (U.S. House, 1945a, 99). Whereas women needed laws, men would have unions to insure their economic security. Both Perkins's and Harrison's analyses were based on their perception of the "typical" woman worker, not of those who desired or were capable of labor patterns and activities more commonly associated with men, such as widowed mothers working to support their families.

The proponents of the ERA took a more aspirational view with regard to the situation of women workers, and were likely to stress the rights of individual women, regardless of what the typical pattern of labor activity for women might currently be. They held up the FLSA, as well as the Public Contracts Act that governed working conditions for government contractors, as models of what would occur if protective labor standards were applied to both sexes. It was clear to the equality advocates, such as Nora Stanton Barney (Elizabeth Cady Stanton's granddaughter), that sensible labor regulations would apply both to men and women, while the insensible ones only marked women as less capable and more dependent, or did little to actually assist them. So, for instance, on hours laws, Barney testified that "excessively long hours are just as bad for men as women" (U.S. House, 1945a, 18). But on other so-called health laws, she was more incredulous: "It is evident these laws are not for women's health, but are discriminatory laws designed to embarrass and discourage women from being employed in certain occupations" (U.S. House, 1945a, 18).

Despite their overall positive review of the FLSA — for example, how the act made it so that protective laws could be applied without regard to gender — the ERA advocates recognized that in practice some labor standards would be de facto of greater difference to women than to men. Yet this recognition only led them to criticize the general conditions under which women labored and to call for more assistance — either through government action or through unionization. So, on the one hand, Barney suggested that the existing "interstate minimum wage" standard that applied to "men and women alike" should be expanded to intrastate industries. On the other hand, she critiqued the role of the gender-neutral minimum wage standard for job categories in which women predominated: "It does not help the status of women to set a wage which is often far below the union wage. . . . It has been the demand for labor, unionization, stiffening the backbones and self-respect of women that have raised the wages of women" (U.S. House, 1945a, 19). Barney and others saw the same general labor conditions that Perkins pointed to in justifying protective labor laws solely for women as an indication of the inadequacy of such laws, whether they were applied to the situation of women workers de jure or de facto.

In the end, the ERA was defeated in the 1940s. But the debate over an equality standard for women at the end of World War II illustrates the way that inequality was presumed and expressed in the differential labor rights that attached to men's and women's civic membership, and shows some of the difficulties that were perceived in pursuing constitutional equality for women. Gender continued to be an acceptable marker of civic difference in the 1940s. Yet the location of these differences was shifting from civil and political rights to social rights. While the opponents of the ERA included both traditional paternalists (concerned with the status of married women) and labor progressives, the more significant voice was that of the labor progressives who defended the creation of new, gendered standards of social rights in relation to labor status. In time, fewer and fewer government officials were willing to defend the legal disabilities of married women; but as the social welfare state grew, the defense of family provisioning for male workers and their dependents became steadfast (Kessler-Harris, 2001). Further, this debate reveals that the equality standard troubled many feminists and their labor allies for two reasons: merely aspirational, it failed to address the immediate, practical concerns of many working women; and equality might be interpreted to mean legal sameness on the basis of male standards of rights and protections. Yet there was another possible outcome in the call for equality: whereby women would be treated increasingly as autonomous individuals at the level of national citizenship, and the United States would represent itself in the international arena as a nation committed to equal rights for all. But that future was still decades away.[7]

Full Employment

Within the various councils of the executive branch, the relationship between labor, civic membership, and the general welfare also was being elaborated. In the early 1940s, the National Resources Planning Board (which had been established by the executive branch) articulated a concept of full employment that linked the right to work with national economic well-being. This initial formulation evolved into a set of proposals by FDR for a modern, *economic* bill of rights to supplement the rights protected in the first ten amendments to the Constitution. In his 1944 State of the Union address, President Roosevelt discussed the implications of industrialization for civic rights. "We have come to a clear realization of the fact that true individual freedom cannot exist without economic security and independence. . . . We have accepted . . . a second Bill of Rights under which a new basis of security and prosperity can be established for all. . . . Among these are: The right to a useful and remunerative job in the industries or shops or farms or mines of the Nation" (Roosevelt, 1938–50, 13:41). The foremost right of the new economic bill of rights was the right to a job.

Further, this right was conceived of as more than a right of civic membership. It also was thought of as a way to manage the national economy and prevent steep economic downturns by encouraging consumption (Brinkley, 1995, chap. 10). Within the councils of the NRPB, full employment was seen as part of both the social and economic program of the New Deal. It was a key element of the administration's demobilization policy. By using taxing and spending measures to encourage economic growth, the government hoped to avoid the massive unemployment that followed the close of the First World War. It also hoped that high and steady wages would mean a growing economy centered on the production and consumption of consumer durables — as befitted the world's leading democratic nation. The war had demonstrated the prowess of the American industrial machine. Now the goal was to retool that machinery to supply the nation with cars and washing machines instead of bombs and tanks.

Women fit into this postwar scenario in two ways, as workers and as homemakers. The staff members of the NRPB were explicit about their desire to treat men and women workers as equal beneficiaries of the full-employment policies, even as they acknowledged women's domestic role: "These provisions, it goes without saying perhaps, apply without discrimination to women and men alike. For women who choose to continue their employment outside the home, facilities and assistance should be given through several measures and agencies here recommended. Women in the home will, of course, share in the aids and opportunities provided for the armed services and war workers" (National Resources Planning Board, 1943, 5). Women, as workers and veterans, were entitled to equal benefits and nondiscrimination.[8] Women as wives, like their children, would benefit indirectly from programs aimed at supporting male workers and veterans. While articulating both a right to employment and an expectation of it as a civic right, the NRPB wished to exempt certain classes from this expectation: "We must plan for full employment. . . . We must plan to do this without requiring work from youth who should be in school, the aged who should be relieved if they wish it, and women who choose to make their contribution in the home" (National Resources Planning Board, 1943, 7–8). Unlike youth and the elderly, women escaped the injunctive here — they were given a choice of home or work, while the old and young were more clearly excused from working.

Yet, in many ways, it appears that this allowance for working women was undermined by a greater tendency to see citizens and workers as men. For despite their policy of nondiscrimination, the NRPB also made clear the gender of their idealized worker and citizen: "Our greatest resource is men-at-work, a resource which is lost forever when men are idle. . . . The full employment that we Americans seek must be, at the same time, free employment, . . . even material prosperity is not worth the price to men who cherish freedom and the dignity of man" (National Resources Planning Board, 1941, 1). The republican ideal of an independent citizen who was the master of his home and family was reinvented under the New Deal. Now there was the male citizen worker whose contributions to society were recognized and rewarded in ways that allowed him to provide for both himself and his family. It was this shift in the understanding of men's civic membership — to being both workers and providers — that cast women's civic membership in a supportive, dependent, and domestic role. Men were still the heads of households, even if these modern households were bound more by relations of affection than authority.

This shift in the civic order and in conceptions of civic membership was represented in several ways. One was in the reconceptualization of civic independence from the realm of negative rights, such as the right to freedom of contract, to the realm of positive rights, including a right to social security for workers and their dependents.[9] Put differently, social ordering now took place within the arena of social rights. Whereas in the nineteenth century the government recognized social differences (and translated them into civic differences) by awarding different civil rights according to one's social status (e.g., coverture), now, as civil rights were being equalized, social hierarchies were recognized and rewarded instead through social rights and provisioning.

The universal civic member of the 1940s was a worker and a veteran, a husband and a father. In recognition of the contributions he made to the nation, this civic member was supported in his role as a provider. It was his rights and position that the government recognized and protected. Through him, wives and children were taken care of as well. When the Full Employment Act was considered by Congress, the question arose as to whether women would be included in the calculation of full employment.[10] In the Senate hearings on the bill, Senator Murdock objected to a provision that exempted those with full-time housekeeping responsibilities from a right to employment. In an exchange with the bill's author, Senator James Murray, Murdock charged, "It seems to me that your exceptions are hardly justified, and rather impose an indignity on . . . one of the fundamental labors of the Nation . . . housekeeping." He went on, "I certainly would not want to deprive the housewife of any opportunity that is open to any other American." In response, Senator Murray defended himself, somewhat sheepishly, "Well, of course, it was not expected that this bill was intended to take the housewives out of the homes and put them into industry or other employment." Murdock rejoined that he, too, favored the role of housewives, "but I do not think that we should make an exception of any class." As a principle, full employment was universal and individual. But at the level of social classes and social order, women were to be preserved in their role as housewives (U.S. Senate, 1945b, 19).

Time and again, in Senate and House hearings on the full-employment bills, both elected officials and the witnesses before them betrayed a political imaginary in which civic members as workers and providers are men:

R. B. MARSTON, LEGISLATIVE-FEDERAL RELATIONS DIVISION,

NATIONAL EDUCATION ASSOCIATION:

I am, however, pretty much disturbed, Mr. Chairman, about the obligation of the Nation to the individual who wants to work and is willing to work, and who has served his country well, who had been a good citizen in his community, who is respected by officers of the law, when conditions arise over which he has no control, and he has a family. . . . We have got to keep him a good American citizen. (U.S. House, 1945b, 156)

NATHAN E. COWAN, LEGISLATIVE DIRECTOR, CIO:

I think the greatest crime on earth is to see an American Parent, a father, who has a half dozen children, and he goes out honestly day after day seeking after work, and he cannot find work. . . . In my mind's eye I go back to these boys that helped win the war, that are the product of deprivation. . . . I wonder if we are the proper caretakers of their heritage if we do not do more than we are doing now. (U.S. House, 1945b, 363)

REPRESENTATIVE GEORGE OUTLAND (CALIFORNIA):

The duties of the citizen have meaning only when balanced against the rights of a citizen. When men are deprived of the latter, they lose faith in justice and order. . . . Full employment in a free, competitive economy is the real road to freedom — freedom for the individual. (U.S. Senate, 1945b, 141)

RALPH E. FLANDERS, PRESIDENT, JONES AND LAMSON MACHINE CO.:

With regard to the right to a job, the corresponding duty of the individual is to be productive, self-reliant, and energetically in search of employment when out of work. To assign the right to individuals who do not possess these qualities is to subsidize idleness and encourage them becoming social parasites. (U.S. Senate, 1945b, 356)

Although the right to work is imagined repeatedly as an individual right, a right like those specified in the Bill of Rights or the Declaration of Independence, it also is seen as a right that is consistent with the nature and social position of men. It is men who lose faith in justice and order when there is no work. It is men who must be kept good American citizens by making work available. Or, in a more demanding view, men must show themselves worthy of the rights they receive by being productive and self-reliant. Where women are imagined, it is not in connection with this right, which is not ever justified as something fundamental to their civic membership. Rather, they serve as a measure of men's rights — of the hopes and despairs of those seeking to work and provide and thereby be good American civic members.

One difference between the House and Senate hearings on the full-employment bills was that no women were called upon to testify in the House hearings, while several women testified before the Senate subcommittee charged with considering the bill.[11] On the Senate side, the housekeeping exemption was ultimately dropped in favor of language that would make the bill's provisions available to those "able to work and seeking work." When consideration of the housekeeping exemption came up on the House side, it typically was part of a critique of the bill, for its inability clearly or practically to define who would be covered under the provisions of the full-employment measures. The chair of the House Committee on Expenditures in the Executive Departments, Representative Carter Manasco (Alabama), repeatedly raised the issue of how one would know whether a woman was a full-time homemaker. "I am just wondering if, under the terms of the House bill she [a homemaker] would be entitled to work on these Federal projects, say after she had completed her housework by 9 o'clock in the morning, if she didn't have any children" (U.S. House, 1945b, 401).

Similarly, Representative Ralph Church of Illinois wondered about women who had domestic servants and asked, "If she doesn't work the very last minute of her time at her household duties she would be entitled to the benefits of this bill?" (U.S. House, 1945b, 182). In critiquing the bill through the housekeeping provision, these representatives offered a portrait of women whose commitment to homemaking was somewhat suspect, because of their reliance on labor-saving devices or on the assistance of paid help in the home. Elsewhere in the hearings, they affirmed their belief in housekeeping and in the family as "a great American institution" (U.S. House, 1945b, 192). But nowhere in the House hearings was the situation or existence of full-time women workers ever considered.

The women who testified in the Senate hearings were more concerned with the situation of working women, and were not satisfied with the suggestion that women would return to full-time housekeeping after the war.[12] Thus, Loula Dunn of the American Public Welfare Association tried to get the senators to expand their understanding and appreciation of women's roles. She testified that in her home state of Alabama during the war years, "more women have worked than ever before.... While some of these women may be glad to quit work, many are the sole support of their families.

Full-employment planning, therefore, should take into account not only the need for some of these women to work, but also the value of their skills in the labor market" (U.S. Senate, 1945b, 193). The expansion that people like Loula Dunn sought to make in the imaginations of the senators — one that was pursued tentatively and carefully — was an acceptance and appreciation of the fact that some women *needed* to work in order to support their families. When there were no fathers, being a good mother meant being a worker as well. Yet it would be some time before this revision was accepted. The secretary of agriculture, Clinton P. Anderson, in discussing the estimates his agency made of the postwar labor force, stated, "It has been argued that at least part of these emergency workers will continue to seek employment after the war and hence should be considered permanent additions to the normal postwar labor force. Perhaps so; but since the estimates of the probable number vary widely and are subject to a great deal of controversy, none of these workers were included in the computation" (U.S. Senate, 1945b, 298). By emergency workers, the secretary meant youth, the elderly, and married women — none of whom were counted on or planned for as part of the postwar workforce.

As the war ended, both labor and industry worried about the possible return of massive unemployment. To cushion the transition back to a civilian economy, women were called upon to return voluntarily to the domestic realm; they were expected to want to return to their homemaking duties when their husbands came back from overseas, in the nation's best interest. As Frederick Crawford, the head of the National Association of Manufacturers said, "from a humanitarian point of view, too many women should not stay in the labor force. The home is the basic American institution" (quoted in Hartmann, 1982, 156). While labor leaders in principle supported a woman's right to a job, they also emphasized the right of male workers to provide for their families. As Emil Rieve, the president of the Textile Workers Union, stated, "If he can bring home enough money himself, the American worker does not want to see his wife, his 16-year-old daughter, and his 70-year-old father trudging off to the mill. . . . He wants to see . . . his wife making a home for the family" (quoted in Hartmann, 1982, 167–68).

These attitudes were reinforced by two institutional measures that gave men an employment preference. The first was the labor seniority system. Most collective bargaining agreements contained a provision for retention by seniority. Since women workers were likely to be hired more recently, they were among the first to be dismissed. This provision was more harmful to women employees over the long term since women tended to be employed more irregularly than men. Second, after the war, veterans (who were over 98 percent male) were given a job preference under the GI Bill. Veterans were to be credited with seniority for their time in military service; they were assured reemployment in the same job or a job at the same skill level where possible; and they were given job protection for one year. Veterans also received preferences for civil service jobs. In effect, many women workers were replaced by men. The result was a temporary decline in women's participation in the labor force and, in the longer term, a shift of women from better paid, more unionized "male" jobs into nonunionized "women's" work in sales, service, and clerical employment (Hartmann, 1982; Chafe, 1991).

The goal of enacting a full-employment policy as part of an economic bill of rights was never fully realized. When Harry Truman replaced Franklin Delano Roosevelt as president, many of the labor progressives in the New Deal administration left, and were replaced by more conservative, business-oriented officials. Further, the public reacted negatively to the high level of strike activity in 1946, after wage and price controls were lifted and workers tried to preserve their wage gains in a period of high inflation. The labor movement was also hurt by its failed campaign to organize the South in Operation Dixie. Organizers were unable to overcome persistent racial animosity and the rise of anticommunist sentiment in that region. Finally, the 1946 elections brought many more Republican conservatives into Congress, and the Taft-Hartley Act of 1947 (which significantly modified the Wagner Act of 1935) effectively ended the progressive trajectory of the labor movement (Brinkley, 1995). Although an Employment Act was finally passed in 1946, it was mostly a budget-planning measure that did little to provide Americans — male or female — with employment as a right of civic membership.

Labor and Gender Jurisprudence in the 1940s

Myriad Supreme Court cases in the 1940s touched on gender, class identity, and labor rights. The facts of these cases dealt with a wide range of circumstances — from bigamy, to racial exclusion by unions, the labor rights of barmaids, and the parental fitness of religious women. Equally diverse were the constitutional issues raised, which extended from due process considerations, to equal protection, the scope of the Commerce Clause, the meaning of the General Welfare Clause, the protection afforded by the Sixth Amendment, and the applicability of the Full Faith and Credit Clause. Despite this range of facts and law, however, certain trends are evident. In the shift from a world of legal status to one of liberal universalism, emphasis was placed on the link between social identities and economic interests. Further, to the degree that collective identities were positively acknowledged, they were cast either as matters of aggregate self-interest that could be treated in representative terms, or as naturalized and traditional, and therefore as something prior to law. Despite growth in expressions of support for individualism and equality, gender typically was cast as a reasonable difference that escaped the rigors of equal protection scrutiny. Finally, in this odd dance between individual equality and naturalized difference, substantive due process reasoning occupied a strategic place for its ability to accommodate different visions of human particularity.

In acknowledging the power of workers to organize and bargain collectively, the Court stated in *N.L.R.B. v. Jones and Laughlin Steel Corp.*, 301 U.S. 1 (1937), that the Commerce Clause empowered Congress to prohibit employers "from engaging in any unfair labor practice affecting commerce" (30). This recognition of congressional authority was extended when the Fair Labor Standards Act was upheld in *United States v. Darby*, 312 U.S. 100 (1941), in which the Court found that the use of the commerce power was not restricted when the object was not the regulation of commerce per se: "Whatever their motive and purpose, regulations of commerce which do not infringe some constitutional prohibition are within the plenary power conferred on Congress by the Commerce Clause" (115). Thus, the ruling overturned *Hammer v. Dagenhart*, 247 U.S. 251, the 1918 case in which the Court struck down, as a misuse of the commerce power, a federal act that prohibited interstate commerce in products produced with child labor. Through the power to act on matters of national economic interest, Congress had asserted the authority to regulate the social order through the regulation of labor conditions. Given that the provisions of the NLRB more often applied to men (since they were more likely to work in unionized industries), and those of the FLSA more often applied to women (since they more often worked in low-wage, nonunion sectors), in the new positive-rights and positive-government regime of the late New Deal, men received the means for collective representation while women received paternalistic regulation.

Once congressional authority to use the commerce power for broad purposes was clearly acknowledged, the Court established the right to organize and bargain collectively as a general welfare matter. In *Phelps Dodge Corp. v. N.L.R.B.*, 313 U.S. 177 (1941), the Court wrote of "the workers' right of self-organization" (182). This collective right was developed in recognition of "the nature of modern industrialism" (183), and the need, under the constitutional principle of promoting the general welfare, to attain "industrial peace" (185). Yet, this modern right of collective bargaining (justified also under the Commerce Clause) was further anchored in First Amendment principles of "freedom of association." The attachment of labor rights to the core freedoms protected in the Bill of Rights is repeated in other cases as well. For instance, in *Thomas v. Collins*, 323 U.S. 526 (1945), the Court threw out a Texas antilabor law for violating the rights of free speech and free assembly of workmen, labor leaders, and unions.

The link between individuals and the collective in the area of labor rights also was articulated by the Court in terms of representation. Three cases (*Steele v. Louisville and Nashville Railroad Co.*, 323 U.S. 192 [1944]; *Tunstall v. Brotherhood of Locomotive Firemen and Enginemen*, 323 U.S. 210 [1944]; *Graham v. Brotherhood of Locomotive Firemen and Enginemen*, 338 U.S. 232 [1949]) came before the Court that involved challenges by African American railroad workers to unfavorable collective bargaining agreements made by the union that represented them but from which they were barred (on the basis of race) from membership. In these cases, the Court compared the union to a legislature. The Court majority wrote in *Steele*, "For the representative is clothed with power not unlike that of a legislature which is subject to constitutional limitations on its power to deny, restrict, destroy or discriminate against the rights of those for whom it legislates and which is also under an affirmative constitutional duty equally to protect those rights" (198). Under modern industrialism, the rights of a worker to labor representation were like the rights of a citizen to political representation, and both kinds of rights were constitutionally protected.

Union rights were recognized by the Court as rights based on organizational and economic interest. The idea that a labor or class identity could be something more — something like a cultural identity, or a marked, ascriptive category, for instance — was rejected. In its discussion of the nature of class identity (in *Fay v. New York*, 332 U.S. 261 [1947] — a jury case), the Court wrote that unlike race or gender, economic position seemed less clearly to place a mark on one's political position or social outlook.

> It would require large assumptions to say that one's present economic status, in a society as fluid as ours, determines his outlook. . . . There is entrepreneur and wage-earner, consumer and producer, taxpayer and civil servant, foreman and laborer, white-collar worker and manual laborer. But we are not ready to assume that these differences of function degenerate into a hostility such that one cannot expect justice at the hands of occupations and groups other than his own. (292)

Race and gender were fixed categories, so the Court believed, but class was not — not in the nation of Horatio Alger, Andrew Carnegie, and Abraham Lincoln, where one born at the very bottom of the economic and social scale could rise to wealth and political power.[13] This faith held true for the (economically privileged) justices of the Supreme Court, even in an age when memories of the Great Depression remained vivid and class had become something other than a pejorative term in American politics. Not only did the presence of economic opportunity prevent class identity from becoming fixed, but the presence of cross-cutting cleavages (even, merely, economic ones) suggested a scenario better characterized as pluralism and a fluidity of interests than a fixed and stratified society.

Class did not appear in the labor opinions as a clearly defined category. It was not readily imagined as a basis for legal and political discrimination, nor as a cultural formation reflected in the lifestyles, rituals, and beliefs of different social groups. If it had substance, it most comfortably was viewed as the basis of differing economic interests and corresponding political outlooks — differences that in themselves might make class relevant to the ideal of a jury that constituted a representative cross section of the community. Class had to be confronted in the years after the Great Depression, when unions were strong and many voters demonstrated class allegiance in their voting behavior and partisan affiliation. But the role of class in politics at a foundational level — where social identity becomes relevant to the terms of civic membership — remained circumscribed in the view of the Court.

As a footnote to the discussion of the Commerce Clause, it is instructive to consider the case of *Mortensen v. United States*, 322 U.S. 369 (1944), where the Court considered the conviction under the Mann Act of a married couple who allowed two women they employed as prostitutes to accompany them on a vacation from Nebraska to Utah. The majority overturned the conviction, saying there was no factual basis for the jury's decision in the case. "The sole purpose of the journey from beginning to end was to provide innocent recreation and a holiday for petitioners and the two girls" (375). Throughout the majority opinion, the prostitutes are referred to as girls (they became women again in the dissents), and the vacation trip is presented as an innocent, familylike excursion (it included a visit to an elderly parent) that suggested a parental relationship between the "girls" and their employers, the married couple. While it was unwilling to explicitly question the statutory legitimacy of the Mann Act, the majority willingly attacked its application.

The dissenting justices were unmoved by this attack. They asserted that the majority should show deference to congressional authority, even as the dissenters shared the majority's disdain for this legislation. "Courts have no more concern with the policy and wisdom of the Mann Act, than of the Labor Relations Act, or any other which Congress may constitutionally adopt. Those are matters for Congress to determine, not the courts" (378). This statement from the minority seems ironic, since the Mann (or White Slavery) Act had been upheld in *Caminetti v. United States*, 242 U.S. 470 (1917), at a moment when the Court was generally unwilling to recognize the authority of Congress to use commerce or taxing powers for social purposes. The Mann Act was treated as an exception to that era's generally strict and conservative jurisprudence. This was another instance when the regulation of women was an exception to constitutional prohibitions on the regulation of men or business. As James Morone (2003) writes (comparing *Caminetti* to *Dagenhart*), prior to the New Deal, "Women fell under federal jurisdiction; widgets did not" (309).

The mention by the dissenters in *Mortensen* of the National Labor Relations Act (NLRA) was also a reminder to the majority justices that the terms of federalism had changed, as the national government entered into new arenas previously regarded as the province of the private sector or the states. It suggested that while some justices might now find the Mann Act problematic, others were equally troubled by the progressive labor ideals embraced by the NLRA. So in both instances, legislative deference was appropriate. While the Court by the 1940s showed some reluctance in enforcing federal statutes that explicitly drew upon social identities to make political distinctions, it was willing to endorse the role of the states or legislatures in making such distinctions.

Contending with Gender Difference: Equal Protection Analysis in the 1940s

During the New Deal, substantive due process reasoning was on the decline, while the use of the Equal Protection Clause to protect individual rights was on the rise. Yet, in cases that applied to women, the opposite may have been true. In the 1940s, the assertion of gender difference (as opposed to equality) was as judicially acceptable as it ever had been, though the use of the Equal Protection Clause to protect women's individual rights was explicitly rejected. These gendered exceptions to the general rule were indicative of the difficulties of incorporating women as persons and full civic members into a liberal constitutional system.

There were a series of jury cases in the 1940s that addressed the exclusion (or overinclusion) of various groups from the jury pools. In instances where the exclusionary practices were based on race, they were typically found to violate the Equal Protection Clause of the Fourteenth Amendment. According to the Court, the "primary concern" of the authors of the Fourteenth Amendment (passed just after the Civil War) was the "preservation" of civil and political rights "from discriminatory action on the part of the States based on considerations of race or color" (*Shelley v. Kraemer*, 334 U.S. 1 [1948], 22). The Court's treatment of gender difference in relation to jury service was quite different. Sex, according to the Court majority in *Ballard v. United States*, 329 U.S. 187 (1946), constituted a legally recognizable form of social difference. The plaintiffs (a mother and son) in this case brought suit after being convicted of mail fraud (they claimed they were soliciting for religious purposes) by a jury from which women were excluded. The Court sided with the plaintiffs. In *Ballard*, the Court suggested that federal discrimination against women jurors in California (where women were eligible for jury service in the state criminal courts) violated the principle that a jury should be drawn from a fair cross section of the community.

In the other major jury cases of this decade, the Supreme Court was concerned with enunciating the principles of equality, individualism, and nondiscrimination (see *Thiel v. Southern Pacific Co.*, 328 U.S. 217 [1946]; *Hill v. Texas*, 316 U.S. 400 [1942]; and *Smith v. Texas*, 311 U.S. 128 [1940]). But in *Ballard*, the logic behind the ruling was somewhat different. As Justice William O. Douglas wrote for the Court majority, "The truth is that the two sexes are not fungible; a community made up exclusively of one is different from a community composed of both. . . . The exclusion of one may indeed make the jury less representative of the community" (193–94). So the primary concern expressed here was not with the right of women as citizens to serve on juries. Rather, it was a concern (covered under the Sixth Amendment) for defendants, that their entitlement to a representative jury would be violated if women were excluded. The Court expressed this concern in substantive terms — as a concern with what the different sexes might bring to the jury, and to the judgment in this particular case. Even where gender difference was treated positively, however, formal inclusion was often accompanied by practical exclusion, as it was in states where women were made eligible for jury service but provided with automatic exemptions from serving.

Indeed, arguments for both equality and gender distinction could be problematic for those seeking rights and access to the public sphere for women under liberal constitutionalism. In his dissent in *Ballard*, Justice Burton noted that gender distinction was an accepted legal principle, but that the trend was toward equality between the sexes, what he referred to as "the general and increasing absence of sound reasons for distinctions between men and women in matters of suffrage, office holding, education, economic status, civil liberties, church membership, cultural activities, and even war service." Yet instead of concluding that gender should be a recognized category under equal protection analysis, Burton finished by suggesting that gender should not be politically relevant at all: "[the above trend] emphasizes the lack of reason for making a point of the presence or absence of either sex, as such, on either grand or petit juries" (205). So for Burton, if women were different, then they could be legally excluded, but if they were the same, they could make no positive demand for legal inclusion. This was the bind for women, discussed by many feminist critics of liberalism (Pateman, 1988; W. Brown, 1995; MacKinnon, 1987; Katzenstein, 1998; Beauvoir, 1989), between a neutral (and typically male) standard of equality and a discriminatory standard of difference.

In the other jury cases that addressed gender exclusion, there is both a recognition that gender was used as a means to legally discriminate and a rejection of the idea that this was politically or constitutionally relevant. In *Fay* the Court addressed a series of objections to the use of blue ribbon juries in New York State. Regarding women's exclusion from jury service, the Court began by noting the historical tolerance of gender classifications by the Supreme Court.[14] "It would, in the light of this history, take something more than a judicial interpretation to spell out of the Constitution a command to set aside verdicts rendered by juries unleavened by feminine influence" (289–90). Yet the opinion also seems to recognize women's political and social progress, even as it proclaims the Court's inability to further that progress with its rulings. Thus, two different attitudes were expressed here — one that framed gender difference as common sense and acceptable, and the other that affirmed the principles of egalitarian liberalism, but then excused itself from the practical application of those principles.

There were other cases in which the Court proclaimed the irrelevance of the Fourteenth Amendment to protection against gender discrimination. In *Goesaert v. Cleary*, 335 U.S. 464 (1948), the Court upheld a Michigan law that banned women from working behind a bar unless they were the daughters or wives of a male bar owner. The majority wrote, "The Fourteenth Amendment did not tear history up by the roots, and the regulation of the liquor traffic is one of the oldest and most untrammeled of legislative powers. Michigan could, beyond question, forbid all women from working behind a bar" (465). The protection of women and their exclusion from the public sphere was based in history, which was not something that even an amendment to the federal Constitution was likely to overcome. Michigan was asserting its rights under the police power to socially order the community so that unattached women would not serve liquor in a public establishment. A similar statement of what the Fourteenth Amendment *did not do* appears in *Fay*: "Until recently, and for nearly a half-century after the Fourteenth Amendment was adopted, it was universal practice in the United States to allow only men to sit on juries" (289). The role of the police power was also discussed by Justice Frankfurter in *Martin v. Struthers*, 319 U.S. 141 (1943): "the Fourteenth Amendment did not abrogate the power of the states to recognize that homes are sanctuaries from intrusions upon privacy and of opportunities for leading lives in health and safety" (153). In the 1940s, federal principles of equality and individual liberty did not reach beyond a certain sphere — they did not reach the home, private establishment, or domestic realm, where women often were regulated instead under the police powers of the states.

Goesaert joined the panoply of infamous cases in which judges took a condescending and dismissive attitude toward claims of gender equality (R. B. Ginsburg, 1978a). In their five-paragraph opinion, the Court majority dismissed the plaintiff's claim that the Michigan law violated the Equal Protection Clause. Gender classifications were presumed to be reasonable. Given that the state could "unquestionably" bar all women from such employment ("Since bartending by women may, in the allowable legislative judgment, give rise to moral and social problems"), the only remaining issue concerned the distinctions made among women. The Court credited the state legislature with recognizing the protective oversight provided by fathers and husbands. Although they rejected this analysis, the dissenters to this opinion did not reject the majority's paternalistic attitude toward women who tended bar. "A male owner, although he himself is always absent from his bar, may employ his wife and daughter as barmaids. . . . This inevitable result of the classification belies the assumption that the statute was motivated by a legislative solicitude for the moral and physical well-being of women" (*Goesaert v. Cleary*, 468). None of the justices expressed concern for the employment rights of women either. Women were not conceived of primarily as workers (in the introduction to the majority opinion, the Court refers to barmaids by recalling the Shakespearian "alewife, sprightly and ribald"), and consequently their civic membership was conceived of differently as well. Gender as a social identity precluded certain other social identities, such as that of a worker, from being attached to civic status (Kessler-Harris, 2001).

Yet there was another case in which the Court willingly applied the Fourteenth Amendment and overturned a law for failing to comply with the Equal Protection Clause: *Skinner v. Oklahoma*, 316 U.S. 535 (1942), in which the Court held unconstitutional a law that mandated sterilization for repeat criminals. In this instance, the Court did not hesitate before asserting its authority. "This case touches a sensitive and important area of human rights. Oklahoma deprives certain individuals of a right which is basic to the perpetuation of a race — the right to have offspring" (536). The classification scrutinized by the Court was not gender based, it was class based. Still, the opinion suggests that the justices were particularly moved by the plight of a male convict who faced the prospect of sterilization. "We are dealing here with legislation which involves one of the basic civil rights of man. . . . Any experiment which the State conducts is to his irreparable injury. He is forever deprived of a basic liberty" (541). With a male plaintiff, the Court recognized that a basic liberty was at stake. Yet in the earlier sterilization case with a female plaintiff (*Buck v. Bell*, 274 U.S. 200 [1927]), no fundamental right was detected. In that case, Carrie Buck, "a feeble-minded woman" who was the "mother of an illegitimate feeble-minded child," fought against a state-ordered sterilization procedure. The Court upheld the order for sterilizing Buck, which it characterized not as something that violated a basic right, but as something that demanded a "lesser sacrifice." Regarding Buck's claim that the procedure violated her rights under the Fourteenth Amendment, the Court wrote, "It is the usual last resort of constitutional arguments to point out shortcomings of this sort" (208). Instead of condemning the effort by the state to sterilize the socially undesirable, the Court offered this chilling praise: "It is better for all the world, if instead of waiting to execute degenerate offspring for crime, or to let them starve for their imbecility, society can prevent those who are manifestly unfit from continuing their kind" (207).[15] In distinguishing their opinion from the ruling in *Buck v. Bell*, the justices in *Skinner* argued that Carrie Buck was afforded due process procedures that defendant Skinner was denied. But the difference in the normative judgments in the two cases went beyond the issue of due process. It was a difference that reflected the different genders of the plaintiffs in each case.[16]

Finally, in another 1940s case, the majority was open and explicit about its use of substantive due process reasoning (in *Skinner*, substantive due process concerns were suggested but not explicitly invoked).[17] In *Prince v. Massachusetts*, the Supreme Court upheld the conviction of Sarah Prince for violating the Massachusetts child labor law when she allowed her nine-year-old niece and ward, Betty Simmons, to engage in religious preaching and efforts to sell religious pamphlets on a public street. The case brought into question the state's authority to regulate two fundamental liberties: "One is the parent's, to bring up the child in the way he should go, . . . [to practice] their faith" (164). The other belonged to the child, who was also entitled to freedom of religion. Against these rights stood the interest of the state "to protect the welfare of children" and to insure "that children be safeguarded from abuses and given opportunities for growth into free and independent well-developed men and citizens" (165).

Despite the gravity of these rights, the Court ruled against Sarah Prince, in a decision that was imbued (according to the dissenting judge [176]) with religious prejudice against the Jehovah's Witnesses. Yet as a preface to the ruling, the Court employed substantive due process reasoning to suggest a sphere of liberty around the family that should be protected from state interference. Both the Court's identification of this sphere of family liberty (what would later be folded into a right of personal privacy) and its rejection of Prince's claims reveal a great deal about the Court's thinking regarding the relationship between gender and civic membership in the decade around World War II.

As discussed in Chapter 3, marriage and family relations were traditionally regulated under state law, where they were constitutionally authorized under the concept of the police power (that is, that the states are entitled to regulate the morals, health, and well-being of their communities). The police power, in the late nineteenth and early twentieth centuries, was one of the primary means by which governments imposed social order on gender and race relations. But with the emergence of a modern, liberal constitutional order the sphere for exercising the police power was shrinking as the role of the federal government grew relative to the state. Did this mean, then, that liberal constitutional principles such as individualism, equality, and universalism would begin to govern marriage and family relations as well? Put differently, were status hierarchies rooted in common law and connected to labor and gender identities being displaced by liberal individualism? Yes and no. Substantive due process could be cast as an individual right to protect one's life, liberty, and property. The *Skinner* decision suggests just such an approach.[18] But the concept of due process liberty could also be used to reassert the importance of traditional, hierarchical status relationships in a way that preserved the significance of gender as an identity of social difference for civic membership. Both of those readings are available in *Prince*.

The notion of parental authority within the family is validated by the Court in *Prince*: "It is cardinal with us that the custody, care and nurture of the child reside first in the parents" (166). Further, the Court was quite clear in its view that it was the exercise of parental authority that was at issue in this case. "The case reduces itself therefore to the question whether the presence of the child's guardian puts a limit to the state's power" (169). Yet in this instance that exercise of parental authority was not respected. Why not? The reasons are hinted at throughout, and they had to do with the role of a mother (or, even less persuasively, a guardian aunt), as opposed to a father. Recounting the events that led to Prince's arrest, the Court wrote, "That evening, as Mrs. Prince was preparing to leave her home, the children asked to go. She at first refused. Childlike, they resorted to tears and, motherlike, she yielded" (162). So maternal emotions overcame a guardian's better judgment. Further on, the Court considers Prince's claim to be defending her freedom of religion rather than her freedom of speech.

> If by this position appellant seeks for freedom of conscience a broader protection than for freedom of the mind, it may be doubted that any of the great liberties insured by the First Article can be given higher place than the others. . . . Heart and mind are not identical. Intuitive faith and reasoned judgment are not the same. Spirit is not always thought. But in the everyday business of living, secular or otherwise, these variant aspects of personality find inseparable expression in a thousand ways. They cannot be altogether parted in law more than in life. (164–65)

Religion was a freedom of the heart, while speech was a freedom of the mind. While the Court denied such rights could be separated, it nonetheless cast Prince (and later Simmons) on the side of heart, intuition, and spirit, rather than mind.

Finally, in questioning Prince's exercise of her parental duties, the Court wrote of street preaching and testimony as "zealous" propaganda that created situations that were "wholly inappropriate for children, especially of tender years, to face." The Court expressed its concern for the possible "psychological or physical injury" entailed, and concluded that parents are not free "to make martyrs of their children before they have reached the age of full and legal discretion when they can make that choice for themselves" (169–70).

In her exercise of religion, Prince was zealous, and her zealousness led her to expose her niece to emotional excitement as well as psychological or physical injury. That danger derived partly from practicing religion on a street corner. Both the nature of the parental error and the fear of the harm that might ensue were cast in gendered terms. There is no mention of a "Mr. Prince" in the Court's opinion. Rather, there is only an emotional aunt who has left the shelter of domesticity to expose her impressionable niece to the harms of the streets. Claims of parental authority were more likely to succeed as substantive due process claims when they were made by authoritative, rational fathers rather than solitary, emotional mother figures.

The lessons to be taken from the *Prince* case, then, are twofold. Under the changing terms of federalism, the sphere in which the states governed social relations was beginning to narrow. Consequently, the federal government became more involved in regulating and recognizing social relations. It did this in various ways, including the use of social programs that rewarded acquired social statuses that were implicitly gendered (for instance, in the dependency allowances offered under Social Security). This was also done through the reformulation of status concerns into constitutional rights. The Court by the 1940s felt more beholden to the principles of constitutional liberalism, but it could still operate within these principles, while giving recognition and respect to social differences, through its particular employment of concepts like due process liberty. Due process liberty (later known as personal privacy; see Chapter 8) could mean both individual liberty and a respect for hierarchical social relations beyond the reach of the state. It was a constitutional concept that could be flexibly applied to human particularity. In *Prince*, while the Court enunciated the principle of due process as a principle of individual parental authority, it also denied the application of this principle to Sarah Prince, whose authority as a parent was undermined by actions and characteristics that were associated with her gender. Thus, constitutionally, there was a trend away from the explicit employment of ascriptive social identities in civic membership, and there was a move to employ universalistic constitutional principles in ways that respected social order and social hierarchies.

After World War II, gender was a form of social difference that could still be politically recognized and accounted for in the making of public policy. Unlike class, which was not clearly understood as a form of social difference, and unlike race, which was a form of social difference that could be recognized constitutionally only in order to be overcome, the *Goesaert* and *Ballard* cases show that gender distinctions were constitutionally tolerable in ways that other social distinctions were not. Even so, certain transitions affected the governance of gender relations that signaled a refiguration of the relationship of gender to civic membership. Traditionally, gender relations were policed under state law and the common law (particularly in the realm of domestic relations), but the domain and the norms of this legal system were shrinking with the rise of the national government and the accompanying spread of liberal constitutional principles over civic membership. Even the rules governing marriage, parenting (*Prince*), and procreation (*Skinner*), were now subject to the scrutiny of the federal courts.[19] The courts responded to the challenge of nationalized civic membership by endorsing the use of social provisioning to publicly reward certain private social roles and arrangements (by giving tax credits and social benefits in connection with marriage, for instance), and by applying the principle of due process liberty in ways that respected traditional, long-standing social arrangements.

In the days of the *Lochner* court, a liberal constitutional principle was articulated to protect a traditional status arrangement in which employers dictated the terms of employment to their employees (Orren, 1991; Tomlins, 1995; Novkov, 2001). By the late nineteenth century, it was no longer proper to regard adult working men (unless they were nonwhite) as beholden to their masters. They were citizens, voters, and producers whose liberty was at stake. So court rulings in labor cases that cited the master-servant tradition in common law became more problematic. Instead, the courts took up the principle of freedom of contract. Ironically, however, while endorsing the principle of "liberty" through the doctrine of freedom of contract, the courts reinforced practices in which workers in increasingly exploitative labor arrangements were anything but free. Only by exercising labor liberty with the backing of strong unions (under the philosophy of labor voluntarism), and by reconceiving civic membership and the relationship to the state (under the philosophy of family provisioning), could working men make their constitutional liberty meaningful. In the process, freedom of contract was cast aside.

Similarly, gender relations were moving from the realm of coverture to the realm of liberal individualism. Here, too, substantive due process liberty smoothed the transition in women's civic status by allowing for the articulation of liberal constitutional principles (once again as liberty, and later, as privacy), and yet tolerating practices of gender hierarchy in the domestic realm. As *Prince* suggests, as the principles of modern liberal constitutionalism became more pronounced, along with the growth in equal protection analysis and its application to sex classification, these developments only accelerated the need to find an alternative constitutional principle for protecting gender arrangements that the Courts and society found desirable and worth preserving.

Conclusion

After the Second World War, women were seen in dualistic terms as both rights-bearing individuals and family dependents. This dualism emerged in discussions of human rights, women's rights, and labor rights. Discussions of the rights of women internationally (see Chapter 6) ran parallel to discussions of the rights of women domestically — the ERA debate, the debate over the provisions of the full-employment bill, and judicial decisions about the rights of women workers (*Goesaert*). The ambivalence of the Roosevelt and Truman administrations over women's place in the modern liberal political order was expressed in these debates over labor rights and human rights.

Even though the United States played an increasingly important role in the arena of international politics and human rights, there was also a tendency toward isolationism and a celebration of what was distinctive about American political culture. After the war, many Americans took a renewed interest in domesticity and revived support for traditional gender norms (May, 1988). At a popular, domestic level, the growth in nationalism, and the faith that American social arrangements contributed positively to our role as a strong and wealthy democracy, worked in a conservative direction to mitigate against social or legal changes in gender relations. After a strong (but failed) effort to pass the ERA in Congress in 1945 and 1946, support for and interest in the amendment receded once more. The amendment did not become politically viable again until the 1970s.

Women presented a particular kind of problem for the U.S. constitutional and political system, since gender played a central part in the way that social roles are organized and maintained, and since the American legal and political system both recognized and helped to create those social roles.[20] Changing, then, were the terms on which that recognition and organization could occur. Instead of a constitutional system that saw women as lacking a legal personality, or as being unfit for political participation, gender differences in law and policy were thought acceptable when they were benign (that is, beneficial to women), voluntary (dependent upon a notion of individual consent or choice), or social and private in nature (emanating from the private realm, or at least situated beyond the reach of national law). Thus, gender stratification shifted out of the realm of civic status and formal legal rights and into the realm of federalism, privacy, benign discrimination (or nonarbitrary classifications), and social policies that recognized and rewarded family provisioning.

SIX

War Service

The nation's experience at war helped to reconfigure the nature of civic membership in the American constitutional order in the 1940s. Coming on the heels of the constitutional and political changes of the early New Deal years, the period around the Second World War solidified the expansion in social citizenship initiated by the Roosevelt administration in the 1930s, and witnessed the creation of new social and political rights related to war service. The 1940s was a time when Americans were extremely conscious of *both* the rights and the obligations that inhered in civic membership, and of the citizenry as a bounded community. The relationship between civic status and national identity adhered quite closely in an era when the contrast to other nations, their political ideals, and presumptions about civic membership were expressed on the battlefield. Civic membership and nationalism were tightly linked by a set of ideals regarding what the American constitutional order represented. The war experience represented itself in constitutional debates about what the nation owed its veterans; in calls that afforded women and minorities new rights in recognition of their war service; in efforts to define who was and was not an American; in controversy over what constitutional protections were owed to the people in a time of national emergency; and in international debates about human rights and social stratification. In a register intended to speak to our enduring commitments and foundational principles, the president, the Congress, the Supreme Court, and the public elucidated the changing terms of civic membership for the polity and nation as a whole.

What effect did the war have on the terms of civic membership in the American constitutional order, particularly with regard to gender? Many historians and political scientists claim that democratically fought wars increase rights claims and contribute to a further development of both political and social citizenship to the benefit of women and minorities (Kryder, 2000; Rousseau and Newsome, 1999; Downing, 1992). For example, in the aftermath of World War II, French women received the right to vote, while in several other nations of Western Europe, women's support of the war effort justified the extension of social benefits to the broader population. In the United States, World War II and the subsequent Cold War inspired and contributed to the success of the civil rights movement for both African Americans and Latinos (Dudziak, 2000; Montejano, 1987). This view contends that while democratically fought wars may not equalize the terms of civic membership for all, they provide women and minorities with new rights claims and social benefits.[1]

Other scholars contend that war and militarism are harmful to women because they contribute to a political emphasis on martial virtues. This perspective suggests that wars may deepen, rather than lessen, gendered political hierarchies (Elshtain, 1990; Enloe, 2000; J. S. Goldstein, 2001; Snyder, 1999). Indeed, these scholars suggest that wars often gender states in profound and pervasive ways. The 2004 presidential campaign in the United States was a reminder of the ongoing significance of veterans' status for national political candidates — a significance that may contribute, particularly in times of war, to the difficulties which women candidates face in mounting viable political campaigns at the national level.

These two views may not be entirely at odds with each other, and in fact both fit the American experience in the Second World War. Following the war, previously marginalized ethnic and minority groups articulated new rights claims and were eligible for new social benefits under the GI Bill.[2] For a time, it also appeared that women would be able to make new rights and equality claims based upon their war service and support. Ultimately, however, the amendment failed to gain the two-thirds support needed in both houses of Congress before being submitted to the states. Further, in the process of securing social provisioning for veterans, the nation reordered the terms of civic membership which resulted in a new hierarchy that recognized the civic virtue of the male veteran as superior to all others. Secondarily, through their association with male veterans, the female dependents of veterans were awarded civic recognition as well. In the aftermath of this war, American social citizenship and rights did expand, but not entirely in an egalitarian direction.

Looking beyond the experience of native-born women, it is important to emphasize that the war had a larger impact on the terms of civic membership for all those under American sovereignty. The war was an experience of civic engagement and sacrifice that deepened political attachments and the sense of national unity. For many (African Americans, Mexican Americans, as well as various ethnic and religious minorities), the war meant increased opportunities to make claims for civic recognition and the enactment of rights. But war also sharpened the boundaries of exclusion, leaving those who did not fit within the American ideal of racialized nationality outside of the civic fold, as Japanese immigrants and Japanese American citizens learned so painfully when they were sent to relocation camps. Given the changing role of the federal government, the shift in the country's place in the international order, and the reshuffled relationship of social identity and civic membership for various social groups, the federal government (and particularly the Supreme Court) frequently was called upon to articulate and specify the effect of these changes on fundamental values and commitments of the American constitutional order.

One of the greatest challenges that the judiciary faced in the 1940s was over how to manage the expansion of constitutional rights principles and national citizenship while still affirming the existence of certain social roles and arrangements that contradicted liberal ideals of universalism and egalitarianism. The Court met this challenge in various ways. Sometimes it enforced the principles of national citizenship and let fall governing arrangements that contradicted these principles. Such a response is evident in some of the cases addressing the civil and political rights of African Americans, where state-sanctioned segregation, exclusion, and unequal treatment of racial minorities was increasingly attacked. With regard to the treatment of immigrants and national minorities, the Court vacillated between two approaches. One approach was premised on racialized nationalism, in which the liberal norms governing civic membership in the constitutional order simply were suspended under the logic of "war necessity." Yet even here, the Court found it necessary to articulate the ideals of liberal constitutionalism, to which the practices of exclusion and detention were extraordinary exceptions. The second approach was based on the principles of inclusive pluralism, under which political allegiance was regarded as socially made and the norms of universal egalitarianism were constitutionally affirmed. Finally, in the area of gender and civic membership, the Court explicitly affirmed the relevance of this social identity to the terms of civic membership, and circumscribed the application of universalistic, egalitarian principles while using other constitutional principles to endorse and protect traditional gender arrangements. The constitutional order was an instrument in the redesign of American society in the 1940s, sometimes in ways that expanded democracy and egalitarianism, and sometimes in a manner that simply reshaped the terms according to which social hierarchies were recognized and politically affirmed.

The war not only reordered American society, it also reshaped the international system. As the war came to a close, the Unites States was increasingly involved in the effort to create international governance regimes. Within the new United Nations, debates quickly emerged about international standards for human rights, including the rights of women and racial and ethnic minorities. The United States was a leading participant in these debates, which reverberated in domestic politics. The war had made apparent the costs of using status demarcations (such as race, religion, or ethnicity) to create a segregated or stratified legal and political order. Carried to the ultimate extreme, such a system could produce policies of mass extermination of populations whose presence was found to be socially malignant (as had occurred under the Nazis). This phenomenon was the common starting point for addressing the ongoing problems of subjugation and inhumane treatment both domestically and internationally.[3] From the perspective of American liberalism, the ideals that stood counter to status-based hierarchy were the ideals of individualism and nondiscrimination. The 1940s was a decade in which a more clearly articulated standard of universalism was represented in a commitment to common rights for all persons. Yet for American policymakers it was problematic to determine where women fit into the ideals of nondiscrimination, universalism, and individualism.

Military Service and Political Rights

May only those Americans enjoy freedom who are ready to die for its defense.

> — TOAST ON THE FIRST ANNIVERSARY
> OF THE DECLARATION OF INDEPENDENCE

The Second Amendment to the Constitution asserts "the right of the people to keep and bear arms." It was a right that was also reflective of a duty — the duty to serve in the militia and contribute to the common defense (Levinson, 1989). As a right, the right to bear arms is both personal and social. Personally, it is what Blackstone called an "auxiliary right" intended to secure an individual's fundamental rights of life, liberty, and property. Socially, and this was especially relevant at the time of the American Revolution, the right to bear arms reflected republican concern with the oppressive potential of a standing army. Thus, a well-regulated militia was important for the "preservation of the entire constitutional structure" (Malcolm, 1994, 143). During colonial times, many colonies mandated that all men — white men, freemen, citizens, masters of families, or householders — should be armed and should bear their arms in public places (Malcolm, 1994, 139). Often these mandates carried with them racial restrictions to exclude blacks and Indians. From at least the founding, then, arms bearing has been intimately connected to civic status and to the political order in America.

There are different ways of understanding the civic virtues involved in military service. Virtue may lie in one's willingness to surrender one's personal autonomy in service to the nation in a time of national need. Or it may lie in one's willingness to risk personal safety and perhaps even to die for one's country. Further, war service may involve not just the risk of death but the willingness to kill for the good of the country. Morris Janowitz (1983) argues that a democratically based military (that is, one based upon universal conscription or voluntary militias) contributes to a democratic culture through "the obligation of the citizen to the nation state" (16), and through the role of military experience in providing civic education. Depending upon how military service is conceived, its civic virtues have been more or less accessible to different social groups.

During the nineteenth century, military service was strongly associated with claims for political rights, while during the twentieth century it also was associated with the development of social citizenship. In the republican ideology of early America, civic members demonstrated their civic virtue through their martial service (Kann, 1991). The civically virtuous, in turn, expected to be granted political rights. In the Jacksonian period, the ideal of the *citizen soldier* was used to challenge the property qualification for voting. Comparing service to rights, one speaker at the Virginia Convention of 1829–30 said, "If landless citizens have been ignominiously driven from the polls, in time of peace, they have at least been generously summoned, in war, to the battlefield. Nor have they disobeyed the summons, or less profusely than others, poured out their blood in defense of their country" (quoted in Shklar, 1991, 48). Democracy in military service provided a claim for a democracy of political rights. The result of this particular effort was an expansion of democracy to include all white men within the category of first-class citizens. The extension of the vote effectively gendered civic membership, thereby creating a civic membership that was divided into separate male and female spheres (Baker, 1984). The connection between voting, military service, and civic membership was sustained after the Civil War when partisanship and the social rewards of civic membership were deeply connected to veterans' status (Skocpol, 1992).

The civic status of African American men was also defined in relation to military service. In *Dred Scott v. Sandford*, 60 U.S. 393 (1857), Chief Justice Roger Taney contemplated the issue of whether African Americans, enslaved or free, were citizens of the United States. In answering that they were not, Taney cited the "first militia law, which was passed in 1792." The law directed every "free able-bodied white male citizen" to serve in the militia. Thus, Taney concluded, "The African race . . . is repudiated and rejected from the duties and obligations of citizenship in marked language" (420). Later, the freedmen would articulate their claims for civic membership rights in terms of their military service in the Civil War. As Frederick Douglass said, "It is dangerous to deny any class of people the right to vote. But the black man deserves the right to vote for what he has done, to aid in suppressing the rebellion. . . . He deserves the right to vote because his services may be needed again" (quoted in Shklar, 1991, 52). Hence Douglass clearly demonstrated his understanding of the logic of war and democracy. Voluntary military service required civic rights and rewards. Formally, African American men were granted full civic membership, including the right to vote under the Fifteenth Amendment, yet in the South and elsewhere, their rights continued to be denied in practice for decades to come. After World Wars I and II, the call for civil and political rights for African Americans was once again justified by their martial service records (Kryder, 2000).

WOMEN AND THE MILITARY

For women, there was also an association between war service and the political rights of civic membership. The effort of women as part of the Sanitary Commission in the Civil War bolstered the claim of the Woman Rights movement to extend the right to vote to women. When women finally did get the right to vote in 1920, President Wilson cited their contribution to the war effort in World War I as justification for his own belated enthusiasm for woman suffrage (Flexner, 1973). Women's war service during the Second World War is credited with prompting renewed support by both parties for an Equal Rights Amendment. Summarizing the congressional debate in 1943, historian Susan Hartmann writes, "Women's tremendous contributions to the war effort earned them equal opportunities: to refuse them their rights was 'a stain on our flag' " (1982, 130). Whether in uniform or outside of it, women's contributions to the national defense validated their civic virtue.

During the Second World War, women participated in the military effort to a greater extent than they ever had before. Some 350,000 women served in the military in World War II, in the women's units that were attached to each branch of the military. For the first time ever, and as a result of pressure from women's organizations and members of Congress, these women were awarded full military rank. The only exception was the WASPs (the Women's Airforce Service Pilots), the women's unit attached to the air force (Merryman, 1998). These women, some of whom died in war service, were not awarded military status until the 1970s. But for the women in the WACs (army), WAVES (navy), SPARS (coast guard), and MCWR (marines), full rank and equal pay were provided. There were still, of course, differences in the treatment of male and female service members. Most women were never sent out of the country. Restrictions prevented the enlistment of married women and prohibited participation of women with minor children. Women were barred from higher ranks and were not generally allowed to supervise male servicemen. Finally, the military's concern for the moral reputation of service women was expressed in policies that restricted their off-duty behavior and prevented the distribution of contraceptives or information about venereal disease to women (Hartmann, 1982, chap. 3; May, 1988, chap. 3).

Shortly after Pearl Harbor, a bill introduced by Representative Edith Nourse Rodgers (R-MA) was given approval by the War Department and brought before the House. The bill called for the creation of a Women's Army Auxiliary Corps (or WAAC, later changed to WAC). In signaling his support for the bill, General George Marshall wrote, "there are innumerable duties now being performed by soldiers that can actually be done better by women" (quoted in Weatherford, 1990, 30). Women would free men for combat, and they would bring their own particular "womanly" skills to the tasks at hand. After WAAC was successfully established, the other armed services followed suit with their own women's auxiliaries.

Military service did not necessarily reduce gender difference. Commenting on women's service within the military during World War II, Christine Williams (1989) writes, "Women and men were often engaged in identical tasks, but official military policy and the dominant ideology of gender perpetuated the division of labor by sex. Thus, women's nontraditional activities were interpreted in ways that supported a traditional sex role arrangement. This meant that women could maintain their femininity in spite of the military's traditional identification as a masculine occupation" (20). The women's auxiliaries originally were envisioned as temporary war emergency measures.[4] Even their proponents, including General Eisenhower, did not foresee women having military careers: "after an enlistment or two enlistments women will ordinarily — and thank God — they will get married" (quoted in Williams, 1989, 22). Further, the work of women in the military corps was strongly gendered. Even when women were given jobs previously held by men, these jobs were regendered to highlight women's special abilities to perform the work: "They are superior to men in all functions involving manual dexterity" (quoted in Williams, 1989, 27). While in some respects, women's military experience contributed to calls for gender equality, in others it helped to affirm the importance of gender difference.

As it had been for previous generations, military service was an important affirmation of masculinity for American men in the 1940s (Hoganson, 1998). Consequently, many of the rank-and-file soldiers and sailors resented the presence of women in uniform. In 1943, a widely publicized smear campaign spread rumors regarding the sexual promiscuity of the members of the women's auxiliaries. This grassroots campaign had such a negative effect on morale and recruitment, that the top commanders began a counterpropaganda campaign to bolster recruitment efforts among women. The women in the service understood the motives behind the slander campaign.

As Brigadier General Jeanne Holm recalled, "In the machismo world of barracks humor, where women and sex are a primary topic, military women had become fair game. Having joined what was a masculine domain, the women were 'asking for it.'" As one WAC commander explained the underlying motive, "Men have for centuries used slander against morals as a weapon to keep women out of public life." (quoted in D. Campbell, 1990, 115)

Both the smear campaign and the counterpropaganda campaign took as their premise the differences between the sexes. For some, the presence of women in the services affected not only their civic status, but the masculinity and political status of men as well (Honey, 1984, 113–19).

In the midst of the war, when it appeared that the effort would continue for quite some time, Congress considered a bill to establish a National War Service under which men and women could be required to give civilian service in war industries. Such an effort had public support. As historian William O'Neill writes in *A Democracy at War*, "In January 1942 Gallop reported that 68 percent of the public favored a labor draft for women aged 21 to 35; among women, the majority rose to 73 percent" (1993, 132). The national service bill exempted women who cared for children under eighteen years of age or for elderly parents. In introducing the bill in the Senate, Senator Warren Austin (R-VT) explained, "We have founded our political life and our social life upon the doctrine of relative equality. . . . Therefore it is necessary to declare an equal liability of all mobile men within the range of 18 years and 65 years of age, and all mobile women within the ages of 18 and 50" (*Congressional Record*, February 8, 1943, S668). Provided that women were not obliged to care for their children, then, they too could be asked to serve their country during wartime, albeit in noncombat positions. Yet this was a distinction that mattered. Austin was interrupted during his presentation of the bill by Senator David Walsh (D-MA), who was concerned about the fate of young men ordered to work in a civilian rather than a military capacity: "The impression among many seems to be that unless one has a military service record, after the war his opportunity for civic advancement, and for political preferment in the future, will be handicapped" (*Congressional Record*, February 8, 1943, S669). For men, the virtues of martial service exceeded the virtues of civilian service. So, too, did the expected rewards.

But the senator need not have worried. The prospect of women being drafted prompted the formation of the Women's Committee to Oppose

Conscription. During a radio interview, the organization's leader, Mildred Scott Olmsted, explained her opposition to the national service idea: "Woman are naturally and rightly the homemakers. . . . They play their part during the war by 'keeping the home fires burning' . . . and by carrying on the services that hold the community together" (quoted in Kerber, 1998, 249). Or, as a member of the Mothers of Sons (another conservative women's group) put it, "this bill would nationalize our women and complete the sovietization of our country" (quoted in Kerber, 1998, 249). Although the opinions of these organizations may have been extreme, many in Congress may have shared their concerns about the consequences of drafting women. The bill was not made into law.

Nurses corps also were attached to the various branches in the military. Nurses often operated closer to combat areas, and were therefore more likely to risk being injured or taken as prisoners of war. Indeed, both fates befell many of the army nurses who served in the Philippines. Some were killed in the intense fighting between the Japanese and American forces in Bataan and Corregidor in 1942. Under horrible siege conditions, these nurses provided the wounded soldiers with both medical attention and feminine nurture. One nurse recalled, "It meant a great deal to the wounded and sick men to have American women to give them the expert care their mothers or wives would have wanted for them" (Weatherford, 1990, 4). When the American forces finally fled Bataan and Corregidor, some nurses became prisoners of war and remained in a Japanese prison camp in Manila until 1945.

The need for nurses motivated President Roosevelt to call for a draft of nurses early in 1945, when it appeared that the war would drag on for some time longer. Congress responded positively to this initiative — a bill to initiate such a draft passed in the House and was pending in the Senate when victory was declared in Europe. The congressional response to this effort stood in contrast to the negative reaction that accompanied the initiative to draft women in the women's military auxiliaries in 1942 and 1943. The reason for the distinction was not a matter of the greater danger to members of the women's auxiliaries as opposed to the nursing corps. Indeed, just the opposite was true — nurses were in greater danger than auxiliary members. Rather, it appears that there was perceived to be a greater need for women nurses, and that their role in the military was more accepted both by men in the military and by the general public. Women nurses did not challenge gender roles in the way that women army or navy officers did.

Popular journals of the early 1940s are full of images of men in uniform. There are fewer, but still frequent, images of women in uniform as well. Yet what is striking about these images is their tendency to portray women nurses rather than women from the military auxiliaries. Thus, for instance, an ad for stockings in *Good Housekeeping* shows a woman in uniform and is entitled, "She's the BUSIEST Woman on the Block." The text reads, in part, "Red cross classes . . . Nurses' aid . . . Bauer & Black Elastic stockings . . . makes it *possible* for her to *do* those important tasks that women *can* do to help win the war" ("She's the BUSIEST Woman," 1944, 226). Another truly extraordinary ad that appeared in *Good Housekeeping* is of a woman in uniform in front of an airplane. It is entitled "I Looked Into My Brother's Face," and tells the story of a nurse treating combat wounded and coming across her wounded brother. The narrative represents a wonderful mixture of female valor and feminine identity.

> And suddenly we were children again, playing nurse and wounded soldier on the battlefield of our yard back home, and I was crying because it seemed so real and I was scared. . . . Out here, I've seen my share of war. . . . And I've stood it, because I'm an Army nurse and that's my job. But a nurse is a woman first. And when someone you love is wounded, something breaks inside, and the war hits home. ("I Looked," 1943, 145)

The ad celebrates this woman's contribution to the war and calls upon the nation to support her and her brother. Yet it is also careful to assure readers of her femininity (and her brother's masculinity) through the recollection of childhood gender-role playing, through an emphasis on her emotional state, and through the assertion that gender identity ("a woman first") trumps any public role. Finally the contribution being celebrated is that of a nurse (a role already deeply feminized), rather than that of a women's auxiliary member.

Once hostilities ended, women's war service was recalled by the advocates of constitutional equality as well. In congressional hearings on the Equal Rights Amendment in 1946, a great deal of stress was put on women's war service as a justification for the amendment (see also the discussion of the ERA in the last chapter). The 1945 New York State Legislature's resolution in favor of the ERA began, "Whereas they have shared equally in the pain and distress which have been involved in the maintenance of the American Republic . . . and are today participating in the battles precipitated by the enemies of freedom" (U.S. Senate, 1945a, 20). Not only was war service cited as evidence of civic virtue, it also was taken as an indicator of women's abilities. As one member of the National Woman Party testified, "During the two wars that have just come to a close no burden has been too great for women to bear; no responsibility too great for them to undertake; no hazard they have not been called upon to meet. . . . They answered every call" (U.S. Senate, 1945a, 46).

At the close of World War II, the parallel was drawn to the close of World War I and that war's contribution to the passage of the suffrage amendment. "Wars are terrible things, but they bring reformations. At the end of World War I, the women's suffrage amendment was passed and made a part of the Constitution of the United States, but women found that they had but one thing and that was the right to vote. . . . Is it too much to expect that at the end of World War II the Congress of the United States would pass onto the states the opportunity to ratify the equal rights amendment?" (U.S. Senate, 1945a, 34). Eventually the amendment was altered on the floor of Congress and it lost support. But the experience of women in the war contributed strongly to arguments in favor of the ERA at the close of World War II.

The association between military service and civic virtue is configured differently for men and women. For men, willingness both to fight and risk one's life for the nation was a clear act of civic virtue. Indeed, for men who were physically able to fight, a lack of willingness to serve in combat was a signal that they were lacking in civic virtue. Women were also expected to support the war effort, but in different ways — by supporting their men, contributing to the economy, aiding the war wounded, or even participating in the women's military auxiliaries. Yet, women's war contributions were sometimes greeted with ambivalence. Ironically, the actions of women in the military auxiliaries sometimes were regarded as less virtuous, because the presence of women in uniform (other than nurses) threatened gender standards. As the next section's discussion of veterans' rights reveals, the nation was more comfortable with rewarding the widows of servicemen than with rewarding women veterans.

Further, international norms and standards were cited by the ERA advocates in an appeal to American national pride. As Agnes Winn of the American Association of University Women noted, it was the women in other nations' delegations who led the effort to write gender equality in the preamble of the United Nations charter (U.S. Senate, 1945a, 2). Nina

Horton Avery, the representative of the National Federation of Business and Professional Women, also suggested that the nation's failure to support the ERA could prove embarrassing on the world stage. "At the United Nations Conference, Russia, Brazil, and San Domingo answered to the roll call that their women citizens enjoyed equality with men. Unfortunately, no Anglo-Saxon could answer 'yes' " (U.S. Senate, 1945a, 29).[5] Yet the purpose of citing international conventions and standards was not just to embarrass the United States into acting on the ERA; it was also meant to inspire the nation to be on the side of world history and progress. Senator Radcliffe quoted the preamble to the UN charter to suggest that it recognized the same principles of "justice and fairness as underlay this [Equal Rights] amendment" (*Congressional Record*, July 17, 1946, S9224).

The war brought into sharp relief the issue of how different nations addressed women's rights, and for many it provided an indication of the distinctions between democracy and totalitarianism, militarism and pacifism. The National Advisory Council of the NWP recalled the experience of women in Germany. "The 'Kinder, Kuche, Kirche' idea of women, coined in Germany long before the advent of Hitler or even Kaiser Wilhelm, has prevented a woman movement [from] ever rising in that most unfortunate country. This fact has, to our mind, largely contributed to Germany's extreme militarism, and the disaster which engulfs that nation today" (U.S. House, 1945a, 26). Similarly, as the hot war ended and the Cold War was set to begin, Attorney George Gordon Battle suggested that the nation was facing an important historical moment: "Certainly now is the time for the leading democracy of the world to testify to its faith in the doctrine of absolute equality so far as the rights of its citizens are concerned" (U.S. House, 1945a, 38). True democracy and equal rights should be pursued not only in the interests of women, but in the interests of the nation as a whole.

Veterans' Benefits and Social Citizenship

Military service is related to civic membership both as a civic obligation and as the source of civic rights. The rights that military service helps to generate are not just political rights, but social rights as well. Since at least the Civil War, veterans' status has served as the most compelling justification for the development of social citizenship in the United States (Skocpol, 1992, chap. 2). Yet the history of veterans' benefits in the United States calls into question several aspects of T. H. Marshall's model of the development of citizenship. According to Marshall (1950), citizenship expands over time to include more rights (first civil, then political, and finally social). Each expansion creates a more universal and robust civic status that contributes to social equality. But the history of veterans' benefits in the 1940s in the United States suggests that the expansion of certain social rights may produce a more narrow and hierarchical, rather than a more universally based, civic membership. And, of course, a social citizenship that is based on veterans' benefits is a social citizenship that is strongly gendered.

MALE VETERANS

The Roosevelt administration began giving serious consideration to veterans' benefits for World War II veterans in 1943. Several concerns shaped its approach to this issue. Administration officials wanted to avoid the experience of the World War I veterans who suffered high rates of unemployment. Further, disgruntled veterans were a politically dangerous group — as those who remembered the Bonus March of 1932 understood (Barber, 2002). Moreover, the enormous size of the demobilization expected at the end of the war meant that the administration would have to think carefully about how to manage the economic and social dislocation that would accompany this task. Finally, the administration wanted to pursue the expansion of veterans' rights within a broader context of the establishment of social rights for all citizens — a project that began with the passage of the Social Security Act in 1935.

As the administration slowly formulated its plans in 1943, the American Legion took the initiative in putting together a comprehensive veterans' benefits bill. The Servicemen's Readjustment Act (popularly known as the GI Bill of Rights) was introduced in Congress in February 1944. The Legion proposal would centralize benefits under one agency, the Veterans Administration; it would authorize benefits equal or better than those given to World War I veterans; and it would allow for the resumption of the civilian status the veterans had before they had entered the military. After debate in Congress over the extent of the unemployment and educational benefits that should be included in the bill, it passed and was signed into law in June 1944. At the signing ceremony, President Roosevelt commented, "apart from these special benefits which fulfill the special needs of veterans, there is much to be done [for reconversion and readjustment]" (Olson, 1974, 19). The administration did not see the GI Bill as a substitute for broader social welfare measures.

The sixteen million veterans of World War II were provided a broad and generous package of preferences and benefits at the end of the war, which included educational benefits, medical benefits, unemployment benefits, low-interest housing and business loans, job training and placement services, and civil service job preferences. Generous as these benefits were, they received further expansion at the end of the war. By 1948, 20.1 percent of the federal budget went to pay for veterans' benefits. The benefits made a substantial impact on the opportunities and social position of veterans. Ten years after the war, a government study found that veterans had higher pay and more education than nonveterans at all age levels. They also owned more homes (Ross, 1969, 289).

Though initially the extension of veterans' benefits proceeded within a vision of the broader establishment of social citizenship, eventually the political justification for these benefits changed. As Congress turned increasingly conservative in the mid-1940s, and as veterans' organizations articulated a logic of political obligation as the justification for veterans' benefits, a separate ideal of martial citizenship developed. Emblematic of this shift is an editorial that appeared in *Stars and Stripes*:

> Unlike our economy minded enemies, who hate to pay for the expense of a war once it is won, unlike those socialistically-minded do-gooders who would make veterans line up at a clinic along with local unfortunates, unlike the American Medical Association that has formed its trust in order to combat socialized medicine and has caught disabled veterans right in the middle, men who have worn the uniform have by that very act been placed by their Government in a class by themselves to be considered above all other classes, and as such the country has so considered them since its inception. (quoted in Mosch, 1975, 6)

Veterans were cast as a political class apart — a class "above all other classes." They were not to be confused with "local unfortunates" who received benefits from the government as a result of socialism or paternalism. The source of this separate civic status was not disability per se, but the simple act of wearing a uniform. Here we see the ideal of martial citizenship being constructed in contrast to the development of social citizenship for the broader population.

The attachment of veterans' rights to civic membership status received further elaboration by the Supreme Court in *Fishgold v. Sullivan Drydock and Repair Corp.*, 328 U.S. 275 (1946):

> The Act was designed to protect the veteran in several ways. He who was called to the colors was not to be penalized on his return by reason of his absence from his civilian job. He was, moreover, to gain by his service for his country an advantage which the law withheld from those who stayed behind. . . . This legislation is to be liberally construed for the benefit of those who left private life to serve their country in its hour of great need. (284–85)

Thus, the benefits and preferences afforded to veterans for their service were intended not merely to compensate them for time lost from their civilian endeavors, but to positively advantage them over nonveterans. Interestingly, in many of the Supreme Court cases that addressed veterans' preferences after World War II, the Court was called upon to adjudicate between claims of labor rights and veterans' rights.[6] In the hierarchy of civic standing of the late 1940s, it is apparent that the *citizen soldier* stood above the *citizen worker*.

FEMALE VETERANS AND VETERANS' DEPENDENTS

Women might have benefited from veterans' rights in two ways — as veterans or as veterans' dependents. Even with the large number of women who joined the armed forces, as a proportion of those who served, women constituted only 2 percent of World War II veterans (Hartmann, 1982, 26). Thus, far more women were likely to be affected by the veterans' dependents category. Further, it seems that the military and the public were more willing to be generous with the wives and widows of veterans than they were with women veterans. Fewer women veterans made claims for benefits for which they were eligible (Willenz, 1994). Those that did sometimes experienced discrimination in the application of benefits. Women veterans were evidently refused reemployment by many private employers, despite their employers' legal obligation to do so. In their efforts to assist female veterans to new job placements, the federal government generally directed them to lower-skilled "women's" jobs. When women veterans sought to claim dependent benefits for their own families, they were obligated to demonstrate their status as the primary economic provider in the family — an obligation not imposed on male veterans. One of the two major veterans' organizations of the period, the Veterans of Foreign Wars (VFW), refused to admit women as regular members and lobbied against benefits for military women (Hartmann, 1982, chap. 3). Finally, since the WASPs were not accorded military status, they remained ineligible for veterans' benefits.

What accounted for the elevation of *male* veterans and their rights over those of female veterans? Was it that there were far more male veterans so they constituted a more effective voting block? There are two problems with this explanation. First, why should male veterans regard themselves as having a separate political interest from female veterans? The presumption of a gender distinction itself needs explaining. Second, no American politician was opposed to veterans' benefits for men in the 1940s. There was a pervasive sense of national obligation to the male veterans. The claims of male veterans rose above distributive political calculations. For instance, in an article written for the *Ladies Home Journal* in 1944, Dorothy Thompson (who usually wrote in favor of women's rights) expressed the view, "If there are not jobs for women and soldiers [after the war], the soldiers will get them, and no one will want or dare to protest" (6). The question was merely who would be able to attach themselves positively to this support for male veterans and use it as a means of gaining support for other social groups or social programs. Male veterans were seen as having a clear claim to civic virtue and social reward. The claims of women — as veterans or as war workers — were not as clear or absolute.

Even in the original legislation, male and female veterans were regarded differently. The civil service preferences, which were expanded in 1944 to include able-bodied, as well as disabled, veterans made this disparity most apparent. During hearings on the act, Representative Charles LaFollette (R-IN) noted that while the wives of disabled servicemen were awarded their husbands' preferences, the husbands of disabled servicewomen were not afforded a similar advantage. LaFollette sought to rectify this inequity, but he faced opposition from those who feared that men might marry disabled servicewomen just to receive their preference. LaFollette commented, "Can we presuppose that every girl that a soldier marries necessarily on the home front makes any real contribution to the war effort? We know, as a matter of fact, that unfortunately some women who have married soldiers are little strumpets" (quoted in Ross, 1969, 194). LaFollette's arguments proved unpersuasive. The amendment failed and the bill was passed with discriminatory benefits for the dependents of male veterans.

A 1946 article published in the *Reader's Digest* found that women veterans were reluctant to claim veterans' benefits and that many felt discriminated against in their search for civilian employment: "In one voice the girls of the Wac, Waves, Spars and Marines complain that prospective employers completely disregard their two or three years experience in the services. Some employers even count it against them, the women veterans believe. . . . Two thirds of a group of 150 women veterans who met recently at the New York Veterans Center felt they had been discriminated against by employers" (quoted in Weatherford, 1990, 106). Employers were not inclined to believe that women learned anything useful in the services, and may have had questions about the moral standing of women veterans, given the slander campaigns of previous years. The army's official history of the WACs confirms these findings (Treadwell, 1954). Discrimination was that much worse for the African American women veterans. Given the public's ambivalence about women's service in the military, women veterans were more reluctant to discuss their war experiences than were their male counterparts in the years that followed World War II (Treadwell, 1954).

A more sympathetic attitude was shown toward the wives and widows of veterans than to many female veterans. Women dependents received a lower level of financial assistance than male veterans under the GI Bill, but many more women received assistance as dependents than as veterans. In a 1948 case, *Mitchell v. Cohen*, 333 U.S. 411, the Supreme Court ruled on whether members of the Coast Guard Reserve were covered under the Veterans Preference Act of 1944. In doing so, the Court offered its interpretation of who the "ex-servicemen" were that the act intended to cover. "Such ex-servicemen are those who completely disassociated themselves from their civilian status and their civilian employment during the period of their military service, suffering in many cases financial hardship and separation from home and family. They formed the great bulk of the regular armed forces during World War II. In the popular mind, they were typified by the full-fledged soldier, sailor, marine or coast guardsman" (418). Thus, the veterans that the government desired to reward and privilege were the full-fledged soldiers, sailors, and marines — the servicemen who left behind their families and jobs to serve the nation. The popular image cited here is a strongly, if implicitly, masculine one. Making the gender of these servicemen more explicit, the Court goes on to discuss their dependents.

> It is true that . . . the Act establishes preference eligibility for the unmarried widows of deceased ex-servicemen. . . . But the preference rights thereby granted are derivative in nature. They are conferred on the widows because of the dislocation and severance from civil life which their deceased husbands suffered while performing full-time military duties and in partial substitution for the loss in family earning power occasioned by their husbands' deaths. . . . The widows of ex-servicemen are in a special category which cannot be compared, in terms of sacrifice or need for reemployment and rehabilitation, with any group of individuals who performed part-time military duties. (420–21)

Several things should be noted here. First, this passage refers to male servicemen and their widows. So the categories of veteran and dependent are clearly gendered. Second, the rights of dependents are derivative rights, not the rights of civic members for themselves, but rights they receive on the basis of their relationship to another civic member. Third, these widows are welcomed into the job market because they have no husbands in that market ("loss in family earning power"). Upon remarriage, widows lose their job-market privileges, since there is now a man in their lives to provide for them. Fourth and finally, war widows fall into a "special category" that justifies the state's protective attitude toward them (filling in the role of the lost husband), just as the state treated women workers in such protective, paternalistic terms.

When FDR first gave his support to the GI Bill in 1944 he saw it as a part of a larger program to expand and establish American social citizenship. But instead of leading to the creation of a more comprehensive system of social security for all Americans, veterans' benefits led to the creation of a separate system of social provisioning for male veterans and their dependents. This consequence furthered the gendering of American social citizenship, such that male citizens — as workers and veterans — were the direct beneficiaries and their female dependents had derivative beneficiary rights through their men.

Racialized Nationalism and Civic Membership

War-related confrontation with diverse nationalities raised questions about the nature of American civic membership and political identity not only along the lines of gender (as suggested in the next section), but also along the lines of race. International conflict created greater self-consciousness of the American community as a nation. Confrontations with immigrants produced varied political responses, some premised on beliefs in a racialized nationalism and some celebrating the ideals of melting-pot pluralism. Nationalism is racialized both when the members of another nation (and their offspring) are perceived as constituting a race, and when American national membership is understood in racial terms. Quite typically in the 1940s, those of Japanese descent, whether they were citizens or residents, were treated as a distinct race. Regarding American national membership, the dialogue varied between assertions of ethnic and racial diversity, and an implicit holding on to a vision of the core nation as white, English speaking, and European in descent.

We begin, then, with the Court's articulation of the principles of civic membership in cases that dealt with the rights of racialized national minorities and immigrants. In these cases, the Court affirmed the nation's commitment to individual rights, free speech, due process, equality, and nondiscrimination. The justices wrote eloquently on the subject of political allegiance as something created in the hearts and minds of men, rather than as something owed on the basis of race or culture. They also celebrated the image of the United States as an immigrant nation, with opportunity for all, that is sought by people around the world as a land of freedom. Yet, ironically and tellingly, some of the most eloquent of these principled statements appear in opinions that affirm policies of discrimination.

The two cases in which the Court upheld the government's policies of discrimination and detention of Japanese-Americans both contain strong statements of nondiscrimination. In *Hirabayashi v. United States*, 320 U.S. 81 (1943), the Court upheld the conviction of an American citizen of Japanese descent for violating a military-ordered curfew aimed only at Japanese immigrants and Japanese-Americans on the West Coast. As a preface to justifying the policy on which the curfew is based, the majority wrote, "Distinctions between citizens solely because of their ancestry are by their very nature odious to a free people whose institutions are founded upon the doctrine of equality" (100). Later, this opinion was frequently cited (and this sentence quoted) in affirmations of the principle of constitutional equality.[7] Similarly, in *Korematsu v. United States*, 323 U.S. 214 (1944), while the Court upheld the conviction of a Japanese-American for failure to comply with an exclusion order, it still reaffirmed the principle of civic equality: "It should be noted, to begin with, that all legal restrictions which curtail the civil rights of a single racial group are immediately suspect" (216). So even as the Court gave its practical assent to a vicious instance of government discrimination (by a supposedly progressive national administration), there was an unself-conscious articulation of a principle that is precisely opposed to the ruling made. What does this case and this opinion stand for then — equality or discrimination? It stands for both, and for the unarticulated relationship between the two.

Superficially, such statements in *Hirabayashi* and *Korematsu* appear either disingenuous or nonsensical. Yet, rather than suggest that these justices were being somehow hypocritical, more can be learned by treating these statements as genuine. There is a deeper logic that connects these statements of principle with these practices of inequality. What is being managed here is the relationship between social (especially racial) difference and civic membership, or the terms on which individuals from any group might belong to "We, the People." The relationship between politics and social order becomes more difficult to articulate in the United States after the 1930s, when the principles of universalism become more inclusive, and the sphere where universalism is applied is expanded along with the role of the federal government (Mettler, 1998). Consequently, the grounds for legitimating hierarchical notions of ascriptive difference in politics become more narrow (except, perhaps, in the area of gender) and more indirect. Social difference itself does not cease to play a significant role in civic membership — rather, the way that role is explained and justified has changed.

Writing about the United States, in the introduction to the 1998 edited volume entitled *Democracy and Ethnography*, Carol Greenhouse contends that "the modern liberal concept of the nation-state maps a place for cultural diversity, but in ways that contain questions of diversity within the state's existing legal and political forms, as if difference is a matter for reconciliation or, even more problematically, for cure" (4). Further, she argues that when "difference cannot be resolved by law" it is cast out of politics, into the realm of "consumer choice," or it may be treated as "unruly" or "polluting." Finally, social difference within liberalism that cannot be appropriately contained within the legal and political realm may be "silenced altogether" (4–5). Even when social difference is found to be in need of political regulation, as it was in the case of the relocation camps, it may be asserted that social difference has no proper place in the political identity of civic membership. Rather, it belongs (if at all) to the realm of cultural affiliation and economic interest — characteristics presumed not to affect one's civic status or national political allegiances.

Despite the Court's repeated willingness to substantiate discriminatory policies premised on racialized nationality, the majority of the Court's justices endorsed decisions that reiterated an idealized version of the immigrant experience, and of the country's welcoming attitude toward immigrants. Indeed, these articulations were often put forth as statements about what distinguished the United States from the nations we fought against in the Second World War. In *Ex parte Mitsuye Endo*, 323 U.S. 283 (1944), the Court approvingly quoted President Roosevelt's views on Japanese immigrants and Japanese-Americans: "In vindication of the very ideals for which we are fighting this war it is important to us to maintain a high standard of fair, considerate, and equal treatment for the people of this minority as of all other minorities" (283).[8] Similarly, in *Ex parte Kumezo Kawato*, 317 U.S. 69 (1942), the Court spoke of the nation's long-standing recognition that even in times of war, immigrants should not be unjustly discriminated against. "Harshness toward immigrants was [seen as] inconsistent with that national knowledge, present then as now, of the contributions made in peace and war by the millions of immigrants who have learned to love the country of their adoption more than the country of their birth" (73). In the same opinion, the Court wrote of the United States as a "country whose life blood came from an immigrant stream" (73).

Such statements could also be made as a critique of the Court majority. In his dissent in *Korematsu*, Justice Frank Murphy wrote of the ideals he felt the Court had violated when it gave constitutional approval to the Japanese relocation camps: "All residents of this nation are kin in some way by blood or culture to a foreign land. Yet they are primarily and necessarily a part of the new and distinct civilization of the United States. They must accordingly be treated at all times as the heirs of the American experiment and as entitled to all the rights and freedoms guaranteed by the Constitution" (243). The United States was a nation made from immigration, a nation that remade the people of foreign lands into Americans, and a nation that "millions of immigrants" had "learned to love" because of the opportunities and freedoms available to them here. In a settler society like the United States, mythical accounts regarding the role of immigrants and the treatment of immigrants are given a central place in the country's nationalist folkloric history (Honig, 2001). Such accounts were validated in the Supreme Court, by both supporters and opponents of policies that discriminated against racialized national minorities. So while the principles of equality and inclusion did not constrain the practices of discrimination and exclusion, they did affect the terms by which social identity was related to civic membership.

Internationalism and Women's Rights

As the Second World War came to a close, President Truman asked Eleanor Roosevelt to join the American delegation to the first General Assembly meeting of the newly founded United Nations in London. Many believed that Truman was acting out of courtesy to the widow of his predecessor, President Franklin Delano Roosevelt. But Eleanor Roosevelt, like her husband, had an expressed interest and commitment to internationalism, and she soon proved herself an able participant in the London proceedings. Indeed, her performance there was so effective that afterward she was asked by UN officials to spearhead the effort to form a Commission on Human Rights. Two years later, that commission, with Roosevelt as its chair, produced the Universal Declaration of Human Rights (UDHR), which was adopted by the UN in 1948.

Around the same time that Roosevelt was traveling to London, the ERA was being debated in the U.S. Senate. Among the leading opponents of the ERA in the 1940s was another group of activist women — social feminists and labor progressives associated with the Democratic Party — who believed that women ought to be protected by the state and shielded from the rigors of a competitive labor market. These women sought to honor and preserve women's role as mothers and to assist those mothers who must work, because there was no man present to care for them, with labor standards laws designed to prevent greedy employers from exploiting their vulnerable female employees. Eleanor Roosevelt counted herself among the social feminists who opposed the ERA because it threatened to overturn protective labor laws for women.

Nor was Roosevelt unique in her advocacy of universal, international rights and special rights for women in the United States. Dorothy Kenyon was a lifelong advocate of civil liberties and a founder of the women's rights project at the American Civil Liberties Union (ACLU) in the 1960s. Kenyon was also the American delegate to the Commission on the Status of Women (CSW) when it was created by the UN in 1946. In this role, she fought for political rights and equal educational opportunities for women around the globe. Yet within the United States, around this same time, she actively campaigned against the ERA.

How do we reconcile the seemingly contradictory positions of Roosevelt and Kenyon with regard to international universal rights for all, and domestic special privileges for American women? Were the rights being conceived of in these separate venues comparable, or were they sufficiently different in their conception and application as to be incomparable? Were these women representative of broader trends among activist women in the United States, or were the ideological positions of most members of the leading women's organizations more coherent and consistent? Finally, what impact did internationalism have on how women's rights were debated in the United States in the 1940s?

In what follows, these issues are cast in the context of the emergence of the United States as a leading modern liberal state within the postwar international order. What I mean by that is three things: that there was in American politics a more express commitment to universal rights for all citizens within the national political arena; that the rights protected included some preliminary commitment to social security measures for citizens; and that the United States promoted its own vision of human rights as universal in the context of international affairs. Within this context of universalism, social rights, and internationalism, the debate over women's rights exposed many of the dilemmas and presumptions that contradicted or conditioned this expression of liberalism. Further, the position of African American women and the outlook of women activists from within this community suggested the existence of a very different set of understandings about liberalism, internationalism, and human rights. The various positions taken in the debates over human rights and the ERA reveal some of the tensions manifest in the transition of the U.S. political regime to a more internationalist and modern, liberal order.

Just as U.S. participation in the founding of the UN was reflected in debates over the Equal Rights Amendment domestically, so too did the debates on the ERA have an impact on the nation's participation in discussions of human rights and women's rights internationally (Mizen, 1947). Three sets of international rights discussions occurred simultaneously in the late 1940s. The first were the deliberations on the Declaration of the Rights and Duties of Man, adopted at the Ninth International Conference of the American States in Bogota, Columbia, in the spring of 1948. Second was the work of the UN's Commission on Human Rights, which resulted in the adoption of the Universal Declaration of Human Rights by the General Assembly of the UN in December 1948. Finally, there was a separate Commission on the Status of Women (CSW) at the UN.[9] Resolutions on equal rights for women formulated by the CSW were adopted by the Economic and Social Council of the UN in August of 1948. A convention on the political rights of women was adopted by the UN General Assembly in 1952.[10] Activists from both the social feminist camp and from the NWP and the World Women's Party for Equality (founded by Alice Paul and Emmeline Pankhurst) were involved in all of these deliberations. These activists clearly saw the battles for international rights and domestic rights as interconnected.

The charter for the UN, written and adopted at the founding conference in San Francisco in 1945, contains a ringing endorsement of human rights and gender equality. As Minerva Bernardino testified in 1947 (as reported in the journal *Equal Rights*), it was Latin American women delegates, whose commitment to international women's rights was established in their work for the Pan-American Union, who "were the authors of the amendment giving women equality in the Charter of the United Nations" (Bernardino, 1947, 4).[11] In contrast, the United States and Great Britain were "the greatest opponents of the inclusion of women in the Charter" (4). Bernardino went on to suggest that the reason that the United States opposed gender equality at the UN founding conference was because of the domestic debate over the ERA. Nonetheless, the inclusion of women in the charter had a positive effect. It inspired several nations in Latin America to grant political rights to women in the late 1940s. It also gave impetus to further efforts within the UN to analyze and address problems of gender inequality worldwide.

Several nongovernmental advocacy organizations were represented at the San Francisco conference. In addition to the women's organizations present there were other groups representing the interests of non-self-governing or subjugated populations. One of these was the NAACP, which sent three representatives to the conference — Walter White, W. E. B. DuBois and Mary McLeod Bethune. All three were involved in transnational networks of rights activists of African descent. DuBois had long been the leading American intellectual of the Pan-African movement, and was also the special research director for the NAACP. Bethune was the president of the National Council of Negro Women, and a leading voice in the civil rights and women's rights communities. White was then the secretary of the NAACP. DuBois would lead an effort to bring the condition of African Americans to the attention of the Commission on Human Rights (CHR). He orchestrated the development of a document, entitled *Appeal to the World*, outlining the situation of African Americans in the United States that was presented to the UN in late 1946. The federal government worked hard to have the document buried, and by this time DuBois and other civil rights leaders were beginning to get caught up in Cold War politics and subjected to red scare defamation. Bethune was among those to distance herself from the left wing of the civil rights movement (she denounced Paul Robeson after his statement at the Waldorf-Astoria Peace Conference in 1949), which included many Pan-Africanists (Lewis, 2000, 543–45). In time, DuBois was dismissed from his NAACP position, momentum was lost at the UN, and the *Appeal to the World* remained unconsidered. Cold War pressure forced the withdrawal of many civil rights leaders from transnational politics.

In the charter, the only commission explicitly named (in Article 68) was the Commission on Human Rights (CHR), which was created in 1946. At first, the CHR included several subcommissions, among them being the Sub-Commission on the Status of Women. But this status changed when the subcommission was elevated to the Commission on the Status of Women in June 1946. (This was done by a unanimous vote of the Economic and Social Council, although concerns were raised both then and later, that women's rights should be considered in the context of human rights.) After the CSW was created, Eleanor Roosevelt moved at the first meeting of the CHR (according to a reporter's summary) that "the question of equality for women be omitted from the proposed [International] Bill of Rights" (Freedom, 1947, 5). Roosevelt explained that the existence of a separate CSW meant that it was appropriate to address there the issue of gender equality. This suggestion was met with strenuous objections by several delegates, including those from India, the USSR, and the Philippines. Consequently, Roosevelt retreated from her original suggestions and moved instead to suggest that means of cooperation and coordination between the work of the CSW and CHR needed to be established.

The creation of a separate women's commission and the initial opposition of Roosevelt to the inclusion of gender issues in the work of the CHR are both suggestive events. Each indicates the degree to which universal human rights were not necessarily imagined as inclusive. Instead, the universal man was indeed (by default at least) a man. Women's rights were regarded as special or specific — they were partial and particular, rather than universal. An interesting discussion on this point appears in a speech Roosevelt gave a couple of years later as she reflected on the deliberations and adjustments that occurred in the formulation of the UDHR. Roosevelt recalled that when the draft declaration of the UDHR was brought before the Third Committee of the General Assembly, the women delegates on the committee objected to the phrase "all men" in the document (E. Roosevelt, 1995, 560).[12] Instead, the committee changed the phrase to "all human beings." Rather than asserting a more advanced awareness of the need to make this document truly inclusive, Roosevelt saw this change as indicating that gender rights in many other parts of the world were less developed, so the universalism of phrases like "all men" could not just be assumed. According to Roosevelt, the other women delegates explained to her, "we are not going to say 'all men' because in some of our countries we are just struggling to recognition and equality. . . . If we say 'all men,' when we get home, it will be 'all men' " (560). In liberal, Anglo-Saxon countries like the United States, the universalism of phrases like "all men" could be assumed, since women had already been granted basic political rights. Yet Roosevelt herself indicated, by her own willingness to exclude gender issues from the agenda of the CHR and by her allegiance to social feminism and protective legislation, that universalism and equality did not always include women. This ambiguity at the core of Roosevelt's understanding of the place of women in politics and human rights reflected a broader difficulty that many American political elites had in bringing women into liberal universalism.

The American representative on the CSW was Dorothy Kenyon.[13] Kenyon was a good friend of Franklin Roosevelt's secretary of labor, Frances Perkins. Kenyon was assigned to work with the CSW partly because of her previous work on behalf of women's causes at the League of Nations in the

1930s. The labor groups and women's committees associated with the League, it should be recalled, strongly endorsed protective legislation for women. Kenyon herself had been a vocal public opponent of the ERA in 1945, sending several letters to the chair of the Senate committee holding hearings on the issue. In her work for the CSW, she presumably endorsed protective legislation as well. But at the UN, the balance of forces now tilted more in the direction of endorsing equality for women, in accordance with the UN charter ("United Nations Commission on Status of Women," 1948). Despite its leadership role at the UN and in the CHR, the United States did not have a particularly strong presence in the CSW in the late 1940s.

The CSW clearly affirmed its call for the equal political rights for women in suffrage and office holding. At the commission's first meeting in 1946, in dealing with economic rights and the matter of protective legislation, the commission began by affirming equality ("no disability should be attached to women on the ground of their sex"), but then went on to allow an exception for maternal health considerations ("special consideration on grounds of health may be given equally to men and women and special consideration to women on grounds of motherhood" ["United Nations Commission," 1948, 8]). The phrase "special consideration" is suggestive here, for it indicates that health-based regulations, even when applied equally to men and women are somehow exceptional and apart from the norm.[14] Maternal health is more exceptional still in the context of labor rights. Yet, over time, the health consideration given by the CSW would be developed into a call for maternity benefits that did not interfere with employment rights. That concern was pressed particularly by the communist countries.

Although its mandate was expanded, and the CSW came to address civil rights and marriage issues in addition to political and economic rights for women, it gained less support from the General Assembly for its recommendations on these issues. When a convention was finally brought to the UN General Assembly for approval in 1951, it was primarily concerned with the political rights of women. Eleanor Roosevelt spoke for the United States in support of the convention, firm in her conviction that women needed more that formal rights — they needed to have their voices heard in the formulation of government policy. As she argued before the assembled delegates, "too often the great decisions are originated and given form in bodies made up wholly of men, or so completely dominated by them that whatever special value women have to offer is shunted aside without expression" (E.

Roosevelt, 1995, 615). Because of their domestic duties, Roosevelt never expected true equality between men and women ("for most women are needed in their homes while their children are small"), but she believed that far greater effort needed to be made to include women in the political process (615).

After affirming U.S. support for the convention, Roosevelt went on to address criticisms raised by the USSR on the position of women in the United States.

> [The representative of Byelorussia said] that one of the great values in the provision of crèches and nursery schools in the Soviet Union was that it permitted a woman to fulfill her role as mother and at the same time share in the public life of her country. We do not think of the role of mother in our country as separating women or denying women a full share in our public life. We feel rather that it is the family which is the center for men and women alike, and for their children, and we try to make it possible for the father of the family to earn enough so that the woman can stay home and care for the children if she wishes. (618)

Several things are striking about this defense of the position of women in the United States. Unlike her statements on race relations, where Roosevelt and other U.S. political leaders clearly felt themselves to be on the defensive against Soviet criticisms of nonegalitarian American policies, Roosevelt was willing to offer a positive portrait of traditional American gender relations. In this portrait, women were mothers and men were workers as well as fathers. For both, their concern for family determined their broader public roles. For women, motherhood was their contribution to public life. Yet interestingly as well, Roosevelt added a note of voluntarism at the end, after having valorized these traditional roles and having made public norms derivative of private norms. The note of voluntarism comes with the phrase "if she wishes" — suggesting that women did not necessarily have to stay home and raise the kids. They could arrange things differently, either by combining motherhood and work (as in the loathed Soviet model), or in the more traditionally acceptable American alternative, by substituting work for marriage and family.[15] The note of voluntarism here connotes individualism, choice, and consent, all liberal values that stand in contrast to the portrayal of women as domestic, dependent, and relational.

Human Rights and Gender Equality

The 1948 meeting of the Pan-American Union (held in Bogota, Columbia) involved a refounding of the organization as the Organization of American States (OAS). Under the charter agreed to at Bogota, the OAS was designed to be a regional organization affiliated with the UN. In addition to the new charter, the nations meeting at Bogota agreed to several treaties and declarations. Among the treaties were two formal conventions concerning the rights of women. The first was the Inter-American Convention on the Granting of Political Rights to Women. Under the terms of this convention, all the signatories, including the United States, agreed to give women equal political rights to vote and be elected to public office. The second convention was the Inter-American Convention on the Granting of Civil Rights to Women, the signing of whose document the United States abstained from on the grounds that civil rights were a state matter under the U.S. federal system. Once again, federalism was used to preserve gender stratification, while at the national level the United States represented itself as committed to equal rights for women. In addition to these two documents, the conference adopted the American Declaration on the Rights and Duties of Man. That document paralleled an earlier declaration by the Pan-American Union on the Rights and Duties of States, adopted in Mexico City in 1945 (Fenwick, 1948).

The American Declaration of the Rights and Duties of Man (ADRDM) served as something of a model for the UDHR, which was adopted later that same year. Yet despite the striking similarities between the two documents, there are some important differences as well in their tone, emphasis, and overall coherence. The ADRDM is more religious, less gender neutral, and includes an explicit discussion of the duties of persons — all things lacking from the UDHR. The first article of the draft version of the ADRDM declared, "Every human being has a right to life," a right that was specified in an earlier draft as beginning at "the moment of conception." This document reflected the greater cultural commonality of the American nations — a commonality that included the predominance of the Catholic faith in Latin America.

The ADRDM is more gender-explicit than the UDHR in ways that seem both self-conscious and unintended. There is a shift back and forth in the ADRDM between references to "man" and "human beings." The preamble calls upon men to conduct themselves "as brothers one to another." References to the rights of persons in the articles are commonly accompanied by the pronouns "he" and "his." This use of a gendered pronoun seems more substantive than accidental in the details of many of the articles, such as Article 5: "Every person has the right to the protection of the law against abusive attacks on his honor, his reputation, and his private and family life"; or in Article 14: "Every person who works has the right to receive such remuneration as will, in proportion to his capacity and skill, assure him a standard of living suitable for himself and his family" (Pan-American Union, 1948, 134 and 135). Likewise, in the chapter on duties, the Declaration cites the "duty of every person to work, as far as his capacity and possibilities permit, in order to obtain the means of livelihood or to benefit his community" (Pan-American Union, 1948, 139). The one place where women are explicitly mentioned in the Declaration is in connection with children, as the recipients of special protection: "All women, during pregnancy and the nursing period, and all children have the right to special protection, care, and aid" (Pan-American Union, 1948, 134). Yet it was also the case that the second article of the Declaration expressed a commitment to equality before the law for all persons regardless of "race, sex, language or creed" (Pan-American Union, 1948, 134). This Declaration was originally formulated by the Inter-American Juridical Committee. There were no women involved in the drafting process. Instead, equality feminists from throughout the Americas concentrated their efforts on the two women's rights conventions. In the end, the conventions (unlike the Declaration) had the force of law, yet it was the Declaration that was cited as creating normative standards for the international community and which made the gendered nature of the document more problematic.

The formulation of the UDHR involved a more deliberative process in which many more women were involved. Further, the UN was already committed, through its charter, to the principle of gender equality — a principle that was explicitly connected in the charter document to the goal of fostering human rights. Extensive discussions were held within the CHR, the Committee on Human Rights, the Third Committee of the Economic and Social Council, the broader Economic and Social Council, and the General Assembly. Within the Third Committee alone, some eighty-one meetings were devoted to discussions of the draft of the UDHR in the fall of 1948. It seems fair to say that the central item of business for the UN in 1948 was the creation and adoption of the UDHR (United Nations, 1948).

Several points of controversy engaged the participants in the formulation of the UDHR. Among these, a few had bearing on the way that women's rights would be understood in the context of human rights. One of the controversies that persisted throughout the deliberations concerned the legal force of the UDHR. The position of the United States was that the Declaration was moral rather than legal in nature. Other nations, however, such as France and Uruguay, saw the Declaration as an explication of commitments made in the UN charter — therefore, all the charter's signatories were legally bound by the UDHR. The communist nations seemed to agree with the position that the document had no legal force, and they cited their concern with this deficiency of the UDHR as reason for their abstentions when it came up for a vote by the General Assembly. Whether or not member nations regarded the document as legally binding mattered because it determined the necessity of domestic compliance with the articles of the Declaration. Article 2, for instance, states that "everyone is entitled to all the rights and freedoms set forth in this Declaration, without distinction of any kind, such as race, colour, sex, language" (Pan-American Union, 1948, 128). In 1948, with regard to both racial and sexual discrimination, the United States (and many other nations) would find it difficult to say that they were complying with this equal protection provision of the Declaration. Instead, by seeing the Declaration as nonbinding, these could be viewed as aspirational principles toward which the nation would strive over time, and that might be used to educate the American population on the importance of certain rights (E. Roosevelt, 1995, 559).

The UN yearbook for 1948 reports two critical comments from Middle Eastern nations regarding the UDHR. The first came from Saudi Arabia, whose representative expressed concern over the "the fact that the Declaration was based largely on Western patterns of culture, which were frequently at variance with the patterns of culture of Eastern States" (United Nations, 1948, 14). Which cultural patterns the Saudi representative may have had in mind were suggested in comments by the Egyptian representative. His comments were summarized as follows:

> Referring to the article in the Declaration concerning the freedom to
> contract marriage without any restrictions as to race, nationality or religion,
> the representative of Egypt explained that in his country as in almost all
> Moslem countries, certain restrictions and limitations existed regarding the

marriage of Moslem women with persons belonging to another faith. Those
limitations, he contended, were of a religious character, sprung from the
very spirit of the Moslem religion, and therefore could not be ignored. (23)

Eventually, the article on marriage ("Men and women of full age, without
any limitation due to race, nationality or religion, have the right to marry
and found a family" [Article 16, number 1]) was unanimously endorsed. But
other articles, and other sections of this same article, seemed to have a modifying effect on this part of Article 16. Thus, in number three of Article 16,
the Declaration states, "The family is the natural and fundamental group
unit of society and is entitled to protection by society and the State" (Pan-
American Union, 1948, 130). Earlier, in the twelfth article, reference is made
to privacy: "No one shall be subjected to arbitrary interference with his privacy, family, home or correspondence, nor to attacks upon his honour and
reputation" (Pan-American Union, 1948, 129). Taken together, these articles
suggest, on the one hand, a pursuit of individual rights and the treatment of
marriage as a consensual legal contract not subject to prohibitive social regulations or obligations.[16] On the other hand, the articles acknowledge a separate realm, in which social and familial regulation occurs, which is apart
from state regulation in the interest of individual rights.[17] This tension
remains unresolved in the document, and may have provided the ambiguity
necessary for these culturally diverse nations to endorse the UDHR.

The final dispute worth noting in the deliberations over the UDHR concerns the resistance of colonial powers, such as Great Britain, to an explicit
statement concerning the rights of populations in nonsovereign territories,
and of racially segregated societies, like the United States and South Africa,
to statements concerning the rights of national minorities. In the end, neither the people of the nonsovereign territories nor national minorities were
explicitly acknowledged in the UDHR. With regard to an amendment proposed by the USSR regarding the rights of minorities, Eleanor Roosevelt
argued that the amendment's "aim was to guarantee the rights of certain
groups, and not the rights of individuals, with which alone the Declaration
was concerned" (United Nations, 1948, 27). With regard to the article on
the draft that referred to the rights of persons in the Non-Self-Governing
Territories, the United Kingdom succeeded in deleting this provision, contending that "every individual was entitled to the rights and freedoms proclaimed in the Declaration, without distinction of any kind" (29). Thus,

claims of universalism and individualism were used against the explicit acknowledgment of rights for subjected populations. The implicit linkage between these groups drew sympathy and solidarity from African American activists interested in both human rights and civil rights.

The history of the simultaneous efforts in the middle and late 1940s to forward human rights and women's rights through the Organization of American States and the United Nations demonstrates several things regarding the advancement of women's rights in this period. First, institutional and political legacies mattered. In particular, the effort to forward women's rights through the Pan-American Union in the 1920s and 1930s (an effort that was pursued by U.S. feminists after they were shut out of the domestic political arena) created an institutional legacy for gender equality in international governance that was immediately felt through the efforts of Latin American women's representatives at the founding convention of the UN in 1945. Second, the degree to which women's political interests were represented in terms of human rights versus more specific concerns with women's rights did not necessarily determine the efficacy of those rights. Within the OAS, women's rights were pursued more independently, but nonetheless effectively, with the 1948 covenants on political and civil rights. The UN provided a weaker commitment in these early years to the efforts of the CSW, but the UDHR was made more inclusive and contained explicit endorsements of gender equality that contributed to the granting of formal rights to women in several nations. Third, gender traditionalism or stratification, compared to racial stratification, was considered more internationally defensible by the United States (and other Western nations) in the 1940s. Only the South Africans dared to be explicit in their defense of racial stratification in the 1940s. But the 1940s and 1950s was a time when many Western nations welcomed the contrast between themselves and the communist countries in gender relations. In articulating the appropriate relationship between gender roles, individual rights, and the political structure, Western nations defended the division between private roles and public rights for men and women. Fourth, social-movement activists may have found it easier to influence political outcomes in the context of the more open, less formed political environments of the international governance organizations. Given the importance of small working groups such as the CSW and the CHR, organizational representatives who were able to be present at the meetings and to lobby the members of these groups were sometimes quite influential. Fifth, the transnational allegiances of movement elites, their understanding of the intersection between human rights and women's rights, and their evaluation of the U.S. position in the world political order, differed for Anglo-American and African American rights activists. African American women activists tended to be less singular in their political perspectives, often aligning themselves with nationalist leaders from various colonies and former colonies, and found themselves quite critical of the political leadership of the American government both domestically and abroad. Sixth, broader international currents — including the increasingly hostile Cold War competition between the United States and the Soviet Union — shaped debates over rights in international forums such as the UN. American representatives were extremely conscious of the efforts of the USSR and its allies to use political inequality in the United States as propaganda in their campaign for the political allegiances of other nations and populations. Yet their reaction to these efforts in the realms of race and gender inequality were quite different. Seventh, later debates over cultural, or community, versus individual rights with regard to women were already present in a less developed form in this period. In UN human rights debates, references were being made in the early 1950s to the barbarism of clitoridectomy. Disputes over religious traditions, marriage age, rights with regard to divorce, and children also appeared in this period.

Conclusion

In both political and social terms, it is hard to underestimate the significance of World War II for the development of American civic membership. It was a war that remains the model of the good war. American victory in this war is still taken as an expression of the virtues of American democratic culture, American economic might, and American patriotism. It was a war that produced a sense of national unity and confidence in our nation's ability to succeed in the face of international challenges. It was a war to which all groups contributed and a war that inspired new claims for political rights on the part of African Americans, Latinos, and women. Yet it was also a war that deepened the gendered hierarchy of civic membership by elevating the civic status of male veterans, and which excluded many from the American civic community through the application of an ideology of racialized nationalism.

Ironically, then, a democratic military victory provided the basis for new civic hierarchies, in which male veterans obtained exclusive title to the status of first-class citizens.

Social scientists often speculate about the failure of the United States to develop more robust social citizenship rights and social welfare policies during the 1930s and 1940s (Noble, 1997; Skocpol, 1992). Often this literature focuses particularly on the failures of the American labor movement to have a citizen's economic status translate into political rights. Yet it may well be that such an approach neglects a more important site for the development of civic rights in the 1940s. Veterans' status provided the most robust claim for social welfare and political entitlement after 1945. When American liberals dreamed in the 1940s of emulating the British effort to establish a cradle-to-grave system of social provisioning and social citizenship, their vision included all of the programs incorporated under the GI Bill (Ritter, 2000b). Veterans' rights did provide the basis for an expansion of social citizenship in the 1940s. But contrary to Marshall's theory, it was an expansion of social citizenship that created a greater degree of political hierarchy than political equality.

This chapter has considered the relationship between war, gender, and civic membership in the United States in the 1940s. Its argument is that the war contributed to the call to extend equal political rights for women and to the development of a social citizenship for male veterans in which women were seen as secondary. Women's war contributions gave strength to claims for civic equality for women. However, claims about the relationship between war service and civic virtue by male veterans ultimately trumped those of female veterans and war workers. The gendering of civic virtue and male military service raised questions about the relative virtue of women's war service. Hence, Congress and the public appeared to be more comfortable with the service of nurses, who were clearly feminized, than with the contributions of women in the military auxiliaries.

In the aftermath of the war, the place where the hierarchy of American social citizenship was most apparent was in the division between male and female citizens. Although veterans' rights were available to all veterans regardless of their sex, they were understood juridically and in popular culture as rights that applied primarily to the men who had seen battle, and secondarily to the wives or widows they left behind. Since gender historically worked as a reliable organizing principle for the development of civic membership, it continued to be an acceptable basis for the reformulation of civic ideals at the end of World War II. The consequence for women was a reversal in the movement toward greater civic equality that had been gaining momentum in the early 1940s. This analysis suggests that civic membership development in the late 1940s proved more regressive than progressive, as the gendered terms of civic membership became more, rather than less, distinct. Yet it is not clear that this was all bad for feminist politics. After the Nineteenth Amendment, the highly mobilized and effective women's movement of the Progressive Era faded. It may be that the reemergence of gender distinctiveness in the late 1940s and 1950s helped to provide the foundation on which the next phase of the women's movement would be built.

This chapter has also included an analysis of constitutional cases involving the rights of immigrants as well as racialized ethnic groups portrayed as un-American during World War II. In these cases, the Court found itself self-consciously dealing with the United States' status as a liberal nation committed to principles of democracy and equality. The result is a series of striking opinions in which the justices struggle to explain and uphold grand constitutional principles while still conceding the importance of concerns over national security and social order. These cases are particularly revealing for what they suggest about how social-order concerns were constitutionally managed at the historical moment when the United States was self-consciously assuming the mantle of the world's leading liberal democracy. In these cases, the universal, individualist ideals of American political philosophy sometimes made it difficult to address directly the relevance of group identity for civic membership, and so other notions — such as culture, competence, or allegiance — were used in their place. The Court's opinions suggested that race and ethnicity could not be *presumed* to have political meaning, either positive or negative, but could be *found* to have such meaning if they were connected to achievement, performance, or patriotism. Further, while it was better to *find* a relationship between Japanese racial identity and a tendency toward disloyalty, under the stresses of the war emergency, such a relationship could be merely presumed. The Court responded to the challenge of nationalized citizenship during the war by articulating its commitment to liberal governance principles and finding new means to enforce social-order relations both within the American community and at the boundaries of the nation.

In an increasingly international context that celebrated human rights and legal individualism, the United States was forced to articulate its position on the rights of women and the civic significance of gender difference. Women presented a particular kind of problem for the U.S. constitutional and political system, since gender played a central role in the way that social roles are organized and maintained, and since the American legal and political system both recognized and helped to create those social roles. What was changing, then, was the terms on which that recognition and organization could occur. Instead of a constitutional system that saw women as lacking a legal personality, or as being unfit for political participation, gender differences in law and policy were thought acceptable when they were benign (that is, beneficial to women), voluntary (dependent upon a notion of individual consent or choice), or social and private in nature (emanating from the private realm, or that were at least beyond the reach of national law). Thus, gender stratification shifted out of the realm of civic status and formal legal rights and into the realm of federalism, privacy, benign discrimination (or nonarbitrary classifications), and social policies that recognized common social values connected to family, culture, and tradition. Just as the American constitutional order permitted the coexistence of civic equality and gender stratification, so too did the emerging international human rights regime embody a dualism concerning the rights of women as individuals and their gendered roles in society.

PART III

Second Wave Feminism

SEVEN

Equality

Starting with *Brown v. Board of Education*, 347 U.S. 483 (1954), *equality* became the mantra of the politically unrecognized in the United States, and the constitutional means by which groups were offered full incorporation into the American civic order. The balance was shifting from a social order in which each had their place, to a public order in which all were recognized as rights-bearing individuals. The Great Migration of African Americans from the rural South to the urban, industrial North; the mechanization of southern agriculture; the embarrassment of U.S. racial practices in the context of the Cold War; and the social impact of the World War II on race relations — all made the institution of racial segregation vulnerable to attack. Responding to this climate of change, after a series of tentative steps during the 1940s (Ritter, 2002), in 1954 the Supreme Court declared segregation of the public schools unconstitutional under the Equal Protection Clause of the Fourteenth Amendment. This declaration initiated a shift in the American constitutional order that changed the terms of civic membership for all Americans, including women of all races.

Inspired by the civil rights revolution, the 1960s and 1970s were a time when women's civic membership also expanded under the rubric of equality. The gains were legislative and judicial. Most of the legislative gains were aimed at increasing economic opportunity for women. These included the Equal Pay Act of 1963, inclusion under Title VII of the Civil Rights Act of 1964, and protection from employment discrimination related to pregnancy under the Pregnancy Discrimination Act of 1978. Gains were also made in the area of education. Women's educational opportunities were greatly expanded by Title IX of the Educational Amendments (to the Civil Rights Act) of 1972. Finally, in an effort to implement sex equality as a broad constitutional principle, Congress passed the Equal Rights Amendment (ERA) in 1972. When the amendment had not yet been secured by three-quarters of the states several years later, Congress voted in 1978 to extend the deadline for adopting the ERA a few more years. The movement to expand women's civic membership through equality was neither steady nor coherent, yet important gains were made during the 1960s and 1970s. When the Reagan administration took office in 1981 and the ERA failed to be adopted by the 1982 deadline, the era in which women's civic membership had expanded through equality measures stalled and lost momentum.

The courts were slower in responding to the calls for gender equality. It was not until the 1970s that the Equal Protection Clause of the Fourteenth Amendment was applied to sex discrimination. Prior to that time, the same court that was declaring itself intolerant of racial discrimination viewed sex classifications in law as rational and benign. Thus in 1961, the Supreme Court found that jury-selection procedures resulting in the virtual exclusion of women from petit juries were reasonable, since "woman is still regarded as the center of home and family life" and therefore may be "relieved of the civic duty of jury service" when it is inconsistent with "her own special responsibilities" (*Hoyt v. Florida*, 368 U.S. 57, 62). Starting with an estate law that favored men over women, the rationality of such arrangements was finally questioned in *Reed v. Reed*, 404 U.S. 71 (1971). Once the gate was opened, the Court moved quickly in applying increasingly rigorous standards of review to legal classifications based upon sex. The equality principle had taken root and was flowering into a constitutional and statutory guarantee that attached to women's civic membership. In a series of cases over the early and mid-1970s, state and federal statutes that contained arbitrary or invidious sex distinctions repeatedly were struck down. Likewise, in another series of cases, the federal courts upheld the Equal Employment Opportunity Commission's (EEOC) belated efforts to enforce the employment nondiscrimination principles of the Civil Rights Act to the situation of women workers. Yet, as quickly as that judicial trend began, it slowed and reversed in places, as more conservative justices forcefully asserted that sex was not the same as race — that sex differences were substantial, so that laws and institutional practices that recognized sex were not necessarily forms of unjust discrimination.[1] After a series of cases in the second half of the 1970s upheld certain forms of "benign" sex classifications, the Court's commitment to gender equality seemed, at best, partial and incoherent.

For the courts, political officials, and the American public, the commitment to equality was qualified and ambivalent when it came to women. Equality, as it was defined in the United States after the *Brown* decision, had a particular meaning. Drawn from the model of race discrimination, equality meant that status distinctions based upon immutable characteristics were not politically or legally relevant — they could not be used to justify differences in the civil or political rights afforded to persons. Grounding this belief in equality was the view that immutable characteristics are superficial, and do not constitute a person's talents or abilities. Over time, the definition of equality became somewhat more robust, yet it remained rooted in the language of individual achievement. Instead of focusing merely on legal discrimination, lawmakers and jurists became interested in instances of discrimination in the broader public realm, including the workplace. Further, the conviction that an individual's talents and abilities ought to be fully expressed and developed led to a strong emphasis on equality of educational opportunities. Yet, since many Americans remained convinced that sex differences run more than skin deep, and that women's social roles should be based on more than the pursuit of individual ambitions, there was a limit to how far they thought the pursuit of equality should go. Even among activists, equality was considered a poor vehicle for expressing some of the concerns and desires of women as citizens. In areas like contraception and abortion, privacy became an alternative principle for expanding the rights of women.

This chapter considers the expansion of women's civic membership under the principle of equality in the 1960s and 1970s. This expansion took place in three phases, which I label economic and presidential, movement based, and judicial. During the first phase, economic and presidential, from 1961 to 1965, rights advocates affiliated with the Kennedy and Johnson administrations pursued measures that would bring women greater equality in the workplace. This phase began with the establishment of the President's Commission on the Status of Women (PCSW) in 1961, continued through the publication of the PCSW's report *The American Woman* in 1963, and reached its apex with the passage of the Equal Pay Act of 1963 and Title VII of the Civil Rights Act in 1964. The phase ended in the mid-1960s with the establishment of state-level commissions on the status of women.

Those state-level commissions helped launch the second, movement-based, phase, which began with the formation of the National Organization for Women (NOW) at a national gathering of state commission members in 1966. In the late 1960s and 1970s, liberal feminist organizations like NOW, Federally Employed Women (FEW), National Women's Political Caucus (NWPC), and the Women's Equity Action League (WEAL) sought to secure the treatment of women as rights-bearing individuals in the public realm. Their focus was particularly on educational and economic equality, but extended as well to financial discrimination, pregnancy and abortion, and cultural representations of women. Many of their efforts were aimed at securing the enforcement of the antidiscrimination measures (contained in the laws and executive orders) passed during the previous few years. Their activities resulted in increased public awareness as well as legislative and judicial gains for women. By the late 1970s, these organizations had focused their resources on the campaign to adopt the ERA, which was then pending before the states.

During the third, judicial phase (which overlaps with the second) from 1968 until the early 1980s, legal-advocacy groups pursued gender equality through the courts. The first advocacy organizations, such as the NOW Legal Defense and Education Fund, and the Center for Law and Social Policy (CLASP), were devoted primarily to securing enforcement of new federal statutes, particularly Title VII and Title IX. Some of the early Title VII sex discrimination cases raised questions about the constitutional significance of sex classifications in law. Then, in the early 1970s, the Women's Rights Project (WRP) of the American Civil Liberties Union, the Center for Constitutional Rights, Human Rights for Women, Inc. (HRW), and the National Women's Law Center (NWLC) attempted to replicate the successful judicial campaign of the NAACP Legal Defense Fund that resulted in the *Brown* decision. The constitutional campaign against sex discrimination brought many successes. Beginning with *Reed v. Reed* in 1971, the Supreme Court applied the Equal Protection Clause of the Fourteenth

Amendment against sex classifications found to be invidious or irrational. This standard was strengthened through a series of cases in the early 1970s that resulted in the articulation of an intermediate scrutiny standard for sex classifications, in *Craig v. Boren*, 429 U.S. 190 (1976).[2] Nonetheless, the Court was generally more tolerant of what it considered "benign" classifications — that is, laws that discriminated in favor of women. Parallel developments were occurring in the area of employment opportunity law. Further, by the middle of the decade, the development of equal protection doctrine in the area of sex was constrained by the public campaign to adopt the ERA. When that campaign failed in the early 1980s, the judicial phase of equality-based civic expansion came to a halt.

The Presidential Campaign for Economic Equality, 1961–1965

The constitutional shift to civic equality was well under way when President Kennedy announced the formation of the President's Commission on the Status of Women (PCSW) in 1961. As the civil rights movement gathered momentum in the South, women began to consider their own position in American society. When *The Feminine Mystique* (Friedan, 1997) was published by Betty Friedan in the early 1960s, it expressed the sentiment shared by many that the role expectations for women — particularly educated, middle-class women — were too confining, and that there was more to life than being a good mother and housewife. The PCSW was formed under pressure from Democratic women activists and at the specific urging of Eleanor Roosevelt (the senior woman in the party) and Esther Peterson, the director of the Women's Bureau and the highest-ranking woman in the Kennedy administration. Both Roosevelt and Peterson were social feminists: they supported women's rights and were particularly sensitive to the concerns of working-class women, but they opposed the Equal Rights Amendment. Peterson (a former union official) wanted to offer practical alternatives to the ERA. She championed measures that would diminish inequities in pay and opportunities between working women and men; abolish the most egregious forms of legal discrimination against women; and promote opportunities for women in education and politics. Yet she remained committed to preserving protective legislation for working women, which was threatened by the effort to adopt an ERA.

One of the first measures to gain the support of the PCSW was the Equal Pay Act. Various versions of an equal pay proposal had circulated in Congress since the Second World War. Two separate equal pay bills were voted up by the House and Senate in 1962, but the conference committee that met to work on the bills failed to reach consensus. The following year, the administration endorsed a specific (more modest) equal pay proposal, which resulted in the Equal Pay Act of 1963.[3] At the signing ceremony for the act, President Kennedy stated that the act "affirms our determination that when women enter the labor force, they will find equality in their pay envelopes" (U.S. Equal Employment Opportunity Commission, 2003). While it was a positive step, the impact of the act was fairly modest, both because equal pay was defined narrowly and because most of the economic inequality between working men and women resulted from the sex segregation of the labor market, rather than from unequal pay for the same position.

A series of hearings were held on the Equal Pay Act in 1962 and 1963 in both the House and Senate. The record from these hearings offers a revealing portrait of public views about the place of working women in American society and their rights as citizens. The witnesses at these hearings included government officials, representatives of women's organizations, business leaders, and union officials. Virtually all of the witnesses began from the presumption that women should be treated fairly and equally — meaning they should receive equal pay for equal work. But in many instances, that stated principle proved to be little more than a hollow utterance, as business leaders and employment attorneys expressed fierce opposition to the legislation and catalogued numerous reasons why they felt it was justifiable to pay women less. For their part, the supporters of equal pay were somewhat torn over whether to support such a limited bill. They nonetheless felt that as both a practical and principled matter, such a law was long overdue.

The supporters of equal pay noted that more women than ever before were members of the paid workforce. The reality of women as workers meant that they could no longer be treated solely as mothers and housewives. Moreover, women's work participation created new opportunities to cultivate and utilize a pool of previously untapped talents. There was a sense, in the early 1960s, that continued national progress depended upon the development of an educated and skilled workforce. The desire to spur new achievements in science, technology, and industry was accentuated by the competitive environment of the Cold War. Just as the Soviets and their allies sought to publicize the evils of American race relations, in their efforts to win over unaligned countries to the Communist bloc, so too did the Russians portray American gender relations as antiquated and exploitative of women. As James Carey, an officer of the AFL-CIO pointed out, the "lack of an equal pay law" in the United States was "grist for the Communist propaganda mills" (U.S. House, 1963, 116). For the sake of the nation, women's work-force participation should be encouraged and rewarded: "Poor use of man-power and womanpower pose handicaps in our race against the Communist bloc of nations" (130). Behind this concern with the Cold War was a more general sense that the rising number of women workers was part of a new modern social reality to which the federal government should respond. The response being sought was one that differentiated us from communist nations in that it involved a commitment to equality and individualism in the public realm, but ongoing support for gender traditionalism in the private realm.

Other nations were also committing themselves to equal pay standards. Secretary of Labor Willard Wirtz testified that the equal pay principle was "widely accepted abroad." He noted that an "ILO [International Labor Organization] convention which sets up standards and procedures for estab-lishing equal pay" had been ratified by thirty-eight countries. Likewise, some witnesses cited international support for the principle of equal pay to suggest that the United States had fallen behind other leading nations (U.S. House, 1963, 87–96). At the Senate hearings in 1963, Esther Peterson urged that "we should not lag behind other nations in correcting injustice in this vital area" (U.S. Senate, 1963, 20). Several witnesses noted that the Treaty of Rome, which established the European Economic Community in 1957, included an equal pay provision. Ruth Thomson of the YWCA also sug-gested that the nation's commitment to international governance would be substantiated by efforts to enact gender equality. "If the United States is to make an effective contribution to groups such as the United Nations Commission on the Status of Women, we must be willing to be counted among those giving full support to measures designed to enable women to be full citizens in our modern world" (U.S. House, 1963, 298). Doubters and dissenters suggested that many European nations were unwilling to support the principle of equal pay with effective practices (U.S. Senate, 1963, 72–73), but for the most part international sentiment was cited in support of gender equality in the workplace.

As Ruth Thomson's testimony suggests, the women's groups that supported equal pay typically did so for principled reasons that focused on issues of democracy, economic justice, and human dignity. The United Church Women saw equal pay as a measure designed to encourage "the full contributions of talents and skills of all citizens" (U.S. House, 1963, 90). Doris Duffy Boyle, testifying on behalf of the American Association of University Women (AAUW), spoke of equal pay as a "democratic imperative" that was "morally just" and "economically sound" (U.S. Senate, 1963, 86). Like many of the other representatives of women's organizations, Minnie Miles, the president of the National Federation of Business and Professional Women's Clubs (NFBPW), connected equal pay to women's civic membership. Many activists still had memories of the suffrage campaign, and for them women's civic membership was a work in progress, or a goal that had yet to be reached. "If women are to accept the responsibility of citizenship, shoulder their economic load, participate in the thinking and action commensurate with today's needs, it is vital that the barriers of wage discrimination between men and women be removed" (U.S. Senate, 1963, 90). To be citizens, women must be recognized as public beings. Thomson of the YWCA, who worked with young women, spoke of the negative impact of wage discrimination on women's self-esteem. She believed that recognition and human dignity were the keys to releasing women's "creative energy and ability" and encouraging their sense of "worth as individuals" (U.S. House, 1963, 300).

Yet it would be a mistake to see these women as gender egalitarians more broadly. There were limits to their advocacy of equality, and virtually all of them expressed support for women's domestic role. Time and again, the supporters of equal pay offered a sympathetic portrait of working women as mothers forced to support their children by the death or disability of their husbands. Dorothy Haener of the United Auto Workers (UAW) reported "that women work for the same reasons that men do, to support themselves and their dependents" (U.S. House, 1963, 123). At the 1963 Senate hearings, the Women's Bureau placed three letters into the hearing record, all of which came from working mothers. One read in part, "I am a mother of two boys, 12 and 9 years of age, and have been their entire support since the baby was 3 weeks old. . . . I am tired of having my children penalized because their mother is a breadwinner and also a woman" (U.S. Senate, 1963, 67). When one congressman expressed concern that equal pay laws might displace women from their jobs, Elizabeth Johnson (who was there to represent the

AAUW), voiced her support for male breadwinners, since "one of women's rights is for their husbands to have a job, and that is often just as important, or more important, for the woman that her husband have a job rather than she have one herself" (U.S. House, 1963, 269). Finally, the most explicit endorsement of gender traditionalism came from an official of the General Federation of Women's Clubs (GFWC), who stated that her organization had no "desire to alter the traditional idea of male supremacy" (a principle she thought that most women supported), yet when it came "to the pay envelope" then "women who are working side by side with men" deserved "equal pay" (U.S. House, 1963, 134). Equality in the public realm was fine so long as it did not displace gender traditionalism at home.

The difficulties of this mixed equality/gender-difference position were most apparent in the discussions of protective legislation. Esther Peterson and other administration officials wanted both to champion equality for working women with regard to pay and to preserve those measures intended to compensate or protect women workers for their economic vulnerability and physical weakness (U.S. House, 1963, 69). Yet the opponents of the Equal Pay Act repeatedly cited these protective measures as evidence that it was legally acceptable to recognize gender difference. Further, they reasoned that protective legislation made it more expensive to employ women which justified the lower wages that women workers received. John Wayman, an employment lawyer working for the Corning Glass Company, stated that gender difference was an "indisputable fact" that had "been recognized for decades by State laws governing hours of work and types of employment for women" (U.S. House, 1963, 138). Similarly, William Miller of the U.S. Chamber of Commerce contended that female employees cost managers more because of "the many and varied laws or working conditions that apply to women employees" (U.S. House, 1963, 165). That sentiment was echoed by Arnold Becker of the American Can Company, who went on to suggest that the "legislation which imposes upon employers certain restrictions in the employment of women" made them less useful employees (U.S. House, 1963, 252). Faced with the contradiction inherent in supporting both equality measures and protective legislation, social feminists — by the publication of the President's Commission on the Status of Women report in the fall of 1963 — had retreated to justifying protective legislation as temporary measures to assist women until fuller equality was possible (President's Commission, 1963, 56).

The testimony of business leaders suggested how dangerous it was to the advocates of equality to recognize gender difference. Not only did this mean that some institutional and legal forms of gender classification were deemed reasonable, it also supported a cultural view that cast sex as a fundamental form of social identification and classification. To help combat the tendency to see sex as inherently meaningful and fundamental, many equal pay advocates drew a parallel between race discrimination and sex discrimination. Representative Edith Green (D-OR) was a longtime advocate of women's rights. She had sponsored equal pay legislation in Congress nine times by the time the final bill came up for passage in 1963. Green was also a tough questioner with a talent for exposing gender bias. One technique that Green used to help her male colleagues and male business executives to understand that gender bias was not reasonable was by talking about race discrimination. At the end of an exchange with Miller of the Chamber of Commerce, Green commented, "the reason there is discrimination [against women], by and large, is the same reason that there has been discrimination against Negroes over the century — because they are a source of cheap labor" (U.S. House, 1963, 175). Later in the hearings she expanded her analysis with a discussion of legal discrimination.

> It seems to me that the discrimination against Negroes over the last hundred years parallels the discrimination against women, or vice versa, that has existed.
>
> I do not think any woman can grow to maturity and want to enter the business world or the professional world and not be keenly aware of the fact that there are not only Jim Crow laws in this country but there are also Jane Doe laws and women must operate under them. (204)

Sonia Pressman, then an attorney with the ACLU (she later worked for the Equal Employment Opportunity Commission in enforcing antidiscrimination laws), made a similar point in more constitutional terms. She noted that "the 14th amendment" and other more recent laws had "reaffirmed the principle that discrimination . . . is abhorrent to our concept of democracy." Cast in this light, the equal pay bill was "an attempt to give women . . . some of the rights already enjoyed by our various minority groups" (U.S. Senate, 1963, 169).

Yet not everyone in the early 1960s was ready to accept this parallel.

When Representative Green pressed Secretary Wirtz about the president's failure to include sex in an executive order banning discrimination in federal employment, the labor secretary justified the deficiency by distinguishing the position of women from African Americans. Wirtz contended that "there is more prejudice in our treatment of minority groups than there is in our treatment of women today" (U.S. House, 1963, 58). Indeed, Wirtz did not think there was "much prejudice" against women, and characterized the prejudice that remained as a "hangover" or "carryover" from an earlier time (58). The "elements . . . inherent in the minority situation" were different and more substantial (58). The labor secretary also recognized differences in the legal treatment of minority workers and women workers, and was willing to make further exemptions in the application of equal pay measures to accommodate those differences (e.g., in relation to laws prohibiting women from working on night shifts). It appeared, then, that to Wirtz and others, the recognition and accommodation of gender difference should not be confused with sex discrimination.

When President Kennedy signed the Equal Pay Act, he offered the principle of gender equality a limited endorsement. Kennedy did not address whether women should enter the labor force, or what sort of equality was due to women beyond the workplace. But equality in pay for women working the same jobs as men was something the president supported. Advocates for the equal pay provision were not blind to the act's limitations. It did nothing to address the inequities inherent in job segregation. It rejected the principle of comparable worth. Nor did it create equal "opportunities for transfers or promotions" or address the situation of women who were unemployed as a result of "widespread . . . discriminatory employment practices" (U.S. House, 1963, 215). But it was a start. Rights activists spoke hopefully about the connection between the Equal Pay Act and civic equality. Yet here, too, the administration offered a limited commitment. In *The American Woman* (nicknamed the "Peterson report" after its most influential author), the PCSW stated that the U.S. Constitution contained the principle of "equality of rights for men and women," although the principle had yet to be established in practice. As a result, the Commission called upon "interested groups" to bring court cases "to the end that the principle of equality become firmly established as a constitutional doctrine" (President's Commission, 1963, 66). Until this strategy had been tested, the commission concluded, "a constitutional amendment need not now be sought" to establish civic equality between the sexes (66). The commission was hopeful that others would take up the pursuit of constitutional equality for women, yet made no commitment of federal support for that goal.

THE ADOPTION OF TITLE VII

Shortly after the PCSW completed its work, Congress took up the issue of racial equality. After defeating a marathon filibuster in the Senate by southern segregationists, Congress passed and President Johnson signed the Civil Rights Act of 1964. Most of the provisions of the act were concerned with discrimination on the basis of race, religion, ethnicity, or nationality. But the seventh title of the act, which addressed economic opportunity, was amended to include a prohibition against discrimination on the basis of sex. The addition of sex to Title VII was originally proposed by Representative Howard Smith (D-VA). Smith was an ardent segregationist who opposed the overall bill. Yet he was also a long-term advocate of women's rights and an ally of the National Women's Party. When Smith proposed this amendment, his motives were probably mixed — it appears that he hoped that his amendment would decrease the likelihood that the law would pass, but also thought it would also improve the bill if it did pass (Harrison, 1980; Brauer, 1983). Women's rights advocates and civil rights advocates were ambivalent in their response to the amendment. The administration opposed it and convinced longtime women's rights advocate Representative Green to vote against it. But most women's rights advocates followed the lead of Representative Martha Griffiths (D-MI) in supporting it. Because of this confused history surrounding the amendment, following the adoption of the act many government officials were reluctant to enforce vigorously the sex discrimination provisions of Title VII. One observer from the period reported Equal Employment Opportunity Commission director Herman Edelsberg as commenting in the mid-1960s that the sex discrimination prohibition of the title was a "fluke . . . conceived out of wedlock" (Bird, quoted in Hole and Levine, 1971, 34).

The inclusion of sex in Title VII was discussed only in the House debate over the Smith Amendment.[4] In that debate, many women representatives from both parties rose to speak in support of the amendment. Their comments make clear that these women thought of the sex discrimination prohibition in constitutional terms. Representative Catherine May (R-WA) was not ready to pass on an opportunity to enact this provision, noting, "We have been trying since 1923 to get enacted in the Congress an equal rights for women amendment to the Constitution" (U.S. Equal Employment Opportunity Commission [EEOC], 1968, 3224). Likewise, Representative Katherine St. George (R-NY) rejected the view that women had already obtained equality, suggesting instead that if the amendment were defeated it would mean a return to the days when women were regarded as chattel. "Of course, women were not mentioned in the Constitution. They belonged, first of all to their fathers, then to their husbands. . . . Why should women be denied equality of opportunity?" (EEOC, 1968, 3220). Finally, Representative Griffiths discussed the provision for equal economic opportunity in terms of the Supreme Court's historic tolerance of legal discrimination against women in employment in the 1948 case of *Goesaert v. Cleary* (335 U.S. 464) — a failure that she read as an affront to the Equal Protection Clause of the Fourteenth Amendment. Expanding on this theme, Griffiths saw the Court's tolerance of sex discrimination as part of a broader distortion of the provisions of the Fourteenth Amendment.

> When the 14th amendment had become the law of the land, a brave woman named Virginia Minor, native-born, free, white citizen of the United States and the State of Missouri, read the amendment and on the 15th of October 1872 appeared to register to vote. . . . In October 1874 [in *Minor v. Happersett*] in 13 pages of tortured legal reasoning the Supreme Court . . . said: "The amendment did not add to the privileges or immunities of a citizen." (EEOC, 1968, 3219)

For Griffiths, the desire to thwart women's claims to civic equality had been used to deform the true meaning and intent of the Fourteenth Amendment. For Griffiths and the other women in the House of Representatives (except Green) in 1964, the time was long overdue for women to be afforded civic equality. Representative Smith's fortuitous amendment to the Civil Rights Act was regarded as an important step toward constitutional recognition and civic equality.

Yet it is important to note that both the proponents and opponents of Smith's amendment were concerned with framing the issue of sex discrimination in relation to race discrimination. Edith Green explained her opposition to the amendment by suggesting that sex discrimination was a less substantial problem than race discrimination. She was concerned that the amendment would put the entire bill at risk: "let us not add any amendment that would place in jeopardy in any way our primary objective of ending that discrimination that is most serious" (EEOC, 1968, 3222). Further, Green suspected the motives of the southerners who supported the amendment: "I remember when we were working on the equal pay bill that . . . those gentlemen of the House who are most strong in their support of women's rights this afternoon, probably gave us the most opposition [on equal pay]" (3221). Some southerners were quite open about their motives, however, as indicated by the comments of Representative Andrews (D-AL): "Unless this amendment is adopted, the white women of this country would be drastically discriminated against in favor of a Negro woman" (3225). Although her tone and analysis was less offensive than that of her southern colleagues, Martha Griffiths made a similar point when she suggested that without this amendment, white women would be more vulnerable to employment discrimination once the Civil Rights Act passed (3217–19). Approaching the issue from a different perspective, Representative Edna Kelly (D-NY) suggested that rights should apply to all citizens. "My support and sponsorship of this amendment and of this bill is an endeavor to have all persons, men and women, possess the same rights and same opportunities" (3224). For some, at least, support for women's rights and civil rights were common causes.

What is striking about the debate that preceded the adoption of the Smith amendment is the presence of both egalitarian and nonegalitarian statements among both supporters and opponents of this amendment. This mix of beliefs in equality and hierarchy is typical of American political discourse and often emerges most sharply when the rights and status of previously subordinated groups are discussed together. Although the presence of such a mixed discourse is prevalent in American political history, the particulars of the mix change depending on the time, place, and specific political actors whose discourse is being analyzed. The particulars of the mix — for instance, the degree to which support for women's economic rights is seen as consistent or inconsistent with support for economic opportunity for African Americans — matter a great deal as indicators of the possibilities for policy enactments, political coalition formation, and legal recognition. The cause of liberal feminism in the 1960s and 1970s was marked, indelibly, by the Second Reconstruction for African Americans. In the case of Title VII, the cause of civil rights provided an opportunity for a major advance in the economic rights of women, even as it exposed ongoing tensions in the way that these groups were politically imagined and positioned relative to one another.

The Women's Movement and Gender Equality, 1966–1979

In the end, more influential than the Equal Pay Act or the final report of the PCSW was the effect of the commission in educating its members about the barriers of legal and institutional discrimination that women faced, and in raising expectations that government should act to remove those barriers. Many future leaders of the liberal feminist movement worked with the PCSW, including Catherine East, Mary Eastwood, Richard Graham, Margaret Hickey, Pauli Murray, Margaret Rawalt, and Caroline Ware (President's Commission, 1963). After the national PCSW had done its work, several organizations were created to propose and monitor further women's rights measures. These included the Interdepartmental Committee on the Status of Women, the Citizen's Advisory Council on the Status of Women, and the State Commissions on the Status of Women (Hole and Levine, 1971, 25). It was at the third annual gathering of state commission members in 1966 that the National Organization for Women (NOW) was born.

Following the success of *The Feminine Mystique*, Betty Friedan was commuting to Washington in the mid-1960s to do research for a new book. During her stays in DC she talked with various women's rights advocates in Congress, on the EEOC, and at the Citizen's Council about how to further the cause of gender equality. Although they were both EEOC commissioners at the time, Richard Graham and Aileen Hernandez believed that the government needed external pressure before it would respond seriously to the challenge of eradicating sex discrimination. They suggested to Friedan that women needed their own civil rights organization — a women's equivalent of the NAACP. Then, at the gathering of state commission members in June 1966, frustration with the government failure to act to enforce Title VII led twenty-eight women to gather in Friedan's hotel room, where they created the National Organization for Women. At the organization's founding conference the following October (also held in Washington) the officers were elected: Betty Friedan as president; Kay Clarenbach, chair of the board; Aileen Hernandez, executive vice president; Richard Graham, vice president; and Caroline Davis, secretary-treasurer (Freeman, 1973; Hole and Levine, 1971; Gelb and Palley, 1982).

Hendrick Hartog has written about constitutional discourse and development from the perspective of social movements. What he calls the "Constitution of aspiration" is expressed historically in the "passionate insistence of various groups that the Constitution must be (in other words, must be made to be) a recognition and an expression of legitimate aspirations" (Hartog, 1987, 1014). It was precisely such an insistence that animated the activists in NOW. Equality is deeply rooted in the cultures and traditions of America; its denial to women was seen a betrayal of their rightful inheritance as Americans. The founding statement of NOW called for "a new movement toward true equality for all women in America, and toward a full equal partnership between the sexes" (National Organization for Women, 1966). Further on, the statement refers to the new organization's purpose, which is to "bring women into full participation in the mainstream of American society now, exercising all the privileges and responsibilities thereof in truly equal partnership with men" (National Organization for Women, 1966). Recalling both the success of other organizations in the fight against race discrimination and the failure of the federal government to implement the recommendations made by the PCSW, the founders of NOW portrayed their group as a civil rights organization for women.

Since its founding, NOW has been the most visible and effective liberal feminist organization in the nation. Other organizations created to address sex discrimination in the 1960s included Women's Equity Action League (WEAL), the Professional Women's Caucus (PWC), and Federally Employed Women (FEW). In 1971, the National Women's Political Caucus (NWPC) was formed. There were also organizations aimed more specifically at preserving and expanding women's reproductive rights, such as the National Abortion Rights Action League (NARAL).[5] Within the labor movement, women from the United Auto Workers were active in supporting women's rights. They were joined in later years by organizations like "9 to 5," which promoted the interests particularly of women office workers. Finally, these liberal feminist organizations joined with older, more established women's groups, like the National Women's Party, the National Association of Business and Professional Women, the American Association of University Women, and the League of Women Voters, in promoting women's rights and political interests. All of the major women's rights organizations joined together in the effort to secure the Equal Rights Amendment in the later part of the decade.

One of the most effective proponents of liberal feminism other than NOW was WEAL. Founded in Ohio in 1968 under the leadership of Elizabeth Boyer, it was formed in dissent to NOW's pro-abortion rights stand.[6] Created as an organization of "feminist respectability" (Daniels, 1991, 584), WEAL members focused on economic and educational opportunity for women. The organization thrived in places like Iowa, where women were reluctant to call themselves feminist but were "acutely conscious of the economic inequities operating against females, and around that issue they have organized and are using every political tactic in the book to change the economic status quo" (Boyer, quoted in Hole and Levine, 1971, 96). Many WEAL members, who tended to be highly educated and professional women, were also active in more traditional women's organizations such as the League of Women Voters. By 1971, WEAL had chapters in forty states.

WEAL led in the effort to obtain equal educational opportunities for women. The organization brought suits against universities and the EEOC, seeking compliance with the provisions of Title VII. According to Dr. Bernice Sandler, head of WEAL's Action Committee for Federal Control Compliance in Education: "If nothing else we have been enormously successful in legitimating the issue of sex discrimination in the academic world. And if we are successful, colleges and universities will not only have to end discriminatory practices, but will also have to develop plans for affirmative action to remedy the effects of past discrimination in admission and employment practices" (quoted in Hole and Levine, 1971, 97). Once Title IX was adopted as part of the Educational Amendments in 1972, WEAL was active as part of the Education Task Force (an umbrella organization of sixty women's rights groups) in pressing the Department of Health and Human Services to issue regulations for implementation. As two political scientists wrote regarding this effort, "Some observers attribute the final release of Title IX athletic guidelines in 1979, which were favorable to feminists, to their efforts to obtain a contempt citation against HEW for continued non-enforcement" (Gelb and Palley, 1982, 5).

What did equality mean to NOW and other liberal feminist groups? Barbara Epstein writes regarding this period, "The idea that women should enjoy full equality with men was a startlingly radical idea then" (Epstein, 2002, 118). Equality activism did not mean political action in the traditional sense. Neither the liberals nor the radicals were especially focused on electoral politics in a substantive and programmatic way. Liberal feminists (except for the NWPC) were only loosely involved in partisan politics, and mostly their involvement there was aimed at pursuing a legal rights agenda. The NOW Taskforce on Political Rights and Responsibilities issued a report in 1967 calling for the organization to "encourage women who hold elected offices to join our organization and/or advocate the Bill of Rights for Women" (National Organization for Women, 1967a). The Bill of Rights referred to here, which was adopted at the national conference in 1967, did not include any reference to electoral politics (although it did call for the adoption of the ERA).

For the liberals, there was a modern-day version of League of Women Voters in the National Women's Political Caucus. This organization encouraged women to participate in electoral politics and suggested that the gender of the candidate mattered for their politics. Yet, the NWPC also shied away from taking substantive positions, preferring to be nonpartisan. Liberal feminists showed a strong sense of rights consciousness. They were more inclined to mobilize public opinion and to pursue judicial remedies than to engage in partisan activities. This orientation on the part of NOW suggests that the liberal feminists were operating in a political and constitutional environment in which civic membership was framed in terms of legal rights instead of electoral politics. This chapter, then, illustrates the long-term implications of the development, in the nineteenth century, of the marginalization of voting as a right of citizenship and of the creation of a constitutional order in which civic membership is understood more in terms of individual rights and less in terms of political participation (see Chapters 1 and 2).

Fundamentally, equality was conceived of by the liberal feminists as legal individualism and public personhood. Of particular concern to the liberal feminists was the status of women at work and opportunities for women in education. The proportion of women in the workforce was steadily expanding in the 1950s and 1960s and yet they were, if anything, losing ground relative to men in terms of job opportunities and remuneration. The growing wage gap between men and women may have been caused by several factors — including the growing gap in educational attainment between men and women; the demographic trend toward earlier marriage and larger families in the post–World War II period; the cultural idealization in this same period of gender domesticity; and the effects of the GI bill in providing increasing economic mobility for a large class of male veterans. Yet despite the social and institutional commitment to a traditional male breadwinner family model, in fact a rising proportion of women were in the labor force, and many of those women were the main financial supporters of their families.

Indeed, working women did not need to think of themselves as feminists in order to see that employment discrimination was harmful (MacLean, 1999). Concern over economic discrimination, particularly after Title VII nullified the conflict over protective legislation, was the issue that united labor movement women with professional women within feminist ranks. For many, the issue was one of dignity. In the late 1970s, Chicana and feminist activist Lupe Anguiano explained her desire to reform the Aid to Families with Dependent Children (AFDC) program by establishing job training programs. "I am convinced that the solution is basically to assist women heads of families in becoming economically self-sufficient so that they may be able to support their families with dignity and respect" (Bird, 1979, 32). Similarly, in an early article on the women's caucuses which formed following the adoption of Title VII, Susan Davis wrote that *"Without exception a principal demand of the women's caucuses is for respect"* (quoted in MacLean, 1999, 52).

Further, many feminists, particularly those with ties to the labor movement or the civil rights movement, saw economic discrimination as a means of dividing subordinated groups against each other to the advantage of owners and employers. When the Coalition of Labor Union Women (CLUW) formed in 1974, it issued a statement that said, "Employers continue to profit by dividing workers on sexual, racial and age lines. . . . The Coalition will seek to encourage women, through their unions, to recognize and take positive action against job discrimination in hiring, promotion, classification and other aspects of work" (Papachristou, 1976, 243–44). Similarly, a group of black nationalist women who organized in Upstate New York in the late 1960s issued a paper contending that "for real change to happen Black women must ally themselves with the have-nots of the world and their revolutionary struggles and withdraw her children from male dominance and educate and support them herself" (quoted in Baxandall, 2001, 237). In her reflections on the common struggles of women and African Americans, Gloria Steinem contended that the issue was a very old one, but one that second wave feminists were unaware of when they started. "There were many painful years of reinventing the wheel before we re-learned organically what our foremothers had discovered and could have taught us: that a false mythology . . . was being used to keep all women and minority men in the role of cheap labor and support system" (quoted in Bird, 1979, 14).

To the degree that the middle-class, professional women in the liberal feminist movement engaged in a broader social critique around the issue of economic discrimination, it was in connection with two issues: the ghettoization of women in low-paying jobs, and reflections on women's social status more generally. In issuing the call for the Women's Strike for Peace and Equality (an event held in 1970 to mark the fiftieth anniversary of the adoption of the Nineteenth Amendment), Betty Friedan reflected on the underappreciated and underremunerated nature of "women's work." She envisioned a day when "the women who are doing menial chores in the offices as secretaries put the covers on their typewriters and close their notebooks and the telephone operators unplug their switchboards, the waitresses stop waiting, cleaning women stop cleaning and everyone who is doing a job for which a man would be paid more [stops working]" (quoted in Hole and Levine, 1971, 92). As for the issue of social regard, many liberal feminists expressed their anger at the derisive treatment of working women by male employers, government officials, and union officials. The founder of FEW, Daisy Fields, described the reactions of members of the Civil Service Commission to the issue of sex discrimination in federal employment: "As soon as the subject changes to equal employment opportunities for women, the condescending smiles appear, a few jokes are made about women's socially acceptable role in our society" (quoted in Hole and Levine, 1971, 99). Or as one United Auto Workers member recounted in 1978, "As women we make up almost half the [union] membership, but when we want something, we get a pat on the head, just like they do to a pet dog" (quoted in Bird, 1979, 31).

Finally, the understanding of the connection between equality and economic opportunity for liberal feminists is revealed in their discussions of pregnancy discrimination. In a 1967 press release discussing their support for a schoolteacher who was fired after giving birth during a sabbatical leave, NOW officials stated,

> Mrs. Hill was deprived of sabbatical study pay, and subsequently fired, after she gave birth to a baby while on sabbatical leave obtaining her master's

degree at Duquesne University. NOW charged the school district has "violated the rights of motherhood, the rights of a married couple to manage its own family, and the basic individual rights of a teacher" and called Mrs. Hill's case "a serious example of employment discrimination based on sex." (National Organization for Women, 1967b)

What stands out here is the emphasis on privacy with the accent on individualism. The school district's offense was that it interfered with a couple's right to "manage its own family" and violated this woman's "basic individual rights." The stress here is not on family, or on a social concern with support for raising children; rather, there is an expectation that so long as a woman can meet her public obligations (in the realm where she is an individual) then she should not be penalized for her private responsibilities. The press release goes on to note that Hill completed her master's degree and took off only one week after having her baby. Other women's rights advocates framed the issue rather differently. Rita Elway, an Asian American activist in the late 1970s, suggested (in a rather sweeping generalization) that "Asian women aren't as much concerned with individual self-expression as white Americans. They are more community oriented." She went on to say, "For Asians, the family always means the extended family, out to the community" (quoted in Bird, 1979, 21). Whatever the merits of Elway's views on Asian culture, it is striking that for the liberal feminists of the late 1960s, rights and justice claims were framed in terms of enabling women to act as unencumbered individuals in the public realm. As the next chapter will suggest, such thinking permeated many women's understanding of abortion rights as well.

WOMEN'S LIBERATION

Of course, there were other feminist organizations besides NOW and its liberal allies. The vision of radical feminists (or the women's liberation wing of the movement) was more ambivalent about the issue of equality. The radicals were more deeply committed to ideas of self-determination and freedom. As two members of the New York Radical Women wrote in 1968, "Our demand is not for equality. . . . We are trying as women to define ourselves" (Hanisch and Sutherland, 1968). Radicals tended to be critical or dismissive of regular, institutional politics. When women activists from the new left marched on Congress demanding peace in Vietnam, some radical feminists came along as well, to "appeal to women not to appeal to Congress" (Firestone, 1968a). In another essay from the New York Radical Women, Shulamith Firestone wrote of the insignificant nature of the suffrage victory in 1920 and suggested that the vote was not very valuable for women today: "For what is the vote worth finally if the voter is manipulated?" (Firestone, 1968b). This perspective on suffrage was reiterated two years later, when radicals visited Alice Paul (the historic leader of the radical wing of the suffrage movement) on the fiftieth anniversary of the adoption of the Nineteenth Amendment and asked her to join them in giving back the vote to the government (Echols, 1989). Paul promptly dismissed the young activists from her home.

Despite their critical attitude toward political institutions and processes, the radicals retained a strongly egalitarian ethos. Their vision of equality focused not on formal political status, but on the organization of sex roles and gender consciousness. In her "Funeral Oration for the Burial of Traditional Womanhood," Kathie Amatniek (1968) spoke of their insistence that men "share the housework and childcare, fully and equally." She also affirmed the view that "love, justice, and equality are the solution." Equality, in this vision, meant the freedom to determine your own life course. "We don't seek to impose anything on women but merely to open up all possible alternatives; . . . We want to be free people, crippled neither by law or custom or our own chained minds" (Hanisch and Sutherland, 1968). As Jo Freeman observes, the liberals were focused on changing institutions while the radicals were focused on changing attitudes (Freeman, 1971). She suggested that women's liberationists shared the view that men and women were fundamentally equal, so that gender differences "demand a critical analysis of the social institutions which cause them" (Freeman, 1971). For all of their deep and trenchant analyses of the effects of sexism on human development, the women's liberationists offered a vision that pointed more in the direction of future self-help movements than to public, community-based approaches to politics. It is also the case, however, as Barbara Epstein observes, that the radicals expanded the domain of political analysis by "insisting that the subordination of women in the public realm could not be separated from the subordination of women in the private realm," so that public equality could not be separated from the private organization of social roles and relations (Epstein, 2002, 118).

The radicals tended to agree with the liberals that the issue of employment rights mattered, but their analysis of why it mattered went further in critiquing both patriarchy and capitalism.[7] In a position paper that was widely circulated and discussed among radical feminists in the late 1960s, Beverly Jones and Judith Brown wrote, "If women, particularly women with children, cannot leave their husbands and support themselves decently, they are bound to remain under all sorts of degrading circumstances" (quoted in Papachristou, 1976, 231). Job segregation and economic discrimination at work contributed to women's subordination at home. Women's work roles were cast to reflect the social understanding of them as women. One activist suggested that secretaries were "working models of the traditional domestic/sexual functionary" (Roche, n.d.). According to socialist feminists Kathy McAfee and Myrna Wood, "In general, because women are defined as docile, helpless, and inferior, they are forced into the most demeaning and mindrotting jobs — from scrubbing floors to filing cards — under the most oppressive conditions where they are treated like children or slaves" (McAfee and Wood, 1970). Writing in the journal *New York Radical Women's Notes from the First Year*, Shulamith Firestone (1968b) talked about women's double duty and the gendered nature of work. Regarding the effect of work on status within families, she noted that working wives "are still considered to be 'helping out.' And when they come home, there's still the housework to do, the child care, the cooking of supper." Liberal feminists tended to separate out the private realm from politics, or call for equal domestic relations as a means of insuring women's public equality. In contrast, the radicals saw the private realm as a place that was often the source of women's subordination, and looked at the public economic realm as an extension or reflection of that private structure of inequality.

The relationship between work and status was influenced not only by gender but also by race. The National Black Feminist Organization (NBFO, formed in 1973) recalled that African American women in the United States had always worked, but were not always appreciated for it: "The black woman has had to be strong, yet we are persecuted for having survived" (National Black Feminist Organization, 1973). Speaking to men in the black liberation movement, they sought to contribute to that effort by "encouraging *all* of the talents and creativities of black women to emerge, strong and beautiful, not to feel guilty or divisive, and assume positions of leadership and honor in the black community" (National Black Feminist Organization, 1973). Black feminists also raised the issue of class relations between middle-class white women and working-class black women: "With the help of the

Black woman, the white woman had free time from mother and housewife responsibilities and could escape her domestic prison overseen by the white male" (quoted in Baxandall, 2001, 236). A young Maxine Waters (then a California Assembly member) wrote in the 1970s about the reason that many African American women were unfamiliar with the virtues of feminism. "When black women ask me about feminism, I explain its importance for them. I tell them that you don't feel sex discrimination until you start moving up the ladder, and competing for jobs that men want" (quoted in Bird, 1979, 24). For African American women, the relationship between work and structures of subordination was figured quite differently than for native-born white women. Black women worked in low-wage jobs, and were sometimes criticized for the strength and independence this gave them relative to black men; their work relations often involved hierarchical relations with white middle-class women; and the effect of *sex* (as opposed to race) discrimination was something felt more clearly only after they had advanced to more desirable employment positions.

The importance of consciousness raising to the women's liberation movement in the 1970s is revealing for the movement at a whole. Overall, the mantra of the liberals was equality and public-realm individualism. It was a philosophy and a program that was limiting to the extent that it failed to grapple with the meaning of gender. Consciousness raising and personal politics spoke to the desire on the part of the radicals to understand the meaning of gender and the nature of a gendered system of social relations (Sarachild, 1978). Consciousness raising developed out of a sense that "scientific" knowledge about women and gender was biased, and that women would learn more about their situations if they tested facts and beliefs against personal experiences. Its use signaled that gender inequality and hierarchy had to be challenged at a deeper level, since ideas about gender roles and differences were justified with appeals to nature, custom, and tradition. Dislodging such beliefs required casting off understandings of oneself and of human nature that had been cultivated since birth. Liberals avoided these issues by treating women as people who lacked a sex (in public), or by disavowing the political relevance of areas of life where gender difference persisted. Radicals took a different, more social psychological approach that sought not to deny but to critically examine the nature of gender. Both of these approaches brought many positive gains in the form of new legal rights and a new social awareness about gender that expanded the range of social roles available to men and women. Yet somewhere in the space between these approaches, a set of political possibilities was lost. For NOW and its allies, the loss was expressed in their struggles with the restrictions of liberal individualism (seen, for instance, in the pregnancy cases). For the radicals, the struggle came in the effort to become politically relevant to governing institutions and in the fight against the tendency (often born from political exhaustion) of feminists to retreat into the culture of self-help.

THE EQUAL RIGHTS AMENDMENT

After the Second World War, the campaign for the ERA languished, and the last congressional hearings on the amendment were held in 1956. The campaign was revived in the 1970s, after the application of Title VII in the late 1960s had invalidated sex-specific protective labor laws. In 1970, the Senate held hearings on the Equal Rights Amendment. After the ERA passed both houses of Congress in 1972, both the AFL-CIO and the YWCA reversed their historic stances on the measure and declared their support for the amendment. The effort to secure the ERA brought together all of the major women's rights organizations during the 1970s.

Despite a great deal of initial support and enthusiasm for the ERA (twenty-two states endorsed the amendment by the end of 1972), the emergence of a rigorous countercampaign (led by Phyllis Schlafly) effectively slowed and eventually halted progress toward the amendment. By 1976, ERA advocates were combating efforts to rescind previously passed approvals of the amendment by the state legislatures. An extension of the period for states to consider the amendment was passed by Congress in 1978, but by 1982 the adoption effort still fell several states short of the three-quarters of states needed to amend the Constitution. That final defeat, coming as it did midway through President Ronald Reagan's first term in office, signaled the end of second wave feminism as a grassroots political movement.[8]

In opening the Senate hearings on the ERA in 1970, Birch Bayh (D-IN) offered his vision of the purpose behind the amendment: "This amendment would outlaw discrimination on account of sex in the same manner and to the same extent that we prohibited discrimination on account of race, religion or national origin in the 14th amendment 100 years ago. This amendment is a sorely needed step in striking down laws still on the books that deny more than half our population the right of first-class citizenship" (U.S.

Senate, 1970a, 1). The failure to fully include and protect women in the Fourteenth Amendment would finally be corrected by the ERA.

Just as the Fourteenth Amendment had denied women recognition as full civic members, likewise the Nineteenth Amendment had fallen short of its promise as an instrument of civic equality. Senator Charles Goodell of New York recalled, "At the time this amendment was passed, it was assumed that a general revision of the laws and practices would follow, ending discrimination against women. Unfortunately, reality has contradicted that optimistic assumption" (U.S. Senate, 1970a, 46). In the case of the Fourteenth Amendment, the principle of equality was not extended to the class of women. In the case of the Nineteenth Amendment, women's equality was asserted, but only in the limited realm of suffrage. Whether the issue was with the text of these amendments or the interpretations given to them by the Supreme Court, neither had proven to be useful vehicles in allowing women "to be treated as whole citizens" (27), in the words of Representative Florence Dwyer (R-NJ).

But others had doubts about the need for a new amendment. By 1970, representatives and senators were not likely to question the principle of constitutional equality, yet they did suggest that the constitutional arsenal was already well-enough stocked to achieve that end. As Senator Sam Ervin (D-SC) stated in his floor speech, given the "equal protection clause of the fourteenth amendment," a "good case can be made for the proposition that it is not necessary to resort to a constitutional amendment to abolish state laws which make unfair discriminations between men and women in employment or any other sphere of life" (U.S. Senate, 1970b, 3). Likewise, Senator Cook (D-HI) suggested that Congress could use the statutory authority granted to it under Section 5 of the Fourteenth Amendment, "to enact equal rights for women through means other than a constitutional amendment" (U.S. Senate, 1970a, 53).[9] Public-realm equality was already constitutionally available. Ervin, however, made clear that the guarantee of equality under the Fourteenth Amendment would, and should, be limited: "To be sure, the equal protection clause may not satisfy the extreme demands of a few advocates of the equal rights amendment who would convert men and women into beings not only equal but alike, and grant them identical rights and impose upon them identical duties in all the relationships and undertakings of life" (U.S. Senate, 1970b, 3). Identical rights and duties in all spheres of life was a bit too much equality for this senator's tastes.

Indeed, Ervin was right in suspecting that the advocates of the ERA were skeptical of the prospect of achieving civic equality through the Fourteenth Amendment. Representative Martha Griffiths acknowledged that it was "possible for the courts of this country to interpret the Constitution to make an equal rights amendment" (U.S. Senate, 1970a, 22), yet she doubted it would ever happen. Testifying just a few months before the *Reed* ruling, she noted that "no woman litigant has ever stood up before the Supreme Court and successfully argued that she is entitled to the equal protection" (22). Similarly, Representative Shirley Chisholm (D-NY) explained her pessimism by highlighting women's absence from the constitutional text: "While the Constitution mentioned Black Americans only in the negative term of three-fourths of a man, at least it did refer to them. It does not refer to the inherent rights of women at all" (33). Advocates of the ERA did not feel that the Constitution had historically provided much hope for women seeking full civic rights. Nor did they think that justices charged with interpreting the Constitution were likely to change that any time soon.

By the time of the extension hearings in 1978, it was clear that the Equal Protection Clause was available as a means of furthering the civic equality of women. Noting the line of cases that began with *Reed v. Reed*, Professor Thomas Emerson of Yale Law School commented, "I think the Supreme Court is being educated. I think the whole equal rights movement has had an impact, not only on the Court, but on the legislatures" (U.S. Senate, 1978, 77). Despite these advances, however, as Senator Edward Brooke of Massachusetts stated, "these enlightened measures have certainly not eliminated many of the discriminatory laws which remain on the books" (49). In particular, several witnesses pointed to the opinion of Justice Powell regarding sex classifications in the *Bakke* case (*Regents of University of California v. Bakke*, 438 U.S. 265 [1978]): "The Court has never viewed such classification as inherently suspect or as comparable to racial or ethnic classifications for the purpose of equal protection analysis" (291). As Assistant Attorney General Patricia Wald summarized, "The evolution of the 14th amendment, as it applies to women's rights, is in the eyes of many proponents of the amendment unsatisfactory and has [created] uncertainty. It is not just a question of application, but it is a question of the standard by which the court will look at sex difference" (76). Further, it was apparent that the Court was waiting for members of the public to decide how much sex equality was appropriate through their deliberations on the Equal Rights Amendment.

Ironically, the efforts of social-movement advocates to enshrine sex equality in the Constitution may have contributed to the Court's hesitation to move forward to extending the Equal Protection Clause to issues of sex discrimination. By the time the amendment drive failed in the early 1980s, Ronald Reagan was president and the push for formal legal equality for women had lost much of its momentum.

Constitutional Equality, 1971–1981

In those years women citizens framed their demands for social equality as legal demands.

— LINDA KERBER, "WRITING FEMINIST JUSTICE"

The Supreme Court did not take up constitutional equality for women until the 1970s. Prior to that time, legal equality was pursued particularly in the context of employment discrimination cases. Some of these early Title VII cases had constitutional implications, and suggest to us now that by the early 1970s there was a court-centered constitutional dialogue about women's civic place. Participants in this dialogue included state courts, lower-level federal courts, legal advocates affiliated with various women's rights and social justice organizations, officials from the executive branch (particularly those working with the EEOC), and, finally, the Supreme Court itself. Together, they created what Julie Novkov (2001) calls a "node of conflict," in which an institutionally structured contest was occurring over the development of constitutional doctrine. Yet the vision and articulation of women's constitutional place by some members of this discursive community (particularly the actors connected with the legal-advocacy organizations) was only taken up in a fractured and limited way by the community's most authoritative institutional actor — the Supreme Court.

This section considers the actors and activities that constituted the discursive community centered on the effort to achieve legal equality for women. The first part of this section examines the early Title VII cases from the late 1960s and early 1970s. These cases reveal the impact that changing public sentiments and social-movement actors were having in promoting a new understanding of women's civic place. They also expose the growing awareness within the legal community of the need for a new constitutional doctrine on women's civic rights and responsibilities. The next part of this section is devoted to a discussion of Supreme Court cases that addressed women's constitutional equality in the 1970s, starting with *Reed v. Reed*, cases that reveal the nature and limits of constitutional equality when it was applied to sex classifications. The third part of this section looks at the organizations that were formed to advance gender equity through the courts. Over the course of the decade, these organizations became increasingly aware of the constraints they faced in operating on the strategic landscape of constitutional doctrine that was applied to sex discrimination. While they pressed to reformulate that doctrine in a more positive direction, they also lamented the incoherent and modest changes that were emerging from the Supreme Court's decisions. By the late 1970s, many had directed their energies to the adoption of an Equal Rights Amendment.

TITLE VII CASES

In the early 1960s, Velma Mengelkoch worked for North American Aviation, a California-based company. When Mengelkoch applied for promotions and overtime work, she discovered that she was ineligible for these opportunities because she was a woman. Mengelkoch sued the company in 1965, alleging violation of Title VII as well as the Equal Protection and Due Process Clauses of the Fourteenth Amendment. The company responded by claiming that it was merely complying with the state's labor laws — which at the time included a provision restricting women to a maximum of eight work hours per day and forty-eight hours per week. The lower federal courts dismissed the case, claiming lack of jurisdiction. Eventually the Supreme Court sent the case back to the lower courts for reconsideration. Upon rehearing, the case made its way to the Ninth Circuit Court of Appeals, which issued an opinion in 1971 (*Mengelkoch v. Industrial Welfare Commission*, 442 F.2d 1119). In considering this case, the appellate court was forced to grapple with Supreme Court precedents that endorsed government paternalism toward women.

The *Mengelkoch* case was also one of the first sex discrimination complaints considered by the EEOC. It was a difficult case for the commission because it forced the commissioners to confront the impact of Title VII on state protective labor laws for women. Both the courts and the EEOC were hampered by the limited floor discussion over the addition of sex to Title

VII during the congressional debates over the act. Aileen Hernandez was the EEOC commissioner assigned to consider the complaint. According the 1966 *Feminist Chronicles* chronology of the movement, in fall 1965 Hernandez "found 'reasonable cause' to believe Mengelkoch was discriminated against by her employer's adherence to state law" (*Feminist Chronicles*, 1995). But when the case came before the full commission, Hernandez's finding was set aside. On a split vote, the commission decided not to pursue the complaint further. Frustrated with the commission's treatment of sex discrimination complaints, Hernandez resigned her position as a commissioner on the EEOC. After she left government service, Hernandez went on to help found NOW, where she became the organization's second president after Betty Friedan stepped down. Meanwhile, under pressure from NOW and other organizations, the EEOC eventually came to recognize that sex-based protective labor legislation contradicted the terms of Title VII.

By the time the *Mengelkoch* case reached the Ninth Circuit, several other Title VII cases had been decided. These cases (discussed below) indicate a growing willingness by the courts to set aside previously accepted practices of protection and paternalism toward women workers. Such paternalistic attitudes had long been encoded in constitutional doctrine. Noting the existence of several Supreme Court opinions from the first half of twentieth century that explicitly endorsed treating women as more dependent and less capable than men, the federal courts in the late 1960s and early 1970s were forced to contend with changing social understandings of men's and women's capabilities and roles.

After Title VII passed, when companies and states sought to defend the application of sex-based protective labor legislation to limit women's hours and job functions, they did so by citing the provision in Title VII that allows for an exception to the nondiscrimination rule in instances of bona fide occupational qualifications (BFOQ).[10] So, in the late 1960s, both the courts and the EEOC were forced to decide whether these laws and rules constituted a BFOQ exception, and the courts, earlier and more firmly than the EEOC, said they did not. In *Rosenfeld v. Southern Pacific Co.*, 293 F. Supp. 1219 (C.D. Cal. 1968), the district court ruled that the California hours and weights legislation did not create or constitute a BFOQ, finding instead that the legislation discriminated against women on account of sex. Similarly, in *Bowe v. Colgate-Palmolive Co.*, 416 F.2d 711 (7th Cir. 1969), the court held that weight-lifting qualifications for jobs could be retained only if it was applied to both men and women on the basis of a "highly individualized test" designed to consider the "individual qualifications" of the employee.

The Title VII case that was a rallying point for feminists was the case of Lorena Weeks, who had applied for a position as a switchman for the phone company and was turned away because of her sex. She then complained to the EEOC, and eventually sued the company for violation of Title VII. Given the rigorous physical demands of the job, the company claimed that the exclusion of women from this position constituted a legitimate BFOQ exception. The court disagreed. In *Weeks v. Southern Bell Telephone and Telegraph Co.*, 408 F.2d 228 (5th Cir. 1969), it found that "the burden of proof must be on Southern Bell" to show this was a legitimate BFOQ, since the "legislative history indicates that this exception was intended to be narrowly construed" (232). Further, the court voiced principled support for Weeks. "Finally, when dealing with a humanitarian remedial statute which serves an important public purpose, it has been the practice to cast the burden of proving an exception to the general policy of the statute upon the person claiming it" (232). Despite her victory in court, Weeks and her supporters would spend several more years seeking full compliance from the company, with the court's order.

As time went on, the courts only became more pronounced in their articulation of the nondiscrimination principle, and more restrictive in their willingness to grant sex-based BFOQ exceptions. In *Diaz v. Pan American World Airways, Inc.*, 442 F.2d 385 (5th Cir. 1971), the majority wrote, "Construing the statute as embodying such a principle [of nondiscrimination] is based on the assumption that Congress sought a formula that would not only achieve optimum use of our labor resources but, and more importantly, would enable individuals to develop as individuals" (386–87). Within the context of statutory interpretation, the federal courts were leaning heavily in the direction of granting women recognition as civic equality. But there were still issues to be navigated within the domain of constitutional law.

The same year that the *Diaz* case was handed down, the Ninth Circuit issued its ruling in *Mengelkoch*. The court's opinion both suggested ways to advance equality without contradicting those previous rulings and raised questions about whether it was time to reconsider the basic holdings in cases like *Muller* and *Goesaert*. In distinguishing Velma Mengelkoch from the plaintiff in *Muller*, the court wrote: "Unlike *Muller*, she invokes the Equal

Protection Clause, and she does so not to preserve the right of employers to employ women for long hours, but to overcome what she regards as a system which discriminates in favor of male employees and against female employees" (*Mengelkoch*, 1123). The court's comment on *Goesaert* suggested that it was not a barrier here and that the principle of equality was taking hold: "We do not regard *Goesaert* as establishing, beyond reasonable debate, that a statute limiting the hours of labor of women in general occupations may not be so discriminatory against females as to offend the Equal Protection Clause" (1124). Finally, in looking at the effect of Title VII, the court opinion suggested that there was good reason to believe that the state law was inconsistent with federal law, and so the state law would be set aside because of the Supremacy Clause of the federal Constitution. The movement toward gender equality, driven by changes in federal statutory law, was having an impact on the way that the federal courts understood women's constitutional standing.

That year, 1971, was also when the Supreme Court handed down its first opinion dealing with the sex discrimination prohibition in a Title VII case (*Phillips v. Martin Marietta Corp.*, 400 U.S. 542 [1971]). Ida Phillips had been refused consideration for a job because she was a mother. Phillips claimed sex discrimination, but the lower court disagreed, ruling that sex plus another factor, such as parenting, was not subject to regulation by Title VII. In oral argument before the Supreme Court, Attorney William Robinson (of the NAACP Legal Defense Fund) attacked the "sex-plus" theory articulated by the lower court: "The point of the statute is that they should be treated as individuals rather than as members of a broad category. . . . [I]f the act permitted discrimination on the basis of sex-plus it would permit discrimination on the basis of race-plus, religion-plus, or nationality-plus" (quoted in Boylan, 1971, 12–13). In its amicus brief supporting Phillips, Human Rights for Women added, "The 'sex-plus' theory of the Fifth Circuit is wrong because under Title VII sex cannot be *even one* element in employment discrimination" (quoted in Boylan, 1971, 20). The Supreme Court agreed that the sex-plus theory must be rejected. "Section 703 (a) of the Civil Rights Act of 1964 requires that persons of like qualifications be given employment opportunities irrespective of their sex. The Court of Appeals therefore erred in reading this section as permitting one hiring policy for women and another for men — each having pre-school-age children" (*Phillips*, 544). Yet the Court also left open the possibility that motherhood could be used to disqualify women: "The existence of such conflicting family obligations, if demonstrably more relevant to job performance for a woman than for a man, could arguably be a basis for distinction under 703 (e) of the Act" (544). This element in the opinion provoked a response from Justice Marshall, who stated, "I cannot agree with the Court's indication that a [BFOQ] . . . could be established by a showing that some women, even the vast majority, with pre-school-age children have family responsibilities that interfere with job performance and that men do not usually have such responsibilities" (545). Marshall was concerned with the effect such a view would have on women's economic opportunities and with their identification as mothers rather than workers. "The Court has fallen into the trap of assuming that the Act permits ancient canards about the proper role of women to be a basis for discrimination" (545). Once again, women's capacity to become pregnant and be mothers proved very problematic for the extension of legal and constitutional equality to them.

EQUAL PROTECTION

Nearly two decades after the Court moved aggressively to dismantle the apartheid regime of racial segregation in the South using the Equal Protection Clause of the Fourteenth Amendment (*Brown v. Board of Education*, 347 U.S. 483 [1954]), the doctrine of equal protection was applied to sex in *Reed v. Reed*. This was the first of several cases brought before the Court by Ruth Bader Ginsburg, who was subsequently appointed the director of the new Women's Rights Project for the American Civil Liberties Union. Of the six cases that Ginsburg argued before the Supreme Court in the 1970s, she won five of them (all, except *Kahn v. Shevin*, 416 U.S. 351 [1974]).[11] Ginsburg also prepared briefs for several other leading equal protection cases in the 1970s. As a result of this line of cases, the Burger Court established an intermediate standard of heightened review for sex classifications under the Equal Protection Clause, placing sex in between the more rigorous review standard applied to suspect classifications, such as race, and the far more deferential reviews applied to nonsuspect classifications, such as residency. The development of the equal protection doctrine in the 1970s was animated primarily by a concern about race; where the Court found that sex did not fit the paradigm being applied to race, it was much more likely to uphold the classification.

Sex Discrimination Doctrine

The doctrine of equal protection as applied to sex was developed over a series of cases in the 1970s. In *Reed*, the Supreme Court overturned an Idaho law that favored men as estate executers for the estates of family members who die intestate. The Court found, "To give a mandatory preference to members of either sex over members of the other, merely to accomplish the elimination of hearings on the merits, is to make the very kind of arbitrary legislative choice forbidden by the Equal Protection Clause of the Fourteenth Amendment" (*Reed v. Reed*, 76). Two years later, in *Frontiero v. Richardson*, 411 U.S. 677 (1973), the majority of the Court struck down military regulations that provided unequally for the dependents of male and female service members. Writing for a plurality of the Court, Justice William J. Brennan stated that sex should be treated as a suspect category for equal protection purposes, given the nation's "long and unfortunate history of sex discrimination" (684). Justice Lewis F. Powell concurred in the opinion, but differed from the plurality on the question of what standard to apply in reviewing sex-based classifications. He called for a more cautious and gradual approach to this issue: "It is unnecessary for the Court in this case to characterize sex as a suspect classification, with all of the far-reaching implications of such a holding" (691–92). One of the reasons to delay the question of which standard to apply, according to Powell, was that the Equal Rights Amendment (which was ratified by Congress in 1972) was then under consideration in the states, so a rush to judicial judgment on the question of gender equality might effectively short-circuit a democratic political process (692).

Brennan, it seemed, had gone further than many on the Court were ready to go, and in the next couple of years there were a few reversals in which the Supreme Court upheld laws that had been challenged as violating the Equal Protection Clause (or its equivalent at the federal level, the Due Process Clause of the Fifth Amendment). These included *Kahn v. Shevin*, *Geduldig v. Aiello*, 417 U.S. 484 (1974), and *Schlesinger v. Ballard*, 419 U.S. 498 (1975). In the first and last of these cases, the Court upheld sex classifications that it viewed as benign or beneficial to women. In the case of *Geduldig*, the Court was unwilling to strike down California's disability insurance system for its failure to provide coverage for pregnant women workers. The Court found that the insurance program was not discriminatory: "There is no risk from which men are protected and women are not. Likewise, there is no risk from which women are protected and men are not" (496–97). Pregnant women, it seemed, were not comparably situated to nonpregnant men, so to deny them coverage for pregnancy was not discriminatory. The analysis in this case suggested the limits of the equality analysis under which sex classifications were being scrutinized.

These cases were followed by another series of positive rulings in which the Supreme Court struck down laws found to violate the Equal Protection Clause. Many of these cases involved instances of discrimination against men, most famously in *Weinberger v. Wiesenfeld*, 420 U.S. 636 (1975), as well as *Craig v. Boren*, 429 U.S. 190 (1976), *Califano v. Goldfarb*, 430 U.S. 199 (1977), *Orr v. Orr*, 440 U.S. 268 (1979), and *Califano v. Westcott*, 443 U.S. 76 (1979).[12] These cases were presented as instances in which a seemingly benign discrimination in favor of women did an injustice to men and, more importantly, represented a substantial discrimination against women outside of their traditional roles as mothers or wives. Thus, for instance, in the *Weisenfeld* case, a young father was denied social security benefits after his working wife died in childbirth because he had not been supported primarily by his wife's wages before she died. Without this support — to which he would have been automatically entitled as a widow — Wiesenfeld could not afford to stay home with his infant son. Ginsburg argued before the Court that this denial was really a failure to fully recognize and reward women workers by providing for their survivors as equally as to the survivors of a male worker. The Court agreed. By the time of *Craig v. Boren*, the Court had settled on an intermediate, or heightened, scrutiny standard for reviewing sex classification laws.

The Reed Brief

Ginsburg's brief in *Reed v. Reed* came to be referred to as the "grandmother brief" for the advocates of gender equality under the law (Ayer, 1994). In arguing that sex should be made a suspect classification (an argument that Ginsburg expected to repeat several more times before the Court responded positively to it [Markowitz, 1992, 345]), Ginsburg built her claim on the foundation of race. She argued that sex was like race, in that "both are highly visible characteristics on which legislators have found it easy to draw gross, stereotypical distinctions" (brief in *Reed v. Reed*, 16). Elsewhere, sex and race are described as "congenital, unalterable biological traits," "physiological characteristics" (18), or "immutable trait[s]" that were imparted by the "accident of birth" (20). The sense given here is that sex and race are mere exteriors, just shells that ought to have no social meaning (or at least no public meaning), and that have no real bearing on the internal qualities and characteristics of the individual. Equality is imagined in this brief in individual terms. Ideally, individuals would not be socially sorted by their racial or gender grouping. Rather, as Martin Luther King dreamed, they would "not be judged by the color of their skin [or by their sex] but by the content of their character" (Martin Luther King, Jr.). Like other suspect categories, sex was viewed as a "characteristic [that] frequently bears no relation to the ability to perform or contribute to society" (Brief for Appellant, *Reed v. Reed*, 20). Unfortunately for this line of attack, it ultimately proved harder to view sex (as opposed to race) as a mere shell, rather than as something more deeply forming of one's identity, inclinations, and talents.[13]

There were other, more complex ways in which gender and race were represented as parallel categories in the *Reed* brief. Both women and African Americans had been limited by the legacy of historic discrimination, rooted for African Americans in the institution of slavery and for women in the institution of coverture. Further, these institutions and the legal statuses created by them, were historically tied to one another: "Historically, the legal position of black slaves was justified by analogy to the legal status of women. Both slaves and wives were once subject to the all-encompassing paternalistic power of male head of household" (Brief for Appellant, *Reed v. Reed*, 16). Under the common law tradition of domestic relations, (white, propertied) men as the masters of their households had authority over and responsibility toward all of the dependent members of those households, including their wives, slaves, servants (or employees), wards, and children. The rights and civic position of women remained imprinted by this legal tradition well into the twentieth century. The historical legacy of coverture and slavery also had a contemporary expression. Quoting the California Supreme Court, from an opinion that established sex as a suspect classification, the *Reed* brief noted that such statuses carried a "stigma of inferiority and second class citizenship associated with them" (21). This analysis of the parallels between racial and gender discrimination offered a more promising premise for equality jurisprudence, since the analysis highlighted the role of the state in the creation of status hierarchies and legal inequality, and since it allowed for more variation and nuance in the presentation of the historic experiences of discrimination among women and African Americans.

Ginsburg later wrote that she developed this argument about the parallel between race and sex because, under the original understanding of the Fourteenth Amendment, sex classification was not constitutionally problematic (R. B. Ginsburg, 1978a, 453). The authors of this amendment, the men who voted for the amendment in Congress, and the jurists who first interpreted the Fourteenth Amendment, all found that there was no constitutional prohibition on state laws that barred women from voting, prevented them from obtaining professional employment or higher education, or denied basic civil rights to women who were married. So if women were to obtain equal protection under the Constitution, to be treated as legal persons and public individuals, it would be on the basis of the evolving interpretation of constitutional principles, as illustrated through the use of social parallels to groups covered under the amendment's original intent.

Race and Gender

The strategy was a successful one, even if it ultimately carried certain costs. Jurists recognized this parallel and responded to it, just as members of the liberal feminist movement were drawing similar parallels to the principles and achievements of the civil rights movement, and as members of Congress were enacting parallel prohibitions to discrimination on the basis of race or sex (most famously in Title VII, then later in the area of education under Title IX of the Educational Amendments Act of 1972). By the 1970s, racial equality provided an unequivocal language of social justice to which the government and the public were fully responsive. If that language could be borrowed effectively by another group, then it was likely to advance substantially its claims to social equality. Further, race had received constitutional recognition as a protected category — a recognition that was not always meaningful in practical terms but which had been made so again since the *Brown* ruling in 1954. In some sense, then, it was inevitable that race would provide the paradigm for civic and constitutional equality.

When the courts took up this parallel in the equal protection cases, they did so in ways that echoed the more simplistic view of the meaning of racial and gender inequality more often then they articulated the complex view of the parallels and connections between those two forms of civic hierarchy. Clearly drawing on Ginsburg's brief, in *Frontiero* Justice Brennan applied the "shell" theory to explaining the error in applying racial or sexual classifications in law: "Moreover, since sex, like race and national origin, is an immutable characteristic determined solely by the accident of birth, the imposition of special disabilities upon the members of a particular sex because of their sex would seem to violate 'the basic concept of our system that legal burdens should bear some relationship to individual responsibility' " (*Frontiero*, 686).[14] Similarly, in his dissent in *Kahn*, Brennan said that gender classifications, "like classifications based upon race," should be subject to strict scrutiny, since they were based on "generally immutable characteristics over which individuals have little or no control" (357). In *Regents of University of California v. Bakke* (which overturned an affirmative action program at the University of California, Davis, medical school), the Court added a further layer to this analysis in suggesting that sex differences were easier to identify and manage in public policy, since there were only two sexes. Even though the Court did not ultimately agree to treat sex to the same level of scrutiny as race, the two categories were viewed together as primary axes of social division and discrimination. "Classifications based upon gender, not unlike those based upon race, have traditionally been the touchstone for pervasive and often subtle discrimination" (*Personnel Adm'r of Massachusetts v. Feeney*, 442 U.S. 272 [1979]). Race was like gender, in that it was a matter of physical exteriors that had little bearing on an individual's talents and abilities, and in that both were the basis of widespread social discrimination.

The more subtle analysis looked in greater detail at the historical creation of racial and gender hierarchies, and focused particularly on its institutional and legal basis. Leading legal advocates of gender equality, such as Ruth Bader Ginsburg and Pauli Murray, provided this kind of analyses. Unfortunately, however, building off the first view of the parallels between race and gender resulted in a tendency in the courts to treat gender discrimination as simply a matter of traditional or outmoded thinking (often seen as benign) with no political history or institutional foundation. Thus, in the *Bakke* case, Justice Powell explained why racial classifications were particularly problematic: "The perception of racial classifications as inherently odious stems from a lengthy and tragic history that gender-based classifications do not share. In sum, the Court has never viewed such classification as inherently suspect or as comparable to racial or ethnic classifications for the purpose of equal protection analysis" (303). Even where the role of government in creating or reinforcing gender inequality was acknowledged, as it was by Brennan in *Frontiero*, the tendency was to see this role as simply a reflection of social mores.[15] Thus, after quoting Bradley's infamous opinion in *Bradwell v. Illinois*, 83 U.S. 130 (1872) ("The paramount destiny and mission of woman are to fulfill the noble and benign offices of wife and mother" [quoted in *Frontiero*, 685]), Brennan writes, "As a result of notions such as these, our statute books gradually became laden with gross, stereotyped distinctions between the sexes" (685).

Equality and Individualism

Not only did the parallel between race and gender limit the equality analysis as it was applied to sex, but there were other problems with the development of equal protection jurisprudence. These problems can be seen in three of the cases where the Court ruled that equal protection did not apply — *Kahn vs. Shevin*, *Geduldig v. Aiello*, and *Personnel Adm'r of Massachusetts v. Feeney*. In *Kahn*, the Court upheld a law providing a tax benefit to widows but not to widowers, since "there can be no dispute that the financial difficulties confronting the lone woman in Florida or in any other State exceed those facing the man" (353). Thus, where a state provided positive assistance to a woman in recognition of her economic status, the law survived scrutiny. Moreover, where the equality standard was not decisive (see also *Schlesinger* and *Califano v. Webster*, 430 U.S. 313 [1977]), women were viewed in group terms under a gendered status of dependency rather than as individuals. What made recognition of this status acceptable to the Court was the view that dependency was an unfortunate, not a government-created, state.

In the *Feeney* case, the opposite problem held. Massachusetts provided a preference for veterans in hiring that effectively barred women from upper-level civil service jobs. Yet the preference was found to be constitutional since it was facially neutral (there was no explicit sex classification used), and did not demonstrate either overt or covert discriminatory intent against women. After all, in addition to all of the women who were excluded, many men were denied the employment benefit as well. Here the Court failed to recognize that the preferred status (veteran) was implicitly and heavily gendered, and that the gendering of that status contributed to the civic recognition that was attached to it (Ritter, 2003). Thus, it seems, the government's recognition of how a status was gendered and what the government's role was in creating such a status was problematic in a couple of ways. These rulings suggest a court that was unable to see the subtle ways in which a government-created status could be implicitly gendered. Further, the Court may have been more able to recognize the existence of negative statuses attached to an oppressed group rather than positive statuses that attached to a favored group. Finally, when negative group status received government recognition as a premise for government action, it was under the presumption that the group basis of such a status should not continue, and that "groupness" itself implied inequality. For true equality to exist, collective identities must be shed or at least made irrelevant to one's civic role. This last element of the Court's logic of equality proved particularly problematic, since there was ultimately a limit to how far the Court was willing to go in according women a status as individuals.

Finally, *Geduldig* shows that to the extent women are particular or different from men, they may not be subject to constitutional equality (see also *General Electric Co. v. Gilbert*, 429 U.S. 125 [1976]). As feminist theorists and law scholars long have noted, the standard of equality is male to the extent that it implies being the same as a man (Beauvoir, 1989; W. Brown, 1995; MacKinnon, 1987). As explained above, in this case the State of California failed to cover women workers for pregnancy and childbirth in its employment disability insurance program. In finding this exclusion constitutionally acceptable, the Court found there was no inequality created since there was not an equal risk faced by men and women for which one sex was covered and the other one was not. In contrast, other cases from the 1970s (*Cleveland Board of Education v. LaFleur*, 414 U.S. 632 [1974], and *Turner v. Dept. of Employment Security of Utah*, 423 U.S. 44 [1975]) ruled in favor of the rights of pregnant working women (a position ultimately codified by Congress in the Pregnancy Discrimination Act of 1978), but these cases were decided on due process rather than equal protection grounds. An implicit issue distinguishing these cases may have been the relationship between pregnancy and a woman's ability and willingness to engage in public economic activity. "Perhaps the *able* pregnant woman seeking only to do a day's work for a day's pay is a sympathetic figure before the Court, while the woman *disabled* by pregnancy is suspect" (R. B. Ginsburg, 1978a, 462). Where rights were to be extended to areas in which women were viewed as physically different from men, equality analysis did not apply.

WOMEN'S RIGHTS LEGAL ADVOCACY

The Women's Rights Project at the American Civil Liberties Union was by no means the only organization or law firm dedicated to the mission of advancing women's rights through the courts. NOW's Legal Defense and

Education Fund (NOW LDEF), founded in 1970 and self-consciously modeled after the NAACP Legal Defense Fund, focused somewhat less on constitutional questions and more on issues of statutory enforcement. In particular, NOW LDEF was heavily involved in securing enforcement of Title VII and Title IX. The Project on Equal Educational Rights (PEER) was created in order to advance educational equity for women and girls. As the effort to secure a national ERA became less certain, the LDEF created the ERA Impact Project to follow the effects of the various state ERAs. Another important legal advocacy group for women's rights was the National Women's Law Center (NWLC), established in 1972 as a project of the Center for Law and Social Policy (CLASP) in Washington, DC. The NWLC focused primarily on reproductive issues, educational rights (it worked closely with WEAL), and family law matters. Other centers and legal organizations active in this period included the Center for Constitutional Rights (led by Arthur Kinoy); Human Rights for Women, Inc.; and the Equal Rights Advocates, Inc., a California-based feminist law firm founded in 1974 by Nancy Davis, Mary Dunlop, and Wendy Williams. In addition, legal advocates for women's rights often found allies in government (e.g., Sonia Pressman Fuentes, a staff attorney for the EEOC) or in the academy (e.g., Barbara Babcock, Herma Hill Kay, and Eleanor Holmes Norton) (Kerber, 2002).

The Women's Rights Project (WRP) was started under the leadership of Ruth Bader Ginsburg in 1972, who was then on the faculty at Rutgers Law School and had just finished working with Mel Wulf of the ACLU on the case of *Reed v. Reed*. The 1972 prospectus that Ginsburg authored for the new WRP identified six areas in which the project would focus its effort to achieve legal equality for women. These included employment discrimination, the use of government aid by private institutions, reproductive rights, educational opportunity, access to government training programs, and credit discrimination (A. Campbell, 2002, 166). The ruling in *Reed* was a victory that inspired further action, but it was also a tentative first step in the direction of constitutional equality that suggested the road ahead would not be easy. In reflecting on the case, Ginsburg wrote, "But the small step forward in *Reed* seems a fair indication that reliance on the judiciary for firm, unequivocal constitutional commitment to equality of rights for men and women is at best a dubious course and certainly an arduous and enervating one" (R. B. Ginsburg, 1972, 8). This combination of determination and pessimism was reflected in the prospectus for the WRP as well, where the founders (Ruth Ginsburg and Barbara Fasteau) of that new effort drew lessons from the experience of the civil rights litigators. "The experience of trying to root out racial discrimination in the United States has demonstrated that even when the arsenal of legislative and judicial remedies is well stocked, social and cultural institutions shaped by centuries of law sanctioned bias do not crumble under the weight of legal pronouncements proscribing discrimination" (A. Campbell, 2002, 165–66). For the women's rights litigators this meant that legal action was but one approach in a broader movement for political and constitutional equality. Ginsburg and the other women's rights attorneys of this era were also deeply involved in the effort to secure the Equal Rights Amendment.

Much of the work of Ginsburg and the WRP has been discussed in the previous section of this chapter. Two issues it would be worth considering further (drawing on Amy Campbell's fine article, as well as Ginsburg's own writings from the period) include the emergence of an intermediate scrutiny standard for sex discrimination, and the effort to use equality reasoning to combat rights denials related to pregnancy. Originally, as indicated by the *Reed* brief, the ACLU attorneys endeavored to have the Court apply a strict scrutiny standard to sex classifications. They did not get that, but they did get an opinion in which the Court quoted from a 1920 case about the need for a classification to bear a "substantial relation to the object of the legislation" — which suggested a standard higher than a mere rational basis.[16] The suggestion of an intermediate standard was developed further when it appeared in the mid-1970s that the majority was prepared to resist the application of a strict scrutiny standard to sex classifications in *Kahn v. Shevin* and *Schlesinger v. Ballard*. The resistance to strict scrutiny, like the ultimate failure of the ERA, suggests the limits of the constitutional equality model for women.

In 1978, Ginsburg wrote an essay in the *Women's Rights Law Reporter* (another product of the legal advocacy movement for women in the 1970s) on the current state of efforts to win constitutional recognition of sex equality. The essay appeared at an interesting moment, during the third phase of the constitutional equality campaign of the 1970s. The first phase — marked by the victory in *Reed* and the establishment of the WRP — was a moment of expansion and hope. The second phase, with reversals in cases like *Kahn* and *Schlesinger*, was a period of retrenchment and reconsideration, when it became apparent that the courts were willing to go only so far in applying the Equal Protection Clause to sex classifications. Then, in the third phase in the later 1970s, the WRP and allied groups modified their strategy, solidifying the recognition and application of an intermediate scrutiny standard to sex classifications.

The key case for this new synthesis, according to Ginsburg, was *Califano v. Webster*. *Webster* upheld a social security benefits scheme based on an employment history calculation that was more favorable to women, in recognition of the discrimination women had historically suffered in the job market. The opinion in this case endeavored to bring together concern over sex discrimination with recognition that unequal benefits could be used to promote gender equity. In Ginsburg's view, the *Webster* opinion explained the balance it was aiming for by building on the finding in *Califano v. Goldfarb*. "When, as in *Webster*, legislation directly addresses discrimination and serves to remedy it, disparate treatment of the sexes, at least as an interim measure, is constitutional. When, as in *Goldfarb*, disparate treatment is rooted in traditional role typing and is not deliberately and specifically aimed at redressing past injustice, differential treatment based on sex is unconstitutional" (R. B. Ginsburg, 1978b, 146). By 1978, the legal advocates of gender equality were ready to accept and make space for such compensatory schemes, provided that they would "preserve and bolster the general rule of equal treatment" between the sexes. Clearer establishment of the general principle of equality still needed to be pursued, according to Ginsburg, who called for adoption of the ERA, which "would give the Supreme Court a clear signal — a more secure handle for its rulings than the fifth and fourteenth amendments" (147). So the concession to compensatory schemes made here seemed less a matter of principle (the liberal legal advocates remained strongly committed to legal individualism and equality), and more a matter of realpolitik.

Indeed, women's rights lawyers lamented the failure by the Supreme Court to apply equality principles to issues related to pregnancy and reproductive rights. When women appeared before the Court fully embodied, the Court was seemingly unable to imagine them as abstracted liberal individuals entitled to equal rights. It preferred to address women's physicality under the terms of substantive due process and privacy — terms that provided a poor foundation for the elaboration of rights and social justice. Ginsburg notes Laurence Tribe's observation that "nothing in the Supreme Court analysis in *Roe v. Wade* or *Doe v. Bolton* turned on the sex specific impact of abortion restrictions" (1978b, 144), and goes on to observe that these cases "barely mention women's rights. They are not tied to equal protection or equal rights theory" (144). Given the Court's very mixed record with regard to pregnancy discrimination claims in employment cases, Ginsburg indicates that there was a distinct absence of broader thinking guiding the Court's approach to the various areas in which sex discrimination and women's rights claims were emerging.

The effort to deal with reproductive rights under the banner of equality was part of the original mission of the WRP, a mission it tried to pursue in the case of Susan Struck, an air force officer who was discharged after she refused to abort an out-of-wedlock pregnancy. The case was dismissed in 1972, before it reached the high court. As Amy Campbell (2002) writes, it was a case that represented a missed "opportunity to link reproductive choice to the disadvantageous treatment of women" (195). Reflecting on the case many years later, Ginsburg wrote, "confronted with Captain Struck's unwanted discharge, might the Court have comprehended an argument, or at least glimpsed a reality, it later resisted — that disadvantageous treatment of a woman because of her pregnancy and reproductive choice is a paradigm case of discrimination on the basis of sex?" (quoted in A. Campbell, 2002, 195). The question was mooted by the Court's decision in *Roe v. Wade*, 410 U.S. 113 (1973). In the end, Congress proved more amenable to the view that pregnancy discrimination played an important role in limiting women's equality and economic opportunity: the Pregnancy Discrimination Act was passed in 1978.

Conclusion

The principle of equality was a powerful instrument in the campaign to expand women's rights in the 1960s and 1970s. It should not surprise us that equality proved such a valuable resource for this campaign. After all, equality was also the doctrine used to expand civic rights for African Americans by the courts and legislatures. Further, the liberal wing of the feminist movement was strongly articulating their demands for economic and political rights in terms of equality, and the ideal of equality had an honored place in the lexicon of American public philosophy. The most venerated line in the nation's founding document rings with the conviction, "We hold these truths to be self-evident, that all men are created equal." Though the reference here is clearly gendered, the principle that status differences should not amount to political differences has been frequently extended in American history to incorporate new groups into "We, the People." The principle of equality proved a potent instrument in the fight for women's rights in the 1960s and 1970s.

Yet, tracing the constitutional expansion of women's civic membership through equality measures in the 1960s and 1970s also reveals the difficulties entailed in fitting women into a liberal conception of citizenship and personhood. While seeking to make women "equal" and thereby erase the significance of gender from women's civic identities, the equality approach was limited by the ways in which the courts found women to be irreducibly different from men, and by the loss of history and political identity entailed when the project of equality succeeded. The desire to preserve a recognition of gender difference ultimately fed into the development of the privacy doctrine (as discussed in the next chapter). Women were left with the political choice between public sameness or private notions of difference. The result for women's civic membership is captured by Wendy Brown in her analysis of gender and liberalism. "The gendered ideological moments of liberalism, then, pertain on the one hand to essentializing gender as difference; on the other, to glossing the social power of gender formation with generic or neutral language" (W. Brown, 1995, 143).

The vision of civic membership that emerges from the equal protection cases is one in which substantive group identities must remain nonpolitical. So long as gender remains relevant to a woman's civic membership (except as a set of practical interests), it is a signal of inequality, and of her failure to be fully absorbed into the ideal of liberal, individuated civic membership. The cost of equality, for women, then, is the cost of their gender.

How are women socially constituted by America's modern liberal constitutional order? As public civic members their gender identities are erased, turned into economic interests or organized group preferences. To be counted as full citizens they are expected to be unencumbered physically and emotionally — without the burdens or benefits of relationality, caregiving, reproduction, sexuality, or vulnerability to battery and sexual assault. To be otherwise evokes the presence of a civic member who is not singular, not rational, not autonomous, and not self-contained. Like race, poverty, and disability, a public-realm gendered identity provokes a political response of protection and regulation rather than full civic recognition.

Yet some advocates of gender equality in the 1960s and 1970s also projected a constitutional vision of an enriched equality that would incorporate recognition of women as physical beings and as caregivers without denying them the opportunity for full participation in the economic and political life of the nation. The shift that these equality advocates sought in our understanding of gender and civic membership was rather like the shift that occurred in the 1930s, when the relationship between labor status and civic membership was reconfigured. That change involved moving from a negative rights regime to a positive rights regime — from freedom of contract to social security and the economic bill of rights. A key to this earlier shift was a reimagining of autonomy and civic membership as being dependent not on an absence of government regulation of work relations, but on government recognition and support for workers as producers and providers. Similarly, an enriched vision of gender equality and civic membership would allow for recognition of women's relationality while still enabling them to pursue public-realm participation. In such a scenario, pregnancy benefits, parental leave, child care, reproductive rights, health care, and other measures would provide for a more substantive civic ideal that was public and equal. Equality would be understood more in terms of equity principles — it would be particularized to enable all citizens to participate and to bring their full selves with them into public and political life. This is a vision of equality that has yet to be realized.

EIGHT

Privacy

The pregnant woman cannot be isolated in her privacy.

— *Roe v. Wade* (1973)

Second wave feminism helped to remake civic membership for American women. Whether it was through the explicit campaigns of liberal feminists to achieve new laws and judicial understandings, or through the more diffuse efforts of the radical feminists to change cultural understandings of sex roles, both contributed to the extension of new rights to women. As discussed in the last chapter, many of the advancements in women's rights were premised on the principle of civic equality in the public realm. In contrast, the motto of the women's liberationists was, "The personal is political." Radicals focused more on personal relations, sexuality, and women's control of their bodies. Many participated in the campaign to protect women's reproductive rights and provide them with full access to abortion services. Their efforts contributed to changes in judicial recognition of women's reproductive rights. A broad expansion of the privacy doctrine in the late 1960s and 1970s (rooted, most often, in the Due Process Clause of the Fourteenth Amendment) was used by the courts to justify government noninterference with such intimate matters as contraception and abortion. This judicial expansion

261

of women's civic membership through the doctrine of privacy in the context of second wave feminism is the subject of this chapter.

So privacy was joined with equality as the means by which the federal courts secured new constitutional rights for women in the 1960s and 1970s. That the principle of equality was relied upon by the courts is not surprising, particularly given the impact of the civil rights movement. It is more surprising that the courts turned to the doctrine of privacy in delineating constitutionally protected rights for women. The use of this doctrine is surprising for several reasons: privacy seems to deny the feminist principle that "the personal is political"; privacy is a principle not readily articulated in terms of social justice; privacy does not draw from the Equal Protection Clause of the Fourteenth Amendment, which was the usual source for expanding civic rights outside of the area of suffrage; and, finally, privacy is associated with the constitutional doctrine of substantive due process, which was widely discredited in the 1930s.[1] Yet there were other ways in which privacy made sense as a way of expanding women's rights: privacy provides a backhanded way of acknowledging the political importance of personal matters; it also makes allowance for those areas in which women appeared irreducibly different from men; and the principle serves as a kind of empty space that could be filled by very different ideas about women and their capacity to act as civic participants. Understanding privacy's complex constitutional and political grounding is central to understanding the changes in women's civic membership that accompanied second wave feminism.

This chapter grapples with the puzzle of privacy and its relationship to women's civic membership. The focus here is primarily legal and constitutional. Larger changes in gender relations and gender politics ignited a sweeping constitutional response that culminated with the *Roe v. Wade* decision in 1973, the landmark decision that legalized abortion and treated it as part of a constitutionally protected right of privacy. In the period before and after this decision, feminist groups and antiabortion advocates reacted both to the legal right to abortion and the constitutional principle of privacy. The debate over privacy in relation to abortion, as well as marriage, family, and contraception, reveals that women were only loosely incorporated into the ideal of a liberal citizen. This chapter argues that the doctrine of privacy was used to extend women's rights for two reasons. First, it built on the historical practice of governing women's civic place through marriage law. Privacy offered a transition from the common law principle of governing women under coverture, to the liberal principle of governing citizens as autonomous individuals. Second, privacy allowed for widely varying views regarding women and their political capacities to be expressed through the same principle. It brought together, under the same constitutional principle, those who saw women as nonpublic beings, dependent upon the good judgment and assistance of men (their doctors), and those who saw them as independent, capable, and decisive individuals.

A Legal Genealogy of Privacy

There is no discussion of privacy in the Constitution, yet the concept is closely related to notions of liberty, which is a guiding principle of American public philosophy and constitutional law. The term *liberty* appears three times in the Constitution — each time as a part of the Constitution that defines the relationship between the government and the people — that is, explicitly or implicitly, in sections that deal with citizenship: the Preamble, the Fifth Amendment, and the Fourteenth Amendment. As a constitutional principle, liberty typically is taken to imply limits on the government's ability to act against people and their property. Beyond these explicit references to liberty, the notion of limits to the government's right to intrude its authority or purview upon the people is expressed in various ways throughout the Bill of Rights. Those who see constitutional privacy as related to liberty, and to individual freedom from government regulation, see it as a principle with an old and central constitutional lineage.

The concept of privacy first appeared in a Supreme Court ruling in the case of *Boyd v. United States*, 116 U.S. 616 (1886), a Fourth Amendment case concerning the seizure of personal papers. The seizure of "private papers" the Court found, was particularly offensive, since (here they quoted an earlier English case) "papers are the owner's goods and chattels; they are his dearest property" (627–28). Although the basic right here was property, it was the nature of the property itself (private papers) that most concerned the Supreme Court. "Breaking into a house and opening boxes and drawers are circumstances of aggravation; but any forcible and compulsory extortion of a man's own testimony, . . . is within the condemnation of that judgment" (630). Several things are suggested here. First, privacy is strongly associated with the constitutional principle of liberty. Second, privacy is represented as something personal and intimate, something that involves a man's thoughts and views. Finally, there is a "penumbra" effect in this case in the link that is made between the Fourth Amendment's protection against unwarranted search and seizure and the Fifth Amendment's prohibition against forcing a person to testify against himself or herself.

BRANDEIS ON PRIVACY

This concept of privacy was further elaborated on in a famous *Harvard Law Review* article by Samuel Warren and Louis Brandeis, published in 1890 (Warren and Brandeis, 1890). In this article, Warren and Brandeis presented privacy as a modern issue that arose from the increasing sophistication of men's intellectual and emotional lives, as well as the development of modern media technologies with which to invade those realms. The right of privacy, according to Warren and Brandeis, amounted to the right "to be let alone" (195). It was not the same as the right of private property, for it had to do not with the protection of things, but of "one's personality" (207) as well as one's "dignity" (214). Though privacy was presented as a new right that responded to new social circumstances, it was also regarded as a right with older common law roots. In their conclusion, Warren and Brandeis wrote, "The common law has always recognized a man's house as his castle, impregnable, often, even to its own officers engaged in the executions of its commands" (220). Privacy, then, was the modern-day equivalent of the common law rights of masters in the domestic realm.[2]

After Brandeis was appointed by President Woodrow Wilson to the U.S. Supreme Court in 1916 he gave further articulation to the concept of privacy, most famously in his dissent to the majority opinion in *Olmstead v. United States*, 277 U.S. 438 (1928), a case that concerned the legality of wiretapping. The Court ruled that to wiretap was not a violation of the Fourth or Fifth Amendments. Brandeis thought otherwise: "The makers of our Constitution undertook to secure conditions favorable to the pursuit of happiness. . . . They sought to protect Americans in their beliefs, their thoughts, their emotions and their sensations. They conferred, as against the government, the right to be let alone" (478). Here privacy appears not as something new, but as something that dates back at least until the founding. Brandeis presented privacy, or "the right to be left alone," as an underlying constitutional principle, as a comprehensive right, and as something that could be located specifically in the Fourth and Fifth Amendments. Privacy is associated with the Declaration of Independence and the "pursuit of happiness." It is also called "the right most valued by civilized men" (478). This right and this pursuit seem decidedly nonmaterial in nature. They reflect, instead, on the inner life of the individual and are associated most heavily with the protected space of the home. Yet despite this lineage, Brandeis's conception of privacy seems quite modern. In the decades to come, this famous dissent would be frequently and positively cited in other court cases dealing with privacy.

THE ROOTS OF PRIVACY IN SUBSTANTIVE DUE PROCESS

The 1920s was an important decade for the development of privacy jurisprudence, not only because of the Brandeis dissent, but also because of the development of privacy in association with the doctrine of substantive due process. Both the Fifth and the Fourteenth Amendments contain Due Process Clauses, which in the Fourteenth Amendment reads, "nor shall any State deprive any person of life, liberty, or property, without due process of law." A similar provision in the Fifth Amendment applied to the actions of the federal government rather than the states. In the late nineteenth and early twentieth centuries, the courts moved beyond procedural concerns when applying the Due Process Clauses to government regulation of property. For the conservative, laissez-faire justices of this period, the Due Process Clause became an instrument for the protection of private business interests from government intrusion. Thus, for instance, the principle of "free contract" was applied to laws regulating labor conditions, most famously in the case of *Lochner v. New York*, 198 U.S. 45 (1905). In the 1920s, the Court would build on the principle of free contract and substantive due process developed in *Lochner* (see Chapter 5), not only in labor cases, but also in cases concerning education.

In the *Lochner* case, the Court found that a New York State law regulating the hours of bakers violated "the liberty of the individual" (53), under the Due Process Clause of the Fourteenth Amendment. *Lochner* set the terms for several decades of jurisprudence on matters of labor legislation and the principle of substantive due process, and in time *Lochner* came to stand for unjustified court interferences with legislative judgments. But in the 1920s, *Lochner* remained good law and Supreme Court Justice James McReynolds was a leading advocate of the doctrine of substantive due process. In a pair of cases from that era, McReynolds applied the principle of substantive due process to matters of education, where he made the connection between liberty and privacy.

The cases are *Meyer v. Nebraska*, 262 U.S. 390 (1923), and *Pierce v. Society of Sisters*, 268 U.S. 510 (1925). As Barbara Woodhouse has written, while these cases are remembered as liberal celebrations of privacy and religious freedom, they also paid heed to "the patriarchal family, to a class-stratified society, and to a parent's private property rights in his children and their labor" (Woodhouse, 1992, 997). At issue in *Meyer* was a Nebraska law forbidding educational instruction in public or private schools in any language besides English. The plaintiff was a teacher who taught reading in a parochial school where the instruction was in German. The Supreme Court found the law violated the Due Process Clause of the Fourteenth Amendment. Under due process, liberty included "the right of the individual to contract, to engage in any of the common occupations of life, to acquire useful knowledge, to marry, establish a home and bring up children, to worship God according to the dictates of his own conscience" (399). The rights violated were contract rights, but more than that, they were rights "long recognized at common law as essential to the orderly pursuit of happiness by free men" (399). The opinion in this case began to outline a realm of life — one that included marriage, procreation, and the raising and educating of children — that would later be seen as protected under the principle of personal privacy. This realm was protected under principles drawn from the common law and rooted in the Constitution. As suggested in the discussion of this case in Chapter 3, this affirmation of "liberty" provided a modern way for the Court to affirm social-ordering principles under the rubric of privacy.

In *Pierce*, the law at issue was an Oregon statute requiring public school attendance until the age of sixteen or the completion of the eighth grade. *Meyer* served as the precedent for the Court's ruling in this case: "Under the doctrine of *Meyer v. Nebraska*, we think it entirely plain that the Act of 1922 unreasonably interferes with the liberty of parents and guardians to direct the upbringing and education of children under their control" (534).

States could not interfere with the rights of parents to direct the upbringing of their children. In the realm where this personal liberty right exists, it is also a duty that falls upon parents to prepare their children for life in the public world. The reciprocal rights and duties that define the parental relationship recall the common law tradition of domestic relations, in which parents (particularly fathers) have rights and responsibilities for their children, as well as for the other dependent members of their households (such as wives and servants). It appears that in one of the earliest cases to articulate a notion of personal privacy, privacy appears as the modern-day equivalent of the private authority of fathers and husbands in the domestic realm.

THE POST-'LOCHNER' ERA

Once substantive due process jurisprudence was discredited during the New Deal, the development of the personal privacy doctrine was forced to take a more tortured constitutional route. The ghost of *Lochner* haunts the development of modern privacy doctrine. Through the 1970s and beyond, judges invoking privacy were forced to explain why they were not repeating the errors of judicial excess made in *Lochner*. Some argued for alternative constitutional grounds for the development of privacy. Others hid their privacy opinions under the cover of equal protection. Finally, some were brave enough to proclaim their use of substantive due process doctrine in connection with privacy, but they were careful to distinguish their use of this doctrine from its use in opinions like *Lochner*. In the end, it seems, substantive due process is at the core of privacy jurisprudence, and it is not as distinct as its proponents would like it to be from the due process approach taken in *Lochner* and *Adkins*.

Early examples of post-*Lochner* difficulties in privacy doctrine appeared in two 1940s privacy cases. The first of the two cases is *Skinner v. Oklahoma*, 316 U.S. 535 (1942) (see Chapter 5). At issue was a state law mandating sterilization for criminals twice convicted of crimes designated as exhibiting "moral turpitude" (536). Justice William O. Douglas wrote for the majority: "We are dealing here with legislation which involves one of the basic civil rights of man. Marriage and procreation are fundamental to the very existence and survival of the race" (541). In using terms like "basic civil rights," "fundamental," and "basic liberty," Justice Douglas suggested the existence of fundamental rights that were beyond the reach of the state. What was wrong with the law was that it interfered with the right of men to have children, a right so important that it cannot lightly be denied, even for criminals.

Other justices on the Court noticed what Douglas was doing, and while they concurred with the ruling, they were troubled by the doctrinal grounds upon which Douglas reached his conclusion. Chief Justice Harlan Stone began his concurring opinion by stating, "I concur in the result, but I am not persuaded that we are aided in reaching it by recourse to the equal protection clause" (543). Stone preferred to rely upon procedural due process doctrine instead. "I think the real question we have to consider is not one of equal protection, but whether the wholesale condemnation of a class to such an invasion of personal liberty, without opportunity to any individual to show that his is not the type of case which would justify resort to it, satisfies the demands of due process" (544). The invasion of personal liberty in the area of procreation was not something the state could do without a strong justification and proper procedures. Justice Robert Jackson agreed with Stone, and seemed to verge on going a step further when he wrote, "There are limits to the extent to which a legislatively represented majority may conduct biological experiments at the expense of the dignity and personality and natural powers of a minority — even those who have been guilty of what the majority define as crimes" (546). Procreation was a right that involved the "dignity and personality" of the individual. Again, although it remains unnamed, substantive due process reasoning is lurking in all of these opinions. Yet even without the open use of substantive due process, as of the 1940s the Court increasingly was willing to say that important personal life choices, like the choice to procreate, are constitutionally protected.

The other 1940s case concerned parental rights. In *Prince v. Massachusetts*, 321 U.S. 158 (1944) (see Chapter 5), the Supreme Court upheld Sarah Prince's conviction for violating a state child labor law. Yet in its opinion, the Court relied upon the Due Process Clause to suggest the existence of a sphere of liberty around the family that was constitutionally protected from state interference. Just as the federal government was becoming more involved in regulating social relations, the Supreme Court was reinventing the doctrine of substantive due process liberty to protect traditional social relations in the name of privacy. Liberty was now conceived of in social rather than economic ones. Social hierarchies could no longer be readily defended as a matter of explicit law, but if those hierarchies were conceived of as emanating from the social and cultural preferences of the community, they might still be preserved and defended.

Privacy reasoning takes on a self-consciously gendered dimension in the 1960s.[3] The issue that provoked this development was state regulation of contraception. From the late nineteenth century until the middle of the twentieth century, most states regulated or prohibited the purchase, sale, distribution, and use of birth control for teenagers, single adults, and married couples. Many states modified their laws in the postwar period on public health and other grounds. Further, the provisions of these laws were often unenforced. Yet the laws still had enough authority to prevent the open and legal operation of birth control clinics in most states, making it particularly difficult for poor women to obtain birth control. It was this restriction that the Planned Parenthood Association was set to challenge when they prepared to open a birth control clinic in Connecticut at the beginning of the 1960s.[4]

Connecticut had a particularly restrictive birth control law that barred doctors from advising married couples on the use of birth control and married couples from using it. The law had been upheld by state courts in 1940 in a ruling (*State v. Nelson*, 11 A.2d 856) that resulted in the closing of all public and private birth control clinics in the state. They remained closed in 1960 when a doctor affiliated with Planned Parenthood and some of his patients sought a declaratory judgment voiding the law on Fourteenth Amendment due process grounds. In *Poe v. Ullman*, 367 U.S. 497 (1961), the majority ruled against Poe and the other plaintiffs, finding that the statute was generally null, since there had been no prosecutions under the birth control law since 1940. The ruling provoked strong dissents from Justices William O. Douglas and John Marshall Harlan.

In a dissenting opinion that quickly became more significant than the majority opinion, Harlan laid out the modern vision for a right of personal privacy and grounded it squarely in substantive due process liberty. Harlan opened the section of his opinion that addressed the constitutionality of the Connecticut law as follows: "I believe that a statute making it a criminal offense for married couples to use contraceptives is an intolerable and unjustifiable invasion of privacy in the conduct of the most intimate concerns of an individual's personal life" (539). Having claimed this ground, Harlan then explained the constitutional principles that were at stake. The Constitution, Harlan explained, must not be read "in a literalistic way" (540).

The Due Process Clause could not be viewed as involving merely procedural safeguards, or as applying narrowly to the specific rights protected by the first eight amendments in the Bill of Rights. Rather, due process provided "an independent guaranty of liberty and procedural fairness, more general and inclusive than the specific prohibitions" of the Bill of Rights (541).

How, then, was one to determine what was included under the liberty guaranty of the Due Process Clause? "The best that can be said is that through the course of this Court's decisions it has represented the balance which our Nation, built upon postulates of respect for the liberty of the individual, has struck between that liberty and the demands of organized society" (542). Tradition, history, judgment, and restraint were the guides upon which the courts must rely in balancing the interests of individual liberty against the demands of organized society. Harlan writes here without fear of the discredited substantive due process jurisprudence of an earlier era. He moves straightforwardly to banish the ghost of *Lochner*. In concluding his general discussion of due process liberty, Harlan wrote, "This 'liberty' is not a series of isolated points pricked out"; rather, it "is a rational continuum which, broadly speaking, includes a freedom from all arbitrary impositions and purposeless restraints" (543).

Coming then to the substance of this case, Harlan made clear what was offensive about the Connecticut law. "In sum, the statute allows the State to enquire into, prove and punish married people for the private use of their marital intimacy. . . . This enactment involves . . . a most fundamental aspect of 'liberty,' the privacy of the home" (550). The "privacy of the home" has been invaded here, despite the fact that there may be no "physical intrusion whatever into the home." It is invaded because the private intimacies of the home must be publicly revealed in the course of prosecuting this law. On the protection of the home, Harlan argued that "the sweep of the Court's decisions, under both the Fourth and Fourteenth Amendments, amply shows that the Constitution protects the privacy of the home against all unreasonable intrusion of whatever character" (550).

Even so, Harlan acknowledged that the privacy violation here differs from the physical invasions of the home that the framers of the Constitution were protecting against in the Third (no quartering of soldiers) and Fourth (no unreasonable search and seizure) Amendments. "But to my mind such a distinction is so insubstantial as to be captious: if the physical curtilage of the home is protected, it is surely as a result of solicitude to protect the privacies of the life within" (551). The life within the home, Harlan suggested, is the private life of the family, and within the family, "it is difficult to imagine what is more private or more intimate than a husband and wife's marital relations" (552). So the *most* private and protected relationship is the relationship of marital sexuality — perhaps because it is imagined to be physically the most interior space of the home. Further, the sex that occurs within marriage is generally regarded as legitimate, honored, and state sanctioned in the marital contract itself. Marital sex "is necessarily an essential and accepted feature of the institution of marriage, an institution which the State not only must allow, but which always and in every age it has fostered and protected" (553). Finally, marital sex is linked to the other areas of recognized personal privacy such as procreation and parenting. It is through marital sex that families are made. For all of these reasons, Harlan would void the law as an invasion of constitutionally protected liberty.

In a few short years, the substance of Harlan's views, if not the constitutional grounds on which they were based, became good law in *Griswold v. Connecticut*, 381 U.S. 479 (1965). Following the Court's ruling in *Poe*, the Connecticut birth control movement determined to open up clinics in the state to find out whether the state law truly was null, as the Court had suggested. Shortly after the first clinic was opened, the state came and shut it down, arresting the state's executive director of Planned Parenthood, Estelle Griswold, and the clinic's doctor, Timothy Buxton (who was also a professor at Yale Medical School). Griswold and Buxton challenged their conviction on Fourteenth Amendment grounds.

The first issue for the Court to settle was one of standing. No birth control users had been charged in this case, only the providers. The Court found that particularly given the "confidential relation[ship]" between patient and physician, the "appellants have standing to raise the constitutional rights of the married people with whom they had a professional relationship" (481). This seemingly innocuous move to elevate the position of the physician to speak for the constitutional rights of patients would have long-term implications in the development of privacy rights for women. When they came to the substance of the case the Court found, "This law, however, operates directly on an intimate relation of husband and wife and their physician's role in one aspect of that relation" (482). So doctors were inserted as a third party (and in later abortion rulings, a second, or even first, party) in the development of privacy doctrine.

When discussing the constitutional grounds for the ruling, the Court (in the majority opinion written by Justice Douglas) shied away from using substantive due process jurisprudence. "Overtones of some arguments suggest that *Lochner v. New York*, 198 U.S. 45, should be our guide. But we decline that invitation" (481–82). Instead, Douglas wrote of a "penumbra" effect from the First Amendment, where privacy is protected from government intrusion. The Bill of Rights contains several enumerated rights, but the constitutional principles behind these rights implies the existence of peripheral rights as well. The reasoning here is certainly more awkward and cumbersome than the due process claim made by Harlan in his *Poe* dissent (which he reaffirmed in a concurrence to *Griswold*). Instead of Harlan's liberty, here we have Douglas's "zones of privacy" attached to various "specific guarantees in the Bill of Rights"; these zones then get transformed into a single zone that demands constitutional protection. The reason for all of this constitutional awkwardness is to avoid the accusation, based on *Lochner*, that the Court was acting as a "superlegislature."

Having designated that there is a constitutionally protected right of privacy (although the terms of that protection and the boundaries of that zone remain unclear), Douglas went on to discuss marriage, which was "a relationship lying within" the constitutionally protected "zone of privacy." In suggesting what is wrong with the Connecticut law, Douglas conjured up images of the police searching the "sacred precincts of marital bedrooms" (485), then wrote, "The very idea is repulsive to the notions of privacy surrounding the marriage relationship" (486). So marriage here is a holy estate, the intimacies of which are protected from state view. What makes such an intrusion so repulsive to Douglas? Is it the exposure of legitimate sex, or the notion of interference in the private domain that ought to be under the control of the marital partners? Rather than clarify his objection, Douglas (who had himself been married several times) delivered a concluding soliloquy on marriage.

> We deal with a right of privacy older than the Bill of Rights — older than our political parties, older than our school system. Marriage is a coming together for better or for worse, hopefully enduring, and intimate to the degree of being sacred. It is an association that promotes a way of life, not causes; a harmony in living, not political faiths; a bilateral loyalty, not commercial or social projects. Yet it is an association for as noble a purpose as any involved in our prior decisions. (486)

In this romantic, grandiose, and deeply liberal (that is, that what is private is not political) vision, Douglas seems to suggest that rights need not be constitutionally created to be constitutionally protected. In one of the stunning reversals in privacy jurisprudence, within a few years of this decision, marriage will be abandoned as the ground for privacy claims in the area of sexuality and reproduction.

In addition to the Douglas opinion in this case were three concurring opinions and two dissents. The most substantial of these was the concurring opinion written by Justice Arthur Goldberg and signed as well by Justices William Brennan and Earl Warren. In this opinion, the justices agreed on the main holding in the Douglas opinion, namely, that the Connecticut law amounted to an unconstitutional intrusion on marital privacy. But privacy was located differently in relation to the Constitution, through reasoning that relied on both the Due Process Clause of the Fourteenth Amendment and the Ninth Amendment's acknowledgment of unenumerated rights retained by the people. Much like Harlan in *Poe*, Goldberg relies on a notion of liberty to ground privacy: "I do agree that the concept of liberty protects those personal rights that are fundamental, and is not confined to the specific terms of the Bill of Rights" (486). According to Goldberg, the Ninth Amendment indicates that there are unenumerated rights retained by the people, and the Fourteenth Amendment's Due Process Clause provides protection for fundamental rights (those that are "so rooted in the traditions and conscience of our people as to be ranked as fundamental" [487]) within the states, under the concept of liberty. Marriage is just such a right. "To hold that a right so basic and fundamental and so deep-rooted in our society as the right of privacy in marriage may be infringed because that right is not guaranteed in so many words by the first eight amendments to the Constitution is to ignore the Ninth Amendment" (491). Goldberg sought here to provide both textual support, through the Ninth Amendment, for his defense of privacy, and to rely upon history, tradition, and precedent in making his claims. Thus, the reliance upon marriage as a way of grounding privacy in the controversial area of sexuality and reproduction is both a way to make a commonsense public appeal (who could be against marriage?), and to create a constitutional argument, using the Ninth Amendment, that presents marriage as an unenumerated right retained by the people.

Shortly after *Griswold*, the Court again affirmed the importance of marriage as a fundamental right. At issue in *Loving v. Virginia*, 388 U.S. 1 (1967), was Virginia's antimiscegenation statutes, which the Court found unconstitutional on *both* equal protection and due process grounds. The equal protection component of the decision addresses the issue of race discrimination. Despite the state's claim that the law applied equally to whites and blacks, the Court cited *Strauder v. West Virginia*, 100 U.S. 303 (1879), to indicate their desire to consider the law's impact on the civic standing of African Americans, and concluded that the law was a clear expression of "invidious racial discrimination" (11) that violated the Equal Protection Clause. Then the Court turned to the liberty component of the Due Process Clause, and the "freedom to marry" (12) that was protected by that clause. Writing for the majority, Chief Justice Earl Warren cited *Skinner*, concluding, "Marriage is one of the 'basic civil rights of man,' fundamental to our very existence and survival" (12). Here marriage was a right of individual choice, but a choice nonetheless that was affirmed as a right "of man." Further, rights considerations that attached to race were more readily addressed through equality for the Court, while those that attached to sexuality and reproduction were more readily addressed through privacy.

Having used marriage as the means by which to justify a constitutional right of personal privacy, the Court quickly moved beyond marriage in the area of sexuality and reproduction. The key ruling for this shift was *Eisenstadt v. Baird*, 405 U.S. 438 (1972), another contraception case. The case concerned Bill Baird, a birth control activist convicted of distributing contraceptives to a single woman at a public lecture in Massachusetts. In an opinion written by Justice Brennan, the Court ruled that the law under which Baird was convicted, "viewed as a prohibition on contraception per se, violates the rights of single persons under the Equal Protection Clause of the Fourteenth Amendment" (444). That is, since married persons had a right to obtain and use contraception, so equally did single people, since "whatever the rights of the individual to access to contraceptives may be, the rights must be the same for the unmarried and the married alike" (453). How had marriage been so readily eclipsed here? Why, suddenly, did marital status amount to an unreasonable classification in this area? Surely, the courts upheld the significance of marital status for legal distinctions in laws regarding the distribution of public benefits, the application of criminal sanctions for various kinds of behavior, and so on. Beyond that, both the majority opinion and the main concurring opinion in *Griswold* grounded the constitutional right to privacy in marriage itself.

This crucial shift in the development of privacy doctrine will be explored further below. What remains to be discussed here is the ground for claiming that marriage was not crucial to privacy in *Eisenstadt*. The shift depended on reconceptualizing the marital relationship. As Brennan wrote,

> It is true that in *Griswold* the right of privacy in question inhered in the marital relationship. Yet the marital couple is not an independent entity with a mind and heart of its own, but an association of two individuals each with a separate intellectual and emotional makeup. If the right of privacy means anything, it is the right of the individual, married or single, to be free from unwarranted governmental intrusion into matters so fundamentally affecting a person as the decision whether to bear or beget a child. (453)

For Douglas in *Griswold*, marriage was sacred. It was represented in terms that spoke of unity ("coming together," "harmony"), rather than individualism. In contrast, Brennan represented marriage as a voluntary association (based upon a contract) of two individuals, and what matters is the right of those individuals to decide whether to bear a child. Here privacy is singular and intellectual; it is about the ability of each person to make choices regarding important matters in their life without governmental intrusion. Just as in the state of nature, men have reason and are therefore capable of self-governance, in America the mature capacity for choice entitles one to control one's reproductive life. But finally, the move away from marriage is still being couched in ways to make it more legitimate and publicly acceptable — the right to privacy is represented as a right to think rather than a right to act; it is a reproductive right rather than a sexual right.[5] These two faces of marriage — as being about unity and harmony in *Griswold* and about individualism and contract in *Eisenstadt* — suggest the split in reasoning about privacy when it came to women. By the late 1960s, some judges were ready to regard women as liberal individuals, even within marriage, while others still saw them in sentimental terms as residing under the protective awning of domesticity. It was a split that would be even more apparent in the cases on abortion.

PRIVACY AND ABORTION: THE *ROE* DECISION

In the late 1960s, both the liberal and the radical wings of the women's movement fought for reform or abolition of state laws restricting the availability of abortions. They were joined in these efforts by many of the members of the birth control movement (particularly from Planned Parenthood), as well as by a growing number of lawyers and legal organizations interested in advancing the rights of women through constitutional challenges. For a time it appeared that the efforts of abortion reform advocates would have the greatest effect in the context of state legislatures. Many states passed abortion reform laws at the end of the 1960s and the beginning of the 1970s. But as these more directly democratic efforts ran into an increasingly vocal and organized pro-life movement, the legislative movement was slowed, and there were even some reversals in states that had already passed reform laws. Consequently, by 1971 or 1972, the movement for abortion reform began to focus increasingly on constitutional challenges to laws restricting abortion. In the wake of *Griswold*, the tactic most commonly taken in these challenges was to advocate abortion availability as part of a right of privacy (Garrow, 1998).

The major ruling on abortion came in *Roe v. Wade*, 410 U.S. 113 (1973), and the companion opinion in *Doe v. Bolton*, 410 U.S. 179 (1973). Justice Harry Blackmun wrote the majority opinion in both cases. After a thorough review of the historical and legal issues involved, the Court held in *Roe* that Texas's restrictive abortion law was an unconstitutional violation of privacy, a right grounded in the liberty protected by the Due Process Clause of the Fourteenth Amendment. Despite the broad impact of the ruling, it was in many ways conditional, as suggested by the language of the summary section: "A state criminal abortion statute of the current Texas type, that excepts from criminality only a life-saving procedure on behalf of the mother, without regard to pregnancy stage and without recognition of the other interests involved, is violative of the Due Process Clause of the Fourteenth Amendment" (164). The Texas law, rooted as it was in nineteenth-century notions of abortion, was unconstitutional because it went too far. It was clear even in this original opinion that it was possible for states to restrict abortions in ways that would withstand constitutional scrutiny.

The Court appeared to go a bit further with the ruling in *Doe*, which overturned Georgia's new abortion reform law. The restrictions specified in the Georgia law, which made some abortions legal but set conditions for when and how an abortion could be obtained, amounted to a denial of privacy. Under the procedures set forth in the Georgia law, appellant *Doe* was denied her application to obtain an abortion. The Court wrote, "This invaded her rights of privacy and liberty in matters related to family, marriage, and sex, and deprived her of the right to choose whether to bear children" (209). The Court here is more affirmative in its view that a woman's right to obtain an abortion cannot be unduly burdened by cumbersome and highly restrictive procedures. Further, because the Georgia law set strict procedures regarding the role of doctors and hospitals in approving and performing abortions, there is a great deal of discussion about the relationship of physicians to the right of privacy. That issue is quite illuminating for understanding the impact of privacy on women's civic membership. But before analyzing that issue further, it will be helpful to discuss the *Roe* ruling in greater detail.

The *Roe* decision was quite controversial, and has come to be broadly criticized by constitutional law scholars. Many people, from the legal profession, the academy, the media, and the movements for and against the right to obtain an abortion, have written about the *Roe* decision. Addressing this huge literature is well beyond the scope of this work. My concern here is with understanding what *Roe* can tell us about the development of privacy doctrine and its impact on women's civic membership. For this purpose, several elements of the decision are of particular interest. The most striking thing about the *Roe* opinion is that it does not confer fully on pregnant women the status of independent persons with a right of privacy. Instead, they are people who need state protection; people who are not alone because of the presence of the embryo or fetus; and people whose choice of an abortion is guided or determined by their doctors. What this means is that the right by which women's civic membership is being expanded is both elusive and conditional for women. It is a right that does not behave like other rights, in the sense of providing a moral calling for justice and recognition. The reason for privacy's presence in this case lies elsewhere — in the history of women's civic place within common law, and in the ability of privacy to tolerate competing conceptions of women's place in the contemporary social order.

To get to the constitutional grounding for abortion, the Court's opinion in *Roe* went on a long detour through the legal history of abortion in the United States. The foundation for this review was the common law legal tradition that governed abortion at the time the nation was established. The Court wrote about its review, "It is undisputed that at common law, abortion performed before 'quickening' — the first recognizable movement of the fetus in utero, appearing usually from the 16th to the 18th week of pregnancy—was not an indictable offense" (132). Thus, the Court moved to defend a woman's right to an abortion by recalling the treatment of abortion under common law, a point the court returned to in the summary section of the opinion: "This holding, we feel, is consistent with the . . . lenity of the common law" (165). This positive reclaiming of early common law jurisprudence is suggestive, since there was also a privacy tradition, under the common law, particular to women: coverture, whereby women legally disappeared from the public realm to be placed under their husband's governance. This other common law tradition, it seems, has an unacknowledged presence in the *Roe* decision, since women never appear in it as full persons before the law.

When the Court approached the issue of privacy, its discussion was framed negatively and conditionally: "The Constitution does not explicitly mention any right of privacy" (152). Yet such a right had been recognized in previous Supreme Court cases. What was privacy? The Court was never explicit, preferring to draw upon previous cases to suggest both the constitutional moorings for such a right (the First and Ninth Amendments, as well as the Due Process Clause of the Fourteenth Amendment), and the activities that privacy was related to (marriage, procreation, contraception, family relationships, child rearing, and education). Placing privacy within the expanse of the Fourteenth Amendment, the Court determined, made the right "broad enough to encompass a woman's decision whether or not to terminate her pregnancy" (153). The Court's most affirmative discussion of privacy and its relation to abortion involves a review of the harms that might ensue were women forced to continue and complete unwanted pregnancies. The possible harms a woman faced were physical, mental, social, and economic. Because of these risks, "the woman and her responsible physician" (153) should be permitted to decide whether her pregnancy should be continued.

Having placed abortion within the domain of privacy, the Court quickly turned to the limits of this right. The right of privacy was limited both at its point of origin, in relation to the woman, and in terms of the countervailing interests of the state. The Court's discussion of privacy's limits in relation to pregnant women is nothing short of startling. In the midst of a section discussing whether a fetus should be recognized as a legal person, Justice Blackmun wrote,

The pregnant woman cannot be isolated in her privacy. She carries an embryo and, later, a fetus. . . . The situation therefore is inherently different from marital intimacy, or bedroom possession of obscene material, or marriage, or procreation, or education, with which *Eisenstadt* and *Griswold, Stanley, Loving, Skinner,* and *Pierce* and *Meyer* were respectively concerned. . . . The woman's privacy is no longer sole and any right of privacy she possesses must be measured accordingly. (159)

Thus, although the right to abortion is premised on privacy, the pregnant woman is never truly in a private situation. Although the Court refused to define the fetus as a legal person, the presence of this unnamed entity is still enough to deny the woman a claim of individuality. Further, this is so despite comparable social situations where privacy is granted even when other people are present — as in the case of marital intimacy, marriage, procreation, or the education of one's children. Indeed, the only other privacy situation that Blackmun named that might involve a person in isolation is in the case of the "bedroom possession of obscene materials." Why, then, is the privacy claim of a pregnant woman more socially compromised than that of sexually active couples or of parents and children? Because for this Court, women are not self-possessed individuals who might be singularly trusted with such important decisions as whether to terminate a pregnancy. After this discussion, the Court's opinion returned to its analysis of whether a fetus is a legal person. It appears that the fetus is not the only being for whom the Court has questions on that issue.[6]

In *Roe,* the Court sought alternately to protect and to guide women. It protected women from the risks of unwanted pregnancy when it allowed them to abort. It protected them as well when it allowed states to establish the circumstances under which second-trimester abortions may be performed. In its discussion of legitimate state interests the Court wrote, "With respect to the State's important and legitimate interest in the health of the mother, the 'compelling' point, in the light of present medical knowledge, is at approximately the end of the first trimester. . . . It follows that, from and after this point, a State may regulate the abortion procedure to the extent that the regulation reasonably relates to the preservation and protection of maternal health" (163). The state's interest in protecting "the mother" from the risks of unwanted pregnancy or the harms of poorly performed abortions may then shift to concern with protecting the fetus in the third trimester. At that point, the state's desire to preserve potential life can be used to justify a ban on all abortions, "except when it is necessary to preserve the life or health of the mother" (164). Whether abortions are to be permitted or prohibited, protecting the "mother" is a guiding state concern.

Finally, when abortion is permitted, the Court relied upon a woman's physician to guide her in her decision to terminate an unwanted pregnancy. The role of the physician in making the abortion decision is so strongly stated as to leave the woman occluded. When abortion is first acknowledged as falling under privacy, it is "the woman and her responsible physician" (153) (for what and to whom is he responsible?) that are left with the decision. More specifically, during the first trimester, "the attending physician, in consultation with his patient, is free to determine, without regulation by the State, that, in his medical judgment, the patient's pregnancy should be terminated" (163). In this instance, the woman is merely consulted and the decision is made by the physician. By the summary section of the opinion, the woman is no longer even consulted: "For the stage prior to approximately the end of the first trimester, the abortion decision and its effectuation must be left to the medical judgment of the pregnant woman's attending physician" (164). While elevating the doctor, the Court explicitly dismisses the idea of a woman deciding on her own: "Appellant and some amici argue that the woman's right is absolute and that she is entitled to terminate her pregnancy at whatever time, in whatever way, and for whatever reason she alone chooses. With this we do not agree" (153). The outright rejection of the possibility that a woman *alone* should make such decisions is striking. It is the doctor who may choose, not the woman.

PRIVACY BEYOND *ROE*

Following *Roe*, the concept of privacy was applied by the Supreme Court to a variety of issues. Other issues that the Court applied the privacy doctrine to during the 1970s included zoning, food stamp provision, the rights of foster parents, possession of obscene materials, private school segregation, Medicaid funding for abortion, the right to marry, mandatory maternity leave, and the rights of unmarried fathers. Among the questions the Court faced in their application of the privacy doctrine were the definition of family and whether all consensual sexual activity was constitutionally protected. Doctrinally in this period, some members of the Court began to bring together due process analysis with equal protection analysis in the area of privacy.[7] Further, the Court returned again to the matters of abortion and birth control in two other major decisions — *Planned Parenthood of Missouri v. Danforth*, 428 U.S. 52 (1976), and *Carey v. Population Services Int'l*, 431 U.S. 678 (1977). In all of these cases, various members of the Court grappled with giving further articulation to privacy as a constitutional concept.

Three cases from 1977 illustrate the Court's concern with what constitutes a family and the degree to which it deserved constitutional protection. In the case of *Fiallo v. Bell*, 430 U.S. 787 (1977), the Supreme Court upheld INS regulations that discriminated against citizenship claims by the illegitimate children of American fathers. Considering the issue from an equal protection standpoint, the Court found that the illegitimate children of American fathers were less likely to have "close family ties" with their fathers than the illegitimate children of American mothers. In his dissent, Justice Thurgood Marshall wrote that the right of privacy applied to children as well as parents and was not restricted by issues of legitimacy. "In addition the statute interferes with the fundamental 'freedom of personal choice in matters of marriage and family life.' . . . The right to live together as a family belongs to both the child who seeks to bring in his or her father and the father who seeks the entrance of his child" (810). In the case of *Moore v. East Cleveland*, 431 U.S. 494 (1977), Justice Lewis Powell carried this logic further, in a majority opinion that struck down a zoning regulation that allowed only for narrowly defined family groups to occupy single-dwelling homes. Noting that they had "long recognized that freedom of personal choice in matters of marriage and family life" were protected under the Due Process Clause, the Court protested against "such intrusive regulation of the family" that made "a crime of a grandmother's choice to live with her grandson" (499). The family was constitutionally protected because it was an institution "deeply rooted in this Nation's history and tradition" (503). Further, the extended family "has roots equally venerable and equally deserving of constitutional recognition" (504). In extending privacy analysis via substantive due process, the Court found it useful to rely upon well-worn public conceptions of what is traditional. The Court was willing to step beyond the nuclear family in its extension of privacy rights, and even beyond the issue of legitimacy, at least in the case of the bonds between mothers and children. But there were limits to how far the definition of family could extend.

Those limits were clearly visible in the third case from 1977, *Smith v. Org.*

of Foster Families for Equality and Reform, 431 U.S. 816. At issue were the rights that foster parents faced with procedures that would deny them continued custody of their foster children. The claim was that the psychological ties developed within foster families made them into real families deserving constitutional protection. Writing for the majority, Justice Brennan denied the claim: "Here, however, whatever emotional ties may develop between foster parent and foster child have their origins in an arrangement in which the State has been a partner from the outset" (836). This was a state-created family that lacked natural (blood-related) bonds; no amount of emotional bonding could make such a family real. The presence of the state here is clearly a decisive factor in determining what was private (or prepolitical) and deserving of constitutional protection. Yet this distinction is striking, since marriage is also a state-created status that involves no blood relation. Despite the reasoning in *Eisenstadt,* however, marriage was not yet broadly regarded as a publicly sanctioned contract between two autonomous individuals. It, too, remains somehow natural, prepolitical, and deserving of privacy protection, even with the looming presence of the state in this institution.

Did the rulings of the 1960s and early 1970s concerning abortion and birth control suggest that consensual sexual relations were covered by a right to privacy? The Court appeared torn about this issue in related rulings. As early as *Osborn v. United States,* 385 U.S. 323 (1966), a Fourth Amendment case, Justice Douglas used his dissenting opinion to rant against government invasions of privacy, particularly in areas of sexuality, including homosexual sex (341–43). Later, Justice Marshall used his dissent in *California v. LaRue,* 409 U.S. 109 (1972), to suggest that consensual sex may be constitutionally protected in light of *Griswold* (132). The issue was discussed more directly in *Carey v. Population Services Int'l,* a case concerning the constitutionality of New York State law prohibiting the sale of contraceptives to minors. There the Court found that "the decision whether or not to beget or bear a child is at the very heart of" the right of personal privacy (685). Hence, as in *Griswold* and *Eisenstadt,* what was protected was a decision or choice, not an act; and further, the Court was concerned with procreation rather than sexuality. Thus, the availability of contraception was protected because "such access is essential to exercise of the constitutionally protected right of decision in matters of childbearing" (688). Yet what this meant for sexuality remained a question. The majority wrote in a footnote to this opinion, "As we observe below, 'the Court has not definitively answered the difficult question whether and to what extent the Constitution prohibits state statutes regulating [private consensual sexual] behavior among adults,' . . . and we do not purport to answer that question now" (689). In his partial concurring opinion, Justice Powell was more definite: "In my view, the extraordinary protection the Court would give to all personal decisions in matters of sex is neither required by the Constitution nor supported by our prior decisions" (703). Framed as a concern with life choices regarding procreation, the Court was willing to extend privacy even to the availability of contraception for adolescents. But framed differently, as a desire to protect sexual freedom, the Court hesitated or balked. Constitutional privacy had not yet displaced the public's ability to morally order social relations. Faith in the judgment and activities of particular private decision makers influenced the Court's willingness to offer them constitutional protection.

Finally, the usefulness and limits of privacy for women became more apparent in *Planned Parenthood of Missouri v. Danforth*. Following *Roe*, Missouri passed an abortion reform law that it hoped would pass constitutional scrutiny. The law had numerous restrictive provisions, which were considered by the Supreme Court; some were upheld, while others were rejected. One of the provisions that was upheld required a woman's written consent to the abortion. "The decision to abort, indeed, is an important, and often a stressful one, and it is desirable and imperative that it be made with full knowledge of its nature and consequences. The woman is the one primarily concerned, and her awareness of the decision and its significance may be assured, constitutionally, by the State to the extent of requiring her prior written consent" (66). The Court concurred with the state's desire to insure that women make well-informed decisions about abortion. They also seemed to express some doubt that an emotional ("stressed") woman, on her own, would make such a decision.

Yet the Court was unwilling to support a provision that required spousal consent. Such a provision contradicted the framework set out by *Roe*. "Clearly, since the State cannot regulate or proscribe abortion during the first stage, when the physician and his patient make that decision, the State cannot delegate authority to any particular person, even the spouse, to prevent abortion during that same period" (69). Nonetheless, the Court realized that consent would be preferable in an ideal situation. "It seems manifest that, ideally, the decision to terminate a pregnancy should be one concurred in by both the wife and her husband" (71). However, if there is a disagreement with the decision made by the woman and her physician, the woman's view must prevail. "Inasmuch as it is the woman who physically bears the child and who is the more directly and immediately affected by the pregnancy, as between the two, the balance weighs in her favor" (71). The Court also rejected a parental consent provision for pregnant minors, not so much because it interfered with the rights of those young women, but because it was an intrusion on the decision-making process of their doctors. In their concurring opinion, Justices Potter Stewart and Lewis Powell suggested that a differently constructed parental consent provision might withstand constitutional scrutiny. The dissenting justices all supported parental notification.

The terms of consent, then, appear central to the Court's willingness to extend a right of privacy to women. Contained within the discussion of consent were varying levels of doubt about a woman's ability and trustworthiness to make a "good" decision on whether to abort. Nearly all of the justices seemed quite reluctant to leave the matter entirely to the woman. Several took comfort in the presence of a responsible male doctor who will guide this decision. The majority upheld the state's effort to insure that the decision be considered with the written consent provision. Greater doubt appears about the role of husbands, as well as the role of parents of pregnant minors. In sum, two competing visions of women in private inform the constitutional debates over abortion and birth control. One is of a woman who is like a man in the private realm — an independent being, master of her own destiny, and capable and deserving of choosing her own life course. The other is of a woman within a domestic domain who depends on the guidance, protection, and authority of others. What is striking about the extension of privacy rights to women in the 1960s and 1970s is how much of the second vision, rather than the first, guided that extension.

Privacy in Focus: The Home, the Doctor, and the Decision Maker

In order to delineate the development of the privacy doctrine more fully, this section examines three revealing positions in the discussions of privacy — that of the home, the doctor, and the decision maker. Historically, in liberalism, the private, nonpolitical realm was a realm in which established authority relationships existed. These relationships were legally represented in the common law of domestic relations, which specified the mutual responsibilities of members of the household. Under the law of domestic relations, masters had authority and obligations to all the dependent members of their household, including their wives, children, servants, and wards. The household, then, was a highly structured place both socially and legally. It was a domain where the male heads ruled apart from the state. In time, of course, the understanding of the home and domestic relations underwent drastic changes. In America, in the late eighteenth and early nineteenth centuries, the ideal of male domestic authority was both democratized and reduced. Any husband or father could be seen as the head of his own household, without the need for an estate or servants to establish the terms of their domestic domain (Stanley, 1998). Yet while more men became masters, the terms of that authority were diminished, as legal reforms removed the legal disabilities of wives under coverture and employees under the master-servant tradition (Orren, 1991; Tomlins, 1995; Ritter, 2000a and 2002). Further, the bonds between husbands and wives, and parents and children, came to be regarded as based as much on affection as on authority. All of these changes in public and legal understanding of the home and the domestic sphere were evident in the emergence and development of the privacy doctrine. The home shifted from being a place of ownership and authority to a place of self-expression, family, and affection.

Although the male master of the house fades as a legal figure, to be replaced by an unattached, autonomous individual, the limits of liberal individualism are exposed in relation to women's civic membership. This shift is most apparent in the application of privacy rights to women. While the husband is gone, standing in his place is the male doctor. For those who are ready to conceive of women as autonomous individuals, the doctor supplies professional expertise to these women. For others, who still want to see women as guided and protected by a male authority, the doctor can make the right decision for the woman, based upon his own good medical judgment. The limitations of a woman's ability to take up the role of an autonomous individual are further revealed in discussions of women as decision makers. Only a few Supreme Court justices in this period are clearly ready to affirm women's capacity to make significant life choices such as whether to have an abortion. Indeed, as the *Roe* opinion reveals, most justices are reluctant to see women as sole individuals at all. Women (particularly when pregnant) are often presented as vulnerable, emotional, and ignorant. Consequently, they are given company in their role as deciders — company which mediates the decision-making process by providing them with guidance or diminishing their authority to decide. Thus, the second model of privacy, of a woman as a dependent being in the domestic realm, seems to dominate the extension of privacy rights to women in the 1970s.

THE HOME

The constitutional concept of privacy emerges in the late nineteenth century in connection with Fourth Amendment concerns about unreasonable searches and seizures. In *Boyd* (1886), the Court began its discussion of privacy with a review of the right of property and prohibitions on trespass. Quoting from a famous 1760s English ruling by Lord Camden, the Court stated, "By the laws of England, every invasion of private property, be it ever so minute, is a trespass. No man can set his foot upon my ground without my license" (627). A man's property was his domain and no one was allowed there without his consent. It was a domain inhabited by a person and that person's possessions — including papers and writings. The home becomes not just a place of material holdings, but of persons and personalities.

This may help to explain why Warren and Brandeis were at pains to suggest that privacy was not about property. Instead, it was something personal, even when it concerned the home. For these scholars, the home was a place to express one's personality beyond the purview of the state. It was also a place of intimate relations. That view of the home is confirmed in *Meyer* (1923), where the Court stated that liberty includes the rights "to marry, establish a home and bring up children" (399). Here a home is a place of family and personal relationships.

By the middle of the twentieth century, the Supreme Court represented the home as being central to the concept of privacy, but what precisely the home is varied greatly from opinion to opinion. It was still a place of possession and female dependence, occupied during the day by the "hospitable housewife, peering on Monday morning around her chained door" (*Breard v. Alexandria*, 341 U.S. 622 [1951], 637). Likewise, the Court affirmed that the Fourth Amendment was premised on the view that "a man's home is his castle beyond invasion either by inquisitive or by officious people" (*Public Utilities Commission v. Pollak*, 343 U.S. 451 [1952], 467). Even as late as 1973, the Court stated that constitutional respect for the "privacy of the home" was "hardly more than a reaffirmation of the principle that 'a man's home is his castle'" (*Paris Adult Theatre I v. Slaton* 413 U.S. 49 [1973], 66).

But other conceptions of the home were emerging as well. In Justice Harlan's famous dissent in *Poe* (1961), the home was protected as a place of family life:

> if the physical curtilage of the home is protected, it is surely as a result of solicitude to protect the privacies of the life within. Certainly the safeguarding of the home does not follow merely from the sanctity of property rights. The home derives its pre-eminence as the seat of family life. And the integrity of that life is something so fundamental that it has been found to draw to its protection the principles of more than one explicitly granted Constitutional right. (551–52)

Likewise, in *Griswold* the home emerges as the "marital home" or, in Powell's opinion in *Carey*, as a place of parental authority. Marshall tried to go further in his *Belle Terre v. Boraas*, 416 U.S. 1 (1974), dissent, suggesting that any companionate relationship could be used to constitute a home. The right to "establish a home" is an essential part of the liberty. The choice of household companions — of whether a person's "intellectual and emotional needs" are best met by living with family, friends, professional associates, or others — involves deeply personal considerations as to the kind and quality of intimate relationships within the home (15–16).

Even for those who still viewed the home primarily as a separate domain beyond state authority, its sanctity for the individual derived from its status as a place to "satisfy his intellectual and emotional needs," rather than as a place of possession. But for some, it was just a place. "The protection afforded by *Stanley v. Georgia*, 394 U.S. 557 (1969), is restricted to a place, the home" (*Paris Adult Theatre I*, 66). After the middle of the century, the home emerged as a realm of intimacy, emotion, relationships, family, personal need, sexuality, and above all, privacy. Yet shadows of an earlier understanding of the home remained, in which men occupied the home more singularly and authoritatively, while the presence of women was more likely to evoke visions of human dependence and interconnection.

THE DOCTOR

In the genealogy of the privacy doctrine presented above, the position of the doctor has already been discussed. Here I seek only to add a couple of elements to that analysis. How did doctors come to be such important figures

in the extension of privacy rights to women? Partly, this occurred acciden-
tally. Doctors were granted standing in *Griswold* because they were at the
forefront of the birth control movement and could be prosecuted for providing contraception to women. Yet this was also a period in which (mostly
male) doctors were widely respected figures, whose judgments about the
physical as well as mental health and well-being of their patients was very
highly regarded. It is also worth remembering, as Reva Siegel discusses, that
doctors led the first pro-life movement in the late nineteenth century, and
based their position then on the claim that they understood the development
of life during pregnancy, while women did not (Siegel, 1992).

Once the doctors were in place as authoritative figures on procreative
issues, they could also be relied upon by judges and legislators to play a
broader role in guiding women. In *Griswold*, doctors were given standing
because they could be prosecuted; but they are also found to have a
"confidential relationship" with the potential recipients of contraception
(*Griswold*, 481). The role of the doctor was expanded greatly in *United States
v. Vuitch*, 402 U.S. 62 (1971), handed down just a couple of years before *Roe*.
At issue was the conviction of Dr. Milan Vuitch in Washington, DC, for performing abortions. The law under which Vuitch was convicted was challenged for vagueness — in particular there was a provision of the law which
allowed a doctor to provide a woman with an abortion in order to preserve
her life or health. A lower court had dismissed the conviction on the finding
that doctors who performed abortions were presumed guilty until proven
innocent, and that the term *health* provided too vague a standard. The
Supreme Court disagreed: "Generally, doctors are encouraged by society's
expectations, by the strictures of malpractice law and by their own professional standards to give their patients such treatment as is necessary to preserve their health. We are unable to believe that Congress intended that a
physician be required to prove his innocence" (71). The Court assumed that
Congress's faith (like its own) in the professional standards of physicians
would have kept them from presuming physicians' guilt in cases of abortion.
As for health, the Court believed this term should be broadly construed to
include mental health, and that the only responsible judges of what was in
the interest of a patient's health were the doctors themselves. "Indeed,
whether a particular operation is necessary for a patient's physical or mental
health is a judgment that physicians are obviously called upon to make rou-
tinely whenever surgery is considered" (72).

In subsequent abortion cases, both *Griswold* and *Vuitch* were cited to establish that doctors had standing to raise concerns regarding the constitutional rights of their patients, and that on matters of health their judgment was preeminent. By the time of *Roe* and *Doe*, the Court had come to lean heavily on the good judgment of doctors, suggesting that they (rather than the women who were pregnant) were the responsible parties in abortion decisions. Such a shift in responsibility was to the women's benefit, it appears. As the Court wrote in *Doe*,

> He, perhaps more than anyone else, is knowledgeable in this area of patient care, and he is aware of human frailty, so-called "error," and needs. The good physician — despite the presence of rascals in the medical profession, as in all others, we trust that most physicians are "good" — will have sympathy and understanding for the pregnant patient that probably are not exceeded by those who participate in other areas of professional counseling. (196–97)

Further, while the Court was quite willing to impose qualifications on the decision-making processes of the woman involved, it was generally unwilling to put such limits on the doctor. Thus, in *Doe*, a legal provision that required a doctor's judgment to be verified by other physicians and a hospital board was overturned. "Required acquiescence by co-practitioners has no rational connection with a patient's needs and unduly infringes on the physician's right to practice. The attending physician will know when a consultation is advisable — the doubtful situation, the need for assurance when the medical decision is a delicate one, and the like" (199).

This faith in the role of the male doctor, and accompanying lack of regard for the judgment of the pregnant woman, began to erode by the latter part of the 1970s. At least some of the justices began to show more deference to the judgment of the women involved. Others also expressed greater suspicion regarding the decisions and actions of doctors — particularly abortion clinic doctors. In the main opinion in *Carey*, there is a move to limit the role of doctors to abortion, because it is a medical procedure, rather than to contraception. It was a shift that involved a rereading of *Roe*: "In cases involving abortions, we have emphasized that the decision to terminate a pregnancy is properly made by a woman in consultation with her physician. See, e.g., *Roe v. Wade*" (*Carey*, 699). In fact, in *Roe* the decision is left to the doctor, who is sometimes called upon to consult with the woman. Now, in *Carey*, the doctor becomes a professional with expertise who may assist the woman in her judgment. Beginning with *Danforth*, questions were being raised about the judgments of doctors. In a partial dissent from the main opinion's ruling that struck down Missouri's parental consent provision, Justice John Paul Stevens wrote, "Similarly, even doctors are not omniscient; specialists in performing abortions may incorrectly conclude that the immediate advantages of the procedure outweigh the disadvantages which a parent could evaluate in better perspective. In each individual case factors much more profound than a mere medical judgment may weigh heavily in the scales" (*Planned Parenthood of Missouri v. Danforth*, 104). Such doubts seemed particularly appropriate to Justices Stewart and Powell, in the case of pregnant minors in relation to their doctors in clinics: "It seems unlikely that she will obtain adequate counsel and support from the attending physician at an abortion clinic, where abortions for pregnant minors frequently take place" (91). Clinic doctors, or doctors who specialize in abortion (there were more women doctors at the clinic), were by now suspect to the Supreme Court. So the changing authority afforded the doctors in these decisions may reflect either the Court's growing faith in the decisional capacities of women, or their loss of faith in the judgment of abortion doctors.

THE DECISION MAKER

In the Supreme Court decisions regarding women and privacy up through the 1970s, women are rarely presented as trustworthy and competent decision makers. This failure is striking, since the right of privacy in liberal theory is premised on the idea that individuals are rational and capable of self-governance. In John Locke's *Second Treatise of Government*, he writes of prepolitical society, "The *state of nature* has a law of nature to govern it, which obliges everyone: and reason, which is that law, teaches all mankind, who will but consult it, that being all *equal and independent*, no one ought to harm another in his life, health, liberty, or possessions" (1980, 9). It is reason that undergirds private liberty. Still, the need for a neutral authority to resolve disputes over property brings people in the state of nature together to form a social compact that creates government, thereby giving up some of their private liberty in the interest of public security. Yet even in Locke, there is an acknowledgment of the nonpolitical authority relationships that exist in the private realm. What is political power, Locke asks? He writes that "the power of a *magistrate* over a subject may be distinguished from that of a *father* over his children, a *master* over his servant, a *husband* over his wife, and a *lord* over his slave" (7). Although one man may hold all these roles, Locke seeks to "shew the difference betwixt a ruler of a commonwealth, a father of a family and a captain of a galley" (7–8). Traditionally, under liberalism, it is not women who in the state of nature are equal and independent (Pateman, 1988; W. Brown, 1995). Rather, they are the subject of their husbands' authority — a private, nonpolitical form of power. The Supreme Court discussions of women as decision makers overlap these two figures — the equal, rational, and independent man of the state of nature is combined with the dependent, previously ruled woman of the private realm.

In many of the Supreme Court rulings reviewed here, it is clear that the right of personal privacy is a right to make a decision about an important life matter. The classic statement of this view comes from *Eisenstadt*: "If the right of privacy means anything, it is the right of the individual, married or single, to be free from unwarranted governmental intrusion into matters so fundamentally affecting a person as the decision whether to bear or beget a child" (453). By implication, other fundamental matters, in addition to procreation, may be included under privacy. By the latter part of the decade, the understanding of personal privacy as decision making was clear. In *Carey*, the Court said "that the Constitution protects individual decisions" (687), in matters such as procreation. In *Whalen v. Roe*, 429 U.S. 589 (1977), the Court spoke of privacy as a right that "protects individual decisions" (599), and in *Zablocki v. Redhail*, 434 U.S. 374 (1978), the Court discussed marriage as being "among the personal decisions protected by the right of privacy" (384). In these instances, the Court suggested that this was what the right of privacy meant from *Griswold*, through *Roe*, and beyond. As a liberal right, privacy is the right of a rational person to make choices without government interference. Privacy (as the pro-choice movement correctly captured) was a right to decide.

It is striking, then, that the right of privacy for women in the latter abortion cases (*Carey, Danforth, Casey*) either erodes or conditions the terms under which a woman decides or consents to an abortion. In some of the companion opinions in *Planned Parenthood of Missouri v. Danforth*, for instance, the Court stressed the importance of the abortion decision as a way of saying that this choice should not be left to the woman alone, particularly if she is underage. A principal concern in the main opinion (discussed above) was to preserve the authority of doctors in the decision-making process. In their concurring opinion, Justices Stewart and Powell wrote regarding the written consent provision that the *Roe* ruling was "not intended to preclude the State from enacting a provision aimed at ensuring that the abortion decision is made in a knowing, intelligent, and voluntary fashion" (*Danforth*, 90). Raising further doubts about the woman's role as a decision maker, Justice Byron White, in his dissent, wrote regarding spousal notification that the Missouri law was "recognizing that the husband has an interest of his own in the life of the fetus which should not be extinguished by the unilateral decision of the wife" (93). Finally, the importance of choice is turned on its head by White in his support for the parental consent provision.

> The purpose of the requirement is to vindicate the very right created in *Roe v. Wade*, supra — the right of the pregnant woman to decide "whether or not to terminate her pregnancy." The abortion decision is unquestionably important and has irrevocable consequences whichever way it is made. Missouri is entitled to protect the minor unmarried woman from making the decision in a way which is not in her own best interests, and it seeks to achieve this goal by requiring parental consultation and consent. (94–95)

In a wonderful twist in reasoning, White explained that it is the importance of the choice being made that leads him to deny a young woman the right to choose.

The Supreme Court was not comfortable with viewing women as decision makers. In this role, women might behave as women — that is, by being emotional and relationally dependent, so the quality of their decision and their ability to reach the "right choice" was in doubt. It was because of this that the state was so likely to provide women with guidance in their abortion choice — most typically that of a male doctor. On the other hand, as the decade wore on, the image of women as rational, autonomous decision makers did begin to take form, and it, too, was discomforting. A pregnant woman acting like a rational, autonomous man was also something that many Supreme Court justices were not ready for, as revealed by their discussion of the spousal consent requirement in *Danforth*. Privacy was supposed to be a matter of mind and not body, but putting women in a position to make a mental determination about what was otherwise supposed to be a defining physical state was perhaps too great a change in gender conceptions to be easily tolerated.

Conclusion

Privacy was the doctrine developed in affording women new civic rights because privacy was legally and ideologically associated with notions of gender difference and dependence. Privacy operated as something of an empty signifier that could be filled differently by different judges and advocates, some who saw women as autonomous individuals and others who saw them as dependent and connected females. Privacy signified the difficulty within the American constitutional order of incorporating women as liberal citizens.

This chapter has argued that the emergence of privacy as a constitutional claim for the expansion of women's rights was due in part to privacy's relation to the common law tradition of coverture. That is not to suggest that privacy grew directly out of the law governing husband and wife relations, or that in modern privacy cases the doctor is a direct stand-in for the husband. Rather, the contention is that the law of coverture brought with it a broader normative universe under which women, married or single, were regarded as dependent persons outside the public realm, under the guidance and authority of male heads of household. So it is the ideals and beliefs of coverture regarding gender relations and social order that get partly reproduced in privacy doctrine rather than the law of coverture itself.

But the claim is also broader than this. Several scholars from law, history, and political science have written about the transition in American law and governance from a common law status regime to a regime based on liberalism and contract (Stanley, 1988 and 1998; Siegel, 1994b; Orren, 1991; Tomlins, 1995; and Ritter, 2000a). As some of these scholars note, the shift away from common law status governance does not imply an end to hierarchy and difference in law and politics. Rather, hierarchy and difference reside in new places in the law, under new normative ideals. In the erosion of coverture, one of the new places where domestic authority relations appear is under the notion of household privacy (Ritter, 2000a). The privacy presented here, which is part of a constitutional theory of substantive due process liberty, is not the same as the household privacy that replaces elements of coverture. But these two notions of privacy may intersect at points, so that constitutional privacy becomes a way to bring women, conceived of as domestic and dependent, into modern liberalism. Tracing these intersections is crucial to the project of understanding how modern liberal governing institutions tolerate status hierarchies.

Observers from other countries are sometimes perplexed that the American abortion rights movement refers to itself as the "pro-choice" movement. Yet given the constitutional framework in which that movement has operated, the label is entirely understandable. Choice is precisely what is being appealed to in the doctrine of privacy. The choice appealed to by the abortion rights movement is fuller and more physically situated than it is for the justices of the Supreme Court. However, for both groups, there is a sense of a constitutional right to determine one's life course which is represented in the doctrine of privacy. Yet the notion of choice also captures what is problematic about privacy for abortion rights advocates. "Choice" seems somehow thin and intellectual when pitted against "life." The notion of choice, in liberal theory, is more intellectual and parsed. It is also contrary to commonsense understandings of gender. It is a male concept, rooted in a notion of autonomy and mental supremacy that clashes sharply with our understanding of the position of a pregnant woman. Finally, it is worth adding that "choice" speaks to the judicial treatment of privacy in another way. Privacy becomes the doctrine of choice for dealing with matters such as abortion and contraception, because it is a concept that tolerates widely different views of what it means and the position of women within it.

What is wrong with grounding the right to an abortion in privacy? (MacKinnon, 1987). In terms of women's civic membership more broadly, rooting rights in privacy has several potentially harmful consequences. One is the denial of a public civic presence to women. Privacy is a negative right that does little to establish women as civic members with public claims of justice. Instead they are cast outside the political realm. Another is the tolerance of notions of difference, which is not problematic in itself, but when difference is understood as being legally and philosophically opposed to equality, then it is problematic. Further, privacy remains an affirmation of the liberal division between public and private under which, historically, authority relations in the household were regarded as natural and prepolitical. Privacy also tends to reaffirm the dichotomy between independence and dependence, autonomy and connection (West, 1988).

Does this mean that privacy should be abandoned? In isolation, privacy provides a dangerous basis on which to advance claims for women's rights. There are two positive arguments for privacy, however. One is the argument put forward by gay and lesbian rights advocates and by critical race theorists that privacy as tolerance or as a prohibition against government intrusion provides important protection for sexual and racial minorities (A. Allen, 1988). The other is the possibility of bringing due process jurisprudence together with equal protection doctrine to provide a more positive claim for women's rights in areas such as sexuality and procreation. Since *Planned Parenthood v. Casey*, 505 U.S. 833 (1992) the Court has clearly affirmed the use of substantive due process reasoning in privacy cases, and in more recent cases, like *Lawrence v. Texas*, 539 U.S. 558 (2003), due process liberty has been increasingly paired with equality reasoning. A constitutional theory that puts together privacy with equality might help to overcome the legal and philosophical dichotomies that have been so harmful to women — equality versus difference, autonomy versus connection, independence versus dependence, and public versus private. Unless these divisions are overcome, on whichever side of the divide women are placed, women will be denied the status of full citizens and full persons in the United States (Lever, 2000).

This analysis suggests that within the U.S. constitutional order, women have never readily fit into the liberal ideal of citizenship. Liberalism proposes a civic membership that separates public selves from private lives and that is grounded in individualism. Under liberalism, economic self-interest motivates political preferences and ascriptive identities are politically irrelevant. Further, liberal citizens are imagined as rational, discriminating (that is, choosing), physically autonomous, and self-sufficient — to the extent that their mental characteristics are emphasized and their physical selves are rendered invisible. Those political subjects that are visible — those that occupy bodies that define their subjectivity, because they are dependent, or not self-contained, for instance — prove troubling for liberalism.

NINE

The Politics of Presence

Hence, there was an explosion of numerous and diverse techniques for achieving the subjugation of bodies and the control of populations, marking the beginning of the era of "bio-power."

— MICHEL FOUCAULT, *The History of Sexuality*

Certain promising political dynamics may be invisible to most of us at the moment because the categories we have for naming them make them invisible. Step outside the categories and suddenly there are new things to see.

— LANI GUINIER AND GERALD TORRES, *The Miner's Canary*

This book began with a question: when did women become civic members of the United States? In pursuit of an answer, the first eight chapters explored the changing terms of women's civic membership from the Civil War through second wave feminism. That journey revealed two dominant legal and political ideals that shaped women's civic membership throughout the late nineteenth and twentieth centuries: the ideal of the domestic, dependent citizen, and its opposite ideal, the liberal, individual citizen. Under the first ideal, women were citizens relationally. They had no direct presence in the public realm, where they were represented by their husbands and fathers. This ideal of civic membership was encoded in coverture, which erased a woman's legal personality upon marriage. Over time, in the twentieth century, women gained standing as legal individuals in the public realm under the terms of liberal citizenship. Yet the presumption of private obligations and a domestic identity limited the degree to which courts and legislatures were willing to embrace the model of liberal personhood for women. Remnants of the old domestic, dependency ideal took up residency in the constitutional doctrine of privacy, where physical difference and relationality were indirectly acknowledged and construed as allowing women voice in their reproductive destinies. The contradictions between these two models of civic membership remains with us today; even now, early in the twenty-first century, there is no clear, coherent understanding of women's civic place in the United States. The issue of women's civic status has yet to be fully resolved.

This final chapter turns to another question: what sort of civic membership should women want? Or, more precisely, what civic ideal should women claim when they assert their status as full members of the American constitutional order? This question asks us to imagine what civic role would work best to express the political interests and identities of American men and women in a fair and just manner. It asks as well what sort of civic membership would enable women to pursue their political interests democratically and efficaciously. By taking the lessons learned from the prior debates over women's civic membership, we can identify the deficiencies inherent in previous ideals of women's civic membership and the promise present in the visions of civic membership offered by women's rights activists and other democratic activists who have aspired for full inclusion within the American constitutional order. After reviewing these previous ideals of women's civic membership, this chapter outlines an alternative — the ideal of a public, embodied citizenship.

The question that frames this chapter contains a political and theoretical presumption: namely, that "women" form a politically meaningful category. My defense for using "women" as a category here is historical and strategic rather than normative in nature. First, following Denise Riley (1988), we can say that it is significant that women historically have been legally and politically constituted as a category. "Women" were afforded different legal rights and duties from men, and women were excluded from most forms of political participation for much of the nation's history. Although its significance may have lessened, sex remains a legally and politically important category in the early twenty-first century. Women as a political category may be thought of as "real" because sex is institutionally inscribed in ways that affect the social experiences and opportunities of all those recognized as female.

Second, though we may start by recognizing sex as an institutionally and legally meaningful category, the category "women" need not be preserved or privileged, except to the degree that participants in a common political project find it useful. From a political perspective, gender may be treated the same way that Lani Guinier and Gerald Torres (2002) treat race, as elaborated in their discussion of "political race": "The concept of political race captures the association between those who are raced black — and thus often left out — and a democratic social movement aimed at bringing about constructive change within the larger community. . . . The project of political race challenges both those on the right who say race is not real as well as those on the left who say it is real but we cannot talk about it" (12). Likewise, "women" may serve as the starting point for a political project that seeks to reimagine gender as a social category that is neither politically invisible nor marked as subjected. In arguing for the pursuit of an embodied, public citizenship, I seek to do three things in relation to "women" as a political category: to make gender visible, and allow for the articulation of gendered experiences and concerns in public life; to make gendered political identity fluid rather than fixed, by suggesting that it is a category of experience and action rather than of distinct rights and duties; and finally, to focus on embodiment in order to have a political, coalitional effect with those who (like women) are cast as politically and legally suspect by their embodiment — racial and ethnic minorities, the disabled, and sexual minorities.

The Lessons of Domestic, Dependent Civic Membership

It is easy to recognize the limits of the domestic, dependent civic membership model for women. Prior to the twentieth century, the norm of coverture regularly was invoked to deny women the opportunities of public civic membership. As expressed by Justice Bradley in *Bradwell v. Illinois*, 83 U.S. 130 (1872), women were unfit "for many of the occupations of civil life" (141); rather, women belonged to the "domestic sphere." In support of this view, Bradley cited the common law principle "that a woman had no legal existence separate from her husband, who was regarded as her head and representative in the social state" (141). On the eve of women's suffrage, the Court again found that "history discloses the fact that woman has always been dependent upon man" (*Muller v. Oregon*, 208 U.S. 412 [1908], 421) — which the Court took to mean that a woman's constitutional liberty rights could be more readily infringed upon than could a man's. Five decades later, as President Kennedy was forming the Presidential Commission on the Status of Women, the Court returned to this old refrain when it found that "woman is still regarded as the center of home and family life," so she could be "relieved from the civic duty of jury service unless she herself determines that such service is consistent with her own special responsibilities" (*Hoyt v. Florida*, 368 U.S. 57 [1961], 61–62). Women's domestic identity, or *special responsibilities*, still excluded them from civic participation, although now that exclusion was framed as voluntary. Even in the midst of second wave feminism, as the Court was pushed to acknowledge a woman's right to control her reproduction under the doctrine of privacy, the majority went on to suggest that since a pregnant woman could not "be isolated in her privacy" her constitutional claims were more limited in nature (*Roe v. Wade*, 410 U.S. 113 [1973], 159). Embodiment and relationality led to a fettering of women's rights.

The ideal of domestic, dependent civic membership is entwined with the history of women's civic subjugation. Yet positive lessons are to be learned from this model of civic membership that may be glimpsed in various movement rhetoric, legislative debates, and court opinions. The main virtue of this model is its acknowledgment of relationality and embodiment as experiences with potential political significance. If domesticity is taken as a realm of activity and experience rather than an ideology or a destiny, then politics and the public realm may open up to the articulation of interests and concerns related to caretaking, family life, and intimacy, on the one hand, as well as violence, dominance, and the needs of the socially vulnerable, on the other. And if dependency is understood as a recognition of need rather than a relationship of subjection, then it might allow for the expression of a broader realm of social experience in politics.

As discussed in Chapter 4, the early women's rights advocates had a vision of women's participation on juries that suggested that they would bring their domestic experiences, and experiences of dependency and vulnerability, with them into politics. Elizabeth Cady Stanton and Antoinette Brown articulated a view of jury service in which gendered experiences like rape, abandonment, and single motherhood would inform women's sense of justice. Oregon briefly experimented with the "mixed jury" model of justice as well (Constable, 1994), when in the early 1920s it instituted a plan in the juvenile justice system that mandated that at least half of the jury members would be women in cases where the victim was an underage girl. The plan failed because the automatic exemption provision for women's jury service made it too difficult to find enough women jurors. Oregon sensed that the gendered experiences of domestic life mattered for women's civic sensibilities, but it was uncertain about whether those experiences called for women's inclusion into the public realm or their exclusion from it. When the federal courts first found that the exclusion of women from jury service was constitutionally problematic, in *Ballard v. United States*, 329 U.S. 187 (1946), they also indicated that women's gendered experiences affected their jury participation. In explaining how gender might matter to jury service, the Court quoted from a lower court opinion in which a hypothetical woman juror was presented as "the mother of five children at whose knee have been instilled in them the teachings of Jesus . . . a sensitive woman, highly spiritual in character" (194–95). Motherhood and religious experience were the things a woman might bring with her into the jury box, without which the justice system would be less broad and community-based.

Two other brief examples from the 1930s and 1940s illustrate the way that a domestic, dependent model offers promising possibilities for structuring an alternative model for women's civic membership. The first example comes from the 1939 amendments to the Social Security Act. The amendments were designed to expand the insurance program, Title II, by adding the wives, widows, and underage children of male workers who were contributing to the program. In considering the terms under which wives and widows would be included, women members of the Federal Advisory Commission proposed adding them not as men's dependents, but as separately entitled recipients who received benefits on the basis of their private (or household) labor contributions. This proposal was rejected because there was not sufficient support in the commission or in Congress for seeing household labor as creating an independent civic entitlement (Kessler-Harris, 1995).[1] Had the proposal been adopted, it would have recognized women's *domestic* contributions as a civic contribution (and would have redefined *work* in the process), while denying that their *dependency* made them indirect civic members, recognized through their attachment to men.

The second New Deal example comes from the benefits given to war veterans in the 1940s. There are different ways of understanding the virtues of military service, all of which highlight the physical and relational sacrifices made by those in the armed forces. Virtue may lie in one's willingness to risk personal safety and perhaps even to die for the nation. Prior to World War II, veteran's benefits were primarily intended to assist those injured or killed in combat.[2] As such, these benefits were a direct recognition of the embodied sacrifice made during war. Yet they were still granted under terms that suggested dependency, since disabled veterans (and their widows) were the main beneficiaries.

During the Second World War, the logic of benefit provision shifted, as all vets were made eligible for benefits that were intended to enable them to have greater social and economic opportunities. The main benefits provided by the Servicemen's Readjustment Act (popularly known as the GI Bill) were educational benefits, medical benefits, unemployment benefits, low-interest housing and business loans, job training and placement services, and civil service job preferences. The virtue of military service may also lie in one's willingness to surrender one's personal autonomy, in the "separation from home and family" (*Mitchell v. Cohen*, 333 U.S. 411 [1948], 418). Even noncombatants could demonstrate virtue, particularly when personal risk was involved. In *Girouard v. United States*, 328 U.S. 61 (1946), the Court highlighted the war contributions of those unable (for religious or other reasons) to bear arms: the "nurses, engineers, litter bearers, doctors, [and] chaplains," many of whom "made the supreme sacrifice" (64). Finally, war service may involve not just the risk of death or injury but a willingness to kill for the good of the country. These physical actions and relational sacrifices were recognized as civic virtues and rewarded with benefits intended to expand social opportunities for veterans.

The 1960s saw the birth of the phrase "the personal is political." Radical feminists offered an understanding of politics that exposed the power dynamics present in family life and personal relations. They called for recognition of the social contribution made by domestic labor. Abortion and childbearing were presented as lived experiences that involved trauma and hardship. As women's rights lawyer Nancy Stearns commented: "I don't think we could possibly underestimate how much women have taught judges, lawyers, and the public. . . . They understood the concept of testimony of experts. . . . But who ever heard of a woman walking into the courtroom talking about something so personal and emotional as back street abortion?" (Goodman, Schoenbrod, and Stearns, 1973, 24–25). Embodiment was central to their understanding of both women's subjugation and their gendered conception of social justice on issues like war, violence, and sexual exploitation. In so many ways, the radical feminist vision uncovered women's experience in the private realm. The result was a deep rethinking of gender roles and the meaning of everyday justice. Yet beyond the realm of the personal, the radicals failed to engage with the broader world of public politics. Consequently, little of the radicals' vision carried over into the higher courts and legislatures, at least in the short term. There, the liberal political vision of civic membership continued to predominate.

The Limits of Liberal Civic Membership for Women

With many qualifiers, it seems fair to say that American political culture and constitutional discourse is largely liberal in its orientation. Over the course of American history, this liberalism, in connection with natural rights philosophy, has fired the constitutional and political imaginations of many aspirants to full civic inclusion. One striking aspect of the history of American radicalism is how often radical political actors have proceeded from the ideals of equality and universalism articulated in such founding documents as the Declaration of Independence (Hartog, 1987). These are arguments from within the American political tradition. The Declaration has been refashioned time and again by those on the margins of public life (e.g., in the Declaration of Sentiments and the "I have a dream" speech) as an assertion of their entitlement as people and as Americans to the promise of the American life. Much has been gained by these campaigns for inclusion under the terms of liberal civic membership.

The second civic ideal that shaped women's civic membership was liberal individualism. Over the course of the late nineteenth century and entire twentieth century some women, particularly native-born white women, came to be seen as legal persons and public individuals under the terms of liberal civic membership. Starting with the adoption of women's suffrage in the early twentieth century, women came to be understood, at least partially, as autonomous individuals in the public realm. The appeal of this ideal to many women's rights advocates is readily apparent. These early reformers, who first learned the principles of social justice from the abolition movement, wanted women's natural rights and civic inheritance to be acknowledged. Women desired to be seen as men's equals, with the same rights, responsibilities, and opportunities as their male counterparts. Yet, the gains always remained partial—women were never fully recognized as civically equal. The experience of women reveals the ways in which the ideal of lib-

eral civic membership itself — as a legal institution and as a normative ideal —
is flawed.

Although women were captivated by the American Dream, they never
readily fit into the liberal ideal of civic membership. Liberalism proposes a
civic membership that separates public selves from private lives and that is
grounded in individualism.[3] Under American liberalism, economic self-
interest is understood as motivating political preferences, and ascriptive
identities are rendered politically irrelevant. Further, in the United States,
liberal citizens are imagined as rational, discriminating (that is, choosing),
physically autonomous, and self-sufficient — to the extent that their mental
characteristics are emphasized and their physical selves are rendered invisible. Those political subjects that are visible — those that occupy bodies that
define their subjectivity, because they are dependent or not self-contained,
for instance — prove troubling for the U.S. constitutional order.

Directly or indirectly, women have always been civically marked as
embodied (through pregnancy, rape, motherhood, sexuality, and domestic
labor), and therefore seen as not fully fit for liberal civic membership.
Consequently, it is important to understand how embodiment is addressed
within liberal constitutionalism — particularly in connection with the regulation of social roles. In earlier times, when civic hierarchy was an accepted
part of the political order, embodiment was directly addressed as a factor
shaping the terms of civic membership. Thus, in *Dred Scott*, legal prohibitions on African Americans that prevented them from occupying various
social roles were taken as evidence that race was a mark of ineligibility for
civic membership.[4] The nineteenth-century constitutional order tended to
be socially constitutive in more direct terms, in its recognition of how social
roles (like those of wife or slave) and the particular embodiments connected
to them (sex, race) determined one's civic membership. Since the mid-twen-
tieth century, the social-design function of the constitutional order has
become more removed and less visible, and the connection made between
social roles and particular embodiments is more remote. Yet we continue to
provide constitutional rewards, recognition, and restrictions on social roles
and relationships of different kinds. Further, the embodied occupants of
these social roles and relationships still matter a great deal for the constitutional response (protective or punitive) they elicit — but less often in terms
that are directly expressed.[5]

Theoretically, liberal constitutional orders reject the relevance of social status for politics. One's race or gender should play no role in determining one's civic status — all citizens should be treated equally. Group-based distinctions that are seen as legally created, discriminatory, or derogatory are rejected in principle. As a result, liberalism has often been effectively mobilized in defense of liberty and individual rights. As discussed in Chapter 1, community and social regulatory concerns have historically operated in tension with constitutional guarantees of individual liberty. Social-order interests have often been cast as opposed to liberty interests — the family versus the individual, the racial order versus the person, and so on — an opposition expressed most powerfully in cases considering the civic status of subordinate groups like women and African Americans.

In practice, social-order concerns and regulations have not disappeared under liberal constitutionalism; they have merely been relocated or transformed. Acceptable liberal legal markers of social difference are based on things like voluntarism or achievement, forms of positive discrimination, and what are regarded as benign forms of classification that reflect pervasive, nonlegal customs or traditions. Another way of recognizing social-order concerns under a modern liberal constitutional order is through various versions of legal dualism that cede authority over social relations to an alternative legal order embedded within a larger liberal legal order. The continued presence of social-ordering laws in our liberal constitutional order suggests that the social-design function of the constitutional order is not adequately addressed through liberal principles.

Three historical examples illustrate the way that liberal constitutionalism contends with gender difference. First, California granted suffrage — and legal personhood — to women in 1913. Yet when Ethel Mackenzie sought to assert her new public identity by registering to vote, not only was she turned away from the polls, but her citizenship was stripped from her as well. Mackenzie had married a foreign national, so under a 1907 statute, she was no longer considered an American citizen. In discussing the constitutionality of the law used to deny Mackenzie her U.S. citizenship, the Supreme Court cited the "ancient principle" of marital unity under which the "identity of husband and wife" is merged and "dominance [is given] to the husband" (*Mackenzie v. Hare*, 239 U.S. 299 [1915], 311). The marital-unity principle derived from coverture — a justification that drew directly from the domestic, dependent model of civic membership.

Yet the Court's reasoning did not end there. Under common law, political allegiance is formed at birth and cannot be alienated. The United States had modified the principle of birth allegiance, but in doing so they added the provision that expatriation must be voluntary. Mackenzie never indicated a desire to forfeit her citizenship. For the Court, the marriage itself was the act of consent by which Mackenzie gave up her citizenship, so the expatriation was voluntary. Thus, Mackenzie was credited with the liberal capacity to consent and contract — only in order to deny her the rights and status of citizenship altogether. A liberal choice resulted in a status-based subjection.[6]

By the 1940s, direct invocations of coverture or marital unity were much rarer. Instead, the precursors of the privacy doctrine were being developed under substantive due process reasoning. So, when Sarah Prince was arrested for violating a child labor statute by allowing her niece and ward, Betty Simmons, to engage in religious solicitation on the streets of Brockton, Massachusetts, she defended herself by citing religious freedom and parental authority. In deciding the case, the Court wove together a defense of constitutional liberty with the recognized values of family and domesticity. Liberty and order were not entirely opposed to each other — in some respects they were concurrent. As the Court wrote, the "primary function and freedom" of parents is to prepare children for their future "obligations," so that they might grow "into free and independent well-developed men and citizens" (*Prince v. Massachusetts*, 321 U.S. 158 [1944], 165–66). Families and their liberty were protected when they functioned as institutions of social ordering. They were subject to infringement when their contribution to social ordering was found suspect. In ruling against Prince, the Court found that "the family itself is not beyond regulation in the public interest," and suggested that Prince had failed in her duty as Simmons's guardian when she allowed her to be "subject to all the diverse influences of the street" (166). The street was no domestic haven. It was a failure that Prince was prone to commit as a woman (particularly a religious one). Prince initially had refused the children's request to go out street preaching that night, when "childlike, they resorted to tears and, motherlike, she yielded" (162). A less emotional, more rational parent — a father rather than a mother — might have received more respect from the Court in his assertion of his "sacred, private interests" (165) and parental authority.

Finally, in discussing the Supreme Court's failure to develop a coherent approach to women's constitutional rights in the 1970s, Ruth Bader Ginsburg highlighted the "meandering course" taken by the Court in pregnancy-related cases (R. B. Ginsburg, 1978b, 144). In *Geduldig v. Aiello*, 417 U.S. 484 (1974), the Court infamously ruled that the exclusion of pregnancy claims from coverage by the California Disability Fund was not discriminatory, because "there is no risk from which men are protected and women are not" (496–97). But another case (*Cleveland Board of Education v. LaFleur*, 414 U.S. 632 [1974]), determined on due process rather than equal protection grounds, decided it was unconstitutional to exclude pregnant women from labor participation. The cases called into question the Court's understanding of discrimination and equality, and how it related to embodied difference between the sexes. Equality was not tied to political participation and civic membership. It had failed to become a broader norm that guided the Court's analysis of discriminatory laws in the way suggested by Kenneth Karst when he posed the question: "Are women to have the opportunity to participate in full partnership with men in the nation's social, political, and economic life? This is a *constitutional* issue" (Karst, 1976, 1036).

Justice Brennan understood this as well when, in his dissent in *General Electric Co. v. Gilbert*, 429 U.S. 125 (1976), he chastened the majority for their failure to consider whether GE had a demonstrated history of sex discrimination (148–53) or to take into account the impact that pregnancy-related employment and benefit exclusions had on women's economic opportunities (153–60). The majority justified the company's exclusion of pregnancy from disability coverage by noting that pregnancy was a "voluntary" condition. Again, the language of liberal choice was used to forgo an analysis of how social experiences connected to physical differences affected equality and participation in public life. The alternative approach that Brennan advocated was one in which the "Court recognized that discrimination is a social phenomenon encased in a social context and, therefore, unavoidably takes its meaning from the desired end products of the relevant legislative enactment, end products that may demand due consideration to the uniqueness of 'disadvantaged' individuals" (159). Yet when a woman's physical being came into view, the limits of the equality analysis that predominated within the liberal constitutional order were evident. Women could only be civically equal if they were unsexed — to acknowledge their embodiment and experiences of gender difference was contrary to the goal of perfecting a color- and sex-blind constitution.

Neither the liberal-individualist nor the domestic-dependent model of civic membership provides women with a strong starting point for participation in civic life. Yet both of these models have positive possibilities that might be recuperated in elaborating a new ideal for women's civic membership.[7] The domestic-dependent model allows for an expression of embodied experiences in politics. Its main limitation is that it denies *public* participation and presence to women. For the liberal-individualist model of citizenship, the opposite holds true. This model provides women with a public role and a claim to rights and a voice within the political sphere. But relationality and embodied experience are denied under liberal civic membership. The persons constructed by legal liberalism are unfeatured and isolated. The alternative ideal outlined below is of an embodied, public civic membership.

Embodied Civic Membership

I propose an alternative ideal of civic membership that is both embodied and public. Gleaning insight from feminist theory, critical race theory, and disability studies, we can critically examine the ways that liberal jurisprudence contends with troubling bodies — such as the bodies of pregnant women seeking abortions, or of disabled persons seeking recognition and accommodation in their lives as workers or as students. This analysis highlights the relationship between physical presence and civic membership — a relationship that should be recast and broadened to include a range of ways of being present in the world, which would imply as well a range of social connectivity that takes us beyond either the autonomous, unfeatured individual or the ascriptively defined member of a specified group. Private existence and social experience should be brought to our public lives in ways that inform our political participation, our sense of justice, and our desires for a representative polity. Too often, when civic membership is given social specificity and presence, it is cast in private terms that encourage essentialism and the political regulation of the socially marginalized. By insisting that civic presence be cast in public terms, we can make it more fluid, self-actualized, procedural (that is, with an emphasis on voice), and empowered.

Why should civic membership be embodied? There are many reasons to fear civic embodiment: it could lead to social regulation, civic disability, essentialism, and political subjection. Under the terms of American liberalism, civic members with bodies are subject to regulation by the state. Physical presence refigures civic subjectivity for those who are seen as racially different, not self-contained (pregnant women and nursing mothers), not autonomous (the disabled), or transgressive and excessive in their physicality, too sexual or prone to violence (immigrants, racial minorities, gays and lesbians, etc.).

Embodiment makes visible social difference and status difference. In contrast, the modern American liberal constitutional order operates under the pretense that there are no differences that politically matter. Historically, civic embodiment has produced political disenfranchisement. Embodiment is considered to be a problem for civic membership for several reasons. It marks you as *dependent* — in the cases of children, wives, the elderly, the disabled, and slaves. It marks you as *irrational* — in the cases of those who are defined by their labor (slaves or servants) or by violence (rapists, murderers, and their victims). It marks you as *diseased* — in the cases of the contagious, the chronically ill, or the mentally disabled, whose condition may be taken as a sign of moral or social failure and whose proximity may be seen as threatening to "healthy" civic members.[8] It marks you as *unvirtuous* or excessively sexual — in the cases of unmarried mothers or gays and lesbians. Finally, it marks you as *unbounded*, as contiguous or continuous with others — in the cases of pregnant women, nursing mothers, and those who are sexually open. These are bodies in need of regulation. They are bodies whose presence disturbs us, so we seek to cordon them off through confinement, rest homes, special schools for the disabled, and prisons; they should not be visible in the public realm. Civic embodiment, in short, is often seen as justification for political regulation or denial.

Nonetheless, I argue for an embodied civic membership for two reasons. First, because embodiment is not always a choice, it is better to try to claim and control the terms of embodiment. By making embodiment visible, the terms under which civic embodiment is created might be made more apparent and subject to critique. In the process of exposing the ways that politically problematic bodies are produced, we may also expose the production of the normal, self-disciplined (and therefore not legally visible) bodies of the civically privileged. Second, embodiment can bring things to civic membership that are positive and productive, such as relationality and the potential for particularity. Further, embodiment allows us to bring a broader range of our social experience with us into civic life, which is important, particularly for those whose lives are primarily figured within households and smaller community settings.

THEORIZING EMBODIMENT

For French social theorist Michel Foucault, modernity is characterized by a regime that has at its center the regulation of the human body. Whereas the premodern age was organized around a sovereignty expressed in the power of death, modern sovereignty is expressed in power over life. Two types of bodily regulation have emerged in the past three centuries, one that involves the disciplining of individual bodies through ideologies and institutions that teach self-mastery, and the other that concerns itself with the broader population (the "species body"), its health, longevity, and rate of growth (Foucault, 1990, 139). Individually, bodies have come to be regarded as machines that should be made to work effectively and efficiently. Collectively, bodies are at the center of the social order that sustains the nation economically, politically, and militarily. This shift to sovereignty over life represented a sea change in the nature of politics, since, "for the first time . . . biological existence was reflected in political existence" (142). This political shift was reflected in the juridical system as well, where instead of distinguishing between allies and enemies in order to administer death to the latter, "the law operates more and more as a norm" that "is increasingly incorporated into a continuum of apparatuses (medical, administrative and so on) whose functions are for the most part regulatory" (144). Distinguishing bodies around this norm also creates new means for enacting social hierarchies. Finally, resistance to this new sovereignty over life takes the body as its object as well, in calls for a "'right' to life, to one's body, to health, to happiness . . . to rediscover what one is and all that one can be" (145).

Foucault's theory of bio-power furthers our analysis of civic embodiment in several ways. First, Foucault presents a view of modernity in which bodies are disciplined and rationalized through techniques of self-mastery. For the liberal individual civic member then, bodies are instrumental and subject to the authority of a reasoning mind.[9] Second, in the domain of regulation of the "species body," the primary subjects are women because of their role in reproduction. Women, in this sense, stand at the center of the state's social-ordering concerns. What this may mean as well is that it is men who are cast as self-mastering individuals, while women are more likely to be seen as part of the human collective. Third, the creation of a legal norm or standard for distinguishing bodies is at the center of the way that law reproduces social hierarchies through its regulation and restriction of nonnormative bodies (see also Garland Thomson, 1997). Fourth, Foucault's comments on the shifting role of law are quite instructive, since they identify the way that law's social-ordering function is shared with other social institutions like the schools, the family, and the health care system. Within a liberal constitutional order, we would expect support for the social-ordering function of these other institutions, and an absence of direct legal regulation of self-mastered individuals whose embodiment is socially unproblematic.

Literary critic and disability theorist Rosemarie Garland Thomson (1997) writes that disability "becomes a repository for social anxieties about such troubling concerns as vulnerability, control, and identity" (6). Disabled bodies disturb the able-bodied, for they serve as a reminder that we all have corporeal limitations. Over time, as we become subject to the vagaries of accident, illness, and aging, physical needs and limitations affect our experiences of the world, our relations with others, and our sense of self. For this reason, Garland Thomson rejects the hard distinction between the disabled and the able-bodied, and suggests instead that disability is much more mutable, context bound, particularized — and therefore universal — than is normally imagined. Yet the able-bodied refuse this commonality, since "the disabled figure operates as the vividly embodied stigmatized other whose social role is to symbolically free the privileged, idealized figure of the American self from the vagaries and vulnerabilities of embodiment" (7). While Foucault illuminates the way that all embodied political subjects are produced, Garland Thomson suggests how the civic embodiment of some serves to elide the civic embodiment of others.

In *Bodies in Revolt* (2005), political theorist and legal scholar Ruth O'Brien contends that disability law can help us to rethink labor relations and the workplace. The book provides an exciting and insightful account of the radical potential inherent in the Americans with Disabilities Act (ADA) of 1990. The legal approach taken in the ADA "turns disability into an open-ended category that is nonessential, ever evolving, and socially constructed" (1). The radical potential of the ADA, according to O'Brien, lies in its ability to bring us toward a *process* view of politics, and away from an *identity-based* approach to politics. According to O'Brien the ADA is an innovative law — innovative because it demands that employers take a *caring, relational* attitude toward their employees; because it encourages *particularity* in accommodation; and because it approaches subjectivity and employment in terms of *enablement* and *activity*. Each of these elements stands in contrast to the usual approach we find in labor law and civil rights law, which cast the relationship between employers and employees as adversarial and economic; which treat people in terms of the class or category they belong to, unable to tolerate the idea that a person could belong to more than one category — often a problem for black women claiming discrimination; and which see identity and ability as fixed and self-contained. Though the radical potential of the ADA has been severely undermined by the Supreme Court, the power of legal discourse extends beyond the realm of doctrine — it affects normative understandings about civic membership and rights as well (Greenhouse, 1994; Merry, 1986 and 1995). In this regard, O'Brien's insights are quite promising for thinking about how embodied civic membership might be imagined and enacted in the United States.

Feminists also have advocated for a "politics of presence" (Phillips, 1995). In arguing for the inclusion of women on juries before the New York State Legislature in the 1850s, Elizabeth Cady Stanton suggested what it might mean to bring social and physical experiences to understandings of justice and the performance of civic membership: "Shall the frenzied mother, who, to save herself and her child from exposure and disgrace, ended the life that had just begun, be dragged before such a tribunal [a judge and jury of men] to answer for her crime? How can *he* judge of the agonies of soul that impelled her to such an outrage of maternal instincts?" (Stanton, Anthony, and Gage, 1881, 597–98). Or, in Sojourner Truth's famous testimonial on the injustices experienced by slave women, "I have borne thirteen children and seen 'em mos' all sold off into slavery, and when I cried out in my mother's grief, none but Jesus heard me! And ain't I a woman?" (Stanton, Anthony, and Gage, 1881, 116). Both Stanton and Truth asserted the importance of embodied gender experiences — like rape, pregnancy, motherhood, and the rending of familial ties under slavery — for women's politics. More recently, Anne Phillips argues in favor of electoral designs that guarantee the representation of political minorities, including women. Her premise is that shared social experiences are an important source of common political interests and ideals. Further, in a legislative context, difference in social experience serves to broaden democratic deliberation in ways that benefit the whole community. *Presence*, for Phillips, means the political inclusion of members of distinct social groups whose lived experiences of gender, race, ethnicity, and the like, help to form their political understandings and views of social justice.

Yet, my advocacy of civic embodiment should not be linked to cultural feminism or an ethics of care. Like Guinier and Torres, the approach taken here seeks to navigate between the shoals of sex (or color) blindness on one side, and identity politics on the other. An emphasis on social experience and embodiment is not meant to suggest either that women are naturally nurturing (Ruddick, 1989), or that heterosexuality as rape is the paradigmatic expression of gender oppression's roots in sexual difference (Dworkin, 1987; MacKinnon, 1987). Bodily differences are made meaningful by social contexts and institutional constructions of those differences. Living in a society that makes race and sex into the justification for different rights, duties, and social opportunities is what makes embodied identities relevant to politics. This is the materiality of race and gender — a materiality that is historically and contextually rooted — and which is too readily ignored by the liberal politics of universal individualism.

To the degree that liberalism allows for recognition of social and embodied difference, it is through the principle of tolerance. Political theorist Wendy Brown seeks to unpack the multicultural vision of an inclusive pluralism that she sees as ultimately premised on an apolitical attitude that reduces sociality, belief, and identity to something to be forborne rather than engaged. Brown connects the rise of religious and political tolerance to modern privacy. Religious and deeply held political beliefs can be tolerated when they are translated into matters of one's private conscience. The effect is to reduce public discourse and democratic politics by making diversity a private matter.

> Tolerance of diverse beliefs in a community becomes possible to the extent that those beliefs are phrased as having no public importance, as being constitutive of a private individual whose beliefs and commitments have minimal bearing on the structure and pursuits of political, social, or economic life. . . . If tolerance fosters both a radical withdrawal from public life that amounts to a kind of social monadism, and requires epistemological and moral relativism in both social and public life, the effect of these requirements on political life is particularly significant. (W. Brown, 1995, 105 and 107)

Brown's insights might be recast this way. Under a modern liberal understanding all civic members are included on terms of equality and universalism, but it is an equality and universalism that is premised on sameness and individualism. Politics is about the public pursuit of economic interests; all else must be left behind in the private or social realm. Yet in late modern society we have come to appreciate that social difference and diversity might matter for politics. These differences are contained through tolerance — through an attitude that renders such differences benign, without ever really confronting or engaging them or seeing what they imply for such things as the institutional production of inequality.

This attitude of tolerance is represented in modern antidiscrimination jurisprudence as well. Thus, the authors of *Whitewashing Race* (M. K. Brown et al., 2003) critique the view that we have no race problem if there is no personal prejudice. "Racial realists conclude that racism has ended because of the massive change in white attitudes toward blacks over the past sixty years" (10). Such beliefs are drawn from surveys that measure racial attitudes among whites. "Because the ideals of equality and formal tolerance are central to American identity, most Americans know the 'correct' answers to such questions" (15). In the eyes of the Supreme Court, too, so long as African Americans, Latinos, and Asian Americans are tolerated, then racial discrimination is not an issue. The Court increasingly has come to focus on invidious intent as evidence of discrimination. Such a view allows American society to ignore social and structural inequality. "Because it extends far beyond individual attitudes, permeating the very structure and organization of American society, race strongly determines the ways in which Americans are treated and how they fare. White Americans, whether they know it or not, benefit as individuals and as a group from the present social pecking order" (15). Whites are in a privileged position in racial terms; it is a privilege that allows them not to see their own racial embodiment and to tolerate, rather than engage, racially embodied others. Embodied experience not only allows us to bring a broader range of social existence into politics; a critical understanding of those experiences brings into focus the concurrence among social institutions as they produce, regulate, and discriminate among civic embodiments.

Public Civic Membership

My vision of public civic membership is based on community. It is civic membership that is enacted in the public sphere and entails coming together, listening, and giving voice to desires for justice, inclusion, and participation. It suggests that civic membership is about more than individualism or domesticity — although it should be a site where people can express their self-interests and reflect their more intimate social lives in whatever ways seem relevant to them. Whereas private civic membership may appear insular, public civic membership empowers aspirations for social justice. It is, in this regard, connected to ideas of popular sovereignty. The promising aspect of publicness comes from its sociality, from its being a place in which we join with others to share insights and articulate interests. Public civic membership promotes the pursuit of social justice: it requires civic members to confront social diversity; it encourages the formulation of principled political appeals that reach beyond the self. Public civic membership emphasizes access, inclusion, and voice. It is civic membership as democracy from the ground up.

Yet, as with civic embodiment, public civic membership or publicness can be dangerous — a danger that is represented, for example, by the panopticon and the mob.[10] By making selves public, those whose behavior is socially offensive or whose social characteristics are unlike those of the majority may be subject to constraint, regulation, and surveillance. A reminder of the dangers of publicness appears in legal scholar Katherine Franke's (1999) work on the Freedmen's Bureau. Franke documents the federal government's efforts following the Civil War to regulate the social behavior of former slaves through the imposition of the institutions of marriage and employment. A more recent example involves the efforts by various states in the 1960s to promote sterilization for women on welfare. Today, the federal government is once again sponsoring social programs aimed at encouraging marriage among the poor. For those who have few economic and social resources, or who are recipients of government benefits, the price for receiving such benefits often includes a public civic membership that is regulatory and punitive. Recalling again the experience of Reconstruction, at that time the government saw the freedmen as embodied subjects in need of the disciplinary institutions of marriage and work. Under the gaze of the Freedmen's Bureau, publicness facilitated the state's scrutiny of the civic subjectivity of former slaves.

Yet, even in this example of an intrusive governmental regulatory regime, public civic membership may have been preferable to a private subjectivity in which former masters were allowed to physically discipline (or kill) their former slaves. Publicness makes possible another kind of scrutiny as well — the scrutiny of democracy, of visibility, and of political debate — which may be used to check personal tyranny or state abuses of authority. This is the scrutiny suggested by the principle of popular sovereignty — an idea that contains within it a promising vision of political action as something that is about more than the pursuit and protection of individual economic interests. Before elaborating on my discussion of popular sovereignty, what follows is a critique of the common alternative to public civic membership — privacy.

PRIVACY

Within the modern liberal constitutional order, privacy is both a realm of liberty and a repository of individualism. Until the nineteenth century, households were ordered around clearly defined and institutionalized social statuses. Under classical liberalism, authority relations within the household were not seen as "political," but they were socially mandated and judiciable under the law of domestic relations. Households were small societies governed by a benevolent master (whose position was ordained by law and by nature) who ruled over his wife, children, wards, servants, and slaves. In the colonies and the early republic, the "head of household" designation was used to award political privileges and assign civic obligations such as voting and militia service.[11] In republican society, the division between public and private was more porous, and the reach of law and institutionalized social authority was extensive. By the nineteenth century, the ideal of male domestic authority was both democratized and reduced. Any husband or father could be seen as the head of his own household, without the need for an estate or servants to establish the terms of their domestic domain (Stanley, 1998). Yet as more men became masters, the terms of that dominion were diminished; reforms removed the legal disabilities of wives under coverture and employees in the master-servant tradition (Orren, 1991; Tomlins, 1995; Ritter, 2000a). All of these changes in public and legal understanding of the home and the domestic sphere were evident in the emergence and development of the privacy doctrine.

Modern privacy as a social space signifies the shrinking of the domestic sphere, as well as its refashioning into a place of family life that stands as a retreat from the rational, competitive, regulatory world of the market and of politics (F. Ginsburg, 1989). In relation to individualism, modern privacy connotes character, interiority, and the thoughts and sentiments of a person that are held beyond the purview of the state or the public.[12] Today's private person seeks to free himself from the disciplined production of civilized members of the community that is the aim of our social institutions. The myth of self-creation is expressed in a libertarian desire to avoid entanglement with public institutions that impose upon the free will of American individualists (Stewart, 2005). The modern descendant of Locke's free man remains free in his mind — in his ability to cultivate his thoughts and sensibilities through culture and self-education. The sentiments of this free man may lead him to create bonds of affection and attachment that result in the formation of homes and families. Sentiments may lead as well to religious or community affiliations. In this regard, modern privacy stands for a chosen, voluntary, self-created person who is entitled to express and further develop this cultivated self without government intrusion (Greenhouse, 1992). Such persons are autonomous and self-ordered; their selves are not socially embedded (except to the extent that they choose to be) or mandated by the community.

There are several dangers apparent in the assertion of privacy as a political principle. First, as feminists have long contended, privacy conceals power relations within the household. Whether the private realm affords the luxuries of self-creation, reflection, and autonomous fulfillment depends upon the social relations and material conditions of one's home. For many — especially poor women — home is a place of personal burden, as one manages the demands and needs of family relations along with the struggle of economic deprivation. Second, privacy sustains the myth of individualism and social autonomy that vitiates the development of an ethic of social responsibility. Privacy is the social imaginary of the gated community, where the gate protects its inhabitants from external dangers, and denies their connection to the world or people beyond the gates. Third, privacy diminishes opportunities for social engagement, engagement that might entail recognition of and dialogue with people whose life experiences and political understandings differ from our own. Finally, privacy gives normative primacy to self and family, and casts them in opposition to the public and community in the way that society is organized.

POPULAR SOVEREIGNTY

The People, according to historian Edmund Morgan (1988), are always a myth. The myth of the people is the myth of the nation, of collective will, of the organic body politic, and of popular sovereignty. Morgan does not mean to disparage this myth. In many ways, *Inventing the People* celebrates the "imagined community" that inspired liberal democracy in Anglo-America (B. Anderson, 1983). The myth of the people can have real effects in promoting democratic accountability. Yet Morgan also seeks to remain critically aware of the dangers of political claiming made on the basis of vox populi.[13]

At the time of the American Constitutional Convention, a debate erupted over the nature of representation and popular sovereignty in a democratic republic. Prior to the convention, the assumption was that republican systems required representation based on small communities. But James Madison offered a radical reformulation of this principle when he suggested that large-scale representation offered positive advantages — particularly in how it can dilute democratic excess and prevent a tyranny of the majority (Federalist Paper 10). Yet for a large-scale republic to be authoritative, it needed popular legitimacy: "To that end he envisioned a genuine national government, resting for its authority . . . on an American people, a people who constituted a separate and superior entity, capable of conveying to a national government an authority that would necessarily impinge on the authority of the state governments" (Morgan, 1988, 267). The need for political authority called for the creation of a new myth. "Madison was inventing a sovereign American people to overcome the sovereign states" (Morgan, 1988, 267). It was an invention that was not born whole from Madison's imagination — the experience of the revolution left the people of the Unites States culturally primed to see themselves as Americans. However, the political understandings that underpinned republicanism in the early national period required reconstructing before the new Constitution could be accepted.

Indeed, many citizens resisted the shift in republican theory that the Constitution represented. Behind the Anti-Federalist critique of the scale of the newly proposed congressional districts and the size of the House of Representatives was a notion of what localism meant for representation. In the Massachusetts debate over the Constitution, William Heath offered this critique: "The representative is one who appears in behalf of, and acts for, others; he ought, therefore to be fully acquainted with the feelings, circumstances, and interests of persons whom he represents: and this is learnt among them, not at a distant court" (Morgan, 1988, 278). Likewise, George Mason of Virginia was opposed to the Constitution, since he believed that representatives "ought to mix with the people, think as they think, feel as they feel, — ought to be perfectly amenable to them, and thoroughly acquainted with their interest and condition" (Morgan, 1988, 279). In other words, localism brought to politics a richer representation of cultural understandings and social identity, and not just refined economic interests. Feelings, circumstances, distresses, wants, and sympathies were all the things that the Anti-Federalists hoped to have their representatives express in national politics.

Another element of the Anti-Federalist critique concerned diversity. Melancton Smith of New York expressed an implicit understanding of the value of diversity in public life. In addition to the educated gentry and economic elite, Smith favored a representative system that promoted the election of "ordinary persons, especially farmers, middling people, the substantial yeomen on the country" (Morgan, 1988, 278). Together with the "natural aristocrats," these ordinary people would create an assembly of balanced interests. In this respect, the Anti-Federalist vision comes close to Anne Phillips's (1995) ideal of a politics of presence, in which different embodied experiences are brought into deliberative democracy.

This powerful Anti-Federalist critique was countered by the Federalist assertion of a sovereign American people as the source of authority in the new constitutional order. Once the Constitution was adopted, the critics of the new constitutional order called for the addition of a Bill of Rights to the Constitution. For the Anti-Federalists (like the Levellers before them (Morgan, 1988, 67–72), a bill of rights represented an effort to reserve an element of sovereignty to the people. This reservation of sovereignty reflected an understanding of the imperfect, or fictive, nature of popular sovereignty and the desire to limit government's ability to act in the name of the people. The Federalists denied the fiction and suggested instead that the constitutional order was the institutionalized expression of the popular will. In this sense, the original Constitution was already a bill of rights. According to James Wilson, "the 'single sentence in the Preamble is tantamount to a volume and contains the essence of all the bills of rights that have been devised' " (Morgan, 1988, 283). Yet ultimately the proponents of the Bill of Rights were successful, and the first ten amendments to the Constitution were passed by the new Congress and ratified by the states.

Legal scholar Akhil Amar (1998) has recovered a different vision of what rights might mean in a working democracy. The traditional view of the Bill of Rights is that they represent an affirmation of individual, personal rights and a protection of minority rights against the oppression of unchecked majorities. Instead, Amar suggests that the original Bill of Rights was an instrument of popular sovereignty intended to affirm democratic practices among a community of citizens within the public sphere.[14] From this perspective, the Bill of Rights may be seen as an extension of the Anti-Federalist vision, designed to protect communities and democracy from potentially abusive exercises of authority by the national government: "The Bill of Rights protected the ability of local governments to monitor and deter federal abuse, ensured that ordinary citizens would participate in the federal administration of justice through various jury provisions and preserved the transcendent sovereign right of a majority of the people themselves to alter or abolish government and thereby pronounce the last word on constitutional questions" (Amar, 1998, xiii). For communities to be seedbeds of democracy, intermediary and locally based associations must be cultivated. The First Amendment, for instance, refers not to individuals, but to the rights of "the people." *The People* are constituted in this amendment collectively — in religious communities, in assemblies, in groups that petition the government, and in reading publics (Habermas, 1989; B. Anderson, 1983).

Why were eighteenth-century Americans so concerned with reserving and affirming the sovereignty of the people? The revolutionary experience must have been formative for the citizenry of the young nation. Central to the colonists' complaints against English rule was the way that claims of sovereign authority were articulated by the king and Parliament. Instead of ruling from above in the name of the people, the American revolutionaries sought to create a government that drew on the understanding and wisdom of the common citizenry from below. To some, the Federalist vision of popular sovereignty went too far in the direction of virtual representation. The assertion that the constitutional order perfectly embodied the popular will suggested that it was an order that was self-justifying and unlimited. This vision of popular sovereignty entailed a vision of community in which the people's will was coherent and transparent, so it could be readily translated into political action by their elected representatives in the federal government. As John Jay wrote in Federalist Paper 2, Americans were "one united people — a people descended from the same ancestors, speaking the same language, professing the same religion, attached to the same principles of government, very similar in their manners and customs," a commonality that had produced in the people a "universal and uniform attachment to the cause of Union" which found its expression in the creation of the Constitution (Hamilton, Madison, and Jay, 1961, 31).

The Federalist vision, and the vision of modern liberal constitutional politics, is predicated on universalism and homogeneity rather than meaningful diversity. It was a critique of that vision that inspired the original Bill of Rights. The Anti-Federalists preferred to rely upon a much messier vision of popular sovereignty that necessitated continuous democratic engagement by the citizenry, not only in elections but also in the broader sphere of public political participation. One should not be romantic about this vision. The democratic community that was the source of this popular sovereignty was still narrowly cast. Recalling "the people" of the founding recalls a community that was both bounded and hierarchically structured, as suggested, for instance, by Judge Taney's majority opinion in the 1857 *Dred Scott* case. However, the idea of popular sovereignty articulated by the Anti-Federalists and expressed in the original Bill of Rights contains within it a promising vision of political action as something that involves more than the pursuit and protection of individual economic interests (Macpherson, 1962). It offers a vision of public civic membership that is richer, more particularized, and more diverse than the one present in most liberal accounts.

DIVERSITY AND ENGAGEMENT

In *Justice and the Politics of Difference* (1990), Iris Marion Young calls for a rethinking of justice such that all members of society are enabled to participate fully and freely in public life and democratic decision making. In a chapter entitled "The Scaling of Bodies and the Politics of Identity," Young describes the way that modern approaches to knowledge — both philosophical and scientific — are premised on a division between mind and body, on the mind's mastery over the body. Further, in terms of social ordering, such views "established unifying controlling reasons in opposition to and mastery over the body and then identified some groups with reason and others with the body" (124). While contemporary political discourse has retreated from explicit public acknowledgment of bodily difference as a marker of political difference, we still see bodies in ways that shape our understanding (both conscious and unconscious) of the social and civic subjectivity of others. Thus, as Garland Thomson (1997) has also suggested, we are often reluctant to engage with the elderly and disabled because they remind us of our own physical fragility and ultimate death. White Americans avoid passing through public spaces occupied by young African American men — whose presence signals to many white citizens the possibility of violence. Likewise, pregnant women may perform a physical presence that threatens dependence, emotionality, and relationality. And some pregnant bodies — those of the young, the poor, the unattached — suggest uncontrolled sexuality. Suburbanization is, in many ways, about creating a space in which its members can be safely protected from the sight of such troubling bodies. Young's work shows how embodied subjectivity can serve as a barrier to political inclusion — recognizing this is an important step in the direction of a more democratic polity in which enacted subjectivities are heterogeneous and flexible.

Given these barriers to inclusion, how can the diversity of experience and realities of social disempowerment that mark the lives of embodied subjects be brought into public politics? One of the great contributions of the radical feminist movement of the 1960s and 1970s was the creation of consciousness-raising groups. In the context of these small groups, women were encouraged to articulate their personal experiences and to analyze them from a social and political perspective. What they learned was that the stuff of everyday life is shaped by social institutions and cultural norms that structure individual choices. Further, in hearing other women confirm their experiences and share similar occurrences from their own lives, these women began to see themselves as part of a common social group — the group of women — and felt more secure in calling upon personal experience as a source of social knowledge. The lessons of consciousness raising were later theorized by feminists as standpoint theory (Hartsock, 1984; Hill Collins, 1990). Part of what gave consciousness raising its power was the creation of knowledge and understandings that contradicted received public wisdom about gender relations.[15]

Two aspects of consciousness raising are worth highlighting here: the first involves *interpretation* and the second involves *solidarity*. It is not enough to say that personal experience matters for politics. For that experience to be made politically meaningful, it must be interpreted in ways that connect what happens to individuals in their families, relationships, and communities to larger social structures. How that interpretation occurs is also relevant — when it draws directly upon personal experience as a valued source of knowledge, and encourages individuals to articulate their experiences, the holder of that knowledge comes to see herself as someone that others may learn from and listen to. That creates a sense of intellectual and social empowerment among those who may not have previously seen themselves as entitled to offer their own views and understandings.

Solidarity is created when members come to see themselves as part of both an interpretive community and a political community, suffering from the same or similar conditions of subjection or inequality, aspiring to a common vision of justice, and committed to collective action to realize that vision. As feminist theorist Nancy Hirschmann writes, "engaging in such communities allows women to see how they have been created, and can create the world; hence it enables women to identify their agency, their ability to act on and shape their contexts, to make choices and act on them. Without such community, then, no 'individual' woman can ever be free" (Hirschmann and Di Stefano, 1996, 69). For the socially disempowered, the first step toward public civic membership and political diversity may be the solidarity of semipublic communities.[16]

Universities have been forced to defend, in recent years, their efforts to enroll a diverse student body. Support for educational affirmative action has lead to a deeper analysis of the value of diversity in education (Bok and Bowen, 2000), and its implications for civic life in a pluralist democracy. A broad review of this research, prepared by educational psychologist Patricia Gurin (2004; in an expert report prepared for the Michigan affirmative action cases), discusses the role that diversity plays in encouraging critical thinking and learning. Drawing on the work of Piaget and others, Gurin notes the tendency that most people have to rely upon preexisting schemas and scripts to guide them through daily life. This reliance on previously developed mental frameworks makes people into passive learners who slot new information and experiences into these already existing frameworks. For active thinking and critical engagement to occur, these frameworks must be disrupted, something that occurs when we are faced by "incongruity and dissonance" of a magnitude to produce "disequilibrium" that forces us to modify or abandon our previous intellectual frameworks. Social diversity, when it is made an active and relevant part of the learning experience, can create such dissonance: "classroom and social relationships that challenge rather than replicate the ideas and experiences students bring with them from their home environments are especially important in fostering cognitive growth" (Gurin, 2004).

Students from diverse educational settings are not only better thinkers, they are better civic members. They are more comfortable dealing with people from different backgrounds, and are better able to comprehend and appreciate assorted points of view. Their exposure to social diversity in college carries over after graduation and results in a stronger tendency to live in racially mixed residential areas, work in diverse settings, and engage in civic activities. The value of diversity in education and democracy depends on conditions that foster interaction among equally situated peers. In community settings, we learn more, and are more likely to consider alternative views of justice and the public good, when we are exposed to competing views, particularly when those views are embodied by people whose social backgrounds are markedly different from our own. Further, Gurin's report suggests that there is value in deeply felt and strongly articulated conflicts over what is true or just — provided that we maintain a minimal standard of respect for others. As we recall from the work of Wendy Brown (2001), to the degree that civility and tolerance are signals of a failure to engage with social diversity in a politically meaningful way, they do little to strengthen democracy. Nor does this engagement with diversity promote conformity — rather, it deepens individuality and a sense of self. For all of these reasons, engagement with diversity in public settings — provided that those settings are predicated on equality and mutual respect — fosters an enriched democratic life in which the identities and interests of all people may be expressed, represented, and considered.

What we learn from the experience of consciousness-raising groups and from efforts to foster diversity in education is that we can create institutional structures that encourage the less powerful to participate in politics, to see themselves as civic members whose life experiences and social concerns matter to society and to the pursuit of justice. Such institutional structures should provide opportunities for solidarity and interpretation among the socially and politically less powerful, and arenas for the meaningful participation at all levels of public life — in schools, libraries, recreation centers, housing boards, community health centers, domestic violence shelters, employee associations, and the juvenile justice system. Wherever public authority is exercised, citizens should be given an opportunity to shape the exercise of that authority. Further, public participation should be structured to foster respect and appreciation for social diversity, by highlighting the contributions that different social groups make to community life, by allowing for multiple avenues for expression and participation in politics (through offering a variety of venues, times, and means of communication), and by cultivating an environment in which all participants are treated as peers or equals. Decision-making structures should be democratic, but they might also include elements that guarantee representation or participation for underrepresented groups. The designing and implementation of such institutional structures would be a first step toward the creation of an embodied, public civic membership that benefits all those who aspire to a political project of democratic inclusion.

Notes

1. The imagination of American civic membership as a status of equality and universalism has, of course, often been in contrast to a historical reality of civic hierarchy. So the claim is not that these liberal principles provide a good description of political reality — rather, it is important to explore the role they play in the American political imagination.

2. A *modern, liberal constitutional order* is defined here as one in which status is explicitly rejected as a basis for political difference in law. All citizens, at the level of national politics and citizenship, are treated as rights-bearing individuals in the public realm. Such an order provides for complete equality in the area of political rights, and presumes the applicability of equality standards and universalism in most other areas. Group-based distinctions that are regarded as legally created, discriminatory, or derogatory are rejected in principle. In practice, in such an order, social-order concerns and regulations have not disappeared, but they have been relocated or transformed. Acceptable legal markers of social difference are based on voluntarism or achievement, forms of positive discrimination, and what are regarded as benign forms of classification that reflect pervasive, nonlegal customs or traditions.

3. The "I have a dream" speech could be read this way — as a ploy to appeal to white Americans based upon their understanding of the nation's commitment to certain ideals, whether or not the historical record shows such a commitment to be real. The most cited line of the speech is this: "I have a dream that one day this nation will rise up and live out the true meaning of its creed: 'We hold these truths to be self-evident: that all men are created equal.'"

4. A document that has always had a significant place in constitutional discourse is the Declaration of Independence.

5. Akhil Amar makes a similar move when he proposes that we overcome the traditional separation in thinking about constitutional provisions that protect personal rights and those that provide for governmental structure. He points to issues of representation and rights designed to protect majoritarianism as doing both (A. R. Amar, 1998).

6. On the creation of legal persons, consider, for instance, Article 1, Section 2 (which includes the Three-Fifths Clause), which offers the following categorization in relation to the formula for representation: "free Persons, including those bound to Service for a Term of Years, and excluding Indians not taxed, three fifths of all other Persons."

7. My thinking on this issue is informed by the social theories of Michel Foucault, who was deeply interested in the issue of how institutions and discourses helped to create persons, both physically and socially. See, for instance, *Discipline and Punish* (1979) and *The History of Sexuality* (1990).

8. According to the dictionary entry that appears on www.findlaw.com, *police power* refers to "the power of a government to exercise reasonable control over persons and property within its jurisdiction in the interest of the general security, health, safety, morals, and welfare except where legally prohibited (as by constitutional provision)."

9. This appears to be the case in Ireland and Israel, for instance. My thanks to Gary Jacobsohn for pointing this out to me.

10. My presumption here is that the meaning of these texts is expressed by the political and institutional actors who interpret them. From that perspective, more than one meaning can be found in these texts, and the meanings that are found there may change over time. Finally, some meanings may achieve an authoritative status (for a time), through political and institutional processes that favor certain interpretations over others.

11. The first words of the Constitution are, "We, the People." The first sentence of the main text of the Declaration is: "We hold these truths to be self-evident, that all men are created equal, that they are endowed by their Creator with certain unalienable Rights, that among these are Life, Liberty and the pursuit of Happiness."

12. This was the case unless they married a foreign national in the late nineteenth or early twentieth century, in which case they were assumed to lose their identity and political allegiance as Americans. Legally, at that point, they were stripped of their U.S. citizenship.

13. The founding document of the suffrage movement was the Declaration of Sentiments, which paraphrased the Declaration of Independence. Likewise, elsewhere in King's "I have a dream" speech (delivered on the steps of the Lincoln Memorial), he says, "When the architects of our republic wrote the magnificent words of the Constitution and the Declaration of Independence, they were signing a promissory note to which every American was to fall heir. This note was a promise that all men would be guaranteed the inalienable rights of life, liberty, and the pursuit of happiness."

14. Negative rights are rights that do not require government action to be substantiated, whereas positive rights are realized through government action.

15. When I say "republican," I have in mind Aristotle, for whom the political realm existed in opposition to the household, and citizens were men who represented their households when they voted and participated in public life.

16. To see how Congress responded to the New Departure by, on the one hand,

taking refuge in the limits implied by the federalist structure of citizenship, and, on the other hand, invoking family governance and corporatist notions of representation, see the Majority Report (issued in 1871) of the Senate Judiciary Committee in response to Victoria Woodhull's memorial to the Senate (Stanton, Anthony, and Gage, 1969, 461–64), and the comments of Senator Merrimon made in 1874 regarding an amendment to a bill on the territories that would have provided suffrage to the women living there (Stanton, Anthony, and Gage, 1969, 552–58).

17. On the debate over the influence of social movements on constitutional development, see, for instance, Rosenberg (1991), Strauss (2001), Siegel (2001), and Forbath (1999).

18. For more on this case, see Chapter 3.

19. Of course, even this limitation on the action of states would be shortly lost, as the Supreme Court found in the *Civil Rights Cases*, 109 U.S. 3 (1883), and later in *Plessy v. Ferguson*, 163 U.S. 537 (1896), that race-based differentiations were allowable under the Reconstruction amendments.

CHAPTER 2. VOTING

1. African American women were also involved in the suffrage campaigns. But the leaders of the national organizations consistently downplayed their contributions and excluded them from national conventions in the interest of obtaining support of white southerners instead. See Rosalyn Terborg-Penn (1998).

2. See interviews with Mary Scully, April 19, 1924, 15; Vira Whitehouse, April 5, 1924, 8; Mrs. Walter Damrosch, April 5, 1924, 30; and Rose Schneiderman, March 22, 1924, 9 and 29 ("Is Woman Suffrage Failing?" 1924).

3. See also, for instance the comment of Gloria Swanson — "But in spite of all that, in spite of the fact that I don't use it, suffrage means more to me than I can possibly put into words. It is a symbol of the freedom of women" ("Is Woman Suffrage Failing?" March 22, 1924, 8).

4. See, for instance, *Minor v. Happersett*, 88 U.S. 162 (1874), *Bradwell v. Illinois*, 83 U.S. 130 (1872), and *Strauder v. West Virginia*, 100 U.S. 303 (1879).

5. For federal law, discriminatory classifications are considered under the Due Process Clause of the Fifth Amendment. Yet it is also worth noting, as Julie Novkov has pointed out to me, that the *Adkins* case contained an equal protection component in its analysis of why a sex classification in labor law was unacceptable. Nevertheless, it is still fair to say that equality failed to become a broader constitutional norm in the area of sex classifications until the 1970s.

6. Holmes wrote, "It will need more than the Nineteenth Amendment to convince me that there are no differences between men and women, or that legislation cannot take those differences into account" (*Adkins v. Children's Hospital*, 569–70).

7. The exception to this being Texas, although in that state, there may still have been relevance to common law rules regarding women's ability to hold office, if not the common law rules of coverture.

8. An excellent example of this is the role that the term *male elector* plays in the interpretation of different courts.

9. See also Boyer (1920), which was part of the Carrie Chapman Catt Citizenship Course, a series of articles that appeared in the journal during 1920 and 1921. In describing the differences between the main parties, Boyer concludes that "whenever the question that comes up has an interest for a particular locality, we forget all about our fundamentals and our traditions and we just vote for the thing that interests us today. That is how it works out" (522).

CHAPTER 3. MARRIAGE

1. An antimiscegenation law is a law which bars marriage between people of different races, particularly between whites and nonwhites. As Taney observed, there were many such laws in the colonial and early national periods. And it should also be noted that new antimiscegenation laws were passed in quite a few states in the Progressive Era, a period when the philosophy of scientific racism predominated.

2. The main laws seeking to abolish polygamy were the Morrill Act of 1862, the Poland Act of 1874, and the Edmunds Act of 1882.

3. At the time, women were allowed to vote in the Utah territory.

4. The most common forms of protective labor legislation in this period were as follows: maximum hours laws; laws mandating rest periods or providing seats for women in certain positions; laws that barred women from night work or from work in "dangerous" occupations; and minimum wage laws. There were some protective labor laws that applied to men as well, but these laws were typically focused on regulating work based upon the job rather than the worker.

5. Among them were Ethel Smith (also of the National Consumers League), Maud Wood Park (Women's Joint Congressional Committee), Rose Sniederman (the Women's Trade Union League), and Carrie Chapman Catt (the League of Women Voters).

6. Examples include mothers' pensions, Aid to Dependent Children, the Sheppard Towner Act, as well as wives' and widows' benefits under both Social Security and the GI Bill.

7. The incorporation of women into the freedom-of-contract regime was only partial because the distinction the Court made between laws regulating minimum wages and those regulating other kinds of working conditions, such as maximum hours. In the later area, the decision in *Muller* still stood and women were still regarded as occupying a distinct legal category.

8. Interestingly, the proposal to pass an amendment enabling Congress to regulate marriage has just been revived in response to the Supreme Court's decision in the Lawrence case (handed down in June 2003) to protect the right of homosexuals to have intimate sexual relations. Christian conservatives and other political conservatives are now concerned that this will lead to a constitutional finding in favor of same-sex marriage, which has lead to the call for a marriage amendment.

9. Prior to this time, several states offered voting privileges to what were referred to as "first paper" immigrant men — those who had filed for citizenship, but had not yet been made citizens (Bredbrenner, 1998). The LWV was also active in the campaign to end voting privileges for immigrants. In this campaign they appealed to postwar nationalist sentiment by noting that veterans were also supportive of the move to strip immigrants of the right to vote (see "Should Aliens Vote?" 1921).

10. Nonetheless, it is important to note that the movement toward fuller inclusion and rights for citizens did not extend to African Americans. Indeed, this was a period of increased repression of African Americans, both illegal (the Ku Klux Klan was undergoing a massive revival) and legal (many states passed new antimiscegenation laws in this era).

11. As Edwin Borchard, an international law expert and law professor at Yale wrote in 1935, "At all events, the Act of 1907, and especially the case of *Mackenzie v. Hare*, which indulged the fiction that by marrying an alien the lady consents to a result 'tantamount to expatriation,' caused the feminist revolution, whose echoes still reverberate at home and abroad. The Cable Act of 1922, the married women's declaration of independence in citizenship, was the result" (Borchard, 1935, 403).

12. On the significance of domestic harmony, also see *Thompson v. Thompson*, 218 U.S. 611 (1910), at 618. Though this is a 1910 case it is widely cited by the state courts in the 1920s and 1930s.

13. Siegel (1996) argues that while the common law right of marital chastisement was abandoned, spousal abuse continued to be juridically condoned. "Instead of reasoning about marriage in the older, hierarchy-based norms of the common law, jurists began to justify the regulation of domestic violence in the language of privacy and love associated with companionate marriage in the industrial era" (2120). Thus, the marital hierarchy was preserved in a modern form (what she calls "preservation through transformation" of a status regime).

14. See Chapter 1's discussion of Justice Benjamin Curtis's dissent in *Dred Scott v. Sandford*.

15. "Other dependent people" refers to Indians, colonized populations, and so on.

CHAPTER 4. JURY SERVICE

1. The concept of equal citizenship may be addressed at three levels. At the broadest level, equal citizenship pertains to civic status. All of those considered as "full" or "first-class" citizens may be thought of as holding the same high civic status. The second conception of equal citizenship is more specifically rights focused, and holds that any differences in the rights afforded to citizens constitute unequal citizenship. Finally, a third conception of equal citizenship examines not only rights and status, but also the duties and obligations of citizens (Ritter, 2000a).

2. The great exception is the decision of *Adkins v. Children's Hospital*, 261 U.S. 525 (1923). Under that ruling, women were loosely incorporated into the *Lochner* regime

(which refers to the case of *Lochner v. New York*, 198 U.S. 45 [1905]) of freedom of contract—that is, they were given the same negative liberty granted to men. For more on this decision, see Zimmerman (1991). For further discussion of this point, see Chapter 1; see also Chapter 2.

3. Jury service is also implicitly treated by the court as a political right. At one point in the opinion the court asks what would happen if whites were excluded from jury service by a majority black population, "thus denying to them the privilege of participating equally with the blacks in the administration of justice" (*Strauder*, 308). Here, jury service is framed as a right of participation.

4. See Justice Fields's dissent in the *Slaughter-House* (48).

5. Indeed, it may be the case that the duties of citizenship matter more for raising one's political status than the rights of citizenship in the United States. For instance, consider the treatment of veteran status as a privileged political status, or the distinction often made in political campaigns and legislative debates between taxpaying and nontaxpaying citizens as indicators of the importance of duties to political status. Such a distinction might help us to understand the current "gays-in-the-military" debate as a claim to duties that would raise a citizen's political status, and the movement toward welfare reform as an effort to lower the political status of nontaxpaying citizens. For a further discussion of the relationship between the duties and rights of citizenship, see Kerber (1998).

CHAPTER 5. LABOR

1. "Freedom of contract" refers to a judicial doctrine prominent in the early twentieth century. Under this doctrine, the due process clause of the Fourteenth Amendment was interpreted to mean that states could not impose many labor regulations on workers or employers without violating their right to liberty—that is, their right to agree to any employment contract that they found beneficial. The doctrine was not applied to women workers in the same way, since they were seen as more vulnerable and in need of state protection.

2. The idea of the "family wage" (an idea that was consistent with the view that male citizens were family providers) was often cited during the Great Depression as a way of pushing women out of jobs. Women workers, on the other hand, were often accused of working only for "pin money," seldom seen as family providers in their own right.

3. For a recent contribution to the debate over the racial motivations behind the South's resistance to the inclusion of agricultural and domestic workers under Title II in the 1930s, see Davies and Derthick (1997).

4. Indeed, the effort to create such an entitlement dates back to the nineteenth century, when women's rights advocates sought to reform coverture with a legal recognition of a wife's economic rights on the basis of her household labor.

5. It is striking, for instance, that in the 1938 revised version of Paul Douglas's *Social Security in the United States* (the original edition was published in 1936) there is

no discussion of survivors' benefits in his lengthy recommendations for how to improve and expand social security.

6. Many, if not most, of the laws that discriminated against women at this time were connected to their status within marriage.

7. Many of the gains of the second wave feminist movement in the 1970s came in the form of legal and constitutional equality—both through statute (especially Titles VII and IX) and through reinterpreting the Equal Protection Clause of the Fourteenth Amendment to forbid many forms of sex classifications.

8. The Women's Advisory Committee and the War Manpower Commission also offered positive views of a woman's right to work and be included under the provisions of full employment (see Chafe, 1991, 155 and 195).

9. For a wonderful illustration of this shift in thinking about the relation between work and citizenship and what it implies about constitutional understandings, see Senator Elbert Thomas's testimony on the full employment bill before the Senate (U.S. Senate, 1945b, 120–25).

10. Alice Kessler-Harris (2001) provides an excellent discussion of the congressional (particularly Senate) debates over the Full Employment Bill in the first chapter of her book, *In Pursuit of Equity*.

11. There were statements included by several women at the end of the printed testimony for the House hearings, including one by economist and labor statistician Edna Lonigan, who wrote to Representative Manasco, "You were good enough to write to me recently that you hoped to include my name among those called to testify before the members of your committee on the full employment bill. When I saw that the committee had closed the hearings I revised the statement for submission in writing. It is herewith enclosed" (U.S. House, 1945b, 1120).

12. Also see the testimony of Mrs. J. B. Caulkins, president of the YWCA (U.S. Senate, 1945b, 747–53).

13. Although social historians, legal historians, and political scientists have since demonstrated otherwise in their analyses of the socially and historically constructed nature of these categories. See, for instance Haney-Lopez (1996); Ignatiev (1995); and Franke (1999).

14. Such cases included, most famously, *Minor v. Happersett*, 88 U.S. 162 (1874), *Bradwell v. Illinois*, 83 U.S. 130 (1872), *Muller v. Oregon*, and *West Coast Hotel v. Parrish*.

15. The opinion in *Buck v. Bell* has now come to be regarded as an embarrassment. In the Stanley Kramer film *Judgment at Nuremberg* (1961)—a fictionalized account of the Nuremburg trials—the German defense counsel reads Justice Holmes's majority opinion to demonstrate that Germany was not the only country that legalized the practice of eugenics.

16. It is also likely that timing contributed to the different reactions in *Buck* and *Skinner*. *Buck* was decided in the 1920s, during the heyday of eugenics, while the *Skinner* ruling was handed down in the 1940s, by which time reports of Nazi atrocities were being publicized. Nonetheless, when the Court was given the option to

overrule *Buck* in the *Skinner* case, they declined to do so, suggesting that the gender of the plaintiff made a difference in their determination.

17. The Due Process Clauses of the Fifth Amendment (which applies to the national government) and Fourteenth Amendment (which applies to the state governments) promise that no one may be deprived of "life, liberty, and property" without due process of law. Under the principle of procedural due process, the Court insures that appropriate procedural safeguards (e.g., that there be a fair hearing and an opportunity for appeal) are implemented before such a deprivation can occur (for instance, before someone is sentenced to the death penalty). Under the principle of substantive due process, the emphasis is on the "life, liberty, and property" part of the clause — meaning that only for the most important causes can a government ever deprive a person of these fundamental rights.

18. See Chapter 8 for the argument that substantive due process reasoning lies behind the veneer of equal protection analysis in *Skinner*. That reasoning appears explicitly in some of the concurrences in this case. After *West Coast Hotel*, many justices were uncomfortable with explicitly using due process analysis. Nonetheless, there was a concern with unspecified fundamental rights that were sometimes placed under the cover of equal protection and that eventually migrated into privacy analysis.

19. Marriage was also increasingly nationally governed through social policies that rewarded the dependent spouses of workers (Social Security) and soldiers (veterans' benefits).

20. Indeed, I think this is true in all nations — that gender is central to the social order, and that the social order is organized and maintained through the legal and political system.

CHAPTER 6. WAR SERVICE

1. By "democratically fought wars" is meant wars with high levels of popular participation, either through conscription or voluntary enlistment (or a combination of the two).

2. There is a debate over whether these claims resulted in actual political gains for various groups.

3. Around the time that the UDHR was being produced, the Committee on Civil Rights (appointed by President Truman) released *To Secure These Rights* — a 1947 report on racial discrimination in this country that included a (for the time) quite progressive and far-reaching set of recommendations on laws and policies to remedy the problem. At the same time, there was a wave of lynchings and race riots in the United States at the close of the Second World War.

4. After the war, in 1948, Congress passed the Women's Armed Services Integration Act, which made the presence of women in the military permanent.

5. The nations cited here as reporting equality suggest the limits of self-reporting when it comes to evaluating legal gender equality.

6. In addition to *Fishgold v. Sullivan*, see *Trailmobile Co. v. Whirls*, 331 U.S. 40 (1947), *Hilton v. Sullivan*, 334 U.S. 323 (1948), and *Aeronautical Industrial District Lodge 727 v. Campbell*, 337 U.S. 521 (1949).

7. Some examples include *Adarand Constructors v. Pena*, 515 U.S. 200 (1995), *Oyama v. California*, 332 U.S. 633 (1948), *Hernandez v. Texas*, 347 U.S. 475 (1954), *Bell v. Maryland*, 378 U.S. 226 (1964), and *Labine v. Vincent*, 401 U.S. 532 (1971).

8. In *Endo* the Court found the petitioner, Mitsuye Endo, was a loyal American citizen and concluded that the War Relocation Authority had no authority to detain her. Her status as a loyal American was confirmed by her brother's service in the U.S. military.

9. The CSW had originally been a subcommission of the Commission on Human Rights, but in June 1946 it was made into a separate commission.

10. Declarations and resolutions were regarded as statements of principle. Conventions, such as the one of political rights for women (1952) or on human rights (1949) were thought to have more binding legal force on the signatories.

11. At the time of this speech, Bernardino was the chair of the Inter-American Commission on the Status of Women and the former vice-chair of the UN Commission on the Status of Women.

12. Roosevelt explained that this committee had a large number of women delegates because its work was not considered to be as important as the work of the other committees.

13. Kenyon would continue to play a significant role in efforts to advance women's rights in the United States. She was the plaintiff's attorney in *Hoyt v. Florida*, 368 U.S. 57 (1961), where a woman convicted of murdering her abusive husband challenged her conviction because of the absence of women on the jury. Although this appeal failed and the Supreme Court continued to endorse practices that led to all-male juries, Kenyon served as a role model and mentor to the next generation of women's rights lawyers. In her filing on *Reed v. Reed*, 404 U.S. 71 (1971) (the first Supreme Court case to successfully use the Equal Protection Clause to strike down a gender discriminatory law), Ruth Bader Ginsburg added Kenyon's name to the brief to honor the role she had played in advancing women's rights (Kerber, 1998).

14. Thus when men's labor or their health is protected by the state, men are somehow feminized.

15. The work or family alternatives for women had been created by women social activists of the Progressive Era. One exemplar of this choice was Jane Addams, the leading figure at Hull House in Chicago, who advocated the interests of poor women with children while herself remaining unmarried and childless.

16. See also, number 2 of Article 16: "Marriage shall be entered into only with the free and full consent of the intending spouses."

17. See also Articles 22 and 27, which make reference to cultural rights, and Article 25, which speaks of a family wage and calls for the protection of motherhood and childhood.

CHAPTER 7. EQUALITY

1. There were several educational equality cases during the 1970s that were contested on the grounds of the Equal Protection Clause. These cases show a similar pattern of resistance (in two 1970 cases), followed by adherence to the equality principle (in two 1972 cases), followed by the reemergence of resistance (in a 1977 case).
For details, see Mezey (2003), table 2.1, page 41. The Title IX cases did not begin
until the very end of the decade (Mezey, table 2.2, page 51).

2. Intermediate scrutiny means a standard of review that is between a rational
basis standard and a suspect classification/strict scrutiny standard. Under the first
standard, the starting presumption is that the classification upon which a law is based
is constitutional, so long as it is rational. Under the strict scrutiny standard, the Court
begins from the presumption that the classification (based typically on race or
national origin) renders the law unconstitutional and that it is the government's burden to show that there is a compelling government interest that justifies the use of
such a classification. Under intermediate scrutiny, the Court begins from a position
of neutrality as to whether a law based on a sex classification violates the equal protection clause.

3. Technically, the Equal Pay Act was an amendment to the Fair Labor Standards
Act of 1938.

4. When the bill from the two houses of Congress went to conference, the Senate conferees retained the sex discrimination provision added by the House to Title
VII. There was no further floor discussion in the Senate after the conference.

5. For more on abortion rights activism in this period, see Chapter 8.

6. At their convention in 1967, NOW adopted a pro-choice plank as part of their
1968 "Bill of Rights." Here is the resolution that was adopted, by a vote of fifty-seven
to fourteen: "NOW endorses the principle that it is a basic right of every woman to
control her reproductive life, and therefore NOW supports the furthering of the sexual revolution of our century by pressing for widespread sex education, provision of
birth control information and contraceptives, and urges that all laws penalizing abortion be repealed" (National Organization for Women, 1968).

7. "Equal employment opportunities must be enforced" (the Chicago Women
Form Liberation Group of 1967, quoted in Papachristou [1976], 229). "Equal pay for
equal work has been a project poo-pooed by the radicals but it should not be because
it is an instrument of bondage" (231).

8. As Mary Katzenstein (1998) has argued, feminism continued to thrive within
various social institutions during the 1980s, including the Catholic Church and the
military. It also had a vibrant presence within the academy.

9. It is worth noting that Cook's suggestion — which Senator Goodell agreed
with — has been recently validated in *Nevada Dept. of Human Resources v. Hibbs*, 538
U.S. 721 (2003), where the Supreme Court upheld the Family Medical Leave Act as
a valid exercise of congressional authority under Section 5.

10. The courts and the EEOC were clear that biological sex differences *did* count

as a bona fide occupational qualification — indeed they were used as an acceptable example of a BFOQ.

11. The cases were *Frontiero v. Richardson*, 411 U.S. 677 (1973), *Kahn v. Shevin*, 416 U.S. 351 (1974), *Weinberger v. Wiesenfeld*, 420 U.S. 636 (1975), *Edwards v. Healy*, 421 U.S. 772 (1975), *Califano v. Goldfarb*, 430 U.S. 199 (1977), and *Duren v. Missouri*, 439 U.S. 357 (1979).

12. The other leading case, in which the petitioner was not a man, was *Stanton v. Stanton*, 421 U.S. 7 (1975).

13. By which I do not mean to suggest that I imagine men to be "naturally" better at math than women. Rather, I believe that the social experience of gender is so deeply formative of our outlooks, developed abilities, and our understanding of ourselves and others, that it is not likely to be readily expunged by declarations of legal gender neutrality.

14. This position is later referenced by Stevens in his concurring opinion in *Craig v. Boren* as the wrong approach to thinking about sex classifications (212).

15. "Neither slaves nor women could hold office, serve on juries, or bring suit in their own names, and married women traditionally were denied the legal capacity to hold or convey property or to serve as legal guardians of their own children" (*Frontiero*, 685). This text draws closely from the Ginsburg brief.

16. The quote is from *Royster Guano Co. v. Virginia*, 253 U.S. 412 (1920), at 415. It appears in *Reed* at 76.

CHAPTER 8. PRIVACY

1. *Privacy is a principle not readily articulated in terms of social justice*: I mean this in two senses — privacy is not a social principle, and it is an antipublic principle. Justice claims, at least when they are made at a general level, seem to be both social and public. Further, it is harder to imagine a social movement making a public claim of principle for something as nonpublic and individualized as privacy. In this sense, liberty seems to be differently located. It seems to be a more public and social claim than privacy.

2. Warren and Brandeis (1890) were arguing mainly for a privacy tort, but years later their argument was taken as having constitutional implications, implications which were developed by Brandeis himself as a Supreme Court justice in the 1920s.

3. For a comment on the unselfconscious, yet still gendered, nature of privacy reasoning before this time, see Allen and Mack (1990).

4. On the history of Connecticut's struggles with birth control in the 1950s and 1960s, see Garrow (1998).

5. For a discussion of competing philosophical conceptions of marriage, see Pateman (1988).

6. The Court's difficulty in treating pregnant women as solitary individuals and full legal persons recalls Robin West's (1988) discussion of gender and assumptions about individualism.

7. This was the case particularly for Justice Marshall. See *Belle Terre v. Boraas*, 416 U.S. 1 (1974), *United States Dept. of Agriculture v. Moreno*, 413 U.S. 528 (1973), *Fiallo v. Bell*, 430 U.S. 787 (1977), *Stanley v. Illinois*, 405 U.S. 645 (1972), and *Zablocki v. Redhail*, 434 U.S. 374 (1978). There were also earlier suggestions of a combination of Equal Protection Clause and Due Process Clause analysis regarding privacy in the cases of *Skinner* and *Loving v. Virginia*, 388 U.S. 1 (1967). Both are cases that deal with privacy and matters of race.

CHAPTER 9. THE POLITICS OF PRESENCE

1. Indeed, the effort to create such an entitlement dates back to the nineteenth century, when women's rights advocates sought to reform coverture with a legal recognition of a wife's economic rights on the basis of her household labor.

2. Nonetheless, after the Civil War, veterans' benefits (which were used to insure partisan loyalty) were widely available in the North. See Skocpol (1992).

3. For more on the autonomy myth that undergirds American civic identity and its implications for gender equality, see Martha Fineman, *The Autonomy Myth* (2004).

4. For the majority, the differences in civic standing determined whether or not one would be counted as a citizen, but for the minority those differences were expressed by there being grades of citizens.

5. An exception to this currently involves the debate over gay marriage. There the public, the courts, and government officials are quite clear that the specific bodies occupying the role of spouse matter a great deal for our willingness to grant civic recognition.

6. This conundrum of choice and subjection for women is discussed by Carole Pateman in *The Sexual Contract* (1988). Pateman approaches the issue theoretically through a discussion of social contract theory. The issue is approached more historically by Pamela Haag in *Consent* (1999).

7. The term *civic ideal* recalls Rogers Smith's important book *Civic Ideals* (1997). My use of the term *civic ideal* is loosely consonant with Smith's, in that we both seek to identify, understand, and critique ideals of citizenship that have been historically expressed in constitutional and political discourse. Of course, our identification of these ideals — both methodologically and substantively — is largely different.

8. Consider, for instance, the social reaction in the 1980s and 1990s to the AIDS epidemic.

9. This strikes me as similar to Locke's view of labor and self-ownership (the roots of right to property). See Uday Mehta's treatment of this issue in *Liberalism and Empire* (1999), 124–25.

10. The panopticon epitomizes the modern idea of surveillance, whereby subjects are constantly observed without seeing those who are watching over them. The concept dates back to Jeremy Bentham's proposal for prison management made in a tract that he published in 1787. The concept was later critiqued by Michel Foucault in *Discipline and Punish* (1979).

11. A slim remnant of this civic category remains today in tax and census designations of "head of household."

12. This is the view of privacy first laid out by Brandeis and Warren in their important 1890 *Harvard Law Review* article.

13. This theme is also explored by Sheldon Wolin (1980) in his critique of the Hamiltonian vision of "the people" in terms of the national unity represented in the constitution.

14. I say "original" because the meaning of the various provisions in the Bill of Rights was fundamentally changed by the adoption of the Fourteenth Amendment and the process of incorporation of the Bill of Rights to apply to actions by the states.

15. Social-movement theorists, and those who study the socially disempowered, often focus on the importance of group interpretations of common experiences in the formation of social justice sensibilities. See, for instance, Carson (1981).

16. Likewise, in Patricia Gurin's (2004) analysis of diversity in education, which was submitted as an expert report for the Michigan affirmative action cases, she finds that minority students in college benefit from solidaristic relationships with other minority students, and that having these relationships makes them more inclined toward democratic participation in diverse settings.

Bibliography

BRIEFS CITED

Brief for Appellant, *Reed v. Reed*, 404 U.S. 71 (1971), no. 70-4.

CASES CITED (LISTED CHRONOLOGICALLY)

Supreme Court Cases

Dred Scott v. Sandford, 60 U.S. 393 (1856).
Butcher's Benevolent Association v. Crescent City Livestock Landing and Slaughter-House Co. [The Slaughter-House Cases], 83 U.S. 36 (1872).
Bradwell v. Illinois, 83 U.S. 130 (1872).
Minor v. Happersett, 88 U.S. 162 (1874).
Reynolds v. United States, 98 U.S. 145 (1878).
Strauder v. West Virginia, 100 U.S. 303 (1879).
Neal v. Delaware, 103 U.S. 370 (1881).
Civil Rights Cases, 109 U.S. 3 (1883).
Ex parte Yarbrough, 110 U.S. 651 (1884).
Murphy v. Ramsey, 114 U.S. 15 (1885).
Boyd v. United States, 116 U.S. 616 (1886).
Plessy v. Ferguson, 163 U.S. 537 (1896).
Holden v. Hardy, 169 U.S. 366 (1898).
Giles v. Harris, 189 U.S. 475 (1903).
Lochner v. New York, 198 U.S. 45 (1905).
Muller v. Oregon, 208 U.S. 412 (1908).
Thompson v. Thompson, 218 U.S. 611 (1910).
Mackenzie v. Hare, 239 U.S. 299 (1915).
Bunting v. Oregon, 243 U.S. 426 (1917).
Caminetti v. United States, 242 U.S. 470 (1917).
Hammer v. Dagenhart, 247 U.S. 251 (1918).
Royster Guano Co. v. Virginia, 253 U.S. 412 (1920).
Fairchild v. Hughes, 258 U.S. 126 (1922).

Leser v. Garnett, 258 U.S. 130 (1922).

Adkins v. Children's Hospital, 261 U.S. 525 (1923).

Meyer v. Nebraska, 262 U.S. 390 (1923).

Pierce v. Society of Sisters, 268 U.S. 510 (1925).

Buck v. Bell, 274 U.S. 200 (1927).

Olmstead v. United States, 277 U.S. 438 (1928).

Funk v. United States, 290 U.S. 371 (1933).

West Coast Hotel Co. v. Parrish, 300 U.S. 379 (1937).

N.L.R.B. v. Jones and Laughlin Steel Corp., 301 U.S. 1 (1937).

Breedlove v. Suttles, 302 U.S. 277 (1937).

Smith v. Texas, 311 U.S. 128 (1940).

United States v. Darby, 312 U.S. 100 (1941).

Phelps Dodge Corp. v. N.L.R.B., 313 U.S. 177 (1941).

Hill v. Texas, 316 U.S. 400 (1942).

Skinner v. Oklahoma, 316 U.S. 535 (1942).

Ex parte Kumezo Kawato, 317 U.S. 69 (1942).

Martin v. Struthers, 319 U.S. 141 (1943).

Hirabayashi v. United States, 320 U.S. 81 (1943).

Prince v. Massachusetts, 321 U.S. 158 (1944).

Mortensen v. United States, 322 U.S. 369 (1944).

Baumgartner v. United States, 322 U.S. 665 (1944).

Steele v. Louisville and Nashville Railroad Co., 323 U.S. 192 (1944).

Tunstall v. Brotherhood of Locomotive Firemen and Enginemen, 323 U.S. 210 (1944).

Korematsu v. United States, 323 U.S. 214 (1944).

Ex parte Mitsuye Endo, 323 U.S. 283 (1944).

Thomas v. Collins, 323 U.S. 526 (1945).

Cramer v. United States, 325 U.S. 1 (1945).

Girouard v. United States, 328 U.S. 61 (1946).

Thiel v. Southern Pacific Co., 328 U.S. 217 (1946).

Fishgold v. Sullivan Drydock and Repair Corp., 328 U.S. 275 (1946).

Knauer v. United States, 328 U.S. 654 (1946).

Ballard v. United States, 329 U.S. 187 (1946).

Trailmobile Co. v. Whirls, 331 U.S. 40 (1947).

Fay v. New York, 332 U.S. 261 (1947).

Oyama v. California, 332 U.S. 633 (1948).

Mitchell v. Cohen, 333 U.S. 411 (1948).

Shelley v. Kraemer, 334 U.S. 1 (1948).

Hilton v. Sullivan, 334 U.S. 323 (1948).

Ludecke v. Watkins, 335 U.S. 160 (1948).

Goesaert v. Cleary, 335 U.S. 464 (1948).

Aeronautical Industrial District Lodge 727 v. Campbell, 337 U.S. 521 (1949).

Graham v. Brotherhood of Locomotive Firemen and Enginemen, 338 U.S. 232 (1949).

Breard v. Alexandria, 341 U.S. 622 (1951).

Public Utilities Commission v. Pollak, 343 U.S. 451 (1952).

Hernandez v. Texas, 347 U.S. 475 (1954).

Brown v. Board of Education, 347 U.S. 483 (1954).

Poe v. Ullman, 367 U.S. 497 (1961).

Hoyt v. Florida, 368 U.S. 57 (1961).

Bell v. Maryland, 378 U.S. 226 (1964).

Griswold v. Connecticut, 381 U.S. 479 (1965).

Osborn v. United States, 385 U.S. 323 (1966).

Loving v. Virginia, 388 U.S. 1 (1967).

Stanley v. Georgia, 394 U.S. 557 (1969).

Phillips v. Martin Marietta Corp., 400 U.S. 542 (1971).

Labine v. Vincent, 401 U.S. 532 (1971).

United States v. Vuitch, 402 U.S. 62 (1971).

Reed v. Reed, 404 U.S. 71 (1971).

Eisenstadt v. Baird, 405 U.S. 438 (1972).

Stanley v. Illinois, 405 U.S. 645 (1972).

California v. LaRue, 409 U.S. 109 (1972).

Roe v. Wade, 410 U.S. 113 (1973).

Doe v. Bolton, 410 U.S. 179 (1973).

Frontiero v. Richardson, 411 U.S. 677 (1973).

Paris Adult Theatre I v. Slaton 413 U.S. 49 (1973).

United States Dept. of Agriculture v. Moreno, 413 U.S. 528 (1973).

Cleveland Board of Education v. LaFleur, 414 U.S. 632 (1974).

Belle Terre v. Boraas, 416 U.S. 1 (1974).

Kahn v. Shevin, 416 U.S. 351 (1974).

Geduldig v. Aiello, 417 U.S. 484 (1974).

Schlesinger v. Ballard, 419 U.S. 498 (1975).

Weinberger v. Wiesenfeld, 420 U.S. 636 (1975).

Stanton v. Stanton, 421 U.S. 7 (1975).

Edwards v. Healy, 421 U.S. 772 (1975).

Turner v. Dept. of Employment Security of Utah, 423 U.S. 44 (1975).

Planned Parenthood of Missouri v. Danforth, 428 U.S. 52 (1976).

General Electric Co. v. Gilbert, 429 U.S. 125 (1976).

Craig v. Boren, 429 U.S. 190 (1976).

Whalen v. Roe, 429 U.S. 589 (1977).

Califano v. Goldfarb, 430 U.S. 199 (1977).

Califano v. Webster, 430 U.S. 313 (1977).

Fiallo v. Bell, 430 U.S. 787 (1977).

Moore v. East Cleveland, 431 U.S. 494 (1977).

Carey v. Population Services Int'l, 431 U.S. 678 (1977).

Smith v. Org. of Foster Families for Equality and Reform, 431 U.S. 816 (1977).

Zablocki v. Redhail, 434 U.S. 374 (1978).

Regents of University of California v. Bakke, 438 U.S. 265 (1978).

Duren v. Missouri, 439 U.S. 357 (1979).
Orr v. Orr, 440 U.S. 268 (1979).
Personnel Adm'r of Massachusetts v. Feeney, 442 U.S. 272 (1979).
Califano v. Westcott, 443 U.S. 76 (1979).
Powers v. Ohio, 499 U.S. 400 (1991).
Planned Parenthood v. Casey, 505 U.S. 833 (1992).
Adarand Constructors v. Pena, 515 U.S. 200 (1995).
Nevada Dept. of Human Resources v. Hibbs, 538 U.S. 721 (2003).
Lawrence v. Texas, 539 U.S. 558 (2003).

Other Federal Cases

McCormick v. United States, 57 Treas. Dec. 117 (1930).
Rosenfeld v. Southern Pacific Co., 293 F. Supp. 1219 (C.D. Cal. 1968).
Weeks v. Southern Bell Telephone and Telegraph Co., 408 F.2d 228 (5th Cir. 1969).
Bowe v. Colgate-Palmolive Co., 416 F.2d 711 (7th Cir. 1969).
Diaz v. Pan American World Airways, Inc., 442 F.2d 385 (5th Cir. 1971).
Mengelkoch v. Industrial Welfare Commission, 442 F.2d 1119 (9th Cir. 1971).
EEOC v. Sears, Roebuck and Co., 839 F.2d 302 (7th Cir. 1988).

State Court Cases

Rosencrantz v. Territory, 5 P. 305 (1884).
Harland v. Territory, 13 P. 453 (1887).
Parus v. District Court, 174 P. 706 (1918).
In re Grilli, 179 N.Y.S. 795 Kings Co. S. Ct. (1920).
People v. Barltz, 180 N.W. 423 (1920).
Commonwealth v. Maxwell, 271 Pa. 378 (1921).
Harper v. State, 234 S.W. 909 (1921).
In re Opinion of the Justices, 130 N.E. 685 (1921).
Opinion of the Justices, 113 A. 614 (1921).
State v. James, 114 A. 553 (1921).
State v. Walker, 185 N.W. 619 (1921).
First Wisconsin National Bank v. Jahn, 190 N.W. 822 (1922).
In re Opinion of the Justices, 135 N.E. 173 (1922).
State v. Chase, 211 P. 920 (1922).
Austin v. Austin, 100 S. 591 (1924).
Dickson v. Strickland, 265 S.W. 1012 (1924).
State v. Kelley, 229 P. 659 (1924).
People ex rel. Fyfe v. Barnett, 150 N.E. 290 (1925).
Palmer v. State, 150 N.E. 917 (1926).
In re Opinion of the Justices, 139 A. 180 (1927).
Moulin v. Monteleone, 115 S. 447 (1927).
Curtis v. Ashworth, 142 S.E. 111 (1928).

Commonwealth v. Welosky, 177 N.E. 656 (1931).

State v. Arnold, 235 N.W. 373 (1931).

Commonwealth v. Rutherford, 169 S.E. 909 (1933).

State v. Nelson, 11 A.2d 856 (1940).

OTHER WORKS CITED

Abbott, G. 1925. "What Have They Done?" *Independent*, October 24, 476.

Ackerman, B. A. 1998. *We the People: Transformations*. Cambridge, MA: Belknap Press of Harvard University Press.

Allen, A. 1988. *Uneasy Access: Privacy for Women in a Free Society*. Totowa, NJ: Rowman and Littlefield.

Allen, A., and E. Mack. 1990. "How Privacy Got Its Gender." *Northern Illinois University Law Review* 10:441–78.

Allen, F. E. 1930. "The First Ten Years." *Woman's Journal*, August 5, 5–7, 30–32.

Alpern, S., and D. Baum. 1985. "Female Ballots: The Impact of the Nineteenth Amendment." *Journal of Interdisciplinary History* 16:43–67.

Altmeyer, A. 1966. *The Formative Years of Social Security*. Madison: University of Wisconsin Press.

Amar, A. R. 1998. *The Bill of Rights: Creation and Reconstruction*. New Haven, CT: Yale University Press.

Amar, V. D. 1995. "Jury Service as Political Participation Akin to Voting." *Cornell Law Review* 80:203–59.

Amatniek, K. 1968. "Funeral Oration for the Burial of Traditional Womanhood." *New York Radical Women's Notes from the First Year*, June. Documents from the Women's Liberation Movement, Special Collections Library, Duke University. http://scriptorium.lib.duke.edu/wlm/notes/#rankin.

"American Declaration of the Rights and Duties of Man." 1949. *American Journal of International Law* 43 (July): S133–S139.

Andersen, K. 1996. *After Suffrage: Women in Partisan and Electoral Politics Before the New Deal*. Chicago: University of Chicago Press.

Anderson, B. 1983. *Imagined Communities: Reflections on the Origin and Spread of Nationalism*. London: Verso.

Anderson, M. 1951. *Woman at Work: The Autobiography of Mary Anderson as Told to Mary N. Winslow*. Westport, CT: Greenwood Press.

Aristotle. 1943. *Aristotle's Politics*. Trans. Benjamin Jowett. New York: Random House.

Ayer, E. H. 1994. *Ruth Bader Ginsburg: Fire and Steel on the Supreme Court*. New York: Dillon Press.

Babcock, B. A. 1993. "A Place in the Palladium: Women's Rights and Jury Service." *University of Cincinnati Law Review* 61:1139.

Baer, J. A. 1978. *The Chains of Protection: The Judicial Response to Women's Labor Legislation*. Westport, CT: Greenwood Press.

Baker, P. 1984. "The Domestication of Politics: Women and American Political Society, 1780–1920." *American Historical Review* 89:620–47.

Barbalet, J. 1988. *Citizenship*. Minneapolis: University of Minnesota Press.

Barber, L. G. 2002. *Marching on Washington: The Forging of an American Political Tradition*. Berkeley and Los Angeles: University of California Press.

Bartlett, K. T. 1993. *Gender and Law: Theory, Doctrine, Commentary*. Boston: Little, Brown.

Basch, N. 1982. *In the Eyes of the Law: Women, Marriage, and Property in Nineteenth-Century New York*. Ithaca, NY: Cornell University Press.

Baxandall, R. 2001. "Re-visioning the Women's Liberation Movement's Narrative: Early Second-Wave African American Feminists." *Feminist Studies* 27:225–46.

Beauvoir, S. de. 1989. *The Second Sex*. Trans. and ed. H. M. Parshley. New York: Vintage Books.

Becker, S. 1981. *The Origins of the Equal Rights Amendment: American Feminism Between the Wars*. Westport, CT: Greenwood Press.

———. 1987. "International Feminism Between the Wars: The National Woman's Party Versus the League of Women Voters." In *Decades of Discontent: The Women's Movement, 1920–1940*, ed. Lois Scharf and Joan Jensen, 223–42. Boston: Northeastern University Press.

Bentham, J. 1995. *Panopticon Letters*. Ed. Miran Bozovic. London: Verso.

Berkowitz, E. 1980. *Creating the Welfare State: The Political Economy of Reform*. New York: Praeger.

Bernardino, M. 1947. "Women of Latin America Advancing Toward Equality." *Equal Rights*, May–June, 4.

Bird, C., compiler. 1979. *What Women Want: From the Official Report to the President, the Congress, and the People of the United States*. New York: Simon and Schuster.

Blackstone, Sir W. 1978. *Commentaries on the Laws of England*. 4 vols. New York: Garland Publishers.

Blair, E. N. 1931. "Why I am Discouraged About Women in Politics." *Woman's Journal*, January, 20–22, 44–45.

"Blessed Are the Bolters." 1920. *Woman Citizen*, October 23, 565.

Bock, G., and S. James, eds. 1992. *Beyond Equality and Difference: Citizenship, Feminist Politics, Female Subjectivity*. New York: Routledge.

Bok, D., and W. Bowen. 2000. *Shape of the River: Long-Term Consequences of Considering Race in College and University Admissions*. Princeton, NJ: Princeton University Press.

Borchard, E. M. 1935. "The Citizenship of Native-Born Women Who Married Foreigners Before March 2, 1907, and Acquired a Foreign Domicile." *American Journal of International Law* 29:396–422.

Boris, E. 1994. *Home to Work: Motherhood and the Politics of Industrial Homework in the United States*. New York: Cambridge University Press.

Bourdieu, P. 1977. *Outline of a Theory of Practice*. New York: Cambridge University Press.

Boydston, J. 1990. *Home and Work: Housework, Wages, and the Ideology of Labor in the Early Republic*. New York: Oxford University Press.

Boyer, I. P. 1920. "Something More on Political Parties." *Woman Citizen*, October 9, 520–22.

Boylan, A. M. 1971. "Ida Phillips vs. Martin Marietta Corporation." *Women's Rights Law Reporter*, 13:11-21.

Brandwein, P. 1999. *Reconstructing Reconstruction: The Supreme Court and the Production of Historical Truth*. Durham, NC: Duke University Press.

Brauer, C. M. 1983. "Women Activists, Southern Conservatives, and the Prohibition of Sex Discrimination in Title VII of the 1964 Civil Rights Act." *Journal of Southern History* 49:37–56.

Breckinridge, S. 1931. *Marriage and the Civic Rights of Women: Separate Domicil and Independent Citizenship*. Chicago: University of Chicago Press.

Bredbrenner, C. 1998. *A Nationality of Her Own: Women, Marriage, and the Law of Citizenship*. Berkeley and Los Angeles: University of California Press.

Brest, P., and S. Levinson. 1992. *Processes of Constitutional Decisionmaking: Cases and Materials*. Boston: Little, Brown.

Brinkley, A. 1995. *The End of Reform: New Deal Liberalism in Recession and War*. New York: Knopf.

Brokaw, T. 1998. *The Greatest Generation*. New York: Random House.

Brown, J. K. 1993. "The Nineteenth Amendment and Women's Equality." *Yale Law Journal* 102:2175–2204.

Brown, M. K., M. Carnoy, E. Currie, T. Duster, D. B. Oppenheimer, M. M. Shultz, and D. Wellman. 2003. *Whitewashing Race: The Myth of a Color-Blind Society*. Berkeley and Los Angeles: University of California Press.

Brown, W. 1995. *States of Injury: Power and Freedom in Late Modernity*. Princeton, NJ: Princeton University Press.

———. 2001. "Reflections on Tolerance in the Age of Identity." In *Democracy and Vision: Sheldon Wolin and the Vicissitudes of the Political*, ed. A. Botwinick and W. E. Connolly, 99–117. Princeton, NJ: Princeton University Press.

Brubaker, R. 1992. *Citizenship and Nationhood in France and Germany*. Cambridge, MA: Harvard University Press.

Burgett, B. 1998. *Sentimental Bodies: Sex, Gender, and Citizenship in the Early Republic*. Princeton, NJ: Princeton University Press.

Burnham, W. D. 1974. "Theory and Voting Research: Some Reflections on Converse's 'Change in the American Electorate.'" *American Political Science Review* 68 (September): 1002–23.

Butler, J., and J. Scott, eds. 1992. *Feminists Theorize the Political*. New York: Routledge.

Butler, S. S. 1931. "I Am Not Disappointed in Women in Politics." *Woman's Journal*, April, 14, 39–40.

Cain, W. E. 1996. "Lincoln, Slavery, and Rights." In *Legal Rights: Historical and*

Philosophical Perspectives, ed. A. Sarat and T. R. Kearns, 53–86. Ann Arbor: University of Michigan Press.

Campbell, A. 2002. "Raising the Bar: Ruth Bader Ginsburg and the ACLU Women's Rights Project." *Texas Journal of Women and the Law* 11:157 ff.

Campbell, D. 1990. "The Regimented Women of World War II." In *Women, Militarism, and War: Essays in History, Politics, and Social Theory*, ed. J. B. Elshstain and S. Tobias, 107–24. Savage, MD: Rowman and Littlefield.

Carson, C. 1981. *In Struggle: SNCC and the Black Awakening of the 1960s*. Cambridge, MA: Harvard University Press.

Catt, C. C. 1920. "How to Conduct Citizenship Schools." *Woman Citizen*, October 23, 580–82.

———. 1923. "Are Women Disappointed in Politics?" *Woman Citizen*, November 3, 14.

Chafe, W. 1972. *The American Woman: Her Changing Social, Economic, and Political Roles, 1920–1970*. New York: Oxford University Press.

———. 1991. *The Paradox of Change: American Women in the 20th Century*. New York: Oxford University Press.

Chused, R. 1983. "Married Women's Property Law, 1800–1850." *Georgetown Law Journal* 71:1359–1425.

Clemens, E. 1993. "Organizational Repertoires and Institutional Change: Women's Groups and the Transformation of US Politics, 1890–1920." *American Journal of Sociology* 98:755–98.

"Conflict of Laws — Jurisdiction: Domicil — Separate Domicil of Women Who Is on Amicable Terms with Husband." 1934. *Harvard Law Review* 47:348–49.

Congressional Record. 1943. 78th Cong., 1st sess., Senate. Washington, DC: GPO.

———. 1946. 79th Cong., 2nd sess., Senate. July 17, 1946, S9224, S9223; July 18, 1946, S9311, S9293, S9294. Washington, DC: GPO.

Constable, M. 1994. *The Law of the Other: The Mixed Jury and Changing Conceptions of Citizenship, Law, and Knowledge*. Chicago: University of Chicago Press.

"Constitutional Law: Police Power, Minimum Wage For Women." 1923. *California Law Review* 11:353–62.

"Constitutionality of Minimum Wage Statutes." 1923. *Columbia Law Review* 23:565–67.

Cott, N. F. 1987. *The Grounding of Modern Feminism*. New Haven, CT: Yale University Press.

———. 1995a. "Across the Great Divide: Women in Politics Before and After 1920." In *One Woman, One Vote: Rediscovering the Woman Suffrage Movement*, ed. M. S. Wheeler, 353–74. Troutdale, OR: NewSage Press.

———. 1995b. "Giving Character to Our Whole Civil Polity: Marriage and the Public Order in the Late Nineteenth Century." In *U.S. History as Women's History: New Feminist Essays*, ed. L. K. Kerber, A. Kessler-Harris, and K. K. Sklar, 107–21. Chapel Hill, NC: University of North Carolina Press.

————. 1998. "Marriage and Women's Citizenship in the United States, 1830–1934." *American Historical Review* 3:1440–73.

————. 2001. *Public Vows: A History of Marriage and the Nation.* Cambridge, MA: Harvard University Press.

Crocco, M. S., and D. B. Brooks. 1995. "The Nineteenth Amendment: Reform or Revolution?" *Social Education* 59:279–84.

Dahl, R. 1989. *Democracy and Its Critics.* New Haven, CT: Yale University Press.

Daniels, A. K. 1991. "Careers in Feminism." *Gender and Society* 5:583–607.

Davies, G., and M. Derthick. 1997. "Race and Social Welfare Policy: The Social Security Act of 1935." *Political Science Quarterly* 112:217–36.

"Declaration of Sentiments." n.d. *National Expansion and Reform, 1815–1880: Reformers and Crusaders*, Seneca Falls Convention, July 1848. Learning Page, Library of Congress. http://memory.loc.gov/learn/features/timeline/expref/crusader/seneca.html.

Dolgin, J. L. 2002. "The Constitution as Family Arbiter: A Moral in the Mess?" *Columbia Law Review* 102:337–406.

Douglas, P. 1938. *Social Security in the United States: An Analysis of the Federal Social Security Act.* New York: Whittlesey House.

Downing, B. M. 1992. *The Military Revolution and Political Change: Origins of Democracy and Autocracy in Early Modern Europe.* Princeton, NJ: Princeton University Press.

DuBois, E. C. 1978. *Feminism and Suffrage: The Emergence of an Independent Women's Movement in America, 1848–1869.* Ithaca, NY: Cornell University Press.

————. 1987. "Outgrowing the Compact of the Fathers: Equal Rights, Woman Suffrage, and the Constitution." *Journal of American History* 74:836–62.

————. 1995. "Taking the Law into Our Own Hands: *Bradwell, Minor,* and Suffrage Militance in the 1870s." In *One Woman, One Vote: Rediscovering the Woman Suffrage Movement*, ed. M. S. Wheeler, 81–98. Troutdale, OR: NewSage Press.

————. 1997. *Harriet Stanton Blatch and the Winning of Woman Suffrage.* New Haven, CT: Yale University Press.

Dudziak, M. L. 2000. *Cold War Civil Rights: Race and the Image of American Democracy.* Princeton, NJ: Princeton University Press.

Dworkin, A. 1987. *Intercourse.* New York: Free Press.

Echols, A. 1989. *Daring to Be Bad: Radical Feminism in America, 1967–1975.* Minneapolis: University of Minnesota Press.

"Education for Citizenship." 1921. *Ladies Home Journal*, February 27, 98.

Edwards, R. 1997. *Angels in the Machinery: Gender in American Party Politics from the Civil War to the Progressive Era.* New York: Oxford University Press.

Elshtain, J. B. 1990. *Women, Militarism, and War: Essays in History, Politics, and Social Theory.* Savage, MD: Rowman and Littlefield.

Enloe, C. H. 2000. *Maneuvers: The International Politics of Militarizing Women's Lives.* Berkeley and Los Angeles: University of California Press.

Epstein, B. 2002. "The Successes and Failures of Feminism." *Journal of Women's History* 14:118–25.

Ernst, D. R. 1998. "Homework and the Police Power from Jacobs to Adkins: Symposium on Eileen Boris. Home to Work." *Labor History* 39 (November): 417.

"Feminist Chronicles." 1966. Feminist Majority Foundation. www.feminist.org/research/chronicles/fc1966.html.

Feminist Chronicles, 1953–1993. 1995. Feminist Majority Foundation. www.feminist.org/research/chronicles/chronicl.html.

Fenwick, C. G. 1948. "The Ninth International Conference of American States." *American Journal of International Law* 42:553–67.

Fineman, M. A. 1995. *The Neutered Mother, the Sexual Family, and Other Twentieth Century Tragedies.* New York: Routledge.

———. 1999. "Symposium, Privacy and the Family, Panel III: What Place for Family Privacy?" *George Washington Law Review* 67:1207–24.

———. 2004. *The Autonomy Myth: A Theory of Dependency.* New York: Free Press.

Firestone, S. 1968a. "The Jeanette Rankin Brigade: Woman Power?" *New York Radical Women's Notes from the First Year*, June. Documents from the Women's Liberation Movement, Special Collections Library, Duke University. http://scriptorium.lib.duke.edu/wlm/notes/#rankin.

———. 1968b. "The Women's Rights Movement in the U.S.: A New View." *New York Radical Women's Notes from the First Year*, June. Documents from the Women's Liberation Movement, Special Collections Library, Duke University. http://scriptorium.lib.duke.edu/wlm/notes/#newview.

"First Jurywomen." 1930. *Women's Journal*, May, 27.

"The First Woman's Platform." 1920. *Woman Citizen*, May 15, 1254.

Flexner, E. 1973. *Century of Struggle: The Woman's Rights Movement in the United States.* Rev. ed. Cambridge, MA: Harvard University Press.

Foner, E. 1995. *Free Soil, Free Labor, Free Men: The Ideology of the Republican Party Before the Civil War.* New York: Oxford University Press.

Forbath, W. 1991. *Law and the Shaping of the American Labor Movement.* Cambridge, MA: Harvard University Press.

———. 1999. "Caste, Class, and Equal Citizenship." *Michigan Law Review* 98:1–91.

Foucault, Michel. 1979. *Discipline and Punish: The Birth of the Prison.* Trans. Alan Sheridan. New York: Vintage Books.

———. 1990. *The History of Sexuality.* Vol. 1. Trans. Robert Hurley. New York: Vintage Books.

Franke, K. 1999. "Becoming a Citizen: Reconstruction Era Regulation of African American Marriages." *Yale Journal of Law and the Humanities* 11:251–309.

———. 2001. "Commentary: Taking Care." *Chicago Kent Law Review* 76:1541.

Fraser, N., and L. Gordon. 1994. "Civil Citizenship Against Social Citizenship." In *The Condition of Citizenship*, ed. B. van Steenbergen, 90–107. London: Sage Publications.

———. 1995. "A Genealogy of *Dependency*: Tracing a Keyword of the U.S. Welfare State." In *Rethinking the Political: Gender, Resistance, and the State*, ed. B. Laslett, Johanna Brenner, and Y. Arat, 33–60. Chicago: University of Chicago Press.

Fraser, N., and S. L. Bartky, eds. 1992. *Revaluing French Feminism: Critical Essays on Difference, Agency, and Culture*. Bloomington: Indiana University Press.

Freedom, V. 1947. "Equality Sought in the International Bill of Rights." *Equal Rights* (May–June): 5.

Freeman, J. 1971. "The Women's Liberation Movement: Its Origin, Structures, and Ideals." Pittsburgh: Know, Inc. Documents from the Women's Liberation Movement, Special Collections Library, Duke University. http://scriptorium.lib.duke.edu/wlm/womlib/.

———. 1973. "The Origins of the Women's Liberation Movement." *American Journal of Sociology* 78:792–811.

Friedan, B. 1997. *The Feminine Mystique*. New York: Norton.

Garland Thomson, R. 1997. *Extraordinary Bodies: Figuring Physical Disability in American Culture and Literature*. New York: Columbia University Press.

Garrow, D. 1998. *Liberty and Sexuality: The Right to Privacy and the Making of* Roe v. Wade. Berkeley and Los Angeles: University of California Press.

Gelb, J., and M. L. Palley. 1982. *Women and Public Policies*. Princeton, NJ: Princeton University Press.

Giles, N. 1944. "What About the Women?" *Ladies Home Journal*, June, 157–59, 161.

Gillman, H. 1993. *The Constitution Besieged: The Rise and Decline of Lochner Era Police Powers Jurisprudence*. Durham, NC: Duke University Press.

Gilmore, G. 1996. *Gender and Jim Crow: Women and the Politics of White Supremacy, 1896–1920*. Chapel Hill: University of North Carolina Press.

Gilroy, P. 1993. *The Black Atlantic: Modernity and Double Consciousness*. Cambridge, MA: Harvard University Press.

Ginsburg, F. 1989. *Contested Lives: The Abortion Debate in One American Community*. Berkeley and Los Angeles: University of California Press.

Ginsburg, R. B. 1971. Comment on *Reed v. Reed*. *Women's Rights Law Reporter* 2:7–8.

———. 1978a. "Sex Equality and the Constitution." *Tulane Law Review* 52:451–75.

———. 1978b. "Sex Equality and the Constitution: The State of the Art." *Women's Rights Law Reporter* 4:143–47.

———. 1979. "Sex Equality Under the Fourteenth and Equal Rights Amendments." *Washington University Law Quarterly* 57:161–78.

———. 1994. "U.S. Supreme Court Justice Ruth Bader Ginsburg Visits John Marshall." *John Marshall Law School Alumni News*, December, 12 and 45.

Goldstein, J. S. 2001. *War and Gender: How Gender Shapes the War System and Vice Versa*. Cambridge: Cambridge University Press.

Goldstein, L. F. 1992. *Feminist Jurisprudence: The Difference Debate*. Lanham, MD: Rowman and Littlefield.

Goodman, J., R. C. Schoenbrod, and N. Stearns. 1973. "*Doe* and *Roe*: Where Do We Go from Here?" *Women's Rights Law Reporter* 1:20–37.

Gordon, L., ed. 1990. *Women, the State, and Welfare*. Madison, WI: University of Wisconsin Press.

Gordon, S. B. 2002. *The Mormon Question: Polygamy and Constitutional Conflict in Nineteenth Century America*. Chapel Hill: University of North Carolina Press.

Graham, S. H. 1996. *Woman Suffrage and the New Democracy*. New Haven, CT: Yale University Press.

Greenhouse, C. J. 1992. "Signs of Quality: Individualism and Hierarchy in American Culture." *American Ethnologist* 19:233–54.

———. 1994. "Commentary: Constructive Approaches to Law, Culture, and Identity." *Law and Society Review* 28:1231–42.

———, ed. 1998. *Democracy and Ethnography: Constructing Identities in Multicultural Liberal States*. Albany: State University of New York Press.

Grossberg, M. 1985. *Governing the Hearth: Law and the Family in Nineteenth-Century America*. Chapel Hill: University of North Carolina Press.

Grossman, J. 1994. "Women's Jury Service: Right of Citizenship or Privilege of Difference?" *Stanford Law Review* 46:1115.

Guinier, L., and G. Torres. 2002. *The Miner's Canary: Enlisting Race, Resisting Power, Transforming Democracy*. Cambridge, MA: Harvard University Press.

Gunew, S., and A. Yeatman, eds. 1993. *Feminism and the Politics of Difference*. Boulder, CO: Westview Press.

Gurin, P. 2004. "The Compelling Need for Diversity in Education" (January 1999). Expert report prepared for the lawsuits *Gratz and Hamacher v. Bollinger, Duderstadt, the University of Michigan, and the University of Michigan College of LS&A*, U.S. District Court, Eastern District of Michigan, Civil Action No. 97-75231; and *Grutter v. Bollinger, Lehman, Shields, the University of Michigan and the University of Michigan Law School*, U.S. District Court, Eastern District of Michigan, Civil Action No. 97-75928. www.umich.edu/~urel/admissions/legal/expert/gurintoc.html.

Haag, P. 1999. *Consent: Sexual Rights and the Transformation of American Liberalism*. Ithaca, NY: Cornell University Press.

Habermas, J. 1989. *The Structural Transformation of the Public Sphere: An Inquiry into a Category of Bourgeois Society*. Trans. Thomas Burger. Cambridge, MA: MIT Press.

Hamilton, A., J. Madison, and J. Jay. 1961. *The Federalist Papers*. Ed. C. Rossiter. New York: New American Library.

Haney-Lopez, I. F. 1996. *White by Law: The Legal Construction of Race*. New York: New York University Press.

Hanisch, C., and E. Sutherland. 1968. "Women of the World Unite — We Have Nothing to Lose but Our Men!" *New York Radical Women's Notes from the First Year*, June. Documents from the Women's Liberation Movement, Special Collections Library, Duke University. http://scriptorium.lib.duke.edu/wlm/notes/#ourmen.

Harper, I. H., ed. 1922. *History of Woman Suffrage*. Vol. 5. New York: J. J. Little and Ives.

Harris, C. 1921. "Practical Politics for Gentlewomen." *Ladies Home Journal*, September, 16.

Harrison, C. E. 1980. "A 'New Frontier' for Women: The Public Policy of the Kennedy Administration." *Journal of American History* 67:630–46.

Hart, V. 1994. *Bound by Our Constitution: Women, Workers, and the Minimum Wage*. Princeton, NJ: Princeton University Press.

Hartmann, S. M. 1982. *The Home Front and Beyond: American Women in the 1940's*. Boston: Twayne Publishers.

Hartog, H. 1987. "The Constitution of Aspiration and the Rights That Belong to Us All." *Journal of American History* 74:1013–34.

Hartsock, N. 1984. *Money, Sex, and Power: Toward a Feminist Historical Materialism*. Boston: Northeastern University Press.

Hartz, L. 1955. *The Liberal Tradition in America*. New York: Harcourt, Brace.

Harvey, A. 1996. "The Political Consequences of Suffrage Exclusion: Organizations, Institutions, and the Electoral Mobilization of Women." *Social Science History* 20:97–132.

———. 1998. *Votes Without Leverage: Women in American Electoral Politics, 1920–1970*. New York: Cambridge University Press.

Hattam, V. 1993. *Labor Visions and State Power: The Origins of Business Unionism in the United States*. Princeton, NJ: Princeton University Press.

Hebard, G. R. 1913. "The First Woman Jury." *Journal of American History* 7:1293–1341.

Hill Collins, P. 1990. *Black Feminist Thought: Knowledge, Consciousness, and the Politics of Empowerment*. Boston: Unwin Hyman.

Hirschmann, N., and C. Di Stefano, eds. 1996. *Revisioning the Political: Feminist Reconstructions of Traditional Concepts in Western Political Theory*. Boulder, CO: Westview Press.

Hoff, J. 1991. *Law, Gender, and Injustice: A Legal History of US Women*. New York: New York University Press.

Hoganson, K. L. 1998. *Fighting for American Manhood: How Gender Politics Provoked the Spanish-American and Philippine-American War*. New Haven, CT: Yale University Press.

Hole, J., and E. Levine. 1971. *Rebirth of Feminism*. New York: Quadrangle Books.

Holland, C. 2001. *The Body Politic: Foundings, Citizenship, and Difference in the American Political Imagination*. New York: Routledge.

Honey, M. 1984. *Creating Rosie the Riveter: Class, Gender, and Propaganda During World War II*. Amherst: University of Massachusetts Press.

———, ed. 1999. *Bitter Fruit: African American Women in World War II*. Columbia: University of Missouri Press.

Honig, B. 2001. *Democracy and the Foreigner*. Princeton, NJ: Princeton University Press.

"I Looked Into My Brother's Face." 1943. *Good Housekeeping*, August, 145.

Ignatiev, N. 1995. *How the Irish Became White*. New York: Routledge.

"Is Woman Suffrage Failing?" 1924. [Interviews with various people.] Pts. 1–5. *Woman Citizen*, March 22, 7–9, 29–30; April 5, 8–10, 30; April 19, 14–16; May 3, 17 and 19; May 17, 24.

Janowitz, M. 1983. *The Political Education of Soldiers*. Beverly Hills, CA: Sage Publications.

Jones, K. B. 1993. *Compassionate Authority: Democracy and the Representation of Women*. New York: Routledge.

Jordan, E. 1920. "Women in the Presidential Campaign." *Ladies Home Journal*, October, 4.

"A Jury of Matrons." 1914. *American Law Review* 48:280.

Kann, M. 1991. *On the Man Question: Gender and Civic Virtue in America*. Philadelphia: Temple University Press.

Karst, K. L. 1976. Review of *Cases and Materials on Constitutional Law*, by Gerald Gunther. *Harvard Law Review* 89:1028–37.

Katz, E. 2000. "Race and the Right to Vote After *Race v. Cayetano*." *Michigan Law Review* 99:491–531.

Katzenstein, M. 1998. *Faithful and Fearless: Moving Feminist Politics Inside the Church and Military*. Princeton, NJ: Princeton University Press.

Katznelson, I., and B. Pietrykowski. 1991. "Rebuilding the American State: Evidence from the 1940s." *Studies in American Political Development* 5:301–39.

Kelley, F. 1922. "The Blanket Amendment." *Woman Citizen*, January 28, 14.

Kennard, F. E. 1931. "Maryland Women Demand Jury Service." *Equal Rights*, March, 7.

Kerber, L. K. 1995. "'Ourselves and Our Daughters Forever': Women and the Constitution, 1787–1876." In *One Woman, One Vote: Rediscovering the Woman Suffrage Movement*, ed. M. S. Wheeler, 21–36. Troutdale, OR: NewSage Press.

———. 1998. *No Constitutional Right to Be Ladies: Women and the Obligations of Citizenship*. New York: Hill and Wang.

———. 2002. "Writing Feminist Justice: Writing Our Own Rare Books." Symposium. *Yale Journal of Law and Feminism* 14:429–50.

Kessler-Harris, A. 1982. *Out to Work: A History of Wage-Earning Women in the United States*. New York: Oxford University Press.

———. 1995. "Designing Women and Old Fools." In *U.S. History as Women's History: New Feminist Essays*, ed. L. K. Kerber, A. Kessler-Harris, and K. K. Sklar, 87–106. Chapel Hill: University of North Carolina Press.

———. 2001. *In Pursuit of Equity: Women, Men, and the Quest for Economic Citizenship in 20th-Century America*. New York: Oxford University Press.

Kettner, J. H. 1978. *The Development of American Citizenship, 1608–1870*. Chapel Hill: University of North Carolina Press.

Key, V. O. 1949. *Southern Politics in State and Nation.* New York: Knopf.

Keyssar, A. 2000. *The Right to Vote: The Contested History of Democracy in the United States.* New York: Basic Books.

King, D. S. 2000. *Making Americans: Immigration, Race, and the Origins of Diverse Democracy.* Cambridge, MA: Harvard University Press.

King, M. L., Jr. n.d. "I Have a Dream." American Rhetoric Web site. www.americanrhetoric.com/speeches/Ihaveadream.htm.

Klarman, M. 2004. *From Jim Crow to Civil Rights: The Supreme Court and the Struggle for Racial Equality.* Oxford: Oxford University Press.

Kleppner, P. 1982. "Were Women to Blame? Female Suffrage and Voter Turnout." *Journal of Interdisciplinary History* 12:621–43.

———. 1987. *Continuity and Change in Electoral Politics, 1893–1928.* New York: Greenwood Press.

Kousser, J. M. 1974. *The Shaping of Southern Politics: Suffrage Restriction and the Establishment of the One-Party South, 1880–1910.* New Haven, CT: Yale University Press.

———. 1999. *Colorblind Injustice: Minority Voting Rights and the Undoing of the Second Reconstruction.* Chapel Hill: University of North Carolina Press.

Kraditor, A. S. 1981. *The Ideas of the Woman Suffrage Movement, 1890–1920.* New York: Norton.

Kryder, D. 2000. *Divided Arsenal: Race and the American State During World War II.* New York: Cambridge University Press.

League of Women Voters. 1924. *A Record of Four Years in the National League of Women Voters, 1920–1924.* Washington, DC: National League of Women Voters.

———. 1930. *A Survey of the Legal Status of Women in the Forty-Eight States,* rev. ed. Washington, DC: National League of Women Voters.

Lemons, J. S. 1973. *The Woman Citizen: Social Feminism in the 1920s.* Urbana: University of Illinois Press.

Lever, A. 2000. "Must Privacy and Sexual Equality Conflict? A Philosophical Examination of Some Legal Evidence." *Social Research* 67:1137–71.

Levinson, S. 1989. "The Embarrassing Second Amendment." *Yale Law Journal* 99:637–59.

Levitan, S., and K. Cleary. 1973. *Old Wars Remain Unfinished: The Veterans Benefits System.* Baltimore: Johns Hopkins University Press.

Lewis, D. L. 2000. *W. E. B. DuBois: The Fight for Equality and the American Century.* New York: Henry Holt.

Lieberman, R. C. 1998. *Shifting the Color Line: Race and the American Welfare State.* Cambridge, MA: Harvard University Press.

Lipschultz, S. 1996. "Hours and Wages: the Gendering of Labor Standards in America." *Journal of Women's History* 8:114–36.

Lipsitz, G. 1998. *The Possessive Investment in Whiteness: How White People Profit from Identity Politics.* Philadelphia: Temple University Press.

Lister, R. 1997. *Citizenship: Feminist Perspectives*. New York: New York University Press.

Locke, J. 1980. *Second Treatise of Government*. Ed. C. B. Macpherson. Indianapolis: Hackett Publishing.

MacKinnon, C. 1987. *Feminism Unmodified: Discourses on Life and Law*. Cambridge, MA: Harvard University Press.

MacLean, N. 1999. "The Hidden History of Affirmative Action: Working Women's Struggles in the 1970s and the Gender of Class." *Feminist Studies* 25:49–79.

MacPherson, C. B. 1962. *The Political Theory of Possessive Individualism: Hobbes to Locke*. Oxford: Clarendon Press.

Maine, Sir H. 1972. *Ancient Law: Its Connection to the Early History of Society and Its Relation to Modern Ideas*. New York: Dutton.

Malcolm, J. L. 1994. *To Keep and Bear Arms: The Origins of an Anglo-American Right*. Cambridge, MA: Harvard University Press.

Marilley, S. M. 1996. *Woman Suffrage and the Origins of Liberal Feminism in the United States, 1820–1920*. Cambridge, MA: Harvard University Press.

Markowitz, D. L. 1992. "In Pursuit of Equality: One Woman's Work to Change the Law." *Women's Rights Law Reporter* 14:335–59.

Marshall, T. H. 1950. "Citizenship and Social Class." In *Class, Citizenship, and Social Development*, by T. H. Marshall, 1–85. Cambridge: Cambridge University Press.

Matthews, B. S. 1926. "Women Should Have Equal Rights with Men: A Reply." *Equal Rights*, May 29, 125–27.

———. 1929. "The Woman Juror." *Equal Rights*, January 19, 26.

———. 1930a. "The Status of Women as Jurors." Pts. 1–5. *Equal Rights*, May 24, 123–25; May 31, 133–34; June 7, 140–41; June 14, 148–49; June 21, 157.

———. 1930b. "The Legal Status of Women in the United States." *Equal Rights*, March 22, 53–55.

May, E. T. 1988. *Homeward Bound: American Families in the Cold War Era*. New York: Basic Books.

McAfee, K., and M. Wood. 1970. "What Is the Revolutionary Potential of Women's Liberation?" Boston: New England Free Press. [Originally entitled "Bread and Roses," this article was first published in the June 1969 issue of *Leviathan*.] Documents from the Women's Liberation Movement, Special Collections Library, Duke University http://scriptorium.lib.duke.edu/wlm/mcafee.

McConnaughy, C. 2004. "The Politics of Suffrage Extension in the American States: Party, Race, and the Pursuit of Women's Voting Rights." Ph.D. diss., University of Michigan.

McCormick, R. L. 1986. *The Party Period and Public Policy: American Politics from the Age of Jackson to the Progressive Era*. New York: Oxford University Press.

McCulloch, C. W. 1920. "Trial by Jury." *Woman Citizen*, October 2, 488, 493, 495.

McDonagh, E. Forthcoming. *Gendering the State: Democratization and Women's Political Leadership*. Chicago: Chicago University Press.

McGerr, M. 1986. *The Decline of Popular Politics: The American North, 1865–1928.* New York: Oxford University Press.

———. 1990. "Political Style and Women's Power, 1830–1930." *Journal of American History* 77:864–88.

Mehta, U. 1990. "Liberal Strategies of Exclusion." *Politics and Society* 18:427–54.

———. 1999. *Liberalism and Empire: A Study in Nineteenth-Century British Liberal Thought.* Chicago: University of Chicago Press.

Merry, S. E. 1986. "Everyday Understandings of Law in Working-Class America." *American Ethnologist* 13:253–70.

———. 1995. "Resistance and the Cultural Power of Law." *Law and Society Review* 29:11–26.

Merryman, M. 1998. *Clipped Wings: The Rise and Fall of the Women's Airforce Service Pilots WASPs of World War II.* New York: New York University Press.

Mettler, S. 1998. *Dividing Citizens: Gender and Federalism in New Deal Public Policy.* Ithaca, NY: Cornell University Press.

Mezey, S. 2003. *Elusive Equality: Women's Rights, Public Policy, and the Law.* Boulder, CO: Lynne Reinner Publishers.

Mill, J. S. 1991. *On Liberty and Other Essays.* Ed. John Gray. New York: Oxford University Press.

Miller, R. J. 1922. "The Woman Juror." *Oregon Law Review* 2:30.

Mink, G. 1995. *The Wages of Motherhood: Inequality in the Welfare State, 1917–1942.* Ithaca, NY: Cornell University Press.

Mizen, M. S. 1947. "An International Bill of Rights." *Equal Rights*, September–December, 30.

Montejano, D. 1987. *Anglos and Mexicans in the Making of Texas, 1836–1986.* Austin: University of Texas Press.

Montesquieu, C. 1949. *The Spirit of the Laws.* Trans. Thomas Nugent. New York: Hafner Publishing.

Montgomery, D. 1993. *Citizen Worker: The Experience of Workers in the United States with Democracy and the Free Market During the Nineteenth Century.* New York: Cambridge University Press.

Morgan, E. S. 1988. *Inventing the People: The Rise of Popular Sovereignty in England and America.* New York: Norton.

Morone, J. 2003. *Hellfire Nation: The Politics of Sin in American History.* New Haven, CT: Yale University Press.

Mosch, T. R. 1975. *The GI Bill: A Breakthrough in Educational and Social Policy in the United States.* Hicksville, NY: Exposition Press.

Muncy, R. 1991. *Creating a Female Dominion in American Reform, 1890–1935.* New York: Oxford University Press.

National Black Feminist Organization. 1973. Statement of purpose. Pamela E. Pennock Web page. www-personal.umd.umich.edu/~ppennock/doc-BlackFeminist.htm.

National Organization for Women (NOW). 1966. Statement of purpose, adopted at the organizing conference in Washington, DC, October 29, 1966. Feminist Majority Foundation. www.feminist.org/research/chronicles/early1.html.

———. 1967a. Report of the Task Force on Political Rights and Responsibilities. Feminist Majority Foundation. www.feminist.org/research/chronicles/early4 .html.

———. 1967b. Press release, November 20. Feminist Majority Foundation. www.feminist.org/research/chronicles/early4.html.

———. 1968. Memorandum [by Betty Friedan, dated January 15] on Second National Conference of the National Organization for Women in Washington, DC, November 18–19, 1967. Feminist Majority Foundation. www.feminist.org/ research/chronicles/early2.html.

National Resources Planning Board. 1941. *After Defense: What? Full Employment. Security. Up-Building America. Post-Defense Planning.* Washington, DC: GPO.

———. 1943. *Demobilization and Readjustment: Report of the Conference on Postwar Readjustment of Civilian and Military Personnel.* Washington, DC: GPO.

National Women's Party. 1946. *Equal Rights Amendment: Questions and Answers on the Equal Rights Amendment.* Washington, DC: GPO.

Nelson, B. 1990. "The Origins of the Two-Channel Welfare State: Workmen's Compensation and Mothers' Aid." In *Women, the State, and Welfare,* ed. L. Gordon. Madison: University of Wisconsin Press.

Noble, C. 1997. *Welfare as We Knew It: A Political History of the American Welfare State.* New York: Oxford University Press.

Novkov, J. 2001. *Constituting Workers, Protecting Women: Gender, Law, and Labor in the Progressive Era and New Deal Years.* Ann Arbor: University of Michigan Press.

———. 2002. "Racial Constructions: The Legal Regulation of Miscegenation in Alabama, 1890–1934." *Law and History Review* 20:225–77.

Nussbaum, M. 1999. *Sex and Social Justice.* New York: Oxford University Press.

O'Brien, R. 2005. *Bodies in Revolt: Gender, Disability, and a Workplace Ethic of Care.* New York: Routledge.

Olson, K. W. 1974. *The GI Bill, the Veterans, and the Colleges.* Lexington: University of Kentucky Press.

O'Neal, E. 1920. "The Susan B. Anthony Amendment: Effect of Its Ratification on the Rights of the States to Regulate and Control Suffrage and Elections." *Virginia Law Review* 6:338–60.

O'Neill, W. L. 1971. *Everyone Was Brave: A History of Feminism in America.* Chicago: Quadrangle Books.

———. 1993. *A Democracy at War.* New York: Free Press.

Orren, K. 1991. *Belated Feudalism: Labor, the Law, and Liberal Development in the United States.* New York: Cambridge University Press.

Pan-American Union. 1948. *American Declaration of the Rights and Duties of Man.* Resolution 30. Final Act, Ninth International Conference of American States, Bogota, Colombia, March 30–May 2.

Papachristou, J. 1976. *Women Together: A History in Documents of the Women's Movement.* New York: Knopf.

Parks, M. W. 1920. "National League of Women Voters Fared Well." *Woman Citizen*, July 10, 152.

Pateman, C. 1988. *The Sexual Contract.* Stanford, CA: Stanford University Press.

———. 1994. "Three Questions About Womanhood Suffrage." In *Suffrage and Beyond: International Feminist Perspectives*, ed. C. Daley and M. Nolan, 331–48. New York: New York University Press.

Pell, Mrs. S. 1931. "Jury Service for Women." *Equal Rights*, November 14, 326–27.

Perkins, F. 1946. *The Roosevelt I Knew.* New York: Viking Press.

Phillips, A. 1993. *Democracy and Difference.* University Park: Pennsylvania State University Press.

———. 1995. *The Politics of Presence.* Oxford: Clarendon Press.

Pildes, R. 2000. "Democracy, Anti-Democracy, and the Canon." *Constitutional Commentary* 17:295–319.

Piven, F. F., and R. Cloward. 1980. *Why Americans Still Don't Vote.* Boston: Beacon Press.

President's Commission on the Status of Women. 1963. *The American Woman: The Report of the President's Commission on the Status of Women.* Washington, DC: GPO.

President's Committee on Civil Rights. 1947. *To Secure These Rights: The Report of the President's Committee on Civil Rights.* Washington, DC: GPO.

Putnam, R. 2000. *Bowling Alone: The Collapse and Revival of American Community.* New York: Simon and Schuster.

"Recent Cases." 1933. *Minnesota Law Review* 18:469–88.

Riesenberg, P. 1992. *Citizenship in the Western Tradition.* Chapel Hill: University of North Carolina Press.

Reiter, D. 1998. "June Democracy and Battlefield Effectiveness." *Journal of Conflict Resolution* 42:259–78.

Riley, D. 1988. *Am I That Name? Feminism and the Category of "Women" in History.* Minneapolis: University of Minnesota Press.

Ritter, G. 1997a. *Goldbugs and Greenbacks: The Antimonopoly Tradition and the Politics of Finance in America, 1865–1896.* New York: Cambridge University Press.

———. 1997b. "Modernity, Subjectivity, and Law: Reflections on Marianne Constable's *The Law of the Other.*" *Law and Social Inquiry* 22:809–27.

———. 1997c. "Regendering Citizenship After the Second World War." Paper presented at the Annual Meeting of the American Political Science Association, Washington, DC, August.

———. 1999. "Gender, Labor, and Citizenship from *Adkins to Parrish.*" Paper presented at the Annual Meeting of the American Political Science Association, Atlanta, September 2–5.

———. 2000a. "Gender and Citizenship After the Nineteenth Amendment." *Polity* 32:301–31.

———. 2000b. "A Common Citizenship for All? Veterans Benefits, Social Security, Gender, and Social Citizenship After World War II." Paper presented at the Annual Meeting of the American Political Science Association, Washington, DC, August 31–September 3.

———. 2002. "Jury Service and Women's Citizenship Before and After the Nineteenth Amendment." *Law and History Review* 20:479–516.

———. 2003. "Of War and Virtue: Gender, Citizenship, and Veterans' Benefits After WWII." *The Comparative Study of Conscription: Comparative Social Research*, ed. L. Mjoset and S. Van Holde, 20:201–26.

Roche, K. n.d. "The Secretary: Capitalism's House Nigger." Pittsburgh: Know, Inc. Documents from the Women's Liberation Movement, Special Collections Library, Duke University http://scriptorium.lib.duke.edu/wlm/sec.

Rodriguez, C. M. 1999. "Clearing the Smoke-Filled Room: Women Jurors and the Disruption of an Old Boys' Network in Nineteenth-Century America." *Yale Law Journal* 108:1805–44.

Roosevelt, E. 1995. *What I Hope to Leave Behind: The Essential Essays of Eleanor Roosevelt*. Ed. A. M. Black. Brooklyn, NY: Carlson Publishing.

Roosevelt, F. D. 1938–50. *The Public Papers and Addresses of Franklin D. Roosevelt*. 13 vols. New York: Random House.

Rosenberg, G. N. 1991. *The Hollow Hope: Can Courts Bring Around Social Change?* Chicago: University of Chicago Press.

Ross, D. R. B. 1969. *Preparing for Ulysses: Politics and Veterans During World War II*. New York: Columbia University Press.

Rousseau, D. L., and B. Newsome. 1999. "Women and Minorities: The Impact of War Time Mobilization on Political Rights." Paper presented at the Annual Meeting of the American Political Science Association, Atlanta, September 2–5.

Rousseau, J. 1972. *On the Social Contract*. Trans. Judith R. Masters. Ed. R. D. Masters. New York: St. Martin's Press.

Ruddick, S. 1989. *Maternal Thinking: Toward a Politics of Peace*. Boston: Beacon Press.

Russell, C. E. 1924. "Is Woman Suffrage a Failure?" *Century*, March, 35 ff.

Salmon, M. 1986. *Women and the Law of Property in Early America*. Chapel Hill: University of North Carolina Press.

Sandel, M. 1982. *Liberalism and the Limits of Justice*. New York: Cambridge University Press.

Sapiro, V. 1984. "Women, Citizenship, and Nationality: Immigration and Naturalization Policies in the United States." *Politics and Society* 13:1–26.

———. 1990. "The Gender Basis of American Social Policy." In *Women, the State, and Welfare*, ed. L. Gordon, 36–54. Madison: University of Wisconsin Press.

Sarachild, K. 1978. "Consciousness-Raising: A Radical Weapon." In *Feminist Revolution: Redstockings of the Women's Liberation Movement*, ed. K. Sarachild, 144–50. New York: Random House.

Savage, C. 1924. "What the American Woman Thinks." *Woman Citizen*, May 31, 19.

Shanley, L., and C. Pateman, eds. 1991. *Feminist Interpretations and Political Theory*. University Park: Pennsylvania State University Press.

Sheridan, E. 1925. "Women and Jury Service." *American Bar Association Journal* 11:792 ff.

"She's the BUSIEST Woman on the Block." 1944. *Good Housekeeping*, August, 226.

Shklar, J. 1991. *American Citizenship: The Quest for Inclusion*. Cambridge, MA: Harvard University Press.

"Should Aliens Vote?" 1921. *Woman Citizen*, September 10, 18.

Siegel, R. B. 1985. "Employment Equality Under the Pregnancy Discrimination Act of 1978." *Yale Law Journal* 94 (March):929–56.

———. 1992. "Reasoning from the Body: A Historical Perspective on Abortion Regulation and Questions of Equal Protection." *Stanford Law Review* 44:261–381.

———. 1994a. "Home as Work: The First Women's Rights Claims Concerning Wives Household Labor, 1850–1880." *Yale Law Journal* 103:1073–1217.

———. 1994b. "The Modernization of Marital Status Law: Adjudicating Wives' Rights to Earnings, 1860–1930." *Georgetown Law Journal* 82:2127–2211.

———. 1996. "The Rule of Love: Wife Beating as Prerogative and Privacy." *Yale Law Journal* 106:2117–2207.

———. 1997. "Why Equal Protection No Longer Protects: The Evolving Forms of Status Enforcing State Action." *Stanford Law Review* 49:1111–48.

———. 1998. "Collective Memory and the Nineteenth Amendment: Reasoning about the 'Woman Question' in the Discourse of Sex Discrimination." In *History, Memory, and the Law*, ed. A. Sarat, 131 ff. Ann Arbor: University of Michigan Press.

———. 2001. "Text in Contest: Gender and the Constitution from a Social Movement Perspective." *University of Pennsylvania Law Review* 150:297–351.

———. 2002. "'She, the People': The Nineteenth Amendment, Sex Equality, Federalism and the Family." *Harvard Law Review* 115:947–1049.

Skocpol, T. 1992. *Protecting Soldiers and Mothers: The Political Origins of Social Policy in the United States*. Cambridge, MA: Harvard University Press.

———. 1996. "Delivering for Young Families: The Resonance of the GI Bill." *American Prospect*, September–October, 66.

Skocpol, T., and G. Ritter. 1991. "Gender and the Origins of Modern Social Policies in Britain and the United States." *Studies in American Political Development* 5 (Spring): 36–93.

Skowronek, S. 1982. *Building a New American State: The Expansion of National Administrative Capacities, 1877–1920*. New York: Cambridge University Press.

Smith, P. 1995 *Democracy on Trial: The Japanese-American Evacuation and Relocation During World War II*. New York: Simon and Schuster.

Smith, R. M. 1989. "'One United People': Second Class Female Citizenship and the American Quest for Community." *Yale Journal of Law and the Humanities* 1:229–94.

———. 1997. *Civic Ideals: Conflicting Visions of Citizenship in US History*. New Haven, CT: Yale University Press.

Snyder, R. C. 1999. *Citizen-Soldiers and Manly Warriors: Military Service and Gender in the Civic Republic Tradition*. Lanham, MD: Rowman and Littlefield Publishers.

Sommers, M. 1993. "Citizenship and the Place of the Public Sphere: Law, Community, and Political Culture in the Transition to Democracy." *American Sociological Review* 58:587–620.

Stanley, A. D. 1988. "Conjugal Bonds and Wage Labor: Rights of Contract in the Age of Emancipation." *Journal of American History* 75:471–500.

———. 1998. *From Bondage to Contract: Wage Labor, Marriage, and the Market in the Age of Slave Emancipation*. New York: Cambridge University Press.

Stanton, E. C., S. B. Anthony, and M. J. Gage, eds. 1881. *History of Woman Suffrage*. Vol. 1. New York: Fowler and Wells.

———. 1887. *History of Woman Suffrage*. Vol. 3. Rochester, NY: Susan B. Anthony.

———. 1969. *History of Woman Suffrage*. Vol. 2. New York: Arno.

Stewart, K. C. 2005. *Ordinary Impacts: The Affective Life of U.S. Public Culture*. Durham, NC: Duke University Press.

Strauss, D. 2001. "The Irrelevance of Constitutional Amendments." *Harvard Law Review* 114:1457–1505.

Taylor, G. E. W. 1959. "Jury Service for Women." *University of Florida Law Review* 12:224–31.

"A Teapot in a Tempest." 1921. *Woman Citizen*, February 5, 949.

Terborg-Penn, R. 1998. *African-American Women in the Struggle for the Vote, 1850–1920*. Bloomington: Indiana University Press.

Thompson, D. 1944. "The Stake of Women in Full Postwar Employment." *Ladies Home Journal*, April 6, 183.

Tocqueville, A. de. 1945. *Democracy in America*. 2 vols. New York: Knopf.

Tomlins, C. 1995. "Subordination, Authority, Law: Subjects in Labor History." *International Labor and Working-Class History* 47:56–90.

Treadwell, M. E. 1954. *The Women's Army Corps*. Washington, DC: GPO.

Tushnet, M. 2004. *The New Constitutional Order*. Princeton, NJ: Princeton University Press.

Universal Declaration of Human Rights. 1949. *American Journal of International Law* 43 (July): S127–S32.

United Nations. 1948. "United Nations Yearbook Summary." Universal Declaration of Human Rights, Franklin and Eleanor Roosevelt Institute. www.udhr.org/history/yearbook.htm.

"United Nations Commission on Status of Women." 1948. *Equal Rights*, January–February, 8–9.

United Nations General Assembly. 1948. Universal Declaration of Human Rights. A/RES/217 A (3), December 10.

———. 1952. Convention on the Political Rights of Women. Treaty Series, vol. 193, no. 2613, December 20.

U.S. Equal Employment Opportunity Commission (EEOC). 1968. *Legislative History of Titles VII and XI of Civil Rights Act of 1964.* Washington, DC: GPO.

———. 2003. "The Equal Pay Act Turns 40." www.eeoc.gov/epa/anniversary/epa-40.html.

U.S. House of Representatives. 1926. Committee on the Judiciary. *Proposal and Ratification of Amendments to the Constitution of the U.S.: Hearing Before the Committee on the Judiciary.* 69th Cong., 1st sess. Washington, DC: GPO.

———. 1945a. Committee on the Judiciary. *Amend the Constitution Relative to Equal Rights for Men and Women: Hearing Before the Committee on the Judiciary.* 79th Cong., 1st sess. Washington, DC: GPO.

———. 1945b. Committee on Expenditures in Executive Departments. *Full Employment Act of 1945: Hearing Before the Committee on Expenditures in Executive Departments.* 79th Cong., 1st sess. Washington, DC: GPO.

———. 1945c. Committee on the Judiciary, Subcommittee no. 2. *Amend the Constitution.* 69th Cong., 1st sess. Washington, DC: GPO.

———. 1963. Committee on Education and Labor. *Equal Pay Act: Hearing Before the Committee on Education and Labor.* 88th Cong., 1st sess. Washington, DC: GPO.

U.S. Senate. 1929. Committee on the Judiciary. *Equal Rights Amendment: Hearing Before the Committee on the Judiciary.* 70th Cong., 2nd sess. Washington, DC: GPO.

———. 1945a. Committee on the Judiciary. *Equal Rights Amendment: Hearing Before the Committee on the Judiciary.* 79th Cong., 1st sess. Washington, DC: GPO.

———. 1945b. Committee on Banking and Currency. *Full Employment Act of 1945, Revised: Hearing Before the Committee on Banking and Currency.* 79th Cong., 1st sess. Washington, DC: GPO.

———. 1945c. Committee on the Judiciary. *Equal Rights Amendment: Subcommittee of the Committee on the Judiciary.* 79th Cong., 1st sess., September 28. Washington, DC: GPO.

———. 1946. Committee on the Judiciary. *Questions and Answers on the Equal Rights Amendment.* Report prepared by Research Department of the National Women's Party. 79th Cong., 2nd sess. Washington, DC: GPO.

———. 1963. Committee on Labor and Public Welfare. *Equal Pay Act of 1963: Hearing Before the Committee on Labor and Public Welfare.* 88th Cong., 1st sess. Washington, DC: GPO.

———. 1970a. Committee on the Judiciary. *"Equal Rights" Amendment: Hearing Before the Subcommittee on Constitutional Amendments.* 91st Cong., 2nd sess. Washington, DC: GPO.

————. 1970b. Committee on the Judiciary. *Equal Rights 1970: Hearing Before the Committee on the Judiciary.* 91st Cong., 2nd sess. Washington, DC: GPO.

————. 1978. Committee on the Judiciary. *Equal Rights Amendment Extension: Hearing Before the Subcommittee on the Constitution.* 95th Cong., 2nd sess. Washington, DC: GPO.

van Steenbergen, B., ed. 1994. *The Condition of Citizenship.* New York: Sage Publications.

Vernier, C. G. 1935. *Husband and Wife.* Vol. 3 of *American Family Laws: A Comparative Study of the Family Law of the Forty-Eight American States.* Stanford, CA: Stanford University Press.

Vernon, M. 1930. "Ten Years of Woman Suffrage." *Equal Rights,* August 23, 227.

Walsh, J. E. 1927. "Justice Served by Women Jurors." *Equal Rights,* February 5, 411.

Warren, S. D., and L. D. Brandeis. 1890. "The Right to Privacy." *Harvard Law Review* 4:193–220.

Weatherford, D. 1990. *History of Women in America: American Women and World War II.* New York: Facts on File.

Weisborg, D. K. 1993. *Feminist Legal Theory.* Philadelphia: Temple University Press.

Weisbrod, C. 1986. "Images of the Woman Juror." *Harvard Women's Law Journal* 9:59–82.

West, R. 1988. "Jurisprudence and Gender." *University of Chicago Law Review* 55:1–72.

Wheeler, M. S., ed. 1995. *One Woman, One Vote: Rediscovering the Woman Suffrage Movement.* Troutdale, OR: NewSage Press.

Willenz, J. A. 1994. "Invisible Veterans." *Educational Record* 75:40–47.

Williams, C. 1989. *Gender Differences at Work: Women and Men in Nontraditional Occupations.* Berkeley and Los Angeles: University of California Press.

Williams, J. 2000. *Unbending Gender: Why Family and Work Conflict and What to Do About It.* New York: Oxford University Press.

Winkler, A. 2001. "A Revolution Too Soon: Woman Suffragists and the 'Living Constitution.'" *New York University Law Review* 76:1456–1526.

"Wives, Husbands, and Votes." 1920. *Ladies Home Journal,* September, 1.

Wolin, S. S. 1980. "The People's Two Bodies." *democracy* 1:11–17.

————. 1989. *The Presence of the Past: Essays on the State and the Constitution.* Baltimore: Johns Hopkins University Press.

"Women Voters Won't Stand for Partisan Slander and Abuse." 1922. *Ladies Home Journal,* August, 8–9.

Women's Rights Law Reporter (WRLR). 1971–79.

Woodhouse, B. 1992. "'Who Owns the Child?': Meyer and Pierce and the Child as Property." *William and Mary Law Review* 33:995–1122.

Young, I. M. 1990. *Justice and the Politics of Difference* Princeton, NJ: Princeton University Press.

Young, L. M. 1989. *In the Public Interest: The League of Women Voters, 1920–1970*. New York: Greenwood Press.

Yu, H. 2001. *Thinking Orientals: Migration, Contact, and Exoticism in Modern America*. New York: Oxford University Press.

Yuval-Davis, N. 1997. *Gender and Nation*. London: Sage Publications.

Zeigler, S. L. 1996a. "Uniformity and Conformity: Regionalism and the Adjudication of the Married Women's Property Acts." *Polity* 28:467–95.

———. 1996b. "Wifely Duties: Marriage, Labor, and the Common Law in Nineteenth-Century America." *Social Science History* 20:63–96.

Zimmerman, J. 1991. "The Jurisprudence of Equality: The Women's Minimum Wage, the First Equal Rights Amendment, and *Adkins v. Children's Hospital*, 1905–1923." *Journal of American History* 78:188–226.

Index

Abbott, Grace, 39
Abortion, 275–80, 283–84, 288–92
ACLU (American Civil Liberties Union), 197
Addams, Jane, 335n15
Adkins v. Children's Hospital (1923), 44, 47–48, 81–82, 91, 94–95, 120, 139–40
ADRDM (American Declaration on the Rights and Duties of Man), 203–4
Affirmative action, 323
AFL-CIO, 239
African Americans: and civic membership, 11–12; and international rights discussions, 199, 207; war service and civic status of, 179–80; women's civil/political status compared to that of, 45–46, 49, 101, 105–6, 114–17, 123, 130, 224–25, 233–34, 241, 249–53. *See also* African American women
African American women: employment discrimination against, 237–38; and international rights discussions, 208; Reconstruction and status of, 15; in suffrage campaign, 329n1; as veterans, 191
After Suffrage (Andersen), 57, 62
Aid to Dependent Children (ADC), 143–45
Aid to Families with Dependent Children (AFDC), 143, 233
Allen, Florence, 43
Alpern, Sara, 57
Amar, Akhil, 319–20
Amar, Vikram, 45, 114–15
Amatniek, Kathie, 236

American Association of University Women (AAUW), 146, 222, 230
American Civil Liberties Union (ACLU), 197
American Declaration on the Rights and Duties of Man (ADRDM), 203–4
American Legion, 187
Americans with Disabilities Act (ADA) (1990), 311–12
The American Woman (PCSW), 218, 225
American Woman Suffrage Association (AWSA), 18, 54
Andersen, Kristi, 54, 57, 62
Anderson, Clinton P., 158
Anderson, Mary, 79
Andrews, George, 228
Anguiano, Lupe, 233
Anthony, Susan B., 17–18, 20, 25, 54, 112
Anti-Federalists, 318–21
Appeal to the World, 199
Aristotle, 37
Austin, Warren, 182
Austin v. Austin (1924), 88
Avery, Nina Horton, 185–86
AWSA (American Woman Suffrage Association), 18, 54

Babcock, Barbara, 255
Baer, Judith, 81
Baird, Bill, 274
Baker, Paula, 55
Ballard v. United States (1946), 164–65, 301
Barney, Nora Stanton, 151–52
Battle, George Gordon, 186
Baum, Dale, 57